UNIVERSITY OF ST. THOMAS LIBRARIES

Black Print Unbound

Black Print Unbound

THE *CHRISTIAN RECORDER*, AFRICAN AMERICAN LITERATURE, AND PERIODICAL CULTURE

Eric Gardner

OXFORD
UNIVERSITY PRESS

Oxford University Press is a department of the University of Oxford.
It furthers the University's objective of excellence in research, scholarship,
and education by publishing worldwide. Oxford is a registered trade mark
of Oxford University Press in the UK and in certain other countries

Published in the United States of America by
Oxford University Press
198 Madison Avenue, New York, NY 10016,
United States of America

© Oxford University Press 2015

All rights reserved. No part of this publication may be reproduced,
stored in a retrieval system, or transmitted, in any form or by any means,
without the prior permission in writing of Oxford University Press,
or as expressly permitted by law, by license, or under terms agreed with the
appropriate reproduction rights organization. Inquiries concerning reproduction
outside the scope of the above should be sent to the Rights Department,
Oxford University Press, at the address above.

You must not circulate this work in any other form
and you must impose this same condition on any acquirer

Library of Congress Cataloging-in-Publication Data
Gardner, Eric.
Black print unbound : the *Christian recorder*, African American
literature, and periodical culture / Eric Gardner.
p. cm.
Includes index.
ISBN 978-0-19-023708-0 (cloth) — ISBN 978-0-19-023709-7 (pbk.) —
ISBN 978-0-19-023710-3 (ebook) 1. Christian recorder of the African American
Methodist Episcopal Church—History. 2. American literature—African
American authors—History and criticism. 3. American literature—African
American authors—Publishing—History—19th century. 4. Literature
publishing—Political aspects—United States—History—19th century.
5. American literature—19th century—History and criticism.
6. Periodicals—Publishing—United States—History—19th century. 7. American
periodicals—History—19th century. 8. African Americans—Intellectual
life—19th century. 9. African Americans in literature. I. Title.
BX8440.G37 2015
287'.83—dc23
2014047141

1 3 5 7 9 8 6 4 2
Printed in the United States of America on acid-free paper

as always, for my family

{ CONTENTS }

Acknowledgments — ix
1. White Houses and Black Print — 1

PART I "Our Church Organ": Toward a Cultural and Material History of the Early *Recorder*

2. "Dense Darkness": Recovering the *Recorder*'s History — 23
3. From Pine Street to the Nation (and Back Again): The Business of the *Recorder* — 61
4. "Their Friends at Home with Papers": *Recorder* Subscriptions and Subscribers — 96

PART II "Would Not Such a Narration Be Worth Reading?": The *Christian Recorder* and African American Literary History

5. "We Are in the World": Reading the *Recorder* in the Civil War Era — 135
6. "So Let Us Hear from All the Brethren": The *Christian Recorder* and Correspondence — 166
7. "That Wished Home of Peace": The Personal and the Political in *Christian Recorder* Elegies — 196
8. Black (Women's) Fortunes and *The Curse of Caste* — 226

Notes — 255
Works Cited — 305
Index — 319

{ ACKNOWLEDGMENTS }

One of the things I learn daily is that being a teacher-scholar means first being a student, so I want to begin by acknowledging how much I've learned and continue to learn from studying the *Christian Recorder* and early Black print culture in general. I'm cognizant of the generations of folks who made that learning possible—individuals too numerous to list comprehensively. Sometimes I look over my shoulder expecting to see Edmonia Highgate or Julia Collins busily writing, Elisha Weaver negotiating with a printer, Jabez P. Campbell carefully collecting issues of the *Recorder*, Daniel Payne arguing with Henry McNeal Turner over doctrine and practice, Benjamin Quarles and Dorothy Porter Wesley reading yellowing newspaper pages. The past reminds me of how much work we need to do in the present and future. Sometimes literally and sometimes figuratively, I've heard the voices of historians and critics closer to my own generation, too—folks like Frances Smith Foster, Carla Peterson, Nellie McKay, John Hope Franklin, and Nina Baym. These intellectual leaders knew—really *knew*—how much we could learn from voices that American culture and the American academy often devalued, dismissed, or ignored, and I am so thankful not only for their work but for their lessons in how to do that work ethically, proudly, even sometimes joyously.

I'm thankful, too, that these folks and some of their colleagues worked to create and shape spaces supportive of research on early Black print. Writing this book would simply not have been possible, for example, if I had not had the support of a year-long fellowship from the National Endowment for the Humanities in 2012–2013 that allowed much-needed time for writing and revising. (That said, any views, findings, conclusions, or recommendations expressed in this publication do not necessarily reflect those of the National Endowment for the Humanities.) Some of my earliest thinking about this book was shaped by experiences tied to a month-long Mellon Fellowship at the Library Company of Philadelphia and the Historical Society of Pennsylvania in 2006 and by a Ruth and Ted Braun Research Fellowship administered by the Saginaw Community Foundation and Saginaw Valley State University (SVSU). Thanks to all of these groups; thanks, too, to Ezra Greenspan for invaluable feedback on the NEH application.

Closer to home, SVSU has actively supported many of my efforts, providing resources during my NEH fellowship year as well as regular travel grants. The library staff has offered significant help in tracking down resources. Faculty, staff, and students in the College of Arts and Behavioral Sciences—and especially the English and history departments, as well as two truly supportive deans (Mary Hedberg and then Joni Boye-Beaman)—have been wonderfully collegial.

I've been especially excited about the growing community of scholars deeply invested in the study and appreciation of African Americanist inquiry and literary history specifically. Several of these folks—again, too many for a comprehensive list—have been wonderfully helpful. I cannot count the ways my work and my practice have been influenced, for example, by John Ernest and Joycelyn Moody. I've also been enriched by talking with and reading the wonderful work of scholars like William Andrews, Nina Baym, Lois Brown, Lara Cohen, Benjamin Fagan, Gabrielle Foreman, Frances Smith Foster, Ezra Greenspan, Teresa Goddu, Leon Jackson, Michael K. Johnson, Barbara McCaskill, Carla Peterson, Reginald Pitts, Hollis Robbins, Jordan Stein, and Ivy Wilson, among several other fellow travelers.

I've been consistently impressed with the dedication of librarians and archivists across the country to both preservation and access. This book would not be possible without the support of folks at institutions like the American Antiquarian Society (with a special nod to Paul Erickson), the Historical Society of Pennsylvania, the Indiana State Library, the Library Company of Philadelphia (especially Phil Lapsansky), the Mother Bethel AME Church Museum and Archives in Philadelphia, and Drew University. I also deeply appreciate the entities who allowed use of the images found in the book, including the Schomburg Center for Research in Black Culture at the New York Public Library; the American Antiquarian Society (especially Jackie Penny); the State Archives of Florida; the Arkansas History Commission; the Greenwood Cemetery Association in Jackson, Mississippi (with special thanks to Bill and Cecile Wardlaw); the Prints and Photographs Division of the Library of Congress; the McLean County Museum of History in Bloomington, Illinois; and the Archives of American Art at the Smithsonian Institution. (Full credits appear with the images.) It is worth noting the mix of larger institutions and more localized entities in these lists, as this volume recognizes how much the academy needs to reach out to diverse communities if we are ever to have a fuller sense of our pasts, presents, and futures. In this vein, I knew when I saw the first subscriber listing from Bloomington, Illinois—where I completed my undergraduate degree—that I'd want to highlight that "unexpected place" in chapter 4, and that gave me a wonderful opportunity to reconnect with Pam and Jack Muirhead and to learn more about African Americans in central Illinois.

The book would not be what it is without feedback provided through a number of public forums. A study of a smaller set of the data considered in chapter 4 of this volume was published in the Summer 2011 issue of *American Literary History*, and Gordon Hutner's smart editing and useful challenges sharpened both that piece and my thinking about this book. A "spin-off" from the project exploring dimensions of Edmonia Highgate's work that are not treated in detail here appeared in Jana Argersinger and Phyllis Cole's wonderful collection *Toward a Female Genealogy of Transcendentalism* (Georgia 2014); their commentary on that piece, as well as that of Kate Adams and Michael Borgstrom, shaped my thinking on this book, too. I had the good fortune to find a missing chapter of Frances Harper's serialized *Recorder* novel *Sowing and Reaping* in the American Antiquarian Society's collection while working on this book, and the folks at both the American Antiquarian Society and *Common-place* who helped with that project gave valuable insight. Panel participants and session attendees at a host of meetings, including the American Literature Association, the Modern Language Association, and the Society for the Study of American Women Writers provided useful feedback, too, as did colleagues involved with my Braun and Warrick lectures at SVSU and with the American Antiquarian Society's Summer Seminar in the History of the Book.

The folks at Oxford University Press have been spectacular. Brendan O'Neill has been a model editor: supportive, challenging, and ever thoughtful. He has my deepest thanks. Stephen Bradley has done everything from answering questions on minutiae to helping with images. The peer readers Oxford engaged provided immensely valuable and constructive critique of the manuscript. Sabrina Hill and Susie Hara helped mightily with production and copy-editing, and Jenny Catchings, with marketing.

There are countless others who helped get these pages into your hands. Please join me in thanking them, too.

Finally, I dedicate this book, like all of my work, to my family—teachers, students, and readers all. The generations surrounding me—my mom and my daughters Abby and Libby—continue to teach me and to bring me great joy. I've lost count of the times my wife Jodie has listened to me talk about this project, has read pages upon pages of drafts, has offered wise and kind counsel, and has reminded me in word and deed of why we teach and learn. They have my thanks and my love.

Black Print Unbound

{1}

White Houses and Black Print

Bishop Daniel Payne rose from the armchair by the fireplace. Short and thin, he was often mistaken for frail during his long life. Historian Benjamin Quarles's assessment is closer to the truth: Payne "looked as though he had been fasting in the wilderness, and he carried himself like a man sent from God" (104). Payne had likely spent much of the last hour praying, arguing, listening, teaching, and preaching. Years after this April 1862 meeting, this lion of the African Methodist Episcopal (AME) Church wrote that he finally felt it was his "duty to withdraw" (*Recollections* 147). As Payne readied himself to go, he took a small magazine and a newspaper from his satchel, and he handed them to the tall, tired man he had come to see. Earnestly, Payne "told him that if he could find a leisure moment to look over" the magazine and the newspaper, "he would see what the A. M. E. Church was doing to improve the character and condition of our people in the republic" (147–148). Then Payne took his leave. One wonders if he glanced back over his shoulder, hoping to see Abraham Lincoln paging through the issues of the *Repository of Religion and Literature* and the *Christian Recorder* that the AME bishop had just gifted him.

Students of African American history know that the meeting between Lincoln and Payne is the kind of moment that most scholars have dismissed, ignored, or simply not known about—that at best it might be treated as a tiny thread in the massive tapestries surrounding Lincoln and the Civil War.[1] Students of Black print culture know that Payne's final gesture, his attempt to deploy African American texts that were not bound books, would, until very recently, not even have garnered much notice. The Lincoln White House was dealing with a war of a size, scope, and character never seen in North America—George B. McClellan's doomed Peninsula Campaign was gearing up—and Lincoln himself, burdened by his office and the death of his eleven-year-old son Willie only two months before, was suffering deep personal pain, too. Add Lincoln's famous willingness to meet with hundreds of petitioners and his White House's incredibly sloppy record-keeping, and it is no wonder that Payne's meeting has received little notice.[2] Decades of obfuscation of Black church action, Black print culture, and Black agency before, during, and after the Civil War undoubtedly sped the removal of the meeting with Payne from American historical consciousness, even as rare scholars attempted to memorialize it.

Comparatively few historians even attend to the question that brought Payne (shown years later in Figure 1.1) to the White House on April 14, 1862: three days earlier, Congress had passed legislation abolishing slavery in the District of Columbia, and Lincoln was deciding whether to sign it into law—something he ultimately did two days after Payne's visit. Now only a footnote to the better-known Emancipation Proclamation, the earlier DC emancipation law demonstrated the North's ambivalence to slavery and to African Americans generally. In addition to encouraging voluntary colonization of enslaved people emancipated through the law, it built on Lincoln's own March 1862 nods toward compensated emancipation; through the law, slave owners in the District were paid for the "loss" of their "property."[3] The resulting contribution to American print culture—a seventy-nine-page *Letter from the Secretary of the Treasury* submitted to Congress and printed in 1864—offers the names of slave owners who petitioned for payment under the law, as well as the names and valuations of their "Persons Held to Service or Labor."[4]

This, of course, is not the story of Lincoln, the Civil War, slavery, and emancipation many want to tell. As Marcus Wood argues, generations have (mis)represented emancipation as a "gift"—certainly not something as crass as the exchange of (government) money for an enslaved person's body and liberty.[5] And we need not belabor the deification of Lincoln in the popular mind. The Lincoln of such fantasies was simply not the Lincoln who, as Michael Burlingame notes in *Abraham Lincoln: A Life*, told friend and Illinois Senator Orville Hickman Browning that the DC emancipation bill "should have been for gradual emancipation" as "now families would be at once deprived of cooks, stable boys &c and they of their protectors without any provision for them" (344).[6] Thus, even the best biographers downplay DC emancipation and ignore both Payne's meeting with Lincoln and his gift of two important Black periodicals.[7]

I open with this discussion of Payne's April 1862 meeting with Lincoln to emphasize the layers of neglect covering so many remnants of American and especially African American history and culture. I submit that uncovering, examining, and contextualizing such remnants might lead us to significant and challenging new questions. Even focusing on Payne's gift of Black print to Lincoln raises a host of concerns: Did Lincoln read the periodicals? What did he do with the copies Payne gave him? Did he hand them off to an aide—or to one of the White House's white or Black servants? What did Lincoln know of Black periodicals generally? Of Black print culture? What kinds of

FIGURE 1.1 *The Bishops' Council of 1892, Philadelphia, PA, from the* General Program . . . of the General Conference of the African Methodist Episcopal Church *(1900). Courtesy of the Manuscripts Collection, Archives and Rare Books Division, Schomburg Center for Research in Black Culture, The New York Public Library, Astor, Lenox and Tilden Foundations. Taken near the end of Daniel Payne's life, this photograph shows Payne (seated fourth from the left) along with a number of key figures in the AME Church and the history of the* Recorder. *Back, from left: Benjamin Tucker Tanner, Moses B. Salter, John Mifflin Brown, Wesley J. Gaines, James A. Handy, Benjamin F. Lee. Front, from left: Abraham Grant, Benjamin W. Arnett, Alexander Wayman, Payne, T. M. D. Ward, and Henry McNeal Turner.*

communities—physical, imagined, or otherwise—would he have witnessed or perhaps even joined by reading?[8]

We might even ask—as this book does—what happens when we leave one of the most expected starting places for a narrative of the Civil War era, the Lincoln White House, and leave as well the towering figure of Lincoln to focus instead on the thousands of African Americans during and after the war who subscribed to, read, supported, wrote for, and/or worked with Black periodicals—African American preachers and teachers, soldiers and domestics, laundresses and barbers, activists and poets. What happens when we conceive of those African Americans—some freeborn, some self-emancipated "fugitives," some "contraband," and some freed only after the war—as agents fighting for rights rather than receiving "gifts"?

This is not a book about Lincoln, though he treads through its pages with some regularity. Nor is this a book about the "traditional" Civil War or the "gift" of emancipation, though the massive set of events referenced (and hidden) within these terms shaped every facet of the world this book considers. Instead, this book begins to tell the story of one of the periodicals Payne handed to Lincoln: the AME's weekly newspaper, the *Christian Recorder*.[9] Focused especially on the years during and just after the Civil War, this is a narrative of a periodical that was conceived by African Americans, edited by African Americans, written primarily by African Americans, and largely distributed by African Americans to an almost completely African American audience—a periodical that, in the midst of a sea of failed print ventures by members of all races in the nineteenth century, survived and influenced a readership across the nation. It is a story critical to any sense of American and African American history, culture, and literature, and it begins with the recognition that Payne's gesture was a most logical thing for an AME Bishop to do, an act that a host of Black Americans would understand and support, and a complex attempt to tell Lincoln much about the "nation within a nation."

To open that story and to set a series of contexts, I want to turn briefly to a different sense of the Lincoln White House. As this study demonstrates, Payne's gift of an issue of the *Recorder* to Lincoln—indeed, any copy of the *Recorder* in white hands or a "white house"—was a comparative rarity. That gift does, though, foreground the hope among many Black activists that print might aid in the battle to convince Lincoln and the broader white populace that, among other things, in John S. Rock's words, "This rebellion . . . means something! Out of it emancipation must spring." Speaking at the 1862 annual meeting of the Massachusetts Anti-Slavery Society, the fiery Rock argued that "While Mr. Lincoln has been more conservative than I had hoped to find him, I recognize in him an honest man, striving to redeem the country from . . . degradation and shame." When Rock's full speech was published in the February 22, 1862, *Recorder*, editor Elisha Weaver (Figure 1.2) said that it should "be hung up in the halls of Congress,—nay, in the house of the President, as an argument on behalf of the black man, that the very same God is the author of both." Readers who knew Weaver were thus invited to picture the stocky, dark-skinned minister—perhaps in his trademark long coat, reminiscent of ministerial robes—walking into the president's office with a hammer, a nail, and a copy of the *Recorder*, then taking a cabinet member's chair over to the fireplace on the office's west wall, climbing up on that chair, and tacking the massive unbound sheet covered with Black print over the portrait of Andrew Jackson that so many contemporary descriptions of the White House reported hanging there.

We cannot assume, though, that the only ways the *Recorder* might enter the Lincoln White House were through Payne's gift or my embroidered version of Weaver's "should." Educated guesses drawn from the *Recorder*'s published

FIGURE 1.2 *Elisha Weaver from James Handy's* Scraps of African Methodist History *(1902). Courtesy of the Manuscripts Collection, Archives and Rare Books Division, Schomburg Center for Research in Black Culture, The New York Public Library, Astor, Lenox and Tilden Foundations. Likely dating from the mid-1860s, this is the only image of Weaver found to date.*

acknowledgments of funds received suggest that there were at least 400 single copy sales of the newspaper in the District of Columbia in the three months prior to Payne's visit to Lincoln, made mainly by two of DC's AME ministers, Daniel W. Moore and James Lynch.[10] If we look more broadly, *Recorder* acknowledgments suggest that there were well over 2,500 single copy sales in the District between 1861 and 1864. The bulk were handled by AME ministers—Lynch, Moore, David Smith, and, later, James Handy and Henry J. Rhodes—but the District also had two enterprising lay agents: Charles O. Moore, "a very worthy and active young man" who sold papers in early 1863, and one of the paper's female agents, Laura Simms, who sold papers between late 1863 and mid-1864.[11] Between 1861 and 1864, those same acknowledgment columns reported at least forty first-time subscribers and at least six renewals from the District—all from individuals who were generally paying for a full year of the paper in advance.[12]

The *Recorder*'s foothold in the District shouldn't be surprising: the 1860 federal census tallied 11,131 free African Americans there and marked over a third of them as literate. (The census also tallied 3,185 enslaved African Americans, though neither their literacy status—which was mistakenly assumed to *always* be illiterate—nor even their names were listed on the separate "slave schedules," where enslaved people were organized by owner and listed only in terms of color, sex, and age.) The AME Church had a strong presence in both Washington proper and in Georgetown, and most of the AME ministers in these locations were strong supporters of Black print culture. Still, while any of the copies distributed through these venues could have made their way to the Lincoln White House, I offer these observations mainly to demonstrate that the *Recorder* was a real presence in the city both immediately before and after Payne's visit with Lincoln.

If we want to consider more likely specific avenues for the paper to enter Lincoln's domain, we should turn to two African Americans with deep ties to the Lincoln family and the White House, Elizabeth Keckley (shown in Figure 1.3) and William Slade. Keckley (1818–1907) was Mary Todd Lincoln's modiste and confidante, now perhaps best known for her 1868 *Behind the Scenes, or Thirty Years a Slave, and Four Years in the White House*. Keckley had already gained Mary Lincoln's respect well before Payne's April 1862 visit; after Willie Lincoln's death in February, Keckley became an essential presence in Mary Lincoln's life.[13] Keckley would join the well-known Fifteenth Street Presbyterian Church in 1865, but her church in the early 1860s was the AME's Union Bethel. From that church, she grew into a leader of the movement to aid the self-emancipating people who were flooding the District—recently enslaved men, women, and children often referred to as "contrabands," reflecting their painful legal status as property in wartime. Keckley was acknowledged in the April 18, 1863, *Recorder* (as "Mrs. Lizzie Keekly [sic]" of Washington, DC) for a full year's subscription. While her subscription status in 1864 and 1865 remain unclear, she again subscribed for a full year later in 1866.[14] Keckley's name was already appearing in the paper before her initial subscription: a November 1, 1862, item, for example, describes her as "Mrs. Keckley, formerly of St. Louis, Missouri, who is now a resident of Washington, D. C.," speaks of her being "empowered to collect funds for the benefit of the contrabands in Washington," and calls her "a member of our Church."[15] More striking is Keckley's own "An Appeal on Behalf of Our People," which appeared in the March 14, 1863, *Recorder* with the signature "Elizabeth Keckley, President

FIGURE 1.3 *Elizabeth Keckley, from Hallie Q. Brown's* Homespun Heroines *(1926), author's collection.*

of the 'Contraband Relief Association.'" It opens by noting that Keckley was "relying on the benevolence and philanthropy of the Christian ministers who peruse the 'Christian Recorder'" to aid the "eight to ten thousand poor men, women, and children, in a most distressing and deplorable condition." Keckley forcefully argues that "This is our seedtime, and doubtless our heavenly Father will cause the seed which is sown in weakness to bear a rich harvest." Her specific use of a Black newspaper as her venue highlights yet another sense of how the *Recorder* was an example of Black print unbound: like Payne and countless others involved with AME print and the paper specifically, Keckley saw entities like the *Recorder* as crucial supports (in multiple senses of that word) to people who were or were hoping to throw off the yokes of slavery and racism.

William Slade (1814–1868) was Lincoln's personal servant, sometime steward, and messenger—in Catherine Clinton's words, Lincoln's "keeper of the keys," in charge of "supervising all the black workers in the Executive Mansion, as well as the arrangements for all public and private functions involving food and service" (160). All accounts mark Slade as a trusted favorite of the president—albeit within Lincoln's racialized worldview. His children played with the Lincoln children in the bowels of the White House, and he washed and dressed Lincoln's body after the president's death.[16] While Slade was an active member of the Fifteenth Street Presbyterian Church (serving as an elder for a number of years), he subscribed for at least two years of the AME *Recorder*: his first subscription was acknowledged in the February 13, 1864, issue, and a renewal was listed in the August 25, 1866, issue. Like Keckley, he was noted several times in the paper before his first recorded subscription, and he eventually also sent a textual contribution.

The earliest mention of Slade seems to be Henry McNeal Turner's September 13, 1862, *Recorder* letter, in which Turner describes attending a festival at the Fifteenth Street Presbyterian Church for relief of the "contrabands" and lists Slade—along with Keckley—among the organizers. Slade's work for the cause led to appearances in *Recorder* letters from Turner in the November 22, November 29, December 6, and December 27, 1862, issues—as well as in a handful of later pieces. Slade continued to be noted occasionally as a community leader: a June 11, 1864, piece of "Washington Correspondence," for example, marks the marriage of one of Slade's "accomplished daughters," and an August 18, 1866, item headed "President Johnson" brags that "The steward of President Johnson's household, Mr. William Slade, is a colored man—his salary is two thousand dollars a year. There are fifty well-backed applicants for the position." Slade's single extant contribution to the *Recorder* was a poem titled "Gems in the Cemetery" that appeared on the front page of the July 21, 1866, issue and mourns "these our loved ones," even as it instructs "cease, weary hearts, thy sad repining, / Thy children, so loved, are not lost; / But enclothed in white raiment, are shining / Safe o'er the dark river they have crossed."

Given that they valued the *Recorder* enough to send both funds and texts, could Keckley or Slade have occasionally shared knowledge gained from, items drawn from, or even copies of the *Recorder* with Lincoln or other members of the Lincoln White House? If we recognize that the Lincoln White House—like many centers of whiteness—was actually much more engaged with Black America than we have often assumed, we can see that getting the paper into that White House could have taken much less than Payne's gift or Weaver's imagined entry.

Still, considering Keckley and Slade in dialogue with Black periodical culture and as subscribers to, subjects of, readers of, and contributors to the *Recorder* foregrounds a much more important issue. Surely those who produced and distributed the *Recorder* hoped the paper would represent Black intellect and potential unbound, would influence the highest levels of national government, and would "be hung up in the halls of Congress,—nay, in the house of the President." But Keckley and Slade's stories remind us that Lincoln was one (white) man. He was separate from, sometimes uninterested in, and sometimes even antagonistic to the struggles of African Americans. For all of his importance, for all of Payne and Weaver's hopes of reaching him, and for all of our contemporary obsessions, Lincoln was not the nation. The myth we have made of that one man has often taken away from our consideration of the other men and women—including Black men and women like Payne, Weaver, Keckley, and Slade—who worked busily to create communities, build coalitions, and strive for social and political change during the period. This book is part of a scholarly tradition that values *their* experiences.

Kate Masur's insightful critique of Steven Spielberg's 2012 film *Lincoln* is instructive about this "other" White House and broader world. Arguing that the film's "African American characters do almost nothing but passively wait for white men to liberate them"—even though, as discussed above, Keckley and Slade were "leaders" in "an organized and highly politicized community of free African Americans"—Masur notes that "It would not have been much of a stretch" for the film "to do things differently. Keckley and Slade might have been shown leaving the White House to attend their own meetings, for example. Keckley could have discussed with Mrs. Lincoln the relief work that, in reality, she organized and the first lady contributed to. Slade could have talked with Lincoln about the 13th Amendment." Masur's piece is an elegant reminder of arguments at least as old as John E. Washington's *They Knew Lincoln* (1942)—that, in and around Lincoln's "white house," there were significant and engaged Black presences. Masur also reminds us of how we continue to treat "emancipation as a gift from white people to black people, not as a social transformation in which African Americans themselves played a role"—of how often we have forgotten the "world of black political debate, of civic engagement and of monumental effort for the liberation of body and spirit."[17] I begin this volume with Daniel Payne's gift of Black print to Lincoln and with recognitions of Elizabeth Keckley and William Slade's connections to the *Christian Recorder* to invoke that world and its importance to American cultural history. I want to remember that world's simultaneous distance from, closeness to, and even overlap with the "white house" that generations of (white) Americans have considered the center of the Civil War and emancipation.

Figures like Payne, Weaver, Keckley, and Slade are still rare in our classrooms and our scholarship not only because of the general discrimination against African American subjects by generations of scholars but also because of the specific inattention to African Americans' faith practices and communities. Recent scholars, however, have recognized that, given the walls the white polity built around almost all public participation, Black churches were key sites of some of the most innovative agitation for sociopolitical change and community-building during the period.[18] But even this understanding has not consistently led researchers to church-related *print*. For a host of reasons—explored most courageously in Frances Smith Foster's work—literary historians have been especially slow to engage with church print even though, according to Foster, "the most consistent and influential element in the first century of African American literary production was Afro-Protestantism" ("A Narrative" 715). "Our cost," Foster and Chanta Haywood thus write, "has been more than imperfect readings of the life and letters of a few individuals. It has rendered our bibliographies inaccurate, our concepts of literary style insufficient. It has perpetuated stereotypes of illiterate African Americans and ignored the agency of African American writers and readers in creating and shaping their tradition as well as the traditions of others. Slighting such contributions is not only a disservice to individuals, perpetuating misreadings of texts, but it ultimately reduces our understandings of the historical relationships among and within various segments of American society" (16).[19]

Texts like the *Recorder* have suffered not only because of the inattention to church print but also because of critical ignorance of and/or inattention to periodicals, specifically newspapers. Select African Americanist historians have known for generations that Black periodicals and especially unbound and often single-sheet (folded) newspapers were crucial to the world Masur describes, and some scholars have cited material from sources like the *Christian Recorder* for decades, often relying on important documentary efforts of the twentieth century like the *Black Abolitionist Papers* and, less so, the *Black Periodical Literature Project*. Still, much recovery work in terms of both building and using such sources remains, and scholars need to not only continue to search the archives but to engage deeply and responsibly with questions of broader access.[20] Literary historians in particular need to reevaluate what they read (and why) much more thoughtfully, especially given recent recognitions that both the circumscribed demands of white abolitionists and the exclusionary practices of "mainstream" white print culture regularly made the nineteenth-century Black press the best—and often the *only*—outlet for many Black authors.[21] To date, arguably only Jacqueline Bacon's *Freedom's Journal* offers the kind of nuanced, contextualized, and archive-centered study of an important individual nineteenth-century Black periodical that is so desperately needed to help a broader population understand just how central Black periodicals were to nineteenth-century Black literature and print culture.

In this frame, William Andrews and Mitch Kachun call the *Recorder* "the closest thing to a national newspaper that black Americans could claim as their own" (xi). During the period at the heart of this study—1860 to 1868, Elisha Weaver's tenure as editor and/or AME Book Steward—the *Recorder* reached across the nation, with subscribers and minister-agents from Massachusetts to California and from Michigan to Mississippi. Those who had watched the paper fail repeatedly after the Church bought *The Mystery* (a Pittsburgh Black newspaper founded by Martin Delany) in 1848 were stunned by its resurrection as a functioning four-page weekly under Weaver. The *Recorder* covered the Civil War but also specifically shared the voices of Black soldiers who wrote letters detailing their own experiences and hopes; not surprisingly, the paper thus featured intense debates about the war, emancipation, reconstruction, and potential places for African Americans in the larger republic. As a handful of recovery efforts have begun to show, the *Recorder* was perhaps even more important to Black literature—publishing texts by many "major" Black authors of the period as well as one of the earliest African American novels, Julia C. Collins's *The Curse of Caste*, and reviewing, discussing, and advertising an amazing array of books, lectures, and dramatic performances. As the AME denominational paper, the *Recorder* also featured a wide range of important sermons, essays, accounts of Church business, and debates on Church policy. As a national "recorder," the paper included notices of marriages and obituaries—often the only print records of critical events in the lives of Black individuals and communities—as well as scores of "Information Wanted" ads submitted by African Americans hoping to repair families torn asunder by slavery and the war.[22] Perhaps most fascinating, it published letters from Black readers across the nation in a time of massive cultural change. As such, the *Recorder* demands consideration in and of itself, but the paper's structure, publication and distribution practices, and content also offer an ideal case study for understanding Black participation in American letters, especially through Black church print and Black periodicals. These diverse and powerful contributions embody Foster's assertion that the Black press offered one of the richest sites for recording and sharing "the words and ideas" that African Americans found "most precious to their own psychic and spiritual (as well as physical or political) survival" (723).

With this in mind, this book is first and foremost a literary history of the *Christian Recorder*. That said, I want to broaden our sense of "literary history" significantly and conceive of such work as an interdisciplinary conversation grounded in the archive, challenging received "history," embracing a wide sense of the "literary," and focused on exploring how individuals and groups used the aesthetic, sociopolitical, and philosophical qualities of published words to address, record, and benefit their lives and those of their fellows. As I have said about similar recovery projects, it is my fervent hope that this book contributes to its own obsolescence: it dreams of a future where memories of the past are fuller, richer, confronted more honestly in their pain and promise, and cared for much more responsibly as we address and improve our present. The book thus builds from scholars of Black letters like William Andrews, Katherine Clay Bassard, Lois Brown, Dickson D. Bruce, Barbara

Christian, John Ernest, Gabrielle Foreman, Frances Smith Foster, Henry Louis Gates Jr., Saidiya Hartman, W. Lawrence Hogue, Barbara McCaskill, Nellie McKay, Joycelyn Moody, Carla Peterson, Joan Sherman, Jean Fagan Yellin, and Rafia Zafar—all of whom stand with a growing number of engaged African Americanists on the shoulders of giants like John Blassingame, John Hope Franklin, Benjamin Quarles, Dorothy Sterling, Dorothy Porter Wesley, and a host of early Black bibliophiles and teachers.

This book also recognizes that our work is both massive and incomplete. Many studies of nineteenth-century Black literature and Black culture still ignore the Black press, much less texts tied to Black faith. Almost all ignore the *Recorder*—even though African Americans of the period recognized it as perhaps *the* most important venue for Black writing. Many such studies also downplay the lessons taught by historians of the book and print in part, perhaps, because most of those historians have so completely ignored African American literature and culture. In attempting to remember the *Christian Recorder* at a critical set of moments in American and African American literature and history, this book thus pairs the fullest study to date of how the physical newspaper moved from composition to the hands of identifiable readers with a rich longitudinal sense of the paper's ideological, political, and aesthetic development. It moves from this material and cultural history to closely and contextually read a sampling of texts in representative genres to not only explore the riches of the paper but also to mark key questions for further consideration. It thus also contributes to four larger debates in American literary studies and histories of American culture—those surrounding our developing senses of nineteenth-century African American literature, of communities and print, of how we have perceived (Black) past(s), and of the nexus of print culture studies and African Americanist inquiry.

First, this study joins rich scholarship over the past decade that reconceptualizes African American literature and that specifically argues that we have been too quick to create canons, define terms, and draw boundaries. In the essential early phases of recovering nineteenth-century African American literature, many scholars placed the slave narrative at the center of the endeavor and often asserted that there were few (if any) texts at the margins. African American authors, this argument went, did not explore a wide range of genres until the end of the nineteenth century. Still, while many African Americanist critics operating under this older model drew sharp limits around the field, some were more open to considering not just a range of slave narratives—those fitting easily into emerging definitions of the genre and those not—but also some other texts and genres. Many (white-centered) Americanists, on the other hand, took the reduction of nineteenth-century Black literature to the slave narrative and reduced even more. Thus, standing in for the slave narrative—a massive and diverse genre that the very word "the" denies—we often have just Frederick Douglass, or more properly, Douglass's 1845 *Narrative*; recognizing some need for gender equity (and, one would hope, simply because of the immense power of the text), Harriet Jacobs's 1861 *Incidents in the Life of a Slave Girl* entered as a complement after Jean Fagan Yellin performed the mammoth work of overturning false and often racist assumptions that *Incidents* was not an original African American work. These two narratives are now standard fare for American literature surveys and anthologies, as part of a pseudo-genealogical narrative of Black letters running from Wheatley/Equiano through Douglass/Jacobs to the Harlem Renaissance (with perhaps a brief stop at Charles Chesnutt or Frances Ellen Watkins Harper along the way). It is also common for dissertations and monographs purporting to be multicultural to have a chapter on either Douglass or Jacobs (or both)—even when no other African American writers and thinkers are studied.[23]

Make no mistake: slave narratives were and are immensely important to any consideration of African American literature and culture. They offer brief but essential windows into the diverse kinds of conditions endured by many, many African American people in the United States before emancipation. Some also demonstrate stunning artistry; Douglass and Jacobs knew how to turn sentences as well as Emerson and Melville, albeit sometimes in different ways. These texts are, simultaneously, the result of great bravery—not only in having endured massive suffering and writing about it but, after the Fugitive Slave Law of 1850, in doing so at great personal risk. But slave narratives were not *all* of nineteenth-century African American literature. That field of texts did not simply include a handful of bound books that focused on men and, less often, women becoming unbound from American slavery, though such texts, again, were crucial. The field was much more diverse in terms of genre, approach, aesthetics, venue, and language and was amazingly dynamic even as it was shaped by systemic oppression. We are only beginning to understand its parameters, and we should have learned long ago that it stretches more broadly—temporally, aesthetically, and sociopolitically—than recent critics' sense of "what was African American literature."[24]

This volume hopes to be both a catalyst for and an example of the continuing recovery of nineteenth-century African American print in all its diversity. Better-known Black writers and activists like Frederick Douglass and Frances Ellen Watkins Harper thus enter the book at various points, and a selection of important white figures from the period—from Lincoln to (a spectral) Thoreau—visit, too. But because this book grows from an ethos of recovery, many of the authors who serve as centerpieces are "new" or "newer" to our contemporary study of (African) American print culture. An implicit and sometimes explicit argument of the book is therefore that until we attend much more to Black periodicals and Black church print, we miss essential pieces of our literary history—like, to note three examples, the fascinating dialogues with American Transcendentalism in the letters of Edmonia Highgate (discussed in chapter 6), the nineteenth-century Black poetry and poetics of figures like George Vashon (discussed in chapter 7), and exciting "firsts" like Julia Collins's *The Curse of Caste* (chapter 8).

Second, this study addresses—and further inserts discussion of African American presences into—questions of print and community that grow from the rich dialogue between critics and historians in answer to Benedict Anderson's *Imagined Communities: Reflections on the Origin and Spread of Nationalism* (1983), especially Trish Loughran's *The Republic in Print: Print Culture in the Age of U. S. Nation Building, 1770–1870* (2007).[25] Specifically, I am hesitant to define community in the binary of Anderson and Loughran. The *Recorder* actually *was*, in some ways—to use Loughran's description of the concepts she sees as most troubling in Anderson's work—the base of "a coherent and connected print culture" and part of an "apparatus that successfully knits together dispersed North American communities" (xviii–xix). That said, building from Loughran's well-founded skepticism, I recognize different senses of "coherent," "connected," and "successfully," and I often speak of a racially specific and racially segregated set of communities functioning within a larger nation-state that was itself in great flux. It seems to me that Loughran's word "knits" opens up possibilities here, as knitting is a mode of joining that allows gaps and holes even as it creates a unitary usable artifact. I hesitate to suggest that any print culture could be like seamless cloth or even sewn or quilted cloth—especially a print culture focused on and created by oppressed peoples. I see "coherence" and "connection" in the midst of gaps—perhaps sometimes because of the gaps—and "success" in both the connecting yarn and the aesthetics and politics of those gaps. I recognize that "local" might not only have geographic meaning, that a textual meeting place for geographically diverse voices might strengthen a national or communal identity, and that the Civil War—the event Loughran sees in some ways as the culmination of the lie of the "nation" as a unified concept—did not divide the AME Church (or African America) in the same ways that it split white America (or, more properly, various white Americas).

The *Recorder* and the AME Church hierarchy that put the paper into motion certainly imagined a national Black community: one of the *Recorder*'s specific charges was to link the various points of what the Church referred to as the "connexion." Print was to knit together an ever-growing, ever-diversifying Church nation (within the Black nation within the nation-state). But print was far from the only joining force, and it needs to be seen within the larger material landscape of AME life, in which, for example, itinerant ministers worked with congregations large and small across the nation. Those itinerant ministers received their charges at regional conferences that met regularly; members of those conferences were linked to each other and to a broader national Church through letters and shared sermons as well as a standard *Discipline* and hymnals and diverse other media and modes (including oral modes); members of those conferences reported to bishops (like Daniel Payne) and sent representatives to national gatherings (called general conferences), which chose bishops, revised the *Discipline* and other Church texts, and debated both national and international Church plans and presences (sometimes quite fiercely).

This AME national community was far from simply imagined. At each node, there was a physical congregation like that shown in Figure 1.4 that met regularly in a specific location (often a physical church building that members of the congregation had built—sometimes with their own hands). Those congregations heard sermons, shared bibles and hymnals, sang together (or debated the appropriateness of singing together), ate together, held each other, and interacted in a host of other ways, some of which reached into their homes and outward into their larger (geographic and other) communities. These physical congregations, church buildings, and ministers were also often the sites/agents for "imagined" rituals that were crucial to not only the spiritual lives of individual congregants but also to the material circumstances of

FIGURE 1.4 *"The Presentation of a Gold Snuff Box to the Rev. R. J. Breckinridge, D.D., in Bethel Church by Rev. Darius Stokes in behalf of the colored people of Baltimore as a gift of gratitude"* (1846). Courtesy of the American Antiquarian Society. A rare early interior view of an important AME Church—including that Church's congregants—this image is also notable because it was submitted for copyright by Daniel Payne.

those congregants: baptisms, marriages, funerals. The itinerant and circuit rider systems so critical to many varieties of Methodism also guaranteed that, over time, these congregants interacted with a range of different ministers with varying approaches to AME theology, church management, community involvement, education, and finance. Church members were sometimes incredibly mobile, and they expected their ministers, church structures, and Church hierarchy to follow suit. Before the Civil War was even finished, for example, the Church launched southern outreach efforts that proved so successful that, by the late-1860s, there were calls for a bishop to live in the South.[26] The speed and power of the Church's southern growth reached almost schismatic proportions by the late nineteenth century.

These recognitions do not demand that we idealize the Church or even the idea of a Black church community, though both were, at times, truly heroic. In all of the nodes of the AME Church and the spaces between them, there were gaps, contradictions, shifts, competing ideologies and personalities, and a host of other divisions. There was sexism, abuse, mismanagement, internalized racism, racism directed toward Native and Asian Americans, class bias, and a host of other ills. These failings and gaps do not mean, though, that the Church was not a national community, both embodied and imagined—a complex, recursive web that consistently attempted to form a more perfect union. The *Recorder* was often—and sometimes intimately—involved in the creation, revision, and joining of this community; that the Church called the paper its "organ" emphasizes its physical connection to Church bodies. As this volume shows, fascinatingly, the *Recorder* became not just a connector but a kind of connection and a kind of community of its own—a network of various nodes within the larger Church, Black "nation," and nation state.

These first two interventions may seem like narratives of progress and agency, and the third set of issues to which this book speaks—mainly through its method—centers on how we interact with and/or re-present the past and suggests that we have oversimplified these concepts in order to dismiss them. I am still struck by the recognition—made by a number of African Americanist critics in diverse ways and diverse venues—that the variations of post-structuralism most dismissive of individual agency and collective progress took hold in the US academy just as African Americans and African Americanists were trying to create a multigenerational wedge into that academy. Simultaneously, such variations of post-structuralism failed to challenge the fantasy that a text is fully realized and fully comprehensible (or playfully incomprehensible) in and of itself and can be judged by modernist or postmodernist conceptions of literary value (and values) formulated and promulgated largely by a white male elite. In this light, Douglass and Jacobs' representative positioning reads like an easy synecdochic tokenism: Douglass and/or Jacobs standing for all nineteenth-century African Americans, and their bound books standing as (non-)objects that need no context. Such moves "give"—in Wood's and Masur's senses—a space or two at the table of literary studies to African Americans, and that "gift" allows us to both ignore these authors' individuality and the host of people not at the table. It also encourages us to ignore the fact that that table was built and set by enslaved and oppressed folks who would be punished if their presence became too felt, and it tragically flattens what should be multidimensional considerations of communities, politics, and aesthetics—to say nothing of the material components of and surrounding texts.

All of these moves highlight literary criticism's dominant presentism. This volume thus attempts to, as Nancy Bentley says of Lloyd Pratt's fascinating "Stranger History," "cultivate a practice of mutual recognition . . . between past historical actors and present ones . . . rather than" deploying a sense of "historical mastery" (150).[27] Pratt concludes that "the role of the intellectual in relationship to the nineteenth century will be neither interpreter nor analyst nor agent of recovery. It will be to provide the transparent medium." While I differ from Pratt's sense of agency and recovery in some ways—including on the possibility of full transparency—I submit that some African Americanists have long practiced something like Jacques Ranciere's "sensitive fabric" (a concept on which Pratt relies heavily), centering our work on piecing together fragments, interrogating gaps, recognizing that our subjects are both far from us and very close, and knowing that, while we may know more about some things than our subjects ever could, we also know much, much less than our subjects did about other things.[28] Thus, the stories in this volume do tell of (and earnestly hope for) progress, but also, as I hope is clear in the above, recognize regression and oppression, both continuing and new. The stories here tell of individuals and communities, but recognize that these people worked with only limited agency and left us only trace presences; the book attempts to tease out those limits—all while recognizing how much we do not know about those individuals and their worlds, implicitly understanding that our agency, too, is limited.

Fourth, these commitments mean that the book directly addresses the new(er) nexus of print culture studies and African Americanist inquiry. It understands even as it sometimes challenges the recognition of Leon Jackson's important *Book History* essay that scholars of Black experiences and scholars "who study books as economic or material artifacts" have often not "listened to, or understood" each other (252). Through its praxis, it recognizes that African Americanist scholars and book historians have both much to teach each other *and* much to learn from each other: neither can assume primacy and neither can assume that long-held beliefs about scholarly practice will not need to be re-explained and sometimes even rethought. Most importantly, neither group of critics and historians can assume that their disciplinary definitions and boundaries will be static.[29] Such dynamism will hopefully allow us to save some of the best features of both disciplines—for example, the commitments of some branches of African American studies to practicing remembrance and recovery as radical political acts that work to ensure justice for oppressed people in the present and future.

This will be a long, ongoing conversation, one in which all involved will need to listen, ask questions, and challenge each other actively as we move forward. Indeed, even in my general use of "print culture" instead of "book history," I issue such a challenge—drawing on dawning African Americanist recognitions discussed above—to understand that bound books are not necessarily the center of nineteenth-century African American or broader American print or literature. In this vein, we must also consider approaches advocated by library and information studies scholars like Christine Pawley, who "considers institutional sites of print as a middle layer that can bridge the gap between structure and agency and between macro and micro views" within (and beyond) the history of reading (73).[30] My emphasis on helping to build approaches to "African American print culture studies" that see all of those terms in symbiosis means that I approach the *Christian Recorder* as, simultaneously, a stunning set of literary texts (broadly defined), a crucial assemblage of sociopolitical commentary on African American life and possibility, and a textual meeting place of diverse African American individuals and ideologies, as well as a collection of physical artifacts that circulated within the larger and often hostile world of American print and that were placed into circulation through acts that demonstrate limited African American agency.

Part I of this volume thus consists of three chapters that explore the cultural place of the *Recorder*; the material conditions of its history, production, and dissemination; and some of the paper's sense of the purposes and powers of print. Chapter 2 provides the fullest history available of the paper's beginnings, its resurrection at the eve of the Civil War, and its structures and management during and after the war. Central to these goals, chapter 2 (re)introduces a crucial figure in the ongoing development of both the AME hierarchy and nineteenth-century Black periodical literature, Elisha Weaver, the driving force behind the paper's 1861 resuscitation and its long-term survival. This consideration of the paper's history leads naturally to further discussion in chapter 3 of the shifting roles tied to the editorial chair (emphasizing operational concerns), as well as the paper's physical spaces, production, finances, approaches to advertising and periodical exchange, and especially distribution—all in dialogue with the denominational, regional, and racial politics governing the paper. Chapter 4 continues the exploration of questions of distribution through combining both qualitative and quantitative analysis of the paper's subscribers who were acknowledged by name in the paper. Building significantly beyond my 2011 study of *Recorder* subscribers in late 1864 and 1865, chapter 4 considers all extant subscription acknowledgments published between January 1861 and December 1867. From such listings, I have been able to identify over 1,100 first-time individual subscribers (including subscribers who sent almost seven hundred renewals) and so to begin to think about both the individuals and the households that represented the *Recorder*'s most likely long-term readers.

Flowing from these gestures toward a cultural and material history of the early *Recorder* and working in some ways as a transition to the rest of the book, chapter 5 opens Part II by exploring how the paper represented acts of reading and writing. It gives special attention to the political, social, cultural, aesthetic, and community-building functions the *Recorder* ascribed to African Americans engaging in such acts. Chapter 5 creates a bridge from the *Recorder*'s history toward chapters that focus more on close contextual study of individual (sets of) texts. Specifically, chapter 5 considers the *Recorder*'s sense of reading as embodied in texts for and/or created by three critical groups of subscribers engaged in a reading/writing nexus: AME ministers, Black soldiers, and single women. Building from this framework, the book's three final chapters are organized around genre and hint at the *Recorder*'s power and range through sampling, again always in dialogue with the paper's goals, structures, and readers.[31] While these later chapters (like parts of chapter 5) often rely on "close reading" of individual, selected texts, they are based on a sense, to use Samuel Otter's words, that "close reading also can be wide and deep" and that we should "examine the workings . . . of lived experience— or, to describe my investment more precisely, of experience as refracted through and considered in literary terms" (16, 18). In this vein, while these chapters offer critical details about the *Recorder*, they are initiatory—designed first and foremost to alert scholars to work that needs to be done much more fully if we are to have a better understanding not just of the paper or the Black press but of nineteenth-century African American and broader American literature and culture and all that followed.

Chapter 6 examines what is perhaps the paper's most important—or, at least, most pervasive—form: correspondence. It emphasizes the development of correspondence as a multifaceted nexus of genres and concerns that challenge contemporary conceptions of both American epistolarity and Black press traditions. To illustrate the wide boundaries of the "letter" and the *Recorder*'s community of print, the chapter's central examples—texts by Daniel Adger and Edmonia Goodelle Highgate—illustrate how studying *Recorder* correspondence can also challenge representations of, for example, Black (inter)nationalism and American Transcendentalism. Chapter 7 focuses on the *Recorder*'s poetry and poetics, with emphasis on the elegy—a form central not only to the paper but also to the larger print culture of the period. Memories and stories of Abraham Lincoln return to the book perhaps most prominently here. However, chapter 7 places the paper's original elegies to Lincoln in dialogue with a host of Black elegies in the *Recorder*—including an amazing rediscovered elegy George Boyer Vashon wrote for his daughter Anne Paul Vashon, as well as a series of poems published in the years surrounding

Lincoln's assassination on the deaths of young AME stalwart Frederick Waugh and Elisha Weaver's wife Mary—to think about how the *Recorder*'s community came together to mourn. Chapter 8 studies Julia C. Collins's *The Curse of Caste*, the (incomplete) serialized novel that ran in the paper between February 25, 1865, and September 23, 1865, and that was recovered and published in book form for the first time in 2006. My discussion of *Curse* considers the novel's "firstness" both among Black women's letters and in the *Recorder*, the shape of its serialization, and its geographic range vis-à-vis the paper's reach, but it focuses on questions of faith and location with attention to the protagonist (light-skinned governess Claire Neville) but emphasis on her darker-skinned caregiver (Juno Hays), a figure largely absent from criticism to date.

All of the chapters in Part II—like the earlier portions of the book—sound refrains critical to the book as a whole: that we need to rethink our conclusions about African American and broader American literature and print culture (to say nothing of figures like Lincoln and Payne); that preexisting models of "community" and "nation" cannot be dropped onto nineteenth-century African American individuals and texts or our (re)presentation of them; that we need to think about (limited) African American agency and not assume presentist superiority; that we need to consider approaches to "book history" that open possibilities for under-represented texts, authors, venues, and groups in ways that critically but also dynamically appreciate the traditions within and surrounding those texts, authors, venues, and groups; that we need to study and consistently reevaluate the multivalence of my title's "Black print" and its optimistic "unbound"; and that each chapter of this volume could be expanded into a book in and of itself.

{ PART I }

"Our Church Organ": Toward a Cultural and Material History of the Early *Recorder*

{2}

"Dense Darkness": Recovering the *Recorder*'s History

"Dear Dr. Tanner," wrote Professor Wiley Lane from his desk at Howard University, "I have just been trying" to direct "a young man [to] the sources of information in regard to the A. M. E. Church, but I am sorry to say that the help I can give him is very limited. As I have several times been questioned in this matter, it occurred to me that you would do a favor to many persons if you would print in the RECORDER an answer to the following question, viz.: What are the sources of exhaustive information in regard to the A. M. E. Church?" The recipient of Lane's February 1884 letter, then-editor of the *Recorder* Benjamin Tucker Tanner, printed both Lane's text and his own response in the March 6, 1884, *Recorder* under the heading "Sources of Information." He prefaced Lane's request with a recognition that "scarcely a week passes by that we are not the recipient of a call for such information."

Before answering Lane's question, Tanner observed that "when a man like Prof. Lane writes this, we can readily imagine the dense darkness of the 'regions beyond.'" Some of Tanner's readers knew that "a man like Prof. Lane" meant an African American just past thirty years old with an AB from Howard, a second AB from Amherst, the honor of being only the third African American Phi Beta Kappa, an MA from Howard, a record of successful teaching, and a professorship of Greek Language and Literature in Howard's College Department.[1] If these achievements were not enough to make Lane familiar to *Recorder* readers, he had also been lauded in the paper for his work on civil rights efforts with luminaries like the aging Frederick Douglass.[2] Less than a year before querying Tanner, Lane had engaged in a very public battle with James Geddes Craighead, the (white) dean of Howard's theology department, over African American education and colonization. The *Recorder* had given Lane's statements—calling out some white educators for racism and paternalism—almost four full columns of its July 26, 1883, and August 9, 1883, issues. That a man "like Prof. Lane" could give only "very limited" help when asked to share the AME past gave Tanner great pause over what had already been lost, forgotten, or simply never known by his readership and the broader nation.

While Lane's query was about Church history generally, it was also centered on Church print: he chose as his expert not one of the Church's bishops but the editor of its newspaper, and he wanted a bibliography of printed sources to appear in print in that newspaper.[3] Tanner complied. His answer first notes "the printed minutes of our Annual and General Conferences" but rightly recognizes that this "source of information . . . can scarcely be obtained by the general public" and might not even be fully extant. Tanner also cites Daniel Payne's 1866 *Semi-Centenary and Retrospection of the African Methodist Episcopal Church*, his own 1867 *Apology for African Methodism*, Alexander Wayman's 1881 *My Recollections of African M. E. Ministers* and 1882 *Cyclopedia of African Methodism*, and his own recently published *Outline of Our History and Government*.

But before listing these books—all part of a kind of Black liberation historiography and all inflected with what Julius Bailey rightly calls "race patriotism"—Tanner (shown in Figure 2.1) emphasizes periodicals. He first notes the *African Methodist Episcopal Church Magazine*, which had been published between 1841 and 1847. But even Tanner, at the heart of AME print culture, notes that "it is difficult to come into possession of a full set" of the *Magazine* and that "indeed, it is questionable whether a full set really exists."[4] He thus emphasizes "the Church organ, the CHRISTIAN RECORDER, formerly the Christian Herald, ordered by the General Conference of 1848 to be published in Pittsburg[h], with Rev. A. R. Green as editor. It has continued until this day. No history of the Church can be written without it, for it is one of the most prolific sources of information relating to our onward progress. Others doubtless have bound copies of the official organ, but the only man we know to possess them is Bishop [Jabez Pitt] Campbell."

What Tanner does and doesn't say about the *Christian Recorder* frames much of this chapter. His mingling of fact, fiction, and omission in his brief historical-bibliographic entry hints at the ways that pieces of the *Recorder*'s own history have been minimalized, hidden, and lost. This chapter thus first provides a brief primer of AME history (with emphasis on AME print) and then explores Tanner's claims about the *Recorder*'s extant presence, birth, and publication history. In part because most "histories" of the early *Recorder* say little more than Tanner and in part because standard bibliographic sources have massive gaps and errors, this chapter's initial argument is that we simply need a fuller sense of the basic elements of the paper: How many issues were published and when? Which issues survive and how did they survive? How did the paper begin? Who were its founders and principal workers? In exploring the latter two questions, the chapter pays special attention to documenting the shifts in and around the *Recorder*'s leadership between 1860 and 1868—beginning with a brief discussion of power structures within the AME Church and then exploring how, following the fits and starts of the 1840s and 1850s, the *Recorder* became a lively nexus for diverse

B. T. TANNER.

FIGURE 2.1 *Benjamin Tucker Tanner, from William J. Simmons's* Men of Mark: Eminent, Progressive, and Rising *(1887). Courtesy of the General Research and Reference Division, Schomburg Center for Research in Black Culture, The New York Public Library, Astor, Lenox and Tilden Foundations.*

voices and a force for developing African American print culture. In this, it emphasizes the shifting power base of Elisha Weaver, the paper's central figure in the 1860s and one of the most important and understudied figures in nineteenth-century Black culture. Building from this work, chapter 3 offers the fullest account of the Civil War–era *Recorder*'s material processes available—one that begins to attend to questions of the paper's publication, structure, funding mechanisms, and distribution, all of which flowed from the Church's conflicting definitions of the paper and its leadership. Taken together, these chapters develop a sense of the *Recorder*'s place and workings in a variety of communities and locations, setting the stage for chapter 4's consideration of the paper's subscribers and for this volume's broader attention to the *Recorder*'s texts.

By the time of Lane and Tanner's exchange, Black church print culture already had a long and complex history as well as an important place in broader Black print—so much so that Frances Smith Foster's narrative "of the interesting origins and (somewhat) surprising developments of African American print culture" begins not with the 1827 birth of *Freedom's Journal* but "with the founding of mutual aid, fraternal, and religious societies in the eighteenth century" ("A Narrative" 719). Stephen Angell and Anthony Pinn describe the AME aspect of these events:

> The origins of the AME Church are complex. The denomination traces its beginnings to the establishment by black Methodist Richard Allen and others of an ecumenical Free African Society in 1787. Over the next three decades, black Methodists underwent a complex differentiation process from white Methodists, on the one hand, and their black Episcopalian and Quaker brothers and sisters in the Free African Society on the other hand. This process culminated in the establishment of the African Methodist Episcopal denomination in 1816 at a conference attended by like-minded African American Christians from Philadelphia; Baltimore; Wilmington, Delaware; Attleborough, Pennsylvania; and Salem, New Jersey. (xiv)[5]

Daniel Coker was asked to be the Church's first bishop, but he declined, paving the way for Allen. Both were deeply interested in print—as were many of their brethren—and so it is no surprise that, only a year later, the Church started the AME Book Concern, which Foster marks as "the first known African American publishing company" ("A Narrative" 721). Such acts embody the fact, according to Foster, that "Afro-Protestant churches, almost from the moment they formally organized, fostered a print culture that included hymnals, church disciplines and record books, history and other textbooks, personal testimonies, sermons, meditations, and inspirational or educational literature" (721). Foster and scholars like Julius Bailey also recognize that, again in Foster's words, "these texts were less prosaic than this description might suggest," in part because they descended from works like Allen and Absalom Jones's 1794 defense of Black Philadelphians' work in the city's yellow-fever epidemic and Coker's stunning 1810 *Dialogue between a Virginian and an African Minister* (721). As Chanta Haywood and Foster argue, as a "center of black life, political, social and religious, the Afro-Protestant church had an obvious imperative to create its own information system. Though the surviving records are fragmentary and details are scarce, it is clear that the establishment of an official newspaper or publishing facility was an immediate priority of each emerging denomination" (22).

While funding was always uneven, the Church valued the Book Concern: Allen was not only the first AME bishop but also the first leader of the Concern, the "Book Steward." AME print production was limited until the 1840s, and Mitch Kachun is generally correct that "before the 1840s, the operations of the Book Concern remained those of a routing agency" (650). Still, the texts they did publish—especially the *Doctrines and Discipline of the African Methodist Episcopal Church* outlining Church law and practice and the AME hymnal—were crucial for many African Americans. There are several reasons for the increased activity of the 1840s and 1850s. Then well into its second generation, the AME Church had grown considerably and become much more geographically diverse. Daniel Payne had an especially massive impact in this period; Angell and Pinn are correct that he "managed almost single-handedly to reorient the position of the AME Church on education from indifference to one of strong support, especially for ministers" (xix). Rising to a bishopric in 1852, Payne, who had been born in South Carolina, brought a strong sense of the Church's responsibility to enslaved African Americans and a deep commitment to print culture. He also sensed possible links between the two, as he knew that immediatist abolitionists—almost nonexistent among white Americans at the time of the Church's founding—had grown into a notable presence in the North and a threatening specter to the white South in part because of print. Payne and the broader nation's engagement with print was made possible by the fact that printing and publishing processes, distribution and mail systems, literacy rates, and regional and national commerce systems had all seen significant improvements by the 1840s. White religious organizations—supported in part by massive numbers of colporteurs—were beginning to spread bibles and tracts far and wide. Payne and his AME colleagues knew that a stronger AME print presence could aid Church work in a host of ways, allow the diffuse pieces of the Church to stay connected, and create spaces for Black voices in a (white) public sphere that continued to exclude, deride, and ignore them. He also knew that a stronger Church print culture would be crucial to his pushes for more educated ministers and a more literate laity.[6]

Foster and Haywood's recognition that "the surviving records" of such early explorations of print by African Americans "are fragmentary" and that "details are scarce" demands that we pause to consider such sources before offering too much more history and analysis. Almost all contemporary scholars who mention the *Recorder* rely heavily on two sets of sources: extant periodical texts and African American-authored histories of the Church and of the Black press written at the end of the nineteenth century. There are, of course, additional primary texts—a handful of autobiographies of select ministers; Church records that, by good fortune, survived; occasional sets of personal papers; the rare diary (like Tanner's from 1860–1861, available online through the Library of Congress); and diverse miscellaneous documents. But coverage is incredibly spotty.

Of special concern is the extant presence of the *Recorder*. Tanner's statement that "others doubtless have bound copies of the official organ, but the only man we know to possess them is Bishop Campbell" was painfully predictive of how close the early *Recorder* has come to being lost. Like many nineteenth-century newspapers, the *Recorder* was probably seen as ephemeral by the vast majority of its readers; copies were thus likely used for insulation, doll stuffing, wrapping paper, kindling, and a host of other household purposes.[7] Some were likely cut up, and some of the pieces may have been pasted on walls or even scrapbooked, as discussed in the fascinating work of Ellen Gruber Garvey.[8] Some were likely thrown away by Black soldiers already loaded down with equipment; others may have been buried with some of those same Black soldiers. Wilberforce reportedly had a full run of not only the *Recorder* but also many other critical AME texts; however, much of their initial collection perished in the fire of 1865.[9] And, of course, many of the libraries and repositories of the period were plagued by racist approaches to collection development, weeding, and preservation that stopped the *Recorder* from reaching or staying on their shelves. In many ways, it is amazing that a significant run of the *Recorder* survived at all, and it is clear that many nineteenth-century historians did not have access to extended runs of the paper.[10]

The fullest set of the *Recorder* was, as Tanner noted, kept by Jabez Pitt Campbell, and it was inherited by Mother Bethel AME Church in Philadelphia. That church's archives and museum continue to carefully preserve Campbell's run. This set was microfilmed in 1973, with film copies deposited with the Historical Society of Pennsylvania, distributed to a number of libraries, and later rereleased by Scholarly Resources/Gale. The Mother Bethel run of Campbell's copies (minus the 1854–1856 issues) was also used for the online version of the *Recorder* owned by Accessible Archives, and it served as the source for the significant excerpts from the *Recorder* that are included in the *Black Abolitionist Papers* (in paper, microfilm, and online formats) and the *Black Periodical Literature Project* (in microfilm with an online index).[11] The digital full-text products are only available through (sometimes quite expensive) fee-based programs, and the microfilm is generally available only at or through select university libraries. The vast majority of students and scholars who use the *Christian Recorder* access it through one of these modes; students scanning any of these products will even note, when images are provided, variations of Campbell's name handwritten on the tops of first pages of some issues. The vast majority of WorldCat records for the *Recorder*—including those for some repositories that erroneously claim paper copies—are for these film or electronic versions. Thus, in short, almost all contemporary citations of the *Recorder* reach back to the Campbell copies.

Paper issues of the *Recorder* from the Civil War and Reconstruction are exceedingly rare, and almost all that are extant are included in the Campbell run. The American Antiquarian Society, for example, has two issues—only one of which (September 14, 1876) is not on the Campbell film. Other nineteenth-century copies noted by the online *Chronicling America* project (sponsored by the National Endowment for the Humanities and the Library of Congress and tied to the federal and state newspaper projects) are housed at the Boston Public Library, Harvard, the Kittochtinny Historical Society of Chambersburg (Pennsylvania), the Moorland-Spingarn collection at Howard, the New-York Historical Society, the New York Public Library, and the Historical Society of Pennsylvania; all seem to duplicate issues on the Campbell film. Drew University has a significant post-1880 collection of paper issues that were being cataloged as this book went to print.

It is possible that there are other paper issues in US repositories that are not fully cataloged, not covered by *Chronicling America*, and/or in private collections. The libraries and archives of many historically Black colleges, for example, remain drastically underfunded—limiting both preservation and cataloging efforts—and some private institutions were not active participants in the federal newspaper project that shaped *Chronicling America*.[12] Church collections often remain uncataloged (and at great risk), and the AME Church has no central archival repository. Further, individuals who were editors, writers, donors, subscribers, single-copy purchasers, and/or advertisers may have left collections to descendants, community groups, or individuals, so uncataloged copies could exist in a range of places. Campbell's foresight—and that of Mother Bethel—in saving seemingly ephemeral objects was thus nothing short of heroic, but individuals hoping to see even a full early *issue* that is freely and openly accessible—much less online—will be disappointed. There are no issues of the early *Recorder* available, for example, through the much-heralded *Chronicling America* project, and proprietary interests among online vendors mean that this situation is unlikely to change in any substantial way.

Further complicating matters, bibliographic and cataloging entries for the early *Recorder* are often deeply inaccurate; indeed, in the course of this study, I found *no* entry for the *Recorder* that is completely correct. The landmark *African American Newspapers and Periodicals: A National Bibliography* (1998), for example, describes the Campbell microfilm at the Historical Society of Pennsylvania as "[v.1, n.1–v.50, n.40] Microfilm [July 13, 1854–Dec. 25, 1902]" (151). The listing's "v.1, n.1" is simply an error, as the July 13, 1854, issue referenced here is actually volume 1, number 16. While the *National Bibliography*'s listing for the microfilm at the Wisconsin Historical Society corrects this error, a greater problem is that both of these listings—like other catalog records—suggest that these institutions' films contain continuous and full extant runs.

The Campbell collection and all of the derivative products in both microfilm and electronic modes are actually significantly incomplete. A careful examination of the mastheads and contents of all issues of the *Recorder* from 1861 to 1868 on the Campbell film reveals at least a dozen fully missing issues and at least thirty more issues that are partial (usually missing at least two of the standard four pages).[13] I say "at least" here because the paper's numbering fell victim to several errors over the years and because there were gaps during the tumult of 1868, so there are likely even more issues missing from the Campbell film.[14] I have found *no* library catalog records that note these gaps—which, when totaled, may equal up to a half-year's worth of missing *Recorder* pages *just* between 1861 and 1868.[15]

It is likely that we have forever lost many more issues than we will ever recover. If racist collection development and weeding policies destroyed many copies in the not-so-distant past, misperceptions that there are full runs of the paper in microform or online (growing from the repeated miscataloging of Campbell derivatives) as well as the continuing pressures on libraries to clear shelves of periodicals may have led institutions to destroy significant runs of the paper more recently. We run a continuing risk that over-simplistic approaches to digitization—like the premature celebration of the possibilities of microforming—will lead individuals and institutions from the Library of Congress on down to similarly dismiss the value of physical, paper remnants of past periodicals.[16] As powerful and exciting as it is, digitization also does not equate to access, especially for those on the wrong side of paywalls. What we have of the *Recorder*, then, demands not only further study but also renewed attempts to find extant copies, preserve them, and make them accessible. Understanding the *Recorder*'s structure, history, and value to students of Black literature and culture may be a first step in these processes.

The murkiness of the *Recorder*'s extant presences, the relative dearth of paper copies, and the lack of wide access to the paper's extant remnants has undoubtedly contributed to the number of errors in accounts of the paper's early history; many scholars simply didn't have access to extant issues. Selective reporting by some church historians and the "life" of errors in scholarship—some of which can be traced back generations to single sources—has surely made this situation worse. Among contemporary scholars, a lack of understanding of AME structures and processes has contributed to even more problems—so much so that, prior to turning to the *Recorder*'s history, I first offer a primer on these structures and processes.[17]

While Richard Newman's biography of Richard Allen usefully challenges definitions of (white) founding fathers within national(ist) schema, there has been little discussion of the AME adaptations and revisions of national governance models. Exploring the "Methodist Episcopal" portion of the Church's identity within a sociopolitical frame that discriminated massively against anything "African," the Church—from its inception—recognized the need for local units to be part of broader and more powerful groups, even if members were also consistently suspicious of allowing too much centrality and too much power to be vested in any one region, church, or individual. By 1852, the AME had developed a complex, evolving, and often-contentious structure to manage and (sometimes) lead a "connection" that was spreading across the nation. As in the US national model, the Church tried to balance "federal" and "regional" bodies and questions, and the AME General Conference included delegates from diverse geographic locations and met every four years (only a few months before each US presidential election). But the AME Church did not have a clear executive head, did not have the bicamerality common in both state and federal US governance models, and did not clearly separate its powers (for example, it had no separate judiciary). AME regional bodies and especially regional conferences shifted *much* more actively than states in terms of both boundaries and character and really have no clear analogy in US politics. Each General Conference saw arguments over moving individual churches from one conference to another as well as regular pushes to change existing conferences and add new conferences.[18] Individual ministers could also move—or be moved—from one conference to another, and sometimes movement up or down power structures necessitated moves from one regional conference to another. Regional conferences were sometimes competitive in their relations with each other and even with the national Church; several conflicts surrounding the Book Concern, for example, centered on the Philadelphia Conference's claims that it was charged with managing that entity. In part because of the difficulties of national meetings—which were expensive, demanded travel, and were shaped by diverse forms of racism, including limits on mobility and assembly within individual locations' "Black laws"—regional conferences met formally each year, and informal groups tied to regional conferences sometimes met more often. Significant power thus sometimes rested within such groups.

Similarly, while the Church had "heads," it emphasized plurality, dialogue, and change in terms of leadership structures. After the 1852 General Conference, the Church had three bishops; after Bishop Willis Nazrey's exodus to the Canada-centered British Methodist Episcopal (BME) Church and the elections at the 1864 General Conference, it had four; later, it would have more. Each bishop was charged with overseeing one or more of the Church's regional conferences, but these assignments generally changed at least every four years. Further, while bishops generally presided at the annual meetings of their regional conference(s), they were almost always joined at such gatherings by other bishops—even to the level of sharing the chair and the duties tied to presiding. They had the notable power of assigning charges to the ministers in their conferences, but this was often a process that included negotiating with other bishops, conference leaders, and sometimes individual congregations and ministers. Bishops were adjudicators for a host of conflicts and could impose diverse sanctions, but their findings could be (and sometimes were, in fierce battles) appealed to General Conference meetings. While some of the bishops' power was formal, much was informal and dependent on being politically savvy enough to build coalitions. Even though the bishops offered a joint message to each General Conference, they were themselves diverse individuals who operated with varying combinations of piety and self-interest, conservatism and liberalism, long-term vision and short-term pragmatism.

Ministers were, of course, a key point of interface between the formal (national) Church organization and local congregations. However, itinerancy and mobility have long been recognized as centerpieces of traditions tied to American Methodism, and so the circumstances of ministers shifted regularly based in part on bishops' appointments. Each AME minister had to balance being a figure of (national) Church control and an advocate for a local congregation's needs and wants—as well as an individual agent within a Church hierarchy, a leader of a local Church congregation, and, in some ways, an employee of both that congregation and the national hierarchy. Further, all of these issues swirled with individual ambition, wages, living conditions, spiritual hopes, and each minister's individual calling. Almost by definition, the annual appointment structure limited individual local power: a minister who stayed with a charge for only a year or two could rarely consolidate the force needed for massive change, and congregations and ministers were always in the mode of getting to know one another. The process also emphasized that the minister was an agent of the larger Church—replaceable by any other qualified agent. Such circumstances could also breed competition; some charges were richer, more active, and/or more prestigious than others. Circuits of several small churches, for example, were often less prestigious and powerful than large congregations who could afford a single minister to attend to their (and only their) needs.

All that said, in other ways, such structures could lend power to select individual ministers. The minister who had held several successful charges throughout a conference could call on laity from several locations to help in both political questions and in securing funds; a savvy coalition-builder could sometimes gain better charges or avoid difficult churches. Such experienced ministers were also often the avenue through which younger ministers entered the Church, and so complex webs of individual debts and friendships could similarly allow ministers to create bases of power from diffuse sources. Further, ministers were also often in short supply—especially in the Church's newer regions—and so circuits and charges could change rapidly, the rate of potential power consolidation in different conferences varied significantly, and Church decisions were sometimes made with the simple goal of having a member of the AME hierarchy present in some fashion in a given location (regardless of whether the hierarchy had a full understanding of that location).

Individual churches were similarly far from static. In addition to the regular creation of new churches as well as divisions of existing congregations (friendly and not), church memberships could vary widely given the mobility (both geographic and sometimes class or sociopolitical) of the period and given that other Black denominations (as well as some white denominations) were often in competition for members. Major churches—Mother Bethel in Philadelphia being archetypal—could be more stable: they often had core members whose families' church presences were multigenerational, buildings that were designed to last, diverse financial holdings, corollary sociopolitical groups (ranging from mutual aid societies to literary clubs), and niches of community involvement. An individual charge could also be loaded with local politics, congregants who knew much more about local circumstances than ministers, and members who had connections to not only local politics but also important figures in the regional or national Church hierarchy. Some congregants and congregations were powerful enough to demand longer terms for ministers who served them well, and some were strong enough to expel pastors who were not to their liking.

That said, certain structures were designed to keep power from individual congregants and congregations. While the laity often had a real presence at annual regional conference meetings, their rights and responsibilities were considerably lesser than those of figures who had reached some level of ordination, and while annual conferences were the site of much important business, most larger issues were addressed solely at General Conference meetings, which often lasted for weeks.[19] Technically, delegates to the General Conferences were there to represent the individual regional conferences, but delegations were almost always full of ordained ministers. Because General Conferences were regularly changing and growing collections of individuals whose actions might be shaped by—in addition to their own deep faith—allegiances to specific theologies, locations, other individuals, factions, traditions, and material concerns, those meetings could, from day to day and even hour to hour, range from high ceremony to confused squabbling to skilled negotiation and coalition-building—much of which left out the laity.

All of these structures were, at least in theory, governed by the *Doctrines and Discipline of the African Methodist Episcopal Church* (the *Discipline*), a text so important that its first 1817 edition followed the Church's formation and was one of the earliest book-length Black publishing endeavors in the nation. While the *Discipline* spent much time on metaphysical matters—such as the trinity, free will, and original sin—it also contained concrete instructions on both ritual and governance. Initially formed from liberal adaptations of various Methodist statements and emphasizing the Church's sense of itself as Wesleyan, the *Discipline* soon grew into an entity specific to the AME world. It was revised every four years, and the General Conference was the sole location of voting on each and every revision. Within these frames, the AME Church was thus far more embodied than Benedict Anderson's "imagined communities" but shared some of their national(istic) features.[20]

Some hoped Church print and especially the *Recorder* would be national normalizing agents, but this inherently meant that Church print could also be a tool to advance individual and factional interests. Complicating matters, the *Recorder*'s publication cycle was much faster than that of the *Discipline* and the General Conference (or even the regional conferences) and much less dependent on broad consensus building. It thus both illustrated and contributed to the fragmentation of an AME national vision and the play of those diverse fragments in different configurations, even as it illustrated and contributed to a more unified operation of the AME community and AME print spaces that reached across the growing nation. Versions of these complex landscapes were the terrain of both the birth and growth of the *Recorder* and the slightly later Church histories—including Tanner's—on which most of the more recent scholarship relies.

Tanner's dating of 1848 as the founding of the *Recorder* (then called the *Christian Herald*)—as part of the growing print presence of this increasingly diverse and complex national community—and his placement of Augustus R. Green as its first editor are correct.[21] At the General Conference that year, the blacksmith-turned-minister was also elected Book Steward, taking over for George Hogarth, who had been the founding editor of the AME *Magazine* and, in Green's words, "a local deacon."[22] Green's election came with several other changes tied to AME print that the General Conference made that year: requiring that book depositories be established in each of the regional conferences, shifting publication of the *Magazine* from a monthly schedule to a quarterly one, and moving the Book Concern from New York to Pittsburgh. Most notably, as Daniel Payne wrote years later, under the Conference's auspices, "a committee was appointed to purchase the paper called *The Mystery*, with the press, types and fixtures" to begin an AME newspaper (220).[23]

Green himself, in the March 1, 1877, *Recorder*, described a rockier solo beginning of the *Christian Herald*. Because his account is absent from scholarship on the paper, it is worth quoting at length:

> As the business [of the Book Concern] was removed from the east, [and] as they had elected me, a western man, I had to negotiate with my predecessor as best I could; as in my election I did not receive one dime for settling with the ex-officer, nor removing the business. I was cast out to sea without oars, compass or chart for four years voyage [the time remaining until the next General Conference]. . . . [I]n the middle of August 1848 I went on to see about my work. Bishop Quinn having sent Rev. E. E. Garey to take my charge in Cincinnati, in the early part of July. After having borne my

expenses from that city to New York, I found my predecessor claiming what was due to him for salary, and all he was responsible for before he would consult to give up anything. Very little that was available was in his hands, except the stereotypes [plates] for Hymn Books. And the claims against it was [sic] $735.00. Some of the brethren in the west thought best not to touch it, but start in the new. I never could consent to such a way [of] doing business. As the credit of the church was at stake, and honesty is the best policy, I agreed with the ex-officer to pay all off as soon as possible. And Aug. 31, 1848, I paid of my own funds in N.Y. $255, and gave my note for the balance. Sept. 30, 1848 I gave my notes for Mystery Printing Press, for $350 and paid cash $150. And then rented my office, and hired my printers, and launched out into the deep. And on the 31st of Oct. we brought out the 1st Christian Herald.

Green here articulates several themes that would resonate through the *Recorder*'s early years: continuing financial problems, limited Church support, difficulties with geographic diversity (here, East/West), and a dual(ing) sense that the *Recorder* and the Book Concern were "businesses" but also moral enterprises shaped by "honesty."

Much has been made by contemporary critics of how "the AME Church ... purchased Martin Delany's Afrocentric and politically charged newspaper *The Mystery* and renamed it the *Christian Herald*," and this genealogy does usefully challenge assumptions about Black Church conservatism.[24] Delany had founded *The Mystery* in 1843 and was, by that point, a key figure in the fascinating and understudied Pittsburgh Black community. While only two issues of *The Mystery* seem fully extant, Robert Levine is likely correct in his sense that the paper was "committed to abolition and the development of black pride" and that, on the map of antebellum reform, the paper held a fairly radical place. That said, Levine is also likely right that "it would be a mistake to overemphasize the influence of this local journal" (27).[25] That none of the early AME histories mention Delany in connection with the *Recorder* might be (mis)read as an attempt to distance the *Recorder* from a man who was sometimes deeply controversial. However, the simple fact is that Delany likely had little—and perhaps nothing—to do with the sale of *The Mystery*: he published his editorial "Farewell to Readers of the Mystery" at the end of 1847, left the paper to a local "Publishing Committee," saw his "Farewell" reprinted in the January 21, 1848, *North Star*, and joined Frederick Douglass as co-editor of that paper well before the sale of *The Mystery* to the AME Church.[26] While Delany's "Farewell" asserted that "The MYSTERY is still afloat, with the solemn promise of the Publishers, to keep her ... in the great struggle for liberty and right," there is little evidence that the paper even, in Levine's words, "appeared irregularly after Delany departed" (39). It was likely defunct when Green purchased its "press, types and fixtures."

So Green began with debt, equipment that was at least five years old, and worn printing plates for hymnals. He seems to have had no real background in printing, editing, or publishing, and his phrasing "hired my printers" emphasizes his need to outsource some work (perhaps, given racist limitations on training in print trades, to white men). While the lack of extant issues and records hampers discussion of the *Christian Herald*, Green later claimed that he published the *Herald* "regular till May 1852, when I resigned the office" of Editor and Book Steward.[27] Most evidence suggests, though, according to a later report from Theodore Gould, that the *Herald* was actually published at best only "with some irregularity" (qtd. in Handy 270).[28]

Church historians did not blame Green for the *Herald*'s failings, though: Payne, for example, recognized him as "possessed of great energy," and Green's successor Molliston Madison Clark said Green "was indefatigable," working "day and night, in his devotion to the interests of the paper."[29] The funding and funding structures for a weekly newspaper were simply not in place. Minister Levin Tilmon's autobiography, for example, said that he had "made some efforts to obtain subscribers" for the *Herald* but had "met with very little success" in large part "because our people here are generally poor" (45–46). Green himself reported to the 1850 Ohio Conference that he had received only $326.74 out of $1,800.00 in promised subscriptions, that individual congregations often could not or would not send support, that two regional conferences had failed to send promised funds, and that simply to get the funds he had in hand, Green had "traveled during the past ten months forty-four hundred and fifty miles" (qtd. in Payne *History* 240). When he stepped down in 1852, the *Herald* was near death.

The next incarnation of the *Recorder*—the period covered by the vague, passive-voice "It has continued" in Tanner's reply to Lane—began with large plans at the 1852 General Conference. In addition to moving the Book Concern and the paper to Philadelphia, the conference voted to change the paper's name to the *Christian Recorder*. One of the *Herald*'s corresponding editors, long-time minister Molliston Madison Clark was chosen to edit the "new" paper—working in concert with William T. Catto, the new Book Steward, and William H. Jones, the Concern's new "travelling agent."[30] Payne called them "three of the best educated men in the Connection" (*History* 279). Clark, a deeply respected friend of Martin Delany, had attended Jefferson College, was multilingual, and was an important figure in the Church. He planned a weekly with an annual subscription price of $1.50—after Green's experiences, theoretically required in advance—that would "not know any social or geographical distinction among our people of East or West, of North or South, but shall be the equal friend of all" and would focus on "1. Religion. 2. Morality. 3. Science and Literature" (qtd. in Payne *History* 279). Some of these high hopes were likely shaped by Payne and Willis Nazrey, two active proponents of AME print who had risen to bishoprics at the same General Conference.

While no issues of Clark's *Recorder* seem extant, Payne's 1891 *History of the African Methodist Episcopal Church* includes excerpts and some description—leading with his own long poem, "Dedicatory Lines to the Recorder." Payne reports that Clark's first issue was published on July 1, 1852, and focused on the General Conference proceedings. Other texts noted by Payne (some of which he reprints) suggest that Clark was already developing the impressive range of authors that would become a hallmark of the later paper: two essays by activist J. W. C. Pennington, two poems and two essays by Frances Ellen Watkins (later Harper), two poems by T. M. D. Ward, and pieces by figures like Mary Still, Jabez Pitt Campbell, Amos Beman, Joshua Woodlin, and Sarah M. Douglass.

The AME leadership was impressed enough that Nazrey used part of his 1854 address to the Baltimore Conference to argue that "If the ministers and people would use their influence in favor of" the *Recorder*, it

> would be sustained. It was the great organ of the Connection, through which we could hear from every part of it. We live too much estranged from one another, and will ever be so until we will support a weekly paper that can connect every portion of the Church by weekly intelligence. That it may shed light and truth among us, it must be ably supported. But that cannot be done without . . . untiring efforts on the part of the ministry. . . . Let us, therefore, be aroused from our sleep. Let us take hold as one man, laughing at difficulties and opposition. O, let us but will it, and it shall be done. (qtd. in Payne, *History*, 306–307)

Nazrey's crystallization of the goals of and for the *Recorder*—to cement and expand the AME's practice of community through print—is powerful. But both the need to say these things and his use of the past tense—"was the great organ"—mark the paper's continuing problems. Catto had resigned after three months as Book Steward, and Clark stepped into that office, too—repeating Green's double charge (Wright 302, Payne 315).

Clark focused his efforts on the Book Concern, where unfinished stock—two thousand copies of the latest *Discipline* and eight hundred hymnals that were not yet bound—worried him; the copies of the *Discipline* were most troubling, as they would become obsolete when the 1856 General Conference met. Clark's report to the 1854 Philadelphia Annual Conference—which appeared in the July 13, 1854, *Recorder*—recommended binding and trying hard to sell as many copies of the *Discipline* as possible. But readying this stock for sale would be expensive; had they done so "and published, weekly, the Recorder, there would be at this time an additional debt of $2200"—more than the worth of the full Book Concern. With regret, Clark recognized "the necessity of suspending the paper . . . after having published three numbers in . . . the conference year . . . comprising 4500 copies." Clark's report was loaded with language suggesting Church anger at his decision, and he defended the choice as one made "between two evils—the accumulation of heavy debt, without probability of payment, and the blame of suspension, until this Conference, whose prerogative it is to order the resumption . . . or sanction the course of . . . suspending it." However, Clark wrote, "Nothing ought to induce the Conference to resume its publication until . . . capital" could be raised. "Every trial without . . . capital will prove an utter failure." Clark tendered his resignation as both Book Steward and editor at that 1854 meeting. He had published fifteen issues of the *Recorder* in his two years as editor. William Jones resigned that year, too, leaving the leadership of the Book Concern completely vacant.

The conference essentially ignored Clark's recommendations. Nazrey appointed Jabez Pitt Campbell (see Figure 2.2) to the AME's Union Church in Philadelphia, and soon after, the Bishops named Campbell both Book Steward and *Recorder* editor—eliding, for the moment, the additional absence caused by Jones's resignation and not publicly commenting on the demands Campbell would face in pastoring a large church on top of his new Book Concern responsibilities. Campbell restarted the *Recorder* with a July 13, 1854, issue, and, ironically, included Clark's recommendations *against* restarting the paper. Counting forward from Clark's paper, he numbered his first issue sixteen. It is the earliest issue of the paper known extant—likely the reason that the *National Bibliography* lists Campbell as the paper's first editor. He seems to have planned to publish biweekly. However, for most of 1855, the

FIGURE 2.2 *Jabez Pitt Campbell and Mary A. Campbell, from* Proceedings of the Quarto Centennial Conference of the African M. E. Church of South Carolina *(1890). Courtesy of the State Archives of Florida.*

paper was, for all practical purposes, a monthly, with almost every issue apologizing for delays and calling for more funding.[31] In the July 11, 1855, issue, Campbell noted that the Philadelphia Conference had authorized him to shift to semimonthly publication until the next General Conference, and the August 18, 1855, issue included some debate about moving from a semimonthly newspaper to a monthly magazine, as "a religious newspaper cannot be sustained" without dependable financial support. The paper skipped a full month in September 1855 and again in February 1856, and the last extant issue from Campbell's time as editor—number 39—came out on March 4, 1856.

Campbell's paper emphasized Church business, though it did attend to literature, the arts, science, and history and expanded the paper's sense of family and children's literature.[32] Still, Campbell's *Recorder* was modest, and his report to the 1856 General Conference was decidedly mixed. On the one hand, he noted that the Book Concern had been officially incorporated in Pennsylvania, that Hogarth's old hymnal plates "had been repaired," and that the Concern was "free from debts to their printer" (qtd. in Payne *History* 333). On the other hand, "in the two entire years they had been able to publish only nineteen numbers of the *Christian Recorder*" (333).[33] Always strapped for cash, the General Conference formally abolished the agent position vacated by Jones. They affirmed the combination of the positions of Book Steward and *Recorder* editor into a single office, and directed Campbell to continue in this role. Campbell later noted with some chagrin that he resigned in June 1858 to pastor full-time but was quickly "elected President of the Board of Trustees for the Book Concern, and by them appointed their Agent ... and bookseller. This appointment made me virtually just what I was before my resignation" (Tanner 170). That said, Campbell, like Clark, turned his energies toward the Book Concern; there is no evidence that he published another issue of the *Recorder*.

Many in the Church who were interested in print turned away from the possibilities of a weekly newspaper after Campbell's 1856 report. Loosely under Payne's initial leadership, a group of several ministers who (like Payne) favored a more educated ministry and laity and who wanted to build print opportunities for such education signed on to edit a new Church quarterly, *The Repository of Religion and Literature and of Science and Art*, whose first issue came out in April 1858.[34] Elisha Weaver, John Mifflin Brown, and Willis Revels (brother to future-Senator Hiram Revels) were listed as publishers. Along with "executive editor" Payne, they joined former *Recorder* editor Molliston Clark, future-Bishop Alexander Wayman, and Savage L. Hammond on the list of editors. Priced at $1.00 per year and planned to run forty-eight pages per issue, the *Repository* attended consciously to those areas Clark had promised in his *Recorder*, especially through essays and other didactic and literary texts. By 1860, the *Repository* had attracted old *Recorder* contributors like Frances Ellen Watkins Harper and Sarah Douglass as well as other important figures in early Black print like Maria Stewart and William J. Wilson.

The *Repository* demands a book-length study of its own, but for our purposes, select facets of its development are important.[35] Though Payne and other editors' work was most prominent, the magazine demonstrated again that there was a significant core of writers who could create diverse content for an AME periodical and that there were readers who wanted such. Perhaps more importantly, the *Repository* offered an alternative funding/support model—one that, in the end, may have pushed the General Conference into action on the questions both of who controlled the *Repository* and what should become of the *Recorder*. Rather than drawing its support from the General Conference or even from regional conferences, the *Repository* was tied to the "literary societies" of the Baltimore, Indiana, and Missouri regional conferences. As a cooperative venture that was distanced, if not totally free, from the bureaucracies of the Book Concern and the General Conference structure (to say nothing of the left-out Philadelphia Conference), the *Repository* had more freedom and adaptability. It also had more solid financial footing. Free of the lingering debt of both the Book Concern and the *Recorder*—remember the advice of Green's "western friends" to start anew—the *Repository* had editors with significant, financially strong charges (Weaver's in Indianapolis, Revels's in St. Louis). It also had the stamp of Payne's bishopric. The new magazine attracted a number of subscribers—reporting, perhaps over-optimistically, that by the end of its first year, it had five hundred subscribers and a profit of $35.[36] For these reasons and because of Weaver's massive investment of time and energy (he had quickly become the journal's center), the *Repository* did not miss an issue in 1858 or 1859. Taken as a whole, it suggested that an AME periodical could be a functioning, financially sound, and cross-regionally collaborative entity; that a Black Church periodical could find both writers and paying readers; and that the AMEC could become a force in shaping Black literature and culture. The national Church took notice, but the events that followed determined that it would be the *Recorder* rather than the *Repository* that would be that force.

Before the General Conference of 1860 had even begun, the Philadelphia Conference—implicitly arguing that the Book Concern was under its management and perhaps that the *Repository* had overstepped its bounds—had snapped up Weaver, naming him their "Publisher and Editor" (Tanner 176). His October 1859 farewell message in the *Repository* said that the magazine was to be left to John Mifflin Brown, who moved the operation to Philadelphia and then to Baltimore. When the General Conference convened in Pittsburgh on May 7, 1860, one of its first acts was to move Weaver from the Indiana Conference roll to the Philadelphia roll, saying that he had "been regularly transferred" (qtd. in Smith 433). But the *Recorder* and the Book Concern quickly became secondary questions at the meeting, as the majority of the delegates focused on increasing rumblings about Nazrey's interactions with Black Methodists in Canada.[37] While there was some attention to questions about "the dispute between the members of the Philadelphia Conference in reference to the Book Concern," Weaver was allowed to present the Concern reports covering 1856–1858 (when Campbell, also in the Philadelphia Conference, was still Book Steward), and 1858–1860 (440).

On May 21—the beginning of the final week of the General Conference—Augustus Green quietly moved that Weaver be appointed Book Steward. In what seems to have been a procedural question, the motion was tabled until the committee on the Book Concern made recommendations. In the meantime, there was jockeying about the *Discipline*'s language on the position—specifically on whether or not the Book Steward and the *Recorder* editor should be a single (combined) appointment. Late on May 24, the next-to-last day of the meeting, the body elected Weaver as the Book Steward and then immediately, on Campbell's motion, "separated" the position of editor from that of Book Steward and asked the bishops "to appoint some minister to a charge in Philadelphia to be Editor" and "give the Editor something for his services, not exceeding $100.00" (461). Campbell's motion and its approval remain somewhat baffling, as earlier, when the Conference was revising the *Discipline*, they had allowed Weaver to insert language that appeared to link the two positions. Further complicating the matter, Campbell's motion inherently made the editor a role that was added to a Church appointment specifically in (and under) the Philadelphia Conference's jurisdiction (458).

Post-Conference events remain hazy. The three bishops—Payne, Nazrey, and senior bishop William Paul Quinn, not fast friends and already tired from Conference battles—may not have been able to agree on an editor, or they may simply have been slow. The Philadelphia Conference that earlier titled Weaver "Publisher and Editor" may not have been in a hurry to agree to a different structure. Even the number of willing candidates is unknown—and it may have been small, as many AME print activists had already resigned from the paper, cast their fortunes with the *Repository*, and/or had other responsibilities. Weaver himself may have slowed the process. What is clear is that Weaver was now the leader of the Book Concern and that its realm included the *Recorder*; by late 1860, he was functioning as the *Recorder* editor. Weaver would remain in leadership roles tied to the Book Concern until 1868, serving longer than any of his predecessors. If we trust the paper's whole numbers—which were occasionally a bit off—this means that Weaver had a hand in 376 issues of the *Recorder* or just over 1,500 pages of print. He edited over 280 of those issues—over 1,100 pages.

Given his importance to the *Recorder* and the fact that he remains relatively unknown, Weaver and his journey to what would be a major role in early Black print culture are worth brief discussion. Born c. 1830 in North Carolina to as-yet-unknown parents, Weaver was in Indiana by the 1840s. We know that he had an uncle, David Weaver, who, according to a December 28, 1861, item, had "moved to the city of New York . . . from Salusbury [sic], North

Carolina." A December 4, 1890, *Recorder* piece places Weaver's birthplace in Fayetteville, North Carolina. But we have few traces of Weaver's youth and family. Tanner's *Apology* says Weaver was "brought up in Paoli," a small town in southeast Indiana, and was schooled by local Quakers (175). By 1846, he was "teaching school" for area African American children "under the auspices of his Quaker friends" (175). Among these "friends" was likely future Earlham president Barnabas Coffin Hobbs, who Weaver referred to in the November 1858 *Repository* as "my old school-master" (131).

He joined the AME Church's Indiana Conference in 1849. Tanner claims Weaver was granted permission by conference leader Quinn to attend Oberlin in 1852 but stayed only "a few months . . . Bishop Payne having called him into active service" (175–176). While Weaver's interactions with Oberlin are undocumented, it is clear that "active service" meant work on both a regional and national scale. Weaver was ordained a deacon and charged with raising funds for missionary work in 1853; by 1854 he was working with a national group on the Bishop Nazrey/Canada question and serving an important charge in Chicago (Payne *History* 295, 313; Handy 202, 205, 214). He was already causing some controversy, too: according to Payne's *Recollections*, Weaver "was impeached in 1857 by his [church] Board for introducing vocal and instrumental music into his Church" (234). He was also venturing into print: he wrote to the *Recorder* from Madison, Indiana, in September 1854, and his February 23, 1856, letter to Toronto's *Provincial Freeman* criticizes racism in Illinois and Michigan.

The late 1850s saw him settle into a large charge in Indianapolis and leadership of the *Repository*. The date of his marriage remains unclear, though it was likely c. 1860. His wife's name was Mary C., and her maiden name was probably Miller. According to the May 22, 1869, *Recorder* obituary for Louisa Miller (Mary Weaver's mother), Louisa Miller, and her husband had moved to Pittsburgh from Virginia in 1846, "having become convinced that justice to their children required them to remove beyond the influences of slavery." Mary was one of these children.[38] The little we know of Mary Weaver's life is discussed further in chapter 7, but the Weavers had at least two children before her death in early March of 1864—Joseph G, who was born c. 1861 and was still alive in 1920, and Elisha, who was born early in 1864 and was still alive in 1930.[39] Elisha Weaver married a second time on November 14, 1866, to Martha Statia of Newark, New Jersey. Bishop Wayman performed the ceremony, which was briefly reported in the November 24 *Recorder*. Statia, the daughter of Isaac and Martha Statia, was about 22 and so more than a decade Weaver's junior.[40] Little is known of her life. The couple had at least two daughters—Nellie, whose death at ten months of age was reported in the July 25, 1868, *Recorder*, and Martha, who was born the following year.[41]

Weaver's June 26, 1873, *Recorder* obituary by an unlisted author says that "the proprieties of the moment forbid that we should remember other than the good he strove to do and this was not a little"; this in some ways signaled Weaver's removal from almost all Church annals. Events leading up to Weaver's exit from the Book Concern—discussed later in the chapter—likely shaped that removal, but his post-*Recorder*, post–Book Concern life may also have contributed. Assigned to Buffalo, New York, Weaver was pulled out not only of the Book Concern but the Philadelphia Conference altogether. A charge of reasonable size, his new church was, nonetheless, not a major post. He stayed there only a year: the June 19, 1869, *Recorder* reported his appointment to Newark's AME Church—a lateral move perhaps influenced by his wife's home there. In late 1870, Weaver seems to have contemplated a return to print: the November 12, 1870, *Recorder* promised "an interesting letter from the Ex-Editor, Rev. E. Weaver" would appear in the November 19 issue. That letter was full of reminders of his successful work with the *Recorder*—opening with "perhaps there are hundreds, yea, thousands, of my old friends . . . who have asked themselves, time and again, where is brother Weaver"—and it hinted that he would write further. No extant evidence suggests he did.

Then-editor Tanner may not have known that Weaver had already reentered American print culture a few months earlier, though as an object rather than an agent. The May 24, 1870, *New York Herald* ran an item headed "A Colored Clerical Artful Dodger" that had the subhead "A Wolf in Sheep's Clothing Unmasked—How a 'Minister' Carried Off a Dead Man's Estate in His Pocket—A Righteous Verdict." In similarly slanted language, the story reported a two-day trial in Essex County, New Jersey, in which a group of relatives of Francis Hedden sued Weaver, claiming that he had conned Hedden into agreeing to a will "in his last hours" that named Weaver as his "sole heir." The unnamed author asserted that the family's lawyer "HANDLED ELISHA WITHOUT GLOVES and alluded delicately yet forcibly to his well known reputation for 'gallantries' in which female members of his congregation figured unpleasantly." The story pointed specifically to "a charge preferred [sic] by a female member of the flock, in which Elisha was accused of having, while escorting her home one night after meeting, assaulted her with criminal intent"—though it noted that a Church inquiry had "not sustained . . . the charge." The author claimed that Weaver had succeeded in "carrying off in his pocket" Hedden's "entire estate."

As with any report on African Americans in a racist white paper like the *Herald*, scholars must approach this text with caution; a comparative dearth of AME records further complicates such work. Francis Hedden died on December 25, 1869, and, as stated in the December 27, 1869, *Newark Evening Courier*, had funeral services in the AME Church that was in Weaver's charge. His will was filed and proved in Essex County on January 4, 1870. It actually did not name Weaver as Hedden's sole heir; in fact, it made specific bequests of furnishings and bedding to four relatives. But it did ignore his wife Sarah and named Weaver as heir to Hedden's house and lot—though the will recognized that the property was currently under a mortgage. The will implicitly told Weaver to sell the property, pay off the mortgage debt, give one of Hedden's relatives $25, and keep what was left. While two additional details could (but need not) be read as suspicious—Hedden signed with only an "x," and Weaver's mother-in-law Martha Statia was one of the will's witnesses—just where between the *Herald*'s con artist minister who fleeced a dying old man on the one hand and an honest minister aiding an illiterate man estranged from (some of) his family in giving a piece of his modest estate to his church on the other remains an open question.[42]

Soon after, Weaver seems to have run into trouble with his local congregation, the New York Annual Conference, and the Church more broadly. Again, records are frustratingly sparse, but three items offer hints. First, a brief note appeared in the January 11, 1872, *Zion's Herald*—the paper of the African Methodist Episcopal Zion church—saying that "Rev. Elisha Weaver, Book Steward, of the African Methodist Episcopal Church, has joined our Church, and been made a Presiding Elder in the Mississippi Conference." Second, a brief "Notice" signed by Weaver appeared in the April 27, 1872, *Recorder* instructing the New York Annual Conference and the presiding bishops "to see to it, that all papers and documents (original) used in my case be brought to the General Conference of the AME Church, at Nashville, Tenn., to accompany the appeal." Finally, notes on the General Conference proceedings published in the June 15, 1872, *Recorder* report that "The minutes of the secret session on Weaver's case were read and submitted for approval. H[enry]. M[cNeal]. Turner moved that the synopsis of the speeches on the case be stricken from the minutes. Carried. Cha[rle]s. Burch moved that the phrase 'indirectly acknowledging the crime' be stricken out. Agreed to by a vote of 65 to 47. On motion the minutes were approved." No actual minutes and no further information on either Weaver's (possible) exodus to the AMEZ Church or his (later) fight at the AME General Conference have yet been located. Except for his obituary, extant issues of this period essentially ignore him; the flurry of post-1870 AME histories mention him rarely when at all.

Though he would be sentenced to obscurity, in 1860 Weaver was a rising force in the AME Church. His new incarnation of the *Recorder* saw its first issue published in early January 1861; while its exact date is not known (as the issue seems to be no longer extant), Benjamin Tucker Tanner—then at a charge in Washington, DC—had received his copy by January 14, 1861, when his diary noted, "I received a letter and paper from Bro. Weaver in Philadelphia." Though Weaver was functioning as editor, he did not so name himself on the paper's masthead. Instead, in and after the January 19, 1861, issue, Weaver noted—in a smaller item that regularly appeared in the first column of the first page—that he was the Church's General Book Steward.

Tensions rose immediately. There were significant rumblings about Weaver jumpstarting the paper—so much so that a "Philadelphia resolution" (noted briefly in the *Recorder*'s June 1, 1861, account of the Philadelphia Conference's annual meeting) asserted, "the General Book Steward and Executive Committee have violated no [church] law in publishing the CHRISTIAN RECORDER. . . ." Weaver's "Editorial Correspondence" of June 22, 1861, briefly marks his pleasure that the New England Conference echoed "the Philadelphia resolution" and that "the Baltimore brethren are of the same opinion, with the exception of one or two." Some forces in the Church not only doubted whether Weaver should be editor but also whether the paper should be published at all.

The first shift at the *Recorder*'s helm happened that July: the July 13, 1861, issue continued to list Weaver as the Book Steward but added "Anthony L. Stanford, Editor" to the masthead. That issue also added (to the first column of the first page) a group of seven "Corresponding Editors" that included former editor Jabez Pitt Campbell, James M. Williams, Grafton H. Graham, future-Bishop Alexander Wayman, Ebenezer T. Williams, Charles Burch, and Liberty Ross—all long-time AME ministers. As most of these men lived far from Philadelphia, they were clearly intended to be regular correspondents rather than a working editorial board. Weaver had prepared readers for some of these changes in his June 29, 1861, "Our New Editor of the Christian Recorder." He recognized Stanford (seen in Figure 2.3), who was to be newly stationed at Philadelphia's Little Wesley, as "a young man of no ordinary ability . . . much beloved by all who know him." But the four paragraphs preceding this lukewarm endorsement of a "young" minister claim that Weaver had actually asked the bishops for an assistant (as the work was "too much for any one man under the heavens to attend to"). The piece reminds readers of Weaver's belief that the General Conference had unified the *Recorder* editor and the Book Steward roles into a single position, and that "the members of the Philadelphia Conference were a *unit*, believing just as we do, that it was all in one." While the bishops "differed a little in relation to who was intended to be, by the General Conference, the editor," Weaver added that "our subscribers" should "not be discouraged," as "we have just as much power now as we had before, with the exception of preparing the leading article and arranging the matter for the paper."

A July 6, 1861, "List of Corresponding Editors to the 'Christian Recorder'" signed by both Nazrey and Payne constructs the situation a bit differently, setting out specific responsibilities for the Book Steward (Weaver) and the "Chief Editor" (Stanford), but also specific rights for Church members: "our preachers and people have the same right as before to columns of the paper." Notably, this "List" does not place Weaver above Stanford; it only differentiates their duties. Below the bishops' signatures, the phrase "subject to amendments, as occasion may require" appears. This "List" was followed immediately by a piece from a frustrated Nazrey titled "The Book Concern" and aimed at articulating "the complicated state of the [church] law, relative to the

FIGURE 2.3 *Anthony L. Stanford, from the official composite photograph of the Senate of Arkansas for 1877. From the Collections of the Arkansas History Commission.*

government of the Book Concern." Nazrey's piece says that while "the General Conference intended to separate the editor and the general book steward"—in line with Campbell's motion—"they have failed to carry out their design by leaving so much of the law as recognises the editor and general book steward concentrated in one person unrepealed." Nazrey's signature on the "List" was thus a compromise made in hopes that the "several parts" of the Book Concern's "government may be made to harmonize."[43]

For all of this tension, Weaver's July 20, 1861, "Communication of the General Book Steward" says that when "the Rev. A. L. Stanford and his good lady" arrived "in a carriage in front of our homestead," "we had a good hearty shake hands, and then bid them enter, where they are to make their home until further arrangements have been made." Stanford's July 13, 1861, "Inaugural and Prospectus" appears guardedly positive, too; it sidesteps the question of the

General Conference's sense of the Book Concern, humbly notes Weaver's praise, calls Weaver "my worthy associate," and says the most important question was whether Church members would "employ a portion of your influence and money" to give the paper "an abundant circulation throughout your cities and towns." Weaver's announcement that he would go on "a Western tour" for two months on "behalf of the Book Concern" probably also gave Stanford some breathing room. Nonetheless, Weaver was never far from the paper, as he sent back regular letters and made soliciting subscriptions a central part of his message wherever he went. While he might not have been the editor, for diverse practical purposes, he was the paper's public face.

As 1861 wore on, the *Recorder* faced a new battle. The earliest extant issue of Weaver's *Recorder* includes a letter from *Repository* editor John Mifflin Brown (shown in Figure 2.4) lauding the paper, linking himself to Weaver ("it takes our Western boys to lead off"), and letting Weaver and readers know that "your old friend, the Repository" could be had "at your book store—No. 619 Pine Street." But as early as the February 23, 1861, *Recorder*, a letter from Savage Hammond says that the Church might not be able to support both a weekly newspaper and a quarterly magazine—that "two little trees... planted in the same soil" might well "impoverish one another." Weaver, a bit clumsily, published an editorial in the same issue asserting that while he did "not oppose the *Repository*," if "both cannot survive, if one only can be... supported at the sacrifice of the other, then we would urge... the higher claims

FIGURE 2.4 *John Mifflin Brown and Mary Louisa Brown, from* Proceedings of the Quarto Centennial Conference of the African M. E. Church of South Carolina *(1890). Courtesy of the State Archives of Florida.*

of *The Recorder*—which belongs to, and is the organ of, the General Conference of our church—to those of the *Repository*, the mere organ of the Literary Society." This conflict, which I have discussed elsewhere, did not flare fully until later that year—when the *Recorder* was already firmly established, the *Repository* was failing, and Brown's interests were turning further South.[44] While the conflict simmered, it might have been safer for Weaver to be out of range and out of the editorial chair. But Stanford was already in trouble: Weaver's September 14, 1861, "Once More at Home" reports returning from his trip and finding "Rev. A. L. Stanford and Mrs. Weaver to have been struggling for life to keep things as near right as possible until we returned."[45]

Weaver's December 14, 1861, contribution notes that, on returning from an "Eastern Tour," he found "The Rev. A. L. Stanford has been somewhat indisposed for several days back, not having been able to attend to his editorial duties properly for some two or three weeks. We feared something serious was the matter, as we observed, in several places through our article . . . 'Our Eastern Tour,' several slight *typographical* errors." Who ran the paper during those weeks is an open question, but the December 14 issue was clearly Weaver's. Ominously, he included an item titled "Editorial Independence" that argues that "every court must have a final authority; so must every newspaper." His letter "To Subscribers and Friends of the Christian Recorder" celebrates the paper's regular issuance during 1861, but notes "we are free and frank to say that there was never a paper published which has met with as much low cunning as the *Christian Recorder* has, and that, too, from sources which we never would have looked for." Not a single piece in this issue bears Stanford's signature.

Weaver quickly called a December 18 meeting of the General Conference's executive committee to address matters tied to the Book Concern. While the December 21, 1861, *Recorder* maintains Stanford's name on the masthead, the editorial content is Weaver's; strikingly, a page two item directs that all *Recorder* correspondence should be sent to Weaver. In the final issue of the year, Weaver's masthead listing as "Editor" foreshadowed a piece headed "Resignation":

> Rev. A. L. Stanford, who had been acting as editor of this paper since the 13th of July, 1861, handed in his resignation to the Committee on the 18th instant, which was accepted by them, and took effect the same day. His reasons for doing so he will himself assign. All that we have to say regarding the matter is, that for the time we have been associated with him, he had proved himself to be a Christian and a gentleman in the discharge of his duty.
>
> The Committee decided that Elisha Weaver should be Editor and General Book Steward, and in perfect keeping with the law as such, declared that all duties devolved now upon him.

Stanford had lasted six months. As per the bishops' July dictate, his place had been "subject to amendments, as occasion may require." Weaver's reporting emphasizes that the Book Steward and the *Recorder* editor should be—as he had argued back in June—"all in one."[46]

Weaver had undoubtedly expended capital in (again) unifying the stewardship and editorship in his portfolio. But with the developing Civil War as well as the growing split between Nazrey and Payne (and the BME and the AME), the Church hierarchy became more willing to let Weaver continue to, in essence, run all of the General Conference-sponsored AME print presence.[47] Initially, he had to fend off continuing complaints from supporters of the *Repository*, but that periodical, which Brown had changed to a smaller monthly magazine, folded in 1863. These few years thus became a crucial building period for the paper—one which included publication of a number of the texts discussed later in this volume and one which set the (national) stage for many more.

Weaver remained essentially unchallenged as both Book Steward and *Recorder* editor until the May 1864 General Conference, where, by Church law, there had to be an election for both positions—or the one combined position. That long meeting in Philadelphia should have been relatively easy for Weaver, and, indeed, Church histories make it sound so: Tanner's 1867 *Apology*, for example, blithely passes over it, three years after calling Weaver only "the gentleman who has twice been elected to this most arduous post" (175). But Weaver started pushing delegates to clarify both the structure and the support for the Book Concern before the 1864 General Conference even began.[48] He steadily maintained his stance that the Book Steward and *Recorder* editor should be one position and that the *Discipline* should be comprehensively revised to reflect such. His desire to consolidate power and many of the delegates' suspicions of centralized authority were again set to clash.

The early days of the meeting were quiet for the Book Concern. In addition to the war, Church leaders continued to struggle with Bishop Nazrey's ties to Canada as well as AME relationships with the African Methodist Episcopal Zion Church (with whom it was contemplating a merger) and with the generally white northern branch of the Methodist Episcopal Church. It had also grown clear that one or more new bishops would be elected at the 1864 General Conference, in part because Nazrey was leaning toward Canada. Weaver offered his initial report on the Book Concern, which included, according to Weaver's May 14, 1864, *Recorder* account, the proud presentation of "three volumes of the *Christian Recorder* to the Conference." A formal resolution of thanks was followed by Payne—not always Weaver's friend—stepping forward, calling for more support for the Book Concern, and, according to C. S. Smith's account, giving $20 himself (469). Amid these good feelings, the Book Concern and *Recorder* were set aside for several days. The structure of Nazrey's exodus was generally resolved, and two new bishops were elected:

Alexander Wayman, by a massive margin in the first round of voting, and Campbell, by a smaller margin in the second.

The first sign of potential difficulty came when the Conference adopted the Book Concern's report with "the exception of that part relating to the Editor and Book Steward, which was referred to the committee on Revision" (479). The issue was not taken up again until the second-to-last day of the Conference—in Weaver's June 11, 1864, words, essentially "left till the very last thing." Two camps had emerged by the morning of Wednesday, May 25, when both Weaver and Willis Revels presented competing sets of suggestions about the Book Concern. While specifics remain unknown, Weaver's general version won, but only after John Mifflin Brown—who had recently shut the doors on the *Repository*—gutted one of Weaver's crucial provisions by adding an amendment "that the office of General Book Steward and Editor be separated" (Smith 490–491). The Pandora's box spilled into the afternoon session, with additional arguments over who the Book Steward and Editor would report to, which regional conference would house him/them, and whether the Book Steward could hire assistant(s).

Sources differ on what happened in the evening session. The June 4 *Recorder* reported that there was a motion "that the Rev. E. Weaver be the General Book Steward and Editor" that "lost," followed by an successful motion "that the election of the General Book Steward and Editor be laid over till to-morrow" and a curious, failed motion that "the publishing committee shall not destroy or change any word or sentence" in the documents tied to the debate. C. S. Smith's 1922 account, supposedly drawn from the minutes and Payne's notes, says that, after the motion to elect Weaver, "Rev. E. Weaver arose, and stated . . . that inasmuch as the General Conference had made the Discipline to contradict itself on the Book Concern, therefore he could not serve while it stood as it is" (491). But Smith then says "Bro. Weaver was elected General Book Steward" only to decline the position the next day (491).

Regardless, it is clear that Weaver again attempted to revise the full *Discipline* and unify the positions on the General Conference's final day. He lost. This time, Brown was nominated as *Recorder* editor and, though a brief and unsuccessful attempt was made to replace Brown's name with that of Benjamin Tucker Tanner, Brown was quickly elected. John A. Warren, an experienced minister but a relative newcomer to the fray, was elected Book Steward.[49] The Conference then voted on a vague, general motion to revise the *Discipline* to allow separate positions and appointed a committee of three—Molliston Clark and Bishops Nazrey and Campbell—"to define the duties of Editor and General Book Steward." Almost as soon as the committee was appointed, however, they had to report back to the General Conference that Brown had decided to resign from the editorship before he even started (Smith 494). During the final evening session, Warren also tendered his resignation. The Conference was moving toward adjournment, and the Book

Concern and the *Recorder* again had no leadership. According to the June 4 *Recorder*, motions to name Weaver as Book Steward and Tanner as Editor were made and then "laid on the table." Payne and several delegates reportedly had to leave to catch departing trains, and the General Conference adjourned until 1868.

Weaver's June 11, 1864, *Recorder* note reports that he was "getting ready . . . to take our dear little children, baggage and all, and return back to the West, or to take work in the Baltimore District, for one year," but at some point soon after the Conference adjourned, (some of) the Church leadership and Weaver seem to have struck a deal—one that embodied the Church's pragmatism in the face of the debate over centralized authority. His note says he was "elected three times before" he "would allow the yoke to remain on us," but he elides the fact that the final "election" was *not* tied to the General Conference. Rather, when the Philadelphia Conference convened soon after the General Conference's adjournment—with Nazrey in the chair and Quinn assisting—it called on its power "per charter" to manage both the Book Concern and the *Recorder* (which reportedly dated from 1856), and it elected seven ministers as "trustees for the Book Concern," with Weaver named chair.[50] These new trustees met three days later at Mother Bethel and agreed quickly, on the suggestion of Bishop Wayman (present as a visitor), to name Weaver both Book Steward and *Recorder* editor. With some largesse, the trustees also approved seeking a new building for the Concern and gave Weaver the power to go about "procuring such help . . . as is necessary." Likely nodding to the broader General Conference and to coalition-building, with Wayman's help, the trustees then named new "corresponding editors" from each of the regional conferences: old editor Anthony Stanford was now listed for the Philadelphia Conference, joined by recent editor-candidate Benjamin Tucker Tanner of the Baltimore Conference; Leonard Patterson, New York Conference; William W. Grimes, New England Conference; Samuel Watts, Ohio Conference; Aeneas McIntosh, Indiana Conference; former editor Molliston Madison Clark, Missouri Conference; and T. M. D. Ward, California Conference.

During the whole process, the *Recorder* had not missed an issue, and the masthead had remained the same. At the final resolution, Weaver crowed a bit, heading his June 11, 1864, *Recorder* letter "Refusal of the General Conference to Receive Our Resignation of the Book Concern." The letter gives two reasons for Weaver's continuation with "the yoke." He wanted to honor his "strong phalanx of friends"—as "letters came pouring in" from "hundreds of regular subscribers . . . which the paper would have lost had we left"—and he "really did not" want "to see our paper go down." Elsewhere in that issue, he would write that "we think that it is high time that our Conference were taking or pursuing a different course. We have now a number of old, worn-out ministers who are now, or might as well be, on the Superannuated [retired] List, and it is high time that our Book Concern was able to do something."

The pattern of Weaver's tenure had emerged: he would remain in power over the Book Concern and the *Recorder* as long as he didn't push too far. The flowering of African American textual culture in the *Recorder* described in the following pages thus happened at the fault lines of not only American print culture but also of the complex, shifting, and growing AME Church community. Weaver may have thought some of the "old, worn-out ministers" might not be around for long, may have misjudged the (informal) willingness of the bishops and the (adjourned) General Conference to continue to allow the Philadelphia Conference to run the Book Concern and the *Recorder*, may have assumed stronger support among the bishops, and may have thought he had more definitive support from the Philadelphia Conference clergy than he did. After the 1864 General Conference, the first time Weaver overreached again, he lost the editorial chair for a period; the second time, he was removed from the *Recorder*, the Book Concern, and the Philadelphia Conference altogether.

Weaver waited until a January 1866 meeting of the bishops and the Book Concern trustees to argue for expansion of the Concern. According to a summary sent by Wayman for publication in the February 3, 1866, *Recorder*, in preparation for that meeting, the trustees asked a set of standard questions on finances but also asked for clarification on "the [church] law regulating the Book Concern." The bishops "gave an elaborate opinion, which was received as satisfactory." So far, so good. Weaver, however, had also contacted the bishops himself—whether with or without trustee input is, at this point, unclear. Both Wayman's piece and one written by Weaver for the same issue agree that Weaver asked "for assistance in conducting the affairs of the Book Concern and the *Christian Recorder*"; Weaver's adds that he hoped specifically for "an assistant out[side] of" the Philadelphia Conference. According to Wayman, Weaver's "communication" to the bishops "was very carefully considered," and they "resolved to grant the General Book Steward's request, so far as it was in their power, in accordance with the spirit and letter of the laws of the General Conference." But then, for reasons that remain unclear, the bishops "appointed Rev. James Lynch, Editor of the Christian Recorder."

The fantasy of a clear "spirit and letter" from the General Conference aside, Lynch (see Figure 2.5) was a fascinating choice. Raised in Baltimore, he was Payne's former student and had taught school briefly, studied with a white Presbyterian minister, and worked in Indianapolis (with Weaver) before receiving his first charge in Galena, Illinois.[51] After pastoring more prestigious churches in Washington, DC, and Baltimore, Lynch worked with Payne to reach out to the newly freed people of the South, starting schools and churches in South Carolina and Georgia.

FIGURE 2.5 *Detail from James Lynch tombstone. Courtesy of Bill Wardlaw, Greenwood Cemetery Association, Jackson, Mississippi.*

Weaver fumed, but had little recourse. His February 3 *Recorder* piece reiterates that he had only asked for an assistant, rails that "WE did not ask our beloved Bishops to appoint an editor, nor to assign any particular post for the assistant," and argues that the Philadelphia Conference and the Book Concern trustees had the sole right to appoint the editor. "In our next issue," it concludes, "we may publish our valedictory." However, Weaver must have been calmed by something or someone. He made a temporary exit of another sort; he left on an extended Book Concern tour soon after the twenty-seven-year-old Lynch's arrival, and the March 10, 1866, *Recorder* includes a letter from him from Norfolk, Virginia. But he remained Book Steward.

Weaver and Lynch's dance had some echoes of Stanford's brief time as editor, but it grew more intense as time passed—in part because Lynch seems to have viewed the editorship as a step toward a bishopric. Lynch initially praised Weaver in the *Recorder*, noting his "indefatigable exertions" in the April 7, 1866, *Recorder* and lauding Weaver's efforts to send the *Recorder* to Black soldiers—saying that "few men ever attempted more and accomplished as much." Still, in an implicit argument for the new configuration splitting the two positions, Lynch asserted that any weaknesses in Weaver's paper happened because "while he was wanted at his editorial desk," Weaver "was out in pursuit of means to publish the paper." Theoretically, he asserted, the split should only aid all. Though Weaver made fewer comments in print, Lynch would later assert, in a June 8, 1867, piece, that Weaver "has steadily maintained the illegality of my appointment, which displaced him" even as he also claimed that there was "the best of feeling" and "no friction whatever" between the two.

The friction increased when Lynch decided to spend less time at the *Recorder* offices; in his absences, his editorial work fell to Weaver. A May 12, 1866, "Apology" notes that Weaver had been "kind enough to do our editorial work last week"—and likely the week prior, too. In August, Lynch spent two weeks in Baltimore and Washington, again leaving the paper to Weaver. In late October and early November, he traveled "to canvas" because Weaver was "prevented from making" the trip "by the demand for his presence in Philadelphia," and the December 22, 1866, *Recorder* includes Lynch's letter from Ohio that opens, "Dear Recorder: It is with pain that I am so long away from home, but I am preparing places for thy reception, and must trust thee a little longer to one to whose nursing care thou are not unfamiliar." For all the language of "nursing care," Lynch was not happy with Weaver and accused him of either sloppy editing or simple malice, specifically claiming in his December 22 letter that "several typographical errors" in the published version of his previous letter "made me say what I did not write." But Lynch did not return.

Weaver began to publicly criticize Lynch in his December 29, 1866, "The Last Number of the Recorder for 1866." While recognizing that "Brother Lynch is doing a great and good work in procuring subscribers to the paper, and in selling our hymnbooks and disciplines"—ironically, the work of a Book Steward—"after our Bishops had appointed our brother . . . as editor, we had hoped to be excused from" editorial duties, "but we were disappointed." Weaver continues, "We had no idea that Brother Lynch would remain away during the holidays, which, to our mind, is the most important part of the year, in which the condition of the paper ought to be defined, and remarks made as to its probable success during the coming year." Weaver took these tasks on himself, reminding readers that "during our connection with the *Christian Recorder* for the last six years, both as editor and publisher, we have performed the labor of two men."

When Lynch stayed in Ohio—sending a letter published in the January 5, 1867, *Recorder* that said he was "still in Cincinnati"—Weaver decided to write the New Year's message himself. Though it promises "Rev. James Lynch will richly feed you on many good things," it adds the language "when he comes home." By the January 26, 1867, issue, Weaver was driven to run this: "WHERE IS BROTHER LYNCH? It is now going on four months since he started on a tour to increase the subscription list of the *Recorder*. We are greatly in need of means. Will he not forward us the means he has on hand?" Ironically, that issue appeared the day *after* Lynch finally returned to Philadelphia. Such complications were not the sole reason for Lynch's resignation later in 1867. Tanner's *Apology for African Methodism*, appearing soon after, notes that "the gentleman has since left the Connexion, and joined the M. E. Church" (178). Historian Leslie Fishel specifies that, "worried by the intransigence of the Methodist Episcopal (ME) Church South" in working with the newly freed people "and fearful of the AME's structural weaknesses," Lynch "tendered his services to the ME Church, North, as a southern missionary." Fishel says "the AME Church did not give up without a struggle; it offered him the pulpit of the mother church, Bethel Church in Philadelphia, in addition to his editorship—two highly prized and influential positions."

However, this analysis isn't fully accurate. The Philadelphia Annual Conference actually appointed Lynch to Mother Bethel (rather than "offering" the post), and that appointment was reported in the June 1 *Recorder*. Lynch's resignation appeared a week later and specifically cites "the great amount of labor this double appointment would involve." Gaining Mother Bethel would have been a coup, but doing it on top of having full charge of the weekly newspaper—his *full-time* appointment from 1866 to 1867—would be a burden, a "double appointment." What also remains unsaid, given Lynch's absences, is the fact that a physical charge at Mother Bethel would have kept Lynch much more firmly in Philadelphia.[52]

Lynch did say "we would attempt" the double charge "with willingness and hope, did not our whole heart say, 'Go South!'" However, he used much of his June 8, 1866, "Valedictory" to articulate the "severe trials" he had faced as *Recorder* editor. He cited the need to balance an "*entire* Connection" of demanding regional groups and political factions, the need to be zealous in the face of "men who consult expedience," the difficulties of dealing with ministers who insisted that their contributions be published, and the pain of working with weak writers who had "laudable ambition but questionable judgment." The Book Concern trustees "reluctantly" accepted his resignation and, according to the June 15 *Recorder*, quickly resolved "that Elisha Weaver fill the editorial chair."[53] This time, beginning with the July 6, 1867, issue, Weaver listed himself on the masthead as "Rev. Elisha Weaver, Editor & Publisher."

Weaver had proven his dedication to AME print time and again. As *Recorder* editor, his name had been in front of congregants across the nation for years, and he had interacted with ministers throughout the connection. As Book Steward, he added to this recognition with travels throughout the Northeast, the Midwest, and, after the Union's victory, the South. While self-interest may have been one motivating factor, the levels of his work and commitment stand unparalleled. As contentious as his time with the Book Concern and the *Recorder* had been, the Church had always returned to him. But as the General Conference of 1868 approached, the stakes were higher and the interactions more complex: Weaver wanted a bishopric.

Rumblings about adding new bishops—and the talk was almost always plural—were already being heard as the Church expanded massively and rapidly into the post-war South. A correspondent from Cincinnati who signed himself/herself "Rector" seems to have offered the earliest print argument for Weaver in the November 16, 1867, *Recorder*:

> We have as many aspirants for this honorable position in our church as we have aspirants for the Presidential chair. We have had a certain character, like Andy Johnson, swing around the circle, disturbing the *Recorder*, and asking of every minister an exchange of views . . . and, after looking on the situation, he retires without hope, leaving the paper and the Church. We have others yet, in the far South and West, who are ever madly ambitious. . . . Suppose the energetic worker of the *Recorder*, who is known by our people better than any other man except Douglass, should run that paper in his interest, for that position, as was done by his late predecessor, what would we think of him? And, yet, if we are to judge men by what they have accomplished in a material way, in behalf of an organization . . . then the present publisher [of the] *Recorder*, the most successful man in that paper . . . *Elisha Weaver* [italics in original] has more claim on the church than any other man. He has . . . energy and ability, and many of the intelligent young and old ministers think as we do.

The jibe at Lynch—both making him "Andy Johnson" and asserting that he had been shopping for a bishopric before leaving "the paper and the Church"—only emphasizes the representations of Weaver's loyalty.

A reply to "Rector" signed "Rectus" commenting on who would be the best new bishop and appearing in the December 21, 1867, issue says in italics, "*Rev. E. Weaver is that man.*" "Rectus" gives Weaver a Lincoln-ian narrative and slaps at Lynch, too—saying Weaver had come "from a log schoolhouse in the Far West where he was engaged in teaching" to become "the most responsible position in the Church—a position in which the ablest men in or out of the Church have failed." While "Rectus" recognizes that Willis Revels, John

Mifflin Brown, and James Shorter were strong candidates, "Rectus" asks, "where is Mr. Weaver's superior as an energetic, faithful worker?" Others echoed this support.[54]

Weaver himself finally wrote a February 1, 1868, editorial headed "Bishops for the AME Church." Donning humility, Weaver's piece notes that the discussion of additional bishops "soon became a personal affair relative to us" and says that he had thus "refrained from saying anything about its importance," feeling "a delicacy in putting these articles in the paper" and publishing them only because "the members of the General Conference have a right to say whom they desire to see ordained as bishop or bishops of the AME Church." Weaver claims that "we are no office-seeker, but if our labors and the faithful performance of duty in the various positions that have been assigned to us, has won the esteem and respect of the young, as well as the old, we cannot help it."

Documentation on the events that followed is exceedingly sketchy. Extant issues from January and February 1868 say nothing about stopping the paper's publication, but the numbering of extant issues of the *Recorder* strongly suggests that only one or two issues were published between February 8, 1868, and April 4, 1868.[55] Only with the April 11 issue did Weaver say that "we were compelled . . . to suspend the publication of the paper until our financial condition could be improved." His language in this piece, headed "The Disappointed Element," is combative—especially when he sarcastically expresses his sorrow about the frustration felt by "that element who rejoiced at the suspension of the *Christian Recorder*," "the disappointed element, who built their structure of joy upon a sandy foundation." He closes with his hope that the General Conference would "place the *Recorder* upon a firm basis. Amen!" Weaver's actions during the paper's suspension are difficult to trace, though it is clear that he visited several sites in the South, and, at the end of April, traveled to Columbus for the Ohio Annual Conference. Nominally, he was traveling as the Book Steward; whether he was also courting votes for a bishopric is an open question. He had, by this point, two clerks, who seem to have been running the *Recorder* office in his absence, albeit with direction in regular letters.

Weaver's complex position at the time of the General Conference of 1868—held in Washington, DC—can be marked in the second lapse in publication around the time the meetings began. The numbering of extant issues suggests that Weaver missed the scheduled May 9 issue (as the General Conference began), and that there were no issues published on May 23, May 30, June 6, or June 13. Given these gaps and the comparative silence of almost all Church histories, we know few specifics on the Conference. Much of the month-long meeting focused on bringing Southern ministers fully into the fold (which the Church did through admitting delegates and restructuring conference boundaries), on establishing possibilities for presiding elders (who would supervise sections of conferences in the absence of a bishop), and on the possibility of uniting with the AMEZ Church (which the AME again declined, albeit with a promise of further study). A committee on episcopacy did recommend electing three new bishops, which the Conference eventually did. James Shorter and John Mifflin Brown—two figures whose names had been suggested in the *Recorder*—were elected along with T. M. D. Ward, leader of California's AME contingent but also well known in the East. (Figure 2.6 shows all of the AME bishops named before 1876.) Weaver was not elected.

Weaver's report in the May 16, 1868, *Recorder* suggests that the Book Concern may have been the subject of immediate unwelcome attention at the Conference. Early on, longtime minister William A. Dove "offered a resolution" on the Concern "that an Investigating Committee should be appointed, which was ordered." Immediately after these events, "a motion was made that the General Book Steward be requested to make his report."[56] Weaver's report expresses bafflement: "This was a new thing under the sun . . . unheard of . . . in the history of all ecclesiastical bodies of which we have ever heard or read—a motion to be entertained before we were organized, and before any of the general officers had made their reports, which was virtually the foreshadowing of something which did not exist." Known surviving documents do not tell more of the work of this "Investigating Committee" or of Weaver's

FIGURE 2.6 *Engraving of AME Bishops and key AME locations by John H. W. Burley (1876). Courtesy of the Prints and Photographs Division, Library of Congress (LC-USZ62-15059). Richard Allen is in the center, with Morris Brown just above him. Clockwise from Brown are William Paul Quinn, Daniel Payne, Jabez Pitt Campbell, T. M. D. Ward, John Mifflin Brown, James Shorter, Alexander Wayman, Willis Nazrey, and Edward Waters. Of special note is the illustration of the* Recorder *office at 631 Pine in the lower right corner.*

Book Concern report, beyond the fact that "The General Book Steward and Editor made his four years' report . . . which was received and referred to the Investigating Committee." Later in the Conference, the Committee on Discipline—and whether this was the *Discipline* or disciplinary action is unclear from the report—"reported articles upon the Book Concern, which were adopted." The June 20, 1868, issue of the *Recorder*—the first with Benjamin Tucker Tanner as the new editor—said that the Conference "readjusted our Missionary and Publishing Branches by the election of new officers, as well as by enacting such laws, as the necessities of the case seemed to demand."

While the exact nature of these "new laws" and "necessities" is hazy, the "new officers" appeared in the June 20 issue. Tanner began his long tenure as editor, and Joshua Woodlin was the new Book Steward. Both were full appointments, and so not yoked to churches. As noted, Weaver was immediately transferred out of the Philadelphia Conference—a move that the General Conference had not made with any of the former editors. Tanner allowed Weaver a short "Editor's Farewell" in his first issue, but this seems to be the last piece Weaver wrote for the paper until 1870. That "Farewell" asserted that he had succeeded "in laying a good foundation" and that "those who may follow will have a much easier time." Still, he said, "in relation to the trials and perplexities of an Editor and General Book Steward, it would be needless for us to speak now, but, suffice it to say, that with us, the greater portion of the time has been a sacrifice; yes, more than, perhaps, will ever be revealed until the day of judgment." While Weaver called Tanner "amply qualified," he gave no praise to Woodlin. He told readers "we hope that you will not be disposed to do less in aid of the *Christian Recorder* than you have done in the past." And he included two barbs, one about the double charge he had fought so long to keep and one that carried reminders of his past threats about subscribers leaving: "There never was a stronger fact or proof that the Book Concern is in far better condition than ever it was before, than by virtue of the election of two, instead of one, to work in our place. . . . And we also turn over into their hands a long list of subscribers: it will be with them to keep them."

Tanner's years would not be without trials—though he was able to hold the editorial chair longer than Weaver and to eventually turn it into a springboard to a bishopric. He did not, though, push for the kinds of changes Weaver did, and for most of his tenure, he always had an associate (sometimes an equal and sometimes a superior) who served in a role like the Book Steward's. Simple growth had made a single combined position untenable, and the broader landscape in which Tanner worked was very different.

Weaver's paper—the subject of the rest of this volume—was rushed into maturity by a massive war and a host of other social, political, and cultural changes, and Tanner and the *Recorder* benefited from all of his battles. The very elements that caused so much struggle over the paper may well have contributed to its richness. Individual and organizational ambitions, factional diversity and strife, regional jockeying, worries over both centralized authority and decentralized chaos (or simply stasis), an abiding sense that the AME Church needed a print presence that it wasn't always willing to pay for, daily life under diverse oppressive circumstances, and the "youth" of the endeavor all shaped the processes and texts described here. The struggles surrounding the editorial chair were part and parcel of the tumult of the Church and the nation. Considering how these factors made (and changed) the pieces of the AME community calls on us to continue to unearth the remnants surrounding the *Recorder* and especially to think more about the material processes of the paper's composition, circulation, distribution, and reception; chapter 3 thus turns to these questions.

{ 3 }

From Pine Street to the Nation (and Back Again): The Business of the *Recorder*

Elisha Weaver walked out of the *Recorder* office at 619 Pine Street in Philadelphia on a chilly day in early February 1866—long before the tumult of 1868 but after he had announced the surprise appointment of James Lynch as the new *Recorder* editor. He was considering what to do next, and his next few steps were metaphorically massive. In the rented row house at 619 Pine, he had made the church's unsteady Book Concern a working venture, and he had not only brought the church organ back to life but also made it a national force among African Americans. Its pages had covered a war like no other, celebrated emancipation, and mourned not only an assassinated President but also Weaver's own wife Mary, who had died in the Weaver family's rooms on the upper floors of that same row house at 619 Pine.[1]

On that cold February day, he walked only a short distance to stop in front of the brick building at 631 Pine, which would soon become the Book Concern and *Recorder*'s new home. With two doors in front (one leading to the upper floors) and a large window in between, it looked more like a shop front than 619 Pine.[2] With mingled pride and pain, he must have remembered the letter "to the Bishops and Ministers of the different Districts of the African Methodist Episcopal Church of America" that he published in the December 16, 1865, *Recorder*. That letter bore his signature as chair of a committee that reported, "It affords us pleasure to inform you, that after nearly fifty years of the organization of our beloved Church, we have at last succeeded in purchasing a house and lot, in a good location, for our Book Concern and paper, No. 631 Pine street, Philadelphia, not far from where we are now doing business." For all of his losses in his attempts to change the Church's governance of the Concern, he had successfully spearheaded efforts to secure a physical space owned by African Americans to house what was fast becoming a center of African American literature and Black print generally.

Basking in that success, Weaver nonetheless probably did not yet have a key to the building. The Concern could not take possession until March 1, 1866, and the building was likely still being used, as it had been off and on for several years, as a boardinghouse.³ But Weaver could look, and perhaps dream a bit. His initial November 4, 1865, announcement of plans to buy the building had suggested that 631 Pine Street could become the site of a full printing business, one that could "teach young men the art of setting type, together with other duties connected with a well-conducted printing establishment." The December 16 letter expands that vision: "here will be the place to educate your young men in the printing business and your young ladies in book-binding, paper-folding, and the selling of books, &c." Though Lynch's appointment must have shaken these hopes, Weaver was probably still praying that 631 Pine Street would become a place that would encourage African Americans to engage even more fully with print.

According to that November 4 announcement, he needed "the sum of fifteen hundred dollars by the 1st of December." He did not get it all; according to his December 16 *Recorder* letter, the Concern had "borrowed money to make the first payment" and would "want the sum of $4,000 by the 25th of April, 1866, in order to carry out the object of our fathers." In the March 17, 1866, *Recorder*, new editor Lynch called again for donations: "brethren, this house is to be paid for." That said, Lynch could still proudly tell readers that "the house is now undergoing some repairs, and will be ready for our occupancy by the 20th inst. And we know that when our Brethren come to Philadelphia, they will be proud to see the AME Connexion possessing such a property."

That AME community members could come to Philadelphia and see, only a short walk from Mother Bethel, a building devoted to African American print culture owned by the AME Church and bought, in part, with their subscription dollars and donations offered a powerful statement. The 631 Pine building (see Figure 3.1 for a later view) was something to be proud of. First, there was the fact of ownership. While the Book Concern and the *Recorder* had been housed at 619 Pine since 1860, in the past, they had bounced around—under Campbell, from 203 Lombard to 719 Russell to 641 Lombard to 639 Lombard, sometimes without much space at all.⁴ Beyond demonstrating economic power and stability, walls and a door offered some protection from the outside world; such physical features made (slightly) safer spaces for the spiritual, the emotional, and the intellectual.

Though it is now combined with 633 Pine into an expensive single-family home—complete with an error-ridden historical marker outside—the building at 631 was striking enough in itself.⁵ Weaver's December 16, 1865, letter notes that "we could not build such a house for that money, to say nothing about the ground, which fronts on two streets, and may be valued at three thousand dollars." Slightly larger than 619 Pine, 631 had a lot that reached

FIGURE 3.1 *AME Book Concern Publication Department building, from* Who's Who in Philadelphia: A Collection of Thirty Biographical Sketches of Philadelphia Colored People *(1912). Courtesy of the General Research and Reference Division, Schomburg Center for Research in Black Culture, The New York Public Library, Astor, Lenox and Tilden Foundations. Compare to the earlier image of 631 Pine included in Figure 2.6.*

back to what is now Panama Street. According to Tanner's *Apology*, this new row house was "quite commodious and is well adapted to the purpose to which it is to be devoted. It is of brick, three stories in height. On the first floor is the store room, large and well filled with a choice selection of the standard books of the day.... A number of other rooms are used for various purposes which the business calls. It is purposed [sic] very shortly to have printing presses placed in one or more of the numerous suit[e]s of rooms, and commence the business in earnest" (43). While Weaver would never live there, some of the upper floors of 631 Pine would initially serve as rooms for Lynch—his single listing in the 1867 *McElroy's* Philadelphia city directory noted "h[ome]. 631 Pine" (808)—and later for boarders.[6] Though the Church would expand its print work after Weaver's exodus—even changing the Book Concern to the "Publication Department"—some of 631 Pine continued to be used as living quarters for select boarders and for employees, including printer James Chisolm in 1872, publisher William H. Hunter in 1873, and agent Theodore Gould in 1882 (*McElroy's* 1872, 323; 1873, 687; 1882, 618).

This mix of business and daily life, of figures tied directly and peripherally to the *Recorder*, of physical space and metaphysical mission, and of community and print all localized many of the issues discussed in the last chapter: during and between most of the larger political battles in the Church, the Book Concern and the *Recorder* continued to operate, and this operation included a bevy of material features and processes. To help understand how the texts discussed later in the volume—and the AME's massive print contributions to African American literature and culture more broadly—circulated, this chapter focuses on the business of the *Recorder*, business concentrated in the buildings at 619 and 631 Pine that both reached out to and received responses from a growing (Black) nation. Specifically, after considering the *Recorder*'s physical spaces, it explores the paper's production processes and editorial work and then studies a set of issues tied to the paper's finances—Church support, advertising and other revenue, and distribution. In examining this last question, it studies the paper's self-promotion (including periodical exchange), its city subscribers and single-copy sales, and its encouragement of both a network of agents (especially minister-agents) and a culture of subscription among AME members, a culture central to chapter 4.

The "store room" Tanner described did not simply signify a place for storage of Book Concern stock, though that was one function of the first floors of both 619 and 631 Pine. He meant a space for an AME Church bookstore. According to the January 19, 1861, *Recorder*, in addition to "Sabbath School Books of various kinds; Question Books; Catechisms, Nos. 1, 2, & 3" and "such" books "as are generally used in the Public Schools," the store at 619 Pine offered "Stationery, Ink, Pens, Paper, Envelopes, and Blank Books." Its centerpiece was a large "show-case" that Weaver had purchased from furniture dealer and Black activist Robert Adger for $43.37 ½ on June

30, 1860. Weaver's other setup costs for the store at 619 Pine, reported in the May 31, 1862, *Recorder*, included buying several books, as well as a ledger, a receipt book and bills, a daybook, envelopes, a feather duster, stamps, inks and sands, "some little toys," paper, wrapping paper, cards, preacher's and exhorter's licenses, various other certificates, a bucket, crayon chalk, pasteboards, matches, pens, coal and wood, wrapping twine, and "valentines." He would later add, among other items, combs, brushes, copybooks, a bell, and a host of "miscellaneous items" and "little articles for the store." According to the February 21, 1863, *Recorder*, customers could even purchase photographs of Shepherd Holcomb, a retired AME minister who had sent some copies to Weaver to sell for twenty-five cents each.[7] Items offered at 631 Pine were similar, and, while the selection likely increased over the years, the sense of an AME bookstore run by African Americans for African Americans dated back at least as early as M. M. Clark and Jabez Campbell's efforts in the 1850s.

Neither 619 nor 631 Pine was especially large: now a triplex, 619 had eighteen feet of frontage space, and perhaps fifty-five feet of depth at the building's deepest point.[8] The 631 Pine building also had eighteen feet of frontage, but it was deeper (at its deepest point, sixty feet). In part because 631 Pine originally had two doors rather than the one door found in 619 (before it was refaced decades later to offer the large door and two display windows seen in early twentieth-century photographs), the 631 building seems to have been more clearly separated between the first-floor store space and the upper levels' living quarters. Whether there was dedicated space for the *Recorder* amid general Book Concern business within either building or whether space was allocated ad hoc remains somewhat of a mystery, as none of the editors said much about the physical processes tied to their work. Weaver did record paying $3 for "a door for the store" on October 23, 1860, but what type of door this was, where it was placed, and what it separated the main store from (if, indeed, it did) all remain unanswered questions. With rooms upstairs for Weaver, his wife, and their young family, space at 619 Pine likely remained at a premium. Weaver had to store—and be ready to mail out—significant numbers of *Disciplines*, hymnals, conference reports, tracts, and bibles, and arrangements would have had to be well-planned, in part because the building was heated primarily by coal stoves.[9]

It is clear that both buildings were always multifunctional. At times, Weaver, for example, also used the space as an information clearinghouse. A December 25, 1865, "Situation Wanted" ad for "a very nice young man"—a "barber by trade" who "can also act as a waiter"—said "You can learn something about him by inquiring at No. 619 Pine St."[10] Several early "Information Wanted" ads that were placed by African Americans searching for family and friends said, as did a January 2, 1864, ad from Mary Dowden of Baltimore, that "any information" could be "left . . . at No. 619 Pine Street." An August 6, 1864, item lists nine individuals whose letters "had been sent to our care"—letters that "remain at our book-store"—and concluded, "Letters are continually sent to our care, for persons of whom we know nothing about. We hope that all persons, who have letters addressed to our care, will call and take them out of the way."

The Weavers' entrepreneurial spirit both for the Book Concern and beyond also centered on 619 Pine. Even before the first issue, Weaver had decided that he would arrange for Philadelphia subscribers' papers to be delivered to their doors. This allowed him to think about utilizing carriers in other ways, and thus a February 14, 1863, item titled "Circulate Your Business" reads, "The carrier of the *Recorder* will circulate through the city, Business Cards, Circular Hand Bills, Bills for Concerts, Exhibitions, Festivals, etc., at reasonable rates. All orders left at the office, 619 Pine Street, will be attended to." In a January 25, 1862 notice, Mary Weaver even encouraged those who were interested in buying or serving as agents for the "Delineator"—a garment drafting product for those who wanted to "learn to cut & fit perfectly" a variety of clothing—to visit her at 619 Pine.[11] Weaver and his colleagues and successors also envisioned the AME bookstore not just as a center of print and commerce but also as a kind of community meeting place, and meetings tied to a host of church issues were held there. Like many liberal bookstores of the period, "our Book Store" was also regularly advertised as a place to obtain tickets for various lectures, fairs, and other events. Such engagement increased after the move to 631 Pine; I have found, for example, advertisements for four lectures in the period by Frances Harper that sent potential attendees to buy tickets at the AME bookstore.[12]

Available evidence strongly suggests that, during the period studied here, one thing that did not happen at either 619 Pine or 631 Pine was printing.[13] That absence is worth brief consideration. As discussed in the last chapter, Augustus Green purchased "the press, types and fixtures" of *The Mystery*, but he also highlighted his own lack of printing experience when he said that he "hired my printers, and launched out into the deep." No early *Recorder* editors had extensive printing experience. Trained as ministers, they were usually managers rather than tradesmen—though Green had briefly been a smith. Weaver and Tanner were on the cusp of a generational shift in African American printing. There *were* Black printers similar in age to the early *Recorder* editors—though scholars have not told much of their story. And while the scholarly silence on enslaved people's work for printers and in printing has often been deafening, we know a bit more about a few early free Black printers.[14] In addition to small clusters tied to William Lloyd Garrison and Frederick Douglass, Bostonian Benjamin F. Roberts (1814–1881, editor/publisher/printer of the *Anti-Slavery Herald* and the *Self-Elevator*); Robert Campbell (1829–1884, teacher at the Institute for Colored Youth and friend of Delany); and especially New Yorker John J. Zuille (1814–1894, originally an apprentice to the *Colored American* and later printer for several Hamilton family ventures) were critical early figures. Still, these men were few and far between, and some of them—Campbell, for instance—shifted in and out of the field. Most African Americans of the time who were interested in printing—like, for example, Peter Humphries Clark of Cincinnati—were frustrated by a host of barriers.[15] It was the generation following these figures that Weaver hoped to help educate through a Black-owned and operated print business that could break the racism of the apprenticeship system.[16] This "coming" generation included men like Frederick Douglass's son Lewis, who grew up interacting with printers for Douglass's newspapers, apprenticed as a typesetter, and eventually became the first African American typesetter at the US Government Printing Office in Washington, DC—though this achievement was quickly tainted by the DC typesetters' union's racist refusal to allow a Black man to join their ranks.[17]

Even if there had been a corps of skilled and ready African American printers in Philadelphia in the early and mid-1860s, the Book Concern was not yet in a financial or physical position to hire them exclusively, and a free-standing enterprise run by Black printers would have had a hard time in a fairly Southern city. Until the church's expansion into the South, which was paired with considerable increases in AME print, the Book Concern couldn't keep many skilled employees at all.[18] There would also have been concerns tied to equipment. Even if the Book Concern moved the *Mystery*'s equipment with them during the 1852 relocation to Philadelphia, that equipment would have been fast aging. It would have also taken up considerable room in what were never spacious or even stable quarters until 1861. Living above such equipment wouldn't have been especially pleasant either. It is thus notable that, while Benjamin Tucker Tanner and his family (including young Henry Ossawa Tanner) moved into the apartments above the Book Concern vacated by Lynch in the mid-1868 and stayed there until 1872, it was only after Tanner bought his own home at what was then 2908 Diamond that his strongest efforts at building in-house printing at 631 Pine began.[19]

In the 1860s, the Book Concern thus recognized that a thoughtfully selected white printer would serve the community better than no printer at all, so Weaver chose a figure who was a known quantity to the Church. His Book Steward's report for 1860 noted paying "Mr. William S. Young" $104 "for printing 3000 copies of Minutes of General Conference."[20] This was the same shop with whom Molliston Clark contracted in 1853 and 1854 and noted in the July 13, 1854, *Recorder* Book Steward's report. A busy and experienced printer, Young kept offices on North Sixth Street (relatively close to the Book Concern), and his own bookstore regularly advertised religious works that he published (ranging from the pamphlet "Loving Jesus" to an edition of *Alger's Pronouncing Bible*) in the *Recorder*.[21] Young also worked regularly with periodicals—including publishing (and printing) monthlies like the *Eclectic Medical Journal* and *The Farmer and Gardener* as well as a religious weekly, the *Christian Instructor*.[22] While Young was not especially active on questions of race, the November 29, 1862, *Recorder* does list him among a group of white Presbyterians who argued for desegregation of city transport.[23]

The business relationship continued until Young's retirement. Soon after printing the 1864 General Conference proceedings, Young ran a card in the June 11, 1864, *Recorder* informing "his friends and the public, that he has disposed of his old, established *Steam Power-Press Printing-Office* TO JAMES B. RODGERS, who will continue the business in all of its branches." The Book Concern and the *Recorder* engaged Rodgers immediately, and he is listed as the printer for, among other items, the minutes of the 1865 Philadelphia Annual Conference, the 1865 edition of the *Discipline*, and the 1868 *Discipline*. An Irish immigrant who also advertised regularly in the *Recorder*, Rodgers expanded Young's plant and sought an even broader base of customers—telling readers of the April 4, 1868, *Recorder* that "Parties residing out of the city can have estimates made for any printing they may desire, and have the work as carefully attended to as though present themselves."[24]

These long-term relationships explain why one of the first things Weaver reported doing in his July 20, 1861, *Recorder* account of Anthony Stanford's arrival was bringing "our new Editor and associate to the office where our paper is printed, and introduc[ing] him to Mr. YOUNG, Mr. BLAKELY, and others,—initiating him to the best of our ability upon his new field of labor."[25] Similarly, on hearing of Rodgers's death, Tanner told readers of the July 11, 1868, *Recorder*: "It is with feelings of the most unfeigned regret that we record the death of James B. Rodgers, Esq. For years he has done our Church printing, leaving upon the minds of all . . . the lasting impress of a gentleman and a Christian."[26] Still, for all the goodwill hinted at by these comments and by the length of the professional relationship, *Recorder* editors left precious little about their interactions with these white printers, so the pressing question of how race shaped those interactions remains unanswered.

Like many periodical editors of the time, *Recorder* editors did complain regularly about both printers' fees and errors. Sometimes discussion of the former was simply a feature of larger duns—as in the January 19, 1861, assertion that "*the printer wants his money!*" Similarly, a December 26, 1863, piece asserts that "paper is still on the rise—from 18 to 23 cents per pound. The printers, too, have been compelled to raise on us." But such calls also recognized that—however "benevolent" they might be—white printers like Young and Rodgers were part of broader power structures. A July 9, 1864, notice, for example, says that "the printers in this city have met together and adopted a scale of prices, which raises the prices enormously high. If they go on in the way they are now doing, we assure our friends that a great many of our weekly papers will have to stop."

Errors were also a source of continuing frustration and occasional humor. Three of the errors in the paper's numbering were blamed on "oversight" by the printer, for example.²⁷ Poet (and later politician) John Willis Menard's March 21, 1863, letter asks to "correct a very laughable error which appears in the last line of the second verse of" his poem "Liberia" in the March 7, 1863, issue: "Please read '*fiends*' and not '*friends*.' Our Liberian friends would be angry at me should they understand me to say that *they would not compromise with friends!* In presenting my best respects to your good printer, please say to him, If he don't keep both eyes open, I shall take the delicate trouble of reporting him to the muses!" Editors would also occasionally blame the printers for losing items, as when Lynch apologized that resolutions from Philadelphia's Banneker Institute "were left out by our printer last week." Sometimes the reverse happened: Weaver's October 5, 1867, "A Blunder" apologized that "a private letter from friend Bolden appeared in our columns last issue" because "by some mistake" it "was placed among the matter for publication and was sent to the printer. We are sorry."

These brief windows into the character of the relationships with the *Recorder*'s white printers also give us some idea of the paper's editorial processes before work reached the printer. Weaver's "A Blunder," for example, confirms what is suggested in a handful of other items: that each week the *Recorder* editor would bring a stack of handwritten texts from 619 and later 631 Pine to the printer, many of which were the actual paper submissions from the paper's various correspondents. While chapters 5 and 6 begin to explore content expectations of the *Recorder* editors, here we need to recognize that the physicality of such texts caused submissions to also be judged on neatness, clarity, and even quality of ink and paper—traits that seem innocuous enough but were actually deeply tied to correspondents' education, class, and background.

Weaver's November 5, 1864, "Hints to Correspondents"—a numbered list of fifteen bits of advice—tells us more about those submissions in language that sometimes emphasizes the links between physical features and editorial evaluation. "Hints" directs writers to, for example,

1. Write with good ink on paper with ruled lines.
2. Leave one page [side] of each sheet blank.
3. Give the written sheet an ample margin all around.
4. Number the pages in order of their succession.
5. Write in a plain, bold hand, with less respect for beauty.

The first three items call not only for good quality supplies—and so having the economic power to gain such—but also for using them judiciously; items two and three mean using much more paper.²⁸ Several of Weaver's fifteen items also require a level of writing skill that demanded that correspondents be fairly well educated. Weaver's thirteenth directive—"Don't depend on the editor to correct your manuscript"—echoes a number of other comments that suggest he wanted to do as little markup as possible.²⁹ Lynch was uniformly condemnatory when he saw what he felt was inadequate writing from incompetent writers, but Weaver waffled more. Writing his year-end message for the December 30, 1865, issue, Weaver paused to reflect on the "many who possess but little education, and can barely write their own name" who "have sent us articles of their own composition." While his conclusions echo Lynch's, as he mocks letters that "would take a Philadelphia lawyer to decipher" and asserts that "duty forbids the publication of matters of no earthly importance to anyone," he did note that "some of these very people have been more active in the support of the paper than many who come under the garb of classical scholars."

When submissions passed muster, they went into the printer's stack. The paper carried Saturday dates, but staff likely picked copies up from the printer's shop late on Fridays, as a February 16, 1861, item notes that subscription papers were "regularly mailed on every Friday night" to subscribers. I have not yet been able to definitively determine when editors took copy to the printer, and this likely shifted a bit with circumstances. Weaver's May 31, 1862, "Notice," for example, stresses that "all articles for the *Christian Recorder* should be in the editor's hands on the Monday previous to the day of issuing the paper, in order to insure their insertion in that week's issue." However, each of the reprinted "Olympus" letters (see chapter 6) appeared in the Philadelphia *Lutheran and Missionary* only two days prior to their publication in the *Recorder*.[30] This tight timeline also opens the question of how often—or whether—editors regularly read proof.[31]

The timeline, the editors' other responsibilities, and the need to use an external printer might raise questions about who made decisions tied to the paper's look and feel, and it is not clear that any of the editors did page design and layout on a consistent weekly basis. That said, editorial comments on items that were "crowded out" because of other content did sometimes appear in the week in which they were left out.[32] This could be the result of editorial experience—eyeballing texts and understanding roughly what would fit—or even of the printer signing such items for the editor. But it seems more likely that there was communication with the editors as type was being set and layout completed. Regardless, it is clear that the editors—and especially Weaver—were in control of broader choices about design, beginning with the size of the *Recorder*'s sheets. As Church historian Richard Wright notes, the *Recorder* under both Clark and Campbell was a small sheet folded once into a newspaper of four pages, each roughly twelve inches wide by sixteen-and-a-half inches high and each with four columns (353). Weaver enlarged the paper considerably: while his *Recorder* was still a single sheet folded once into a four-page newspaper, his seven-column pages were each twenty inches wide by twenty-six-and-a-half inches high.[33] Even as late as his January 3, 1863, "Christian Recorder, Two Years," Weaver was bragging of the "mammoth sheet" and the *Recorder*'s "present large size and form."

The size of the *Recorder* was certainly a statement of presence, but it was also very much emblematic of Weaver's utilitarian design. He packed in as much content as possible—using small type, little white space, and comparatively few illustrations outside of the handful found in advertisements and in select features designed for children and families (generally standard engravings appearing only on pages three and four). Even the masthead spoke to utility. The striking image some African Americanists are familiar with—the words "Christian Recorder" in stylized capitals on a scroll over an image of the globe with sub-Saharan Africa at the fore and, wrapping the bottom of the globe, the Biblical caption "Ethiopia shall soon stretch out her hands unto God" (Figure 3.2)—was not Weaver's; it was Tanner's, created more than a year after he became editor. Weaver's masthead was much more simple. For most of the period studied here, it offered simply "The Christian Recorder," centered, in severe capitals; a line underneath noted, in more ornate type, that the paper was "Published by the African Methodist Episcopal Church in the United States, for the Dissemination of Religion, Morality, Literature and Science"; and a smaller line underneath listed the date, the paper's numeric information, and, later, the names and titles of *Recorder* leaders.

Weaver's paper also evinced a conscious visual organization—one likely of benefit to both editors and printers (in terms of layout and design) and readers (in terms of finding different types of texts). Some of that organization borrowed from other papers of the period, and some was the *Recorder*'s own.[34] The first column of the first page always began with business information—material on the Book Steward and the Book Concern, rates for subscription, rates for advertising and single-copy sales, and lists of corresponding editors. In most issues, this material was followed by a poem or poems—often headed (in ornate type) "Poetry"; at times, this section was replaced by related content like hymn lyrics. The rest of page one usually offered original items of the

FIGURE 3.2 *Masthead of the September 14, 1876,* Christian Recorder. *Courtesy of the American Antiquarian Society. The masthead of Benjamin Tucker Tanner's* Recorder *was much more ornate than that used during Weaver's era.*

most interest, including many of the texts studied in this volume; this was also the space in which many letters from soldiers and others that carried national news appeared—like, for example, some of the recently republished letters of Henry McNeal Turner.[35] Material tied more directly to church business—including more letters, conference reports, and so forth—often appeared on the paper's internal pages, as did items that could not fit on page one. Page two generally included editorials and other items compiled by the editor with headings like "Personal" and "City Items." Announcements ranging from upcoming Church-related meetings to marriages generally occupied these internal pages, too, as did obituaries. Advertisements were generally relegated to pages three and four, and they usually shared these pages with various notices, spillover of page two texts, and, especially, "family literature" that included short fiction, poetry, didactic texts, and brief snippets of trivia. Pages three and four were also the places where reprints from other newspapers and periodicals—including those run by white owners, often with religious ties—most commonly appeared; that said, such items, especially when short, were regularly used as filler to round out a column or a page throughout the paper. Jumps from one page to another were comparatively rare, especially among page one texts. Significant design variations, such as the heavy black column borders in the first issue after Lincoln's assassination, discussed in chapter 7, were even more rare. This regular look and feel suggests that, while editors likely grouped and ordered the various texts in the stack that went to the printer, they did not have to participate in all phases of layout each week, as the paper's design parameters were fairly settled.

The editors did the vast majority of the work described above, but they did not always do it all. As discussed in the last chapter, it is clear, for example, that much of this kind of work fell to Weaver during Lynch's absences. But even when Weaver held the editorial chair and had no official assistant, he was required to travel at times. Records on Book Concern employees seem almost nonexistent, and I have found no records of specific clerks prior to 1864; it also seems doubtful that there would have been sufficient funds to pay a long-term clerk. As noted earlier, Mary Weaver spent time on the shop floor, and she may also have done some limited editorial work, too. But just who did the work of the paper during Weaver's early absences remains unclear. Weaver seems to have used his "three elections" after the 1864 General Conference to convince the Philadelphia conference to allow him to hire clerks. He did have two clerks—both local young African American men—in 1865.[36] Both likely covered for Weaver during his 1865 absences, and his February 18, 1865, piece notes that "during our visit to the State Convention . . . our assistant" made corrections to a letter from Peter Gardiner that Gardiner was quite unhappy about.[37] The loss of these clerks at the end of 1865 may have precipitated Weaver's request for an assistant—and so also precipitated Lynch's appointment.[38] Such clerks, however, had little editorial control.[39] Often, the larger problem was the reverse: editors had to do too much non-editorial work. As late as the August 6, 1870, issue, Tanner—who had succeeded in getting more of the assistance Weaver pined for—was demanding more church support, as such would allow not only "a larger paper" but "a better one," as "such help could be employed as would make the whole machinery work" and prevent "General Officers" like the Book Steward and the Editor from having "to act as clerks, mail boys, folders, pastors, [and] answer scores of letters every week, and then travel not a little in order to raise the necessary means."

The work described above to bring the *Recorder* into print each week—and so the preparation and distribution of texts key to the period's African American literature and culture—could not take place without funding and a broad community presence. The remainder of this chapter thus focuses on those "necessary means"—and especially on various forms of fundraising and/or distribution. The scarcity of funds was one of the few constants for the Book Concern, and the goal to distribute the *Recorder* (and Church texts more generally) as widely as possible was another. After discussing some of the ways the paper pushed supporting entities for funding, the chapter explores the *Recorder*'s three main modes of obtaining funds, all of which were tied to various senses of and participation in AME and broader Black and national communities. First, for almost all of the period, the paper was partially subsidized by the Church via the Book Concern and various other entities. Second, the paper regularly included advertising. Finally, the paper brought in funds from its distribution—though not all circulation brought funds, and the paper had to continually prod to get such funds. Such questions of distribution foreground the considerations of subscribers, readers, and reading that are key to chapter 4.

Detailed budgets and accounts have not yet been found for either the Book Concern or the *Recorder*, and the published versions of reports that Weaver gave to the Philadelphia Annual Conference, the General Conference, and various other groups are abbreviated and sometimes even contradictory. By the January 14, 1865, issue, Weaver estimated that it now cost "over two hundred dollars per week to get the *Recorder* out."[40] Given prices in 1865—$2.50 for an annual subscription or six cents for a single copy—the paper would need either 4,160 paid full-year subscriptions or over 173,000 single-copy sales to reach the $10,400 that Weaver's somewhat-offhand weekly estimate suggests. Though evidence suggests the print run might have reached these levels, the *Recorder* may never have come close to bringing in such funds.

A call or calls for funds—from the Church and/or to delinquent subscribers or other debtors, new subscribers, or donors—thus appeared in almost every single issue during the period studied here. As the sea of dead nineteenth-century periodicals grew larger, readers would have known that threats to cease publication were serious; Candy Gunther Brown estimates the "average life expectancy of any paper" of the time at "from two to four years" (154). The earliest of Weaver's calls emphasizes two regular themes: that every penny counted and that, as noted in Molliston Clark's 1854 resignation, the paper needed "a capital"—an endowment. A long July 13, 1861, item headed "Newspapers Suspended" reminded readers that "many religious newspapers have been suspended in consequence of the embarrassments created by the war": "some papers are printed on a diminished sheet; others, once in two weeks, and many have been abandoned." The issues of December 14 and 21, 1861, speak directly and in depth about suspending the *Recorder*—something Weaver had threatened as early as the November 16 issue—even though "there was never a time in the history of the AME Church when the connexion stood more in need of a weekly organ." The piece urges "each minister, class leader, steward, trustee, and member of the church, or any lady or gentleman" to "take the matter in hand," and even promises to send the paper free to anyone who would "Procure us *Ten* annual subscribers, and send us the $20."[41] And by the end of the year, Weaver published this simple "Notice": "Unless those in arrears settle their accounts immediately, and our friends manifest their interest in our success, by prompt remittances, we will be obliged to suspend our paper at the beginning of the year."

The paper did not stop, but Weaver's threats and those of other editors became regular reading in the *Recorder* with variations over time.[42] While Weaver's early calls included requests for fundraising and other donations, and while such efforts never stopped, he began to emphasize that the best "fund-raising" was soliciting new cash subscriptions. His February 13, 1864, "A Timely Hint" tells those who "wish the RECORDER to continue on its important mission of imparting and diffusing religious knowledge and general intelligence among the colored people in all parts of this country" to show "us what influence you hold over your neighbors and friends in the way of persuading them to subscribe for the paper."

The editors paired such calls with a range of duns.[43] The thrust of such duns was generally personal responsibility—but always within a larger moral and religious framework, as in the June 9, 1866, "An Editorial Brutus," which asserts "as you don't pay, we dun you.... Who is there so mean that he don't pay his printers? If any, let him shout, for he's the man we're after. His name is Legion, and he's owing us for one, two, three, four, and five years." In this frame, the acknowledgments columns studied below and in the next chapter functioned as a kind of reverse dun. Still, the *Recorder* did also, at times, threaten more public and specific duns; an October 19, 1867, "Notice" claims that "the Trustees of the AME Book Concern have authorized us to say to our friends who are in debt ... for papers and books, that if they do not forward the amounts due us, the said Trustees will publish their names, with the amounts of their indebtedness opposite, in the columns of the *Recorder*" and concludes with "Remember the Apostolic command—'Owe no man anything.'"[44]

Calls for Church subsidies evolved, too. In some ways, such support was a godsend, as secular papers (especially those without organizational ties) had no such recourse, but it also added more layers to what were already complex negotiations with bishops, General Conferences, and regional conferences over power and action. Subsidies were often an issue of real contention and so something Weaver initially preferred to talk about indirectly. He made a point of writing in the February 16, 1861, issue, amidst the controversy over whether the paper should have been restarted at all, that "we have not taken one cent of what little income there is from our Book Concern, but have made the paper pay its own way." The March 16, 1861, and March 30, 1861, issues repeat this claim—arguing in the latter that "It has not, as yet, cost the Connexion any thing—not one cent—though the Connexion is in debt to the RECORDER." That said, he did not—and could not—continue to draw such sharp lines, and even these early claims weren't really accurate, as Book Concern funds went toward his salary, house and office rent at 619 Pine, and several other expenses. Thus, broader support for the Book Concern—and the *Recorder* within that frame—became the focus of Weaver's later direct appeals for Church subsidies.

Records are unclear about how much money was really and specifically collected as "Two-Cent Money"—the levy on Church members established at the 1844 General Conference to support the Book Concern—or about what percentage was to go (and/or actually went) to the Book Steward. At least in the early years (say, 1845 to 1852), the total, Church-wide income from this tax reportedly never passed $1,000 annually (Wright 517). An August 9, 1862, piece notes that "the mere pittance of the Two cent money amounts to little or nothing . . . and the small amount that we have got from the Conferences annually, so far, would not pay the expenses which necessarily must accrue in three months' operations." Still, as early as the October 5, 1861, *Recorder*, the paper was chastising ministers and congregants who did not submit Two-Cent Money, and it continued to do so for the next several years—so much so that successful ministers' recommendations for how to collect the Two-Cent Money became an occasionally appearing genre in itself.

It was much easier to call for and praise donations from individual churches and other sources. Perhaps the earliest (quasi-)external entity to step forward to aid Weaver's paper was the Publication Society of Philadelphia, a group of African American women and men who Weaver praised in the January 19, 1861, issue. They sponsored events like an "entertainment"—advertised in the April 20, 1861, issue—that featured some of Mother Bethel's choir. They seem to have turned into the more gender-specific "Female Publication Society," led by Mary Still (the sister of activist William Still), whose ties to the *Recorder* were deep and rich. Over the next few years, their donations took not only the form of cash but also "a fine new and splendid suit" for Weaver noted in the April 18, 1863, issue. Similar groups from places like Carlisle,

Pennsylvania; Flushing, New York; West Chester, Pennsylvania; and Zanesville, Ohio, made one-time group donations to the paper. The November 24, 1866, *Recorder*—in an item submitted from Lynch's western tour—even noted that "a number of ladies of Cincinnati, Ohio, after listening to the address of the Editor of the *Christian Recorder*, resolved to hold a fair for the benefit of the same, that type and a printing press may be obtained"—though I have yet to find much further reporting of these plans.[45]

Lynch's address in Cincinnati does, though, highlight another mode of fundraising. Weaver, Lynch, and even occasionally Stanford traveled during their terms to visit diverse churches and present the needs of the Book Concern and the *Recorder*. Weaver became so famous for pushing for subscriptions that Tanner's *Apology* describes him "as the man whose first question is: 'How do you do?' and the second, 'Will you subscribe for the *Recorder*?'" (176) Though such visits often emphasized subscriptions, they also heavily encouraged "free will offerings" to support the paper. Weaver regularly reported amounts collected, sometimes even criticizing churches that did not contribute enough. When such events were announced ahead of time, it was not uncommon to see Weaver use language similar to a November 12, 1864, "Notice": "We hope that . . . we shall receive . . . a free-will offering" and "We hope that all our friends will come fully prepared."

While many donations were noted in editors' comments, just over one hundred donations during the period of this study were actually included in the paper's "Acknowledgments" columns. Many of these were donations from church collections made by distant ministers, but some were from individuals—often, but not always, subscribers. Perhaps most interesting among these, coming mainly in 1864, were a small group of contributions designated, as Lizzie Hart's September 3, 1864, acknowledgment read, "to send the *Recorder* to a Soldier." Like pushes to get copies into the hands of Black soldiers through other means discussed below, these contributions were not simply an example of individual financial support for the paper; they were also concrete actions by *Recorder* supporters to aid the paper's broader (potential) textual community and to testify to the value of African American writing and reading.[46] These funds coming into 619 Pine (and later 631 Pine) emphasized—perhaps more than any others—that the monies solicited by the Book Concern were designed to help the Church reach outward and that both the physical location of the Philadelphia store and the material of the *Recorder* were conduits for linking a larger AME community.[47]

While many donations and much of the formal AME funding were tagged for general operations, the *Recorder* did occasionally make requests (and demands) for more specifically targeted support.[48] Perhaps the most direct appeal for Church funds came when the 1867 Philadelphia Conference found the Book Concern to be massively in debt—in part from the purchase of 631 Pine and in part from other operating costs. They called on the connection to raise $7,025, and specified amounts that each individual regional conference should contribute. Reports on attempts to raise this money appeared almost weekly throughout July, August, and September with increasing intensity. A September 28 piece, for example, asserts that "this question can be shirked no longer," and an October 12 item is simply headed "Pay Up!" By the December 14 issue, Philadelphia ministers were promising "Mass Meetings in our churches" to press for support for the Book Concern, as "the ministers have not generally responded to the recommendation of the Philadelphia Conference." That same issue carries a piece called "A Cry for Help" that urges "preachers in debt to the Book Concern, and the subscribers and agents in debt to forward the money" in "one united effort . . . to meet our claims and . . . save the credit of the Book Concern." Not enough did—perhaps because they had heard the paper cry wolf once too often. While extant issues from early 1868 do not speak of this fundraising attempt directly, its failure may have precipitated the February and March 1868 suspension.

Even when they came, funds from the sources above were never enough to run the *Recorder*, so, like most newspapers of the period, the paper also relied on advertising revenue. Ignored by almost all scholars who treat the early Black press (most of whom dismiss the *Recorder*'s ads as a secular, capitalist intrusion), the paper's ads also attempted to create a print community—or, at least, interface with the *Recorder*'s existing community—in ways that intertwined sometimes-contradictory ideas of faith and capitalism to agitate for radical change in African Americans' socioeconomic, religious, and political positions. A subset of ads also embodied the smaller and more specific Black business/AME community of Philadelphia. Space prevents me from fully exploring all of the questions tied to such ads, but, to hint at their contours and to consider how ads functioned within the quasi-separate artifact of an "issue," I here offer discussion of the ads in one issue—the February 25, 1865, *Recorder*.

Readers of that issue saw the first installment of *The Curse of Caste*; a reprint of three Greek hymns translated by British evangelical John Mason Neale; a piece of Henry McNeal Turner's "Army Correspondence"; a letter from Sergeant James Payne, an African American soldier stationed near Richmond; an unsigned article on "Colored Troops"; letters from locations as diverse as Louisville, Chicago, Brooklyn, Galesburg, and Allegheny City; an article copied from the New York *Evening Bulletin* on "Negro Suffrage"; and a host of shorter items ranging from a call to produce soldiers' "comfort bags" to brief reports on a lecture by Frederick Douglass and from obituaries to reprints about developments in Africa (from the *Episcopal Standard*) and in North Carolina (from the *Raleigh Whig*). As usual, the back page was devoted to family literature, and this issue, under headings like "Child's Cabinet," included poetry, short moralistic fiction, and texts copied from sources like the *Presbyterian*.

Page three ads took almost two of that page's seven columns, and page four ads took three full columns—in both cases, a bit less than usual. At this point in the paper's history, all of its advertising was guided by brief principles that regularly appeared on the paper's front page—opening with "We solicit Advertisements of all descriptions, suitable for a religious newspaper." What is initially striking in the guidelines is Weaver's attempt to combine the acts of advertising and subscribing: ads no longer than eight lines could be inserted for a full year for $10 "paper included" or $8 "without the paper." Such ads could alternately be inserted for six months for $6, three months for $4, or one month for $1, and these shorter terms came only "paper included."[49] All ads needed to be submitted with "cash." While many papers of the period provided more information on a wider range of sizes and terms, fewer emphasized the receipt of the paper so heavily. Arguably, the *Recorder* was pushing advertisers to become readers—and recognizing that readers might become advertisers—thus bringing commerce directly into the political and religious frameworks of the paper's communities of reading and writing. Also, though many papers of the period talked much more about short-term rates, the *Recorder* did not foreground such strategies. At least eight of the ads in this issue were encoded "1y"—one year.[50] While the *Recorder* was certainly attempting to ensure the funds tied to a long-term ad, strings of more expensive short-term ads would actually have generated more money than the cheaper long-term ads. This approach may have been governed by the editors' time constraints, but I also submit that, on purpose or not, these terms set up more extended presences for readers, so that the solicitation of "Advertisements of all descriptions, suitable for a religious newspaper" can be seen as a more connected form of endorsement, the forming or reinforcing of community.

These links were heavily emphasized in the Book Concern's own advertising in the paper. Weaver used an ad to praise Mary Still (then the paper's Philadelphia agent), and he separately advertised the Church "Book Depository," promising that "we keep on hand" Sabbath School books, a "good assortment of such books as are generally used in the Public Schools," as well as "stationary, inks, pens, paper, envelopes, and blank books." Several times larger than these brief ads—generally known as "cards"—was the ad headed "Our Own Bookstore" that offered a long list of titles that arguably represented the texts the Church (and Weaver especially) thought a literate Christian should want: Bibles, hymnals, the AME *Discipline*, a long list of faith-centered books for young readers, pop religious books by white writers like Daniel Wise and Maxwell Gaddis, an extensive list of books tied to missionary work, and old standbys like John Bunyan's *Pilgrim's Progress*. These titles shared space on the list (and on AME bookstore shelves) with several seemingly more secular works like *The Lives of Lincoln and Hamlin*, Joshua Giddings's *Exiles of Florida*, the *Boys' and Girls' Book of Birds*, even bowdlerized versions of *Robinson Crusoe* and the *Iliad*. These ads emphasize that Weaver saw the store at 619 Pine (and later at 631 Pine) as both (and simultaneously) church-centered and commercial ventures deeply shaped by both faith and capital; they also highlight the fact that the commerce of the book trade and the act of advertising for such were part and parcel of the *Recorder*'s larger push for multiple literacies within an African Methodist Episcopal framework. Select Black-authored books were also included—Solomon Northup's narrative as well as shorter theological tracts—but this larger ad's focus was the insertion of African Americans as *readers* and consumers of print.[51] This ad ends with the nexus of capital exchange, participation in print culture, and racial literacy and uplift—"We hope that brethren of our connexion and friends will send orders, accompanied with the cash, for such works as they . . . ought to study—also the Sabbath Schools—so that our Depository may leave an upward . . . tendency."

Some of the *Recorder*'s external ads advanced similar values. Among the thirty-five other ads in the issue—mainly short cards but also some longer ads—those tied to print culture stand out. W. H. Decordover's Periodical Depot in Philadelphia—which stocked the *Recorder*—advertised that it always had "daily and weekly papers on hand" and offered a brief list of samples: the *New York Ledger*, the *Anglo-African*, and *Harper's Weekly*. Placing these three titles together is amazing: a white story paper, a fairly radical Black paper, and a white family paper. In such a short gesture—one designed for a Black church paper—Decordover's ad suggested a full integration of Black print into American print; as if speaking even further to such, the ad promised that (Black *Recorder*) readers would find "also, stationery." An ad from Winston and Thomas, a periodical depot in New Orleans, did not list specific titles but similarly placed African Americans as both (multilingual) readers and writers—noting "a large assortment of School Books, French Books . . . Phrenological Journals" and "novels" as well as "paper, envelopes, pens," and "ink." Weaver took space on page two—as he sometimes did for advertisers—to specifically endorse this store, which, he said, "always" had single copies of the *Recorder* "on hand" and could reliably facilitate subscriptions to the paper. A similar assertion of Black reading and writing (and a rich range of other literacies) is also exhibited in the ad for the young African American–centered Avery College—endorsed by George Vashon—and, more broadly, by quasi-ads like the announcements for lectures and other events, which Weaver sometimes placed as ads and sometimes included on page two as short news items.[52]

This national sense of a linked *Recorder* community of businesses and consumers was played out in microcosm in the ads placed by Philadelphians. Reminding readers (then and now) that a natural secondary function of the *Recorder* was to serve as the Black newspaper of Philadelphia, these ads also led by example—in suggesting that a strong Black community (with clear anchors in print) could function within the broader landscape of capitalism. Some readers would certainly recognize the names in the various Philadelphia ads from other columns of the paper—both "City News" features and other reportage—but the geographic cluster of addresses would be notable to anyone who had visited the city. In addition to the Book Concern, other Pine Street advertisers included the Philadelphia Intelligence Office, "Eclectic" physician James C. Clark, and Georgina Gleaves's "Trimmings and Fancy Goods"; within easy walking distance from the Book Concern were S. Shorter Hawkins's clothing store (615 Lombard), Mrs. H. S. Duerte's undertaker services (634 Lombard), Thomas J. Bowers's Coal Yard (639 Lombard), Mrs. C. E. Harding's dry goods store (713 Lombard), Charles Brister's restaurant (717 Lombard), the Olive Branch Boarding House (814 Lombard), James W. Brown's steam dying business (123 S. 5th), Charles Magarge's wholesale paper and rag business (32 S. 6th), the Bustill family hair care business (403 S. 6th), Thomas Charnock's undertaker services (427 S. 6th), Mrs. M. Bennett's "herb doctress" office (468 S. 7th), Jane Johnson and Ann Wear's funeral shrouding (618 S. 8th), William A. Longfellow's surgery/dentistry practice (1126 Rodman), and James J. Spellman's office, from which he offered "military instruction" (1021 South). These advertisers endorsed print on multiple levels—choosing to spend funds on advertising in the *Recorder*, assuming that subscribers would be likely customers, and demonstrating multiple literacies through the range of their occupations.[53]

Such ads also argue for a rising Black professional class whose boundaries were limited by racism but who nonetheless spoke for the capitalist-inflected uplift ideals espoused repeatedly by the paper—in some ways, a kind of proto-Garveyism. Taken another way, they also offer a remembrance—a "recording," if you will—of Black professionalism in a kind of liberation historiography of Black-to-Black commerce and of attempts at self-sufficiency within Black communities. The repeated rhetorics of professionalization in these ads not only answer minstrel-show stereotypes in popular white advertising (the "Brack Doctor," for example) but also emphasize Black potential in a "new" nation.

Consider, for example, the large illustrated ad for the famous Bustill family hair business, which included wigs, hair jewelry, hair care products, grooming supplies, and, of course, barbering and styling services. Its language and claims mark not simply professionalism but also expertise, even exclusiveness. Its focal point is a striking illustration of a racially indeterminate woman—likely a stock cut of a nominally white woman. Published in a paper that discussed all sorts of "white" African Americans, including the *Curse of Caste*'s Claire (making her first appearance in this issue), this ad plays with racial boundaries even as it emphasizes a Black-run capitalist venture.[54] The Bustill name alone also reminds readers that commerce interfaced with politics and that capital could become agency. Regular readers of the paper would recognize Joseph Bustill from the *Recorder*'s reports of the Pennsylvania State Equal Rights League; the Social, Civil, and Statistical Association of the Colored People of Pennsylvania; various groups protesting transit discrimination in Philadelphia; and a committee that planned a lecture series that featured Douglass and Harper. They might even remember Sarah Bustill's work with the Ladies Union Association, which was also reported in the *Recorder*. Given Weaver's consistent argument that Black political action expressed faith, it seems clear that his "uplift theology" extended to commerce and that ads that were "suitable for a religious newspaper" could do Black community work.

Another page two puff piece by Weaver suggests the parameters of this community of AME advertisers and consumers—though, ironically, by separating an advertiser from that community. The puff piece calls for "Special Attention" to a patent medicine ad for a book of recipes for cures for "Fits, Consumption, and Dyspepsia" written by Oliver Phelps Brown, a white doctor in Jersey City. The puff piece does give the expected praise—seemingly copied from something written by Brown claiming that his product will make the sick "rejoice in the knowledge" of "a specific remedy." However, the piece is also careful to note that the ad came to the *Recorder* through a recent innovation in advertising—an external ad agency. Far from offering the kind of personal (and personalized) praise Weaver gave Winston and Thomas, for example, his puff piece tells readers that he "procured" this ad "through John Holmes and Co., City and Country Advertising Agency," of New York.[55] While Weaver ends with a characteristic phrase—"we refer our readers to his advertisement"—it is almost as if he was simultaneously distancing himself, carefully marking who was in the *Recorder*'s community and who wasn't. Weaver was engaging in capitalist practice but also questioning it—accepting advertising but also clearly marking it as from someone not known to him, publishing claims but also beginning to equip readers to evaluate those claims.

Contemporary readers might see the presence of a patent medicine ad suspiciously, but such ads were not automatically seen as breaching the *Recorder*'s community-centered advertising at the time. As the *Recorder* was carving out an alternative space in the American print landscape, it also explored potential links to other alternative spaces. By 1865, the paper was already beginning to ally itself with homeopathic physicians, in part because some white homeopaths (especially some spiritualists) sometimes proved a bit more liberal on race issues and in part because African Americans who had been barred from American medical schools often turned to homeopathy.[56] The February 25, 1865, issue thus includes *five* other ads for medical practitioners—at least four of whom were Black, some of whom practiced alternative medicine, some of whom made claims like Brown's, and all of whom demand further study. The *Recorder* recognized that such ads served customers and practitioners who were denied marketplace spaces and so provided a community service to African Americans not only in greater Philadelphia but also those passing through Philadelphia and those using mail order.

These ads' paired sense of public announcement and public request points toward similar items in the paper that also did important cultural work. In the February 25, 1865, issue, there were announcements of diverse events, as well as two obituaries, two marriage announcements, and one "Information Wanted" listing. Obituaries and marriage announcements had long been a feature of the Black press, in part because white papers were often loath to publish such material from African Americans and in part because the broader white culture dismissed and insulted the suggestion of strong Black families. Both types of texts demand further study, and chapter 7 hints at some of the parameters of obituaries through its examination of *Recorder* elegies. For our purposes here, it is important to note that these public announcements both informed far-flung members of the AME community of major events in the lives of family and friends and reinforced the paper's larger radical move to recognize Black love in print. The paper was thus quite hesitant about charging for such notices, though in the end, it did. Weaver's February 13, 1864, "Marriage Notices, &c." gently asserts "when we take the liberty of requesting those brethren forwarding marriage notices for insertion in our columns to be considerate enough to enclose 25 cents for every such notice, we do not wish to be considered as avaricious or grasping. The paper needs every aid possible." Here and elsewhere, Weaver assigned the responsibility of such fees to the minister performing the (church-sanctioned) ceremony of marriage, suggesting that "the brother officiating receives his customary fee, and we think he should not object to devoting so small a sum to the publishing of the notice."[57] But both Weaver's more-terse March 26, 1864, "Marriages" and Lynch's December 22, 1866, "Marriage Notices" note, to use Lynch's language, that "we cannot publish any more notices unless they are accompanied with the money." Weaver's February 13, 1864, piece carefully says that the fee for marriage announcements "extends to all notices, with the exception of announcements of death," but, in early 1867, the paper finally began charging for obituaries, too. Raising the marriage notice rate to thirty cents for four lines or less and to the standard ad rate for longer marriage notices, Lynch also set the rate of "twelve and a half cents per line of nine words" for all "obituaries, notices, acknowledgments, and all matters of a private nature"—a discount from the new ad rate of fifteen cents per line, but a charge nonetheless. While the paper was happy to promote the community functions embodied in these notices, it recognized costs for doing so.

Terms of the "Information Wanted" ads that African Americans placed in hopes of finding family and friends—often lost through slavery—are tougher to trace. The ads began to appear in earnest in 1863 and continued for much of the rest of the century. Many of these ads carry language asking pastors to read them from their pulpits, and those who knew of reunions were asked to share such stories. On the whole, they mark a stunning use of print to (attempt to) rejoin families and communities—one that reaches beyond specific print literacies (into the orality of church services and word-of-mouth), one that should be read in dialogue with slave narratives (as many are exceedingly brief slave narratives in themselves), and one that demands much further study.[58] Their naming of relatives and friends served valuable public genealogical functions, while their listing of brief details of family life and especially their naming of formerly enslaved people's former owners mark yet another liberationist approach to history. "Information Wanted" ads that appeared in the *Recorder* had their own heading and looked, visually, like short cards. Most were marked with insertion information—in terms of either time (e.g., "1 mo.") or number of insertions (e.g., "3t," for three times), and this implies—though does not directly state—that such ads fell under the "matters of a private nature" that received the discounted rate after 1867.[59] Such ads also had complex community functions beyond their personal goals: they held out the (often slim) hope of reuniting Black families, which the Church recognized as crucial to community development; they functioned in some ways as gestures of mourning from individuals stuck without definite resolution of their losses; they offered a stunning rebuttal to the most common antebellum ads "looking" for Black people—those from masters seeking self-emancipating people (and, in this, they certainly challenge the capitalism that dominates other ads); and they again emphasized the ways in which the *Recorder* functioned as a community of voices, as a "recorder" of stories that often could not or would not be told within white print.

Recording and sharing African American stories—even those in such ads and notices—was, of course, one of the paper's central goals, and such sharing meant working actively on questions of distribution alluded to above. Each week, the printed paper needed to go out into the world, and for the aesthetic, intellectual, and emotional processes of reading to take place, first the material processes of printing and dissemination had to happen. The rest of this chapter and much of the next thus build from the discussion of the mechanics of the paper to explore the ways distribution-centered fundraising was tied to larger senses of building an AME community and creating spaces for African American literature and print broadly.

First, though, we need to briefly turn to the most notable form of distribution *not* tied to income—periodical exchange, a barter process of content and reputation rather than coin—in part because, in addition to serving other functions, involvement in such exchange was marketed as a reason for readers to buy both single copies of and subscriptions to the *Recorder*. From its inception, the *Recorder* was both an advocate for and an active participant in the exchange process—the sending of a free copy of the paper to an editor of another periodical who agreed to do the same in return. To date, I have located over four dozen periodicals noted as exchanging with the *Recorder*; there were clearly a number of others. Such trade—discussed usefully by scholars like Meredith McGill and Leon Jackson but still understudied vis-à-vis Black print culture—had multiple layers. It provided a key basis for reprinting, which was an immensely common practice in nineteenth-century periodicals, and it offered editors across the nation local news and commentary they might otherwise never see. One of the *Recorder*'s goals was thus to enter exchange relationships with periodicals from all corners of the nation—and sometimes beyond (as seen in Weaver's early exchange with Augustus Green's Ontario-based BME *True Royalist*). *Recorder* editors regularly noted with special interest when they secured distant exchanges, as when Weaver told of how he was "truly glad to find our friends in the Pacific State doing what they can for the elevation of our people" in announcing an exchange with the San Francisco *Pacific Appeal* in the June 21, 1862, *Recorder*. Such diversity also offered the potential for better reprints, and so Weaver's New Year's message for 1863 promised, among other things, that "we shall secure the best selections which our numerous exchanges afford."

Recorder editors also saw reputational value in their exchange list; Lynch's May 12, 1866, "Our Book Concern" notes not only the length of the exchange list but also the fact that the paper "has on its exchange list the ablest papers, religious and secular, that are published in the country." At times, the *Recorder* conceived of American print culture as a gathering; Weaver's September 27, 1862, "Exchanges," for example, opens, "We acknowledge the following exchanges which came to our office during our absence, and with which we neglected to shake hands in our last." Implicit in such work—reading as "shaking hands," exchanging papers as a gift of introduction—are assertions that the *Recorder* was worthy of broad notice within American print culture and that the editors were breaking racial barriers to enter the "club" of print leaders.[60] From this vantage, the paper could support others in the field, as it did when its June 9, 1866, issue praised the *Loyal Georgian* as "one of the ablest of our exchanges published under the auspices of colored men.... It would be better for the Chattahoochee river to dry up than for this paper to be suspended. We say to the colored men of Georgia, never let it die." But beyond simply praising (and sometimes criticizing) the Black papers it exchanged with, the *Recorder* also used its exchange position to evaluate the white press, as when Weaver praised the *Philadelphia Tribune* in the March 30, 1861, issue for its "good size, fair type, and well conducted [pages]. We like this paper for many reasons, one of which is, because it has the right view of national subjects."

Such exchange copies were among those that the staff at the *Recorder* office—first at 619 Pine and then at 631 Pine—prepared for mailing each week. A significant number of papers, though, were first set aside for delivery to or pickup by the paper's Philadelphia subscribers—the first component of the paper's fundraising via distribution. Packets containing larger numbers of copies—for sale by agents and ministers or for other bulk distribution—and copies for individual mail subscriptions were also wrapped, addressed, and brought to the post office. Additional copies were set aside if the Book Steward or editor had a trip coming up soon. With the exception of exchange copies, all of these modes were centered on bringing money into the Concern even as they performed a host of other functions.

Just what the paper's circulation was at any given point remains hazy. Weaver's calls for subscribers often relied on hyperbole. When he demanded, as he would do repeatedly from 1863 on, that the Church produce "Ten Thousand Subscribers for the Christian Recorder," in a November 12, 1864, call, he was far from reality. Rather than offering specific numbers for actual circulation, he was much more likely to say something like—as he did in the January 3, 1863, issue—"the circulation is larger than it has ever been since the organization of the AME Church." Lynch or Weaver reported a circulation of 5,000 in an item reprinted in the November 19, 1867, Philadelphia *Evening Telegraph*. The 1869 *Rowell's* offers no circulation information, but the volumes for 1870, 1871, and 1872 list a circulation of 2,500—and for 1873, a circulation of 2,800. Tanner's March 2, 1876, report places circulation at 4,000. Wright's 1916 *Encyclopedia* asserts that, while "the circulation has varied," "up to Editor Tanner's time it was always very small"—though he misses several details regarding Weaver's period. All of these numbers must also be placed in context. Some copies may have been read only by a single person but, given the various modes of reading common in the nineteenth century, many copies were likely shared among a number of people (in a family, a neighborhood, a military unit, or a church, for example) and/or read aloud. This meant that any given copy of the paper could "circulate" to many readers—even those who couldn't yet "read" because they lacked a full command of alphabetic literacies. We also cannot equate any circulation numbers directly with funding, as several of Weaver's duns (and some of Lynch's) speak of subscribers who remained on the rolls even though they had not paid for some time.[61] Weaver had actually begun the paper by sending gratis copies—writing in an April 20, 1861, piece that he had "sent of each issue a copy to all [ministerial] brethren whose address was known to us" with the expectation that they would donate, subscribe, and solicit subscribers. Some did, and some did not.

Weaver initially set the subscription price at $2.00 per year; rising paper costs and deep financial need brought the price to $2.25 at the beginning of 1863 and to $2.50 in 1865. Weaver not only defended these raises in print but tied them to broader national trends, even asserting that his "worthy and distinguished cotemporary" the *Weekly Anglo-African* was "right and proper" in raising its annual subscription from $2.25 to $2.50—just before the *Recorder* did the same. Lynch attempted a tiered system—stated in the January 5, 1867, *Recorder*, of $2.50 per year for laypeople, "strictly in advance" (though he also added, curiously, "if not paid within three months from date of subscription, three dollars and fifty cents will invariably be charged"); and $2 in advance (or $2.25 if not advanced) for clergy. Single-copy prices began at four cents, though they went up to five cents, and then, in 1865, to six cents.

Subscribers who lived in the city of Philadelphia had three options for receiving their papers. They could have them mailed, an option almost none of them chose given the additional postage fees discussed below. They could pick them up at the *Recorder* office—thus bringing more of the paper's community into 619 Pine and later 631 Pine—an option at least some chose. Finally, they could have their papers delivered, though this option itself went through three distinct incarnations. Early on, the paper encouraged city subscribers to pay for each individual issue as it was delivered, though by March 30, 1861, Weaver was already reminding such subscribers that "we are depending upon the income . . . every week" and that subscribers needed to "remember that the carriers cannot deliver the papers for nothing." By December 21, 1861, Weaver informed city subscribers that they would need to "pay their $2.00 in advance, to us, or at our office" for their subscriptions. Under this revised delivery model, "the carriers will have nothing to do but to collect one penny for their services"; this approach, Weaver asserted, "will *make carriers more active*" in delivering papers in a timely fashion.[62] More and more, however—and especially during Lynch's tenure—the paper urged Philadelphia subscribers to pay not only their subscriptions but also their delivery fees in full, in advance. Those who did were even offered a small deal: the January 20, 1866, issue offered city subscribers the paper for either "$3.00 per year, delivered at your house or place of business, or $2.50 per year, and the subscriber paying the carrier one penny per week." Delivery options for city subscribers offered significant convenience, not only because the paper was brought to a subscriber's doorstep but also because the *Recorder* employed and supervised the carriers.[63] The paper promised, in the March 30, 1861, issue, that any city subscriber not receiving a paper on time could contact the editor, who would "see whose route it is in, and have it attended to." That said, city subscribers also had to contend with more direct duns from the Concern: in the February 2, 1867, issue, Weaver told "our Philadelphia subscribers who are in arrears" that "we shall call upon those who do not come and pay for their papers."

The *Recorder* did not list the vast majority of city subscribers in its acknowledgments columns, and the paper was vague about how many city subscribers it actually had. Weaver's February 9, 1861, "Visit to New York" ends with a note that "we supply in Philadelphia over 400 per week," though his December 27, 1863, "Notice to Our City Subscribers" asks Philadelphians to subscribe "to the amount of $500," which, at the 1863 rate ($2.25/year), would have equated to just over 220 subscriptions. Some of the difference between these numbers may be accounted for by single-copy sales—from the AME bookstore, from Decordover's, and from individual ministers in the city, for example. But it is likely that Weaver's December 23, 1865, call for "1000 Cash Subscribers from Philadelphia" went far beyond wishful thinking.

That said, significant distribution—and some income—also came from single-copy sales not only in Philadelphia but in several other locations, and this phenomenon is worth some exploration, in part because editors always hoped that such single-copy sales would bring in subscribers. Further, while there were clearly a handful of shops that carried the *Recorder*, the vast majority of single-copy sales went through the same conduit as subscriptions: the paper's agents, often AME ministers. Most of what we know about single-copy sales—beyond stray references to shops like Decordover's—comes from acknowledgments of agents, which were sometimes included in the lists with the individual mail subscriptions discussed in the next chapter.[64] However, those acknowledgments were almost always for bundles of copies, and this means that we can often only trace the copies in these bundles to agents (rather than specific homes or customers). This specific subset of acknowledgments is also both incomplete and sometimes confusing. During 1861 and 1862, the acknowledgments columns often labeled funds from single-copy sales as "for papers." While this label was used sporadically after, it became quite rare by 1865, and many later acknowledgments that were likely "for papers" or for combinations of papers and other items from the Book Concern were not labeled clearly. All of the editors were also uneven in reporting how many copies they distributed on their own.[65]

While it is difficult to judge how many copies went out for single-copy sales, we can mark the total funds acknowledged as "for papers" in extant issues. In 1861, $165.42 was so acknowledged; in 1862, $113.45; in 1863, $139.35; in 1864, $130.40; in 1865, $13.65; in 1866, $15.00; in 1867, $6.40; thus totaling $583.67. While the totals in 1865–1867 are clearly artificially lowered by the lack of clear labeling, the numbers suggest that at least 4,100 copies of the paper were acknowledged in this way in 1861, and close to 3,000 in each year after, up to 1865. While these numbers may initially sound large, shifting them into weekly averages shrinks their power: the 1861 numbers suggest an average of less than 80 copies each week, and the later years are lower. There was also considerable monthly fluctuation: Weaver reported $43.78 in such funds in March 1861 and $35.45 in November 1861, for example, but only $1 in September 1861 and nothing in August 1861. While such work must be tentative, breaking these acknowledgments down by state also suggests that these copies went to areas where, as discussed in the next chapter, subscriptions were thinner—as New York accounted for $116.70 (almost 20%) of the total funds acknowledged in this fashion and Massachusetts accounted for $44.17 (7.6%), while neither state accounted for large numbers of subscriptions.[66]

Weaver himself engineered the largest bulk purchase of single copies. On October 9, 1863, he visited George H. Stuart, the President of the US Christian Committee (USCC) and a Philadelphia businessman. The USCC, founded by

YMCA members, provided a host of assistance to Union troops, including distributing moral literature in the form of books, tracts, and periodicals.[67] (See Figure 3.3 for one USCC location.) Weaver asked that the *Christian Recorder* be added to the titles to be "circulated among our brave colored soldiers, who have freely volunteered for the defense of their bleeding country." In Weaver's October 17, 1863, *Recorder* account, Stuart, "like a Christian, examined our paper, and at once ordered 1000 copies, to be sent to our soldiers." Weaver hoped Stuart would "increase it to three, five, or ten thousand" and noted that "many of the white soldiers will be glad to have our paper," too. Weaver did not report whether he gave the USCC a special rate for the papers. Further, the time during which the USCC bought and then distributed copies of the *Recorder* is also unclear. However, Lynch's February 27, 1864, letter from Beaufort, South Carolina, to then-editor Weaver notes that "about three hundred copies . . . are distributed from Hilton Head weekly" and "while the number may not be so large as that *every* week, yet a great many copies are seen by soldiers and civilians." When the Christian Commission considered post-war mission changes, the *Recorder* worriedly carried an item in the June 10, 1865, issue reminding the Commission that a standing military force "to garrison the forts, and man the navy" would still need papers like the *Recorder*. Lynch's May 12, 1866, assertion that Weaver "through the Christian

FIGURE 3.3 *U.S. Christian Commission at Richmond, Virginia (1865). Courtesy of the Prints & Photographs Division, Library of Congress (LC-B8171-3371).*

Commission" supplied "four thousand copies of the Recorder weekly—cheering the hearts of our gallant boys" may be an overstatement—as that number far surpassed some estimations of the paper's full circulation—but it is clear that Weaver's partnership with the USCC did move a significant number of papers into the camps and the lives of Black soldiers. Some likely saw the paper regularly over a period of time, and some probably saw only a sample issue. Importantly, some became subscribers.[68]

Predicting single-copy sales was likely a difficult proposition. When Weaver resurrected the paper, he underestimated how many copies he would need, noting, for example, in the February 23, 1861, issue, that "all of last week's issue (No. 6) are gone, and we could dispose of some fifty copies more if we had them." Because he never wanted the opposite problem—unsold copies that he had paid to print—he attempted to take both orders and payments from agents in advance whenever possible, with success in the former and repeated failure in the latter. By the mid-1860s, he was addressing as many duns to agents as he was to subscribers—often considering both in a single paragraph. His August 8, 1863, dun says "we cannot get along unless you send us the money" and specifically chastises "some of our agents who get a great many papers" and "let their account run . . . up to twenty-five or thirty dollars, and sometimes more." Given single-copy prices and compensation rates discussed below, $30 could equate to as many as 750 copies.

The paper was vague as to how agents would be compensated—perhaps in part because, as discussed below, editors at times argued that all members of the Church should be "agents." That said, traces suggest that compensation for single-copy sales worked like the structures for carriers—and so that an agent would earn between a penny and a penny and a half for each copy sold. Weaver's February 2, 1867, "A Proposition," for example, offers one hundred copies to "any minister or agent"—indeed, "anyone"—who sent $4.00; fifty copies, $2.00; or twenty-five copies, $1.10. This discounted rate opened the window for agent compensation, and his "Proposition" said "They can sell the paper at six cents per copy and the postage will only cost a half-cent per paper."[69] To broaden their options—and to further support the paper—agents were also encouraged to solicit and handle subscriptions. While more ministers than lay agents seem to have done such work, Weaver seems to have created a structure, noted in the January 2, 1864, issue, that allowed "all agents ordering quantities of the paper to supply weekly subscribers" to "be charged at the rate of three dollars and fifty cents per hundred—and to be settled for promptly every two weeks."[70] Though we still do not know how much it cost the *Recorder* to produce a single copy, we should recognize that these kinds of discounts, while they certainly aided sales and distribution, took a bite out of any profits. The paper thus consistently emphasized more traditional individual mail subscriptions.

The *Recorder*'s central strategies for garnering mail subscriptions—ideally full-year subscriptions paid in cash in advance—had much in common with other Black newspapers, as all were effectively shut out of many of the developments in marketing and distribution pioneered by white periodical publishers generally and evangelical publishers in specific.[71] As noted above, a very small number of outlets were willing to carry the *Recorder*, and the various forms of cross-state colportage were more tied to books and pamphlets and often denied to Black agents because of discriminatory practices regulating Black movement. Thus, at the heart of the *Recorder*'s philosophy was the creation of a culture of mail-based subscription within a set of moral imperatives to circulate and (financially) support the paper.

A basic strategy in such solicitation was an appeal based on the periodical's importance; Weaver asked readers of the October 15, 1864, issue, for example, "What is the use of our brave heroes falling in the strife for advancement, if we at home are too mercenary to subscribe $2.50 to a paper that is shedding the rays of intelligence over our benighted people throughout the land?" A month later, a man who had been among those "brave heroes," Quartermaster Sergeant James H. Payne of the 27th US Colored Troops responded: "I hope the brethren will not fail to use all the energy possible to sustain such a noble paper. . . . It goes forth as a messenger, delivering tidings of joy and intelligence. . . . It visits the family at home and the soldier in the field. . . . Is it not a marvel that such a paper should be found in this land of oppression, where every thing has worked against us?" In short, as Weaver asserted in the December 9, 1865, *Recorder*, publishing the paper *and* subscribing were "duties"—national, racial, and religious duties; in making these claims, Weaver could have been writing for any Black newspaper of the time—any of which might call their paper a rare and important outlet for African Americans "to plead your cause, the cause of justice and right, before the nation."

Still, similarities in tone and content masked significant philosophical and operational differences. Weaver's December 30, 1865, year-end message, in addition to echoing the sense that the paper could offer a crucial voice to African Americans and be a vehicle for both long-free and the newly freed people, claims that "it is utterly impossible for the Church to reach all her members without it. It is impossible for the Church to keep pace with the progressive world without it. . . . A paper like the Christian Recorder gives vivacity to the Church. It informs the ministers from one end of the connexion to the other, of what they are all doing, and what is necessary for a greater concert of action." Consonant with the calls of Bishop Quinn and so many of the early supporters of a Church paper discussed in the last chapter, Weaver was also reminding readers that they needed to take a *religious* paper, as he had in a host of calls like the February 8, 1862, "Four Questions about a Paper," which lectured, "A family without a religious paper . . . is really an object of pity" and "a fit field for missionary labour." Notably, this piece also argues that "It is not enough that you borrow" a paper "from your friend or neighbor," as "in this case your reading will be desultory and interrupted, and the feeling of dependence on another, will take from you both the pleasure and profit of the perusal." In other words, subscription was simply necessary.

As the *Recorder* layered responsibilities to Church and God onto the political responsibilities of ensuring Black participation in print-based public spaces, so, too, did it weave Church structures into distribution efforts. The *Anglo-African*, the *Pacific Appeal*, and the *Elevator*, for example, all relied heavily on localized agents in a business-centered arrangement; the latter two papers often published lists of agents on their front pages. While Black periodical agency remains almost completely unstudied, we know that these agents were almost always tied to small regions—sometimes as specific as the towns in which they resided (though Philip Bell represented the whole West Coast for the Hamilton family). They were often respected members of their communities and had other, well-established careers; being a periodical agent was secondary, never central. Such local agents could be seen as a mode of moving periodical subscription from the "thin trust" that "we repose in strangers" that is almost solely "predicated on a belief that those whom we do not know will behave in . . . socially acceptable ways" toward the "thick trust" that embodies "the confidence we have in those we already know" both personally and as neighbors engaged in "economic exchanges . . . embedded in ongoing social relations" (Jackson 154).

The *Recorder* did have some lay agents who worked in these ways and who emphasized subscription as much or more than single-copy sales. Almost as soon as he resuscitated the paper, Weaver appointed a Philadelphia "canvassing agent," Andrew Burris, a well-known musician and music teacher with deep ties to both church and community. Burris not only solicited subscriptions but also sold advertising and collected donations. Though he did not stay in this role long, his connections to the paper continued—including setting up a benefit concert for the *Recorder* on February 26, 1862, and another later concert to raise funds to send copies of the paper to Black soldiers on April 21, 1864.

One of the most fascinating of the paper's lay agents followed Burris: Mary Still, the sister of Underground Railroad activist William Still. Mary Still had a long history of supporting the AME Church and AME print. She wrote for the *Recorder* before Weaver entered, and she continued to send occasional letters for more than a decade after he left. Her work with the various Philadelphia publication societies is noted above, and her pamphlet "An Appeal to the Females of the African Methodist Episcopal Church" had appeared in 1857. Referred to throughout much of 1863 as "our city and county Canvasser," she was, in Weaver's June 28, 1862, words, "a warm and ardent friend of our people" as well as "a persistent advocate of educational and literary attainments." While Weaver represented her as a friendly schoolmarm—"friends may know her by the wearing of glasses, and by the pleasant smile that is ever lingering on her matronly countenance"—her existence reminds us of the fact that women were an essential part of the paper's support, were skilled (sometimes more so than their male counterparts) at raising funds, and carved out diverse roles tied to the paper. Because Philadelphia subscribers were almost never listed in the paper's acknowledgments, we have only a limited sense of how many subscriptions she secured—though her long engagement with the paper suggests she had some success. When she began traveling more, she was more regularly tied to specific acknowledgments, as when a January 14, 1865, editorial credited her with sending in a dozen cash subscriptions.[72] That said, it was rarer for lay agents to be acknowledged for getting subscriptions. While roughly 940 of the 2,545 likely first-time subscribers discussed in chapter 4 were paired with some note that suggests a conduit for their subscriptions, the vast majority of those listed conduits are ministers.[73]

Lay and clergy agents' collection of subscription money at times bridged over into collecting donation for the Book Concern broadly. However, while this function did not add any compensation for agents, it did open up wider possibilities for scams. As early as July 13, 1861, Weaver ran an item titled "Imposters" that asserted that "There are some scamps making a living under the garb of the *Christian Recorder*" and that "the penitentiary would be too good" for them. He reminded readers that, beyond ministers, the names of "any other agents . . . will appear in the *Recorder*." In the April 11, 1868, issue, he even had to warn that "when we were in Weldon, North Carolina, a few days ago, we heard of some one, who, just two days before our arrival, declared himself to be Elisha Weaver, editor of the *Christian Recorder*." Weaver's notice labeled this man "a villain and a thief."

Such "villains" surely discouraged the Church hierarchy from appointing lay agents not well known to them and to local communities, and neither compensation nor supervisory structures encouraged any emphasis on lay agents. Thus, almost all of the *Recorder*'s "agents" were AME ministers—men who were not only well known within individual communities but also in broader conference regions. In theory, even in the framework of itinerancy, this created a ready-made "thick trust" situation with a given minister's present and past churches. Weaver revised and strengthened this "thick trust" system by intertwining his agents' responsibility with their clerical duties: he treated securing subscriptions as an extension of preaching. He told readers more than once, as he said in the November 26, 1864, issue, "every itinerant preacher is an agent for the Book Concern and the organ of the Church, and should consider himself such. This is a well established rule with the mother (Methodist) Church and her ministers." A May 10, 1862, piece says "Let every minister preach on the subject of the *Recorder*, and never allow three weeks at any time of the year pass over his head without having the subject of the *Recorder* and Book Concern brought up." Weaver's July 20, 1861, "The Great Work and Its Demands" offered this succinct summary: "The *Recorder* has a special claim on the ministry.... Ministers, fellow-laborers in the vineyard of Christ, I wish to impress this on your hearts and consciences that we, each and all, have a duty to perform." That duty was to set the paper's "demands and wants frequently and plainly before the people of their various charges" and secure Two-Cent Money, other donations, single-copy sales, and especially subscriptions.

Editors—especially Weaver—regularly praised ministers for handling subscriptions (or at least single-copy sales) in language that emphasized such ties to pastoral duties. In lauding Rev. John Tibbs in the July 23, 1864, issue for "working hard to get subscribers" "like a faithful shepherd," Weaver asserts that "this is what every itinerant minister ... ought to do." He praised a young Rev. Theophilus Steward in the same issue even more frankly: "He has also raised the ... number of *subscribers* ... in his little charge up to sixty copies or more per week, and ... gets the cash and pays as he goes.... [W]hy cannot all of our ministers do like Bro. Steward? Are we doomed to harp upon this subject forever? Come, brethren, what excuse have you to offer?"

Extant evidence suggests that ministers' successes on these issues varied widely. In terms of single-copy sales, some ministers had pockets of success: James Lynch was acknowledged nine times during 1861 and 1862 for a total of $23, and George Weir was acknowledged nine times during 1861 for a total of $20.50. Others had longer-term presences: future–Bishop Richard Cain was acknowledged eight times between 1861 and 1864 for a total of $39.25, and George Rue was acknowledged seven times between 1862 and 1865 for a total of $21.85. Single-copy sales were no predictor of success in getting subscriptions. Of these four ministers, Lynch, Weir, and Cain were each acknowledged only once as the direct conduit for a subscriber listed in the acknowledgments; Rue was so listed fourteen times. Among ministers most often listed as subscription conduits—usually with a "per" and their name following a subscriber's information—the most successful were William Dove, who sent four subscriptions from Chicago in 1862 and then thirty from New Orleans in 1864 and 1865; Page Tyler, who sent seventeen from Mississippi and Louisiana in 1864; and Theodore Gould, though the vast majority of his thirty-nine listings came after he was appointed "Travelling Agent" in 1867.

Some of the ministers less successful at aiding the paper did attempt to explain themselves. Almost from the paper's beginning, Weaver heard the refrain from "some of the brethren" that, as the April 20, 1861, "Our Paper" noted, "their people are too poor, at least through the winter" to support the *Recorder*. Weaver responded simply, "Where there is a will, there is a way." Lynch echoed him in the September 29, 1866, issue: "Our experience is this: in all places where our church organ is not subscribed for, the fault is with the minister, and not the people. Some of our ministers on the poorest appointments, send the names and money of subscribers continually."

When Weaver learned that Rev. J. P. Underwood had left several weeks of his *Recorder* unclaimed at a Pittsburgh post office (which advised Weaver to stop sending the paper), Weaver published an October 7, 1864, item headed with Underwood's name that asked, "Why is this, Brother Underwood? Have you grown weary in the Master's service?" Weaver's August 24, 1861, "A Few Words on Behalf of the Recorder" demurs naming a specific minister, but chastises "a dear brother" who told him "I cannot sell papers on Sunday; it is wicked" in these words: "I wonder if that dear brother has not since then suffered his salary to be collected on Sabbath, and if so, did he not, in the case of the *Recorder*, 'strain at a gnat?' and in the case of his own salary had he not since 'swallowed a camel?'" Weaver continues, "If we, as ministers, would work more for the general good of the Church, and less for personal and individual interest . . . far greater would be our blessings." Weaver's November 24, 1864, editorial bluntly reminds "young ministers" who did "not sufficiently interest themselves" in the Book Concern and the *Recorder* that they were breaking "a well established rule" and "a written law . . . in the New Discipline, page 226, 7th paragraph" and suggesting that "the Conference will do well to call these recreant brethren to an account at its next meeting." He concludes that "our Bishops should stringently examine . . . these faithless and careless shepherds." Weaver thus combined praise (in all senses of that word) and brimstone to foster ministerial "agents" with *both* deep local respect and deep connections to the national church organization—a kind of doubled thick trust network.

While Weaver sometimes asserted that current subscribers had a duty to work with the ministry to bring others to the fold—a version of Candy Gunther Brown's "priesthood of all believers" (167)—he saw gathering subscriptions as first and foremost a ministerial duty. Those who wanted a Black—and specifically a Black Christian—presence in print had to subscribe and had to foster the subscription of others. In this vein, Lynch told the contributors who had sent "a half bushel of communications" that "those who write for our paper" should "*get subscribers also*, as nothing puts a correspondent on better terms with the editor and the publisher than getting subscribers for the paper." This ethic of subscription was reinforced in rhetoric ranging from correspondents who signed their work "I subscribe myself" to repeated calls for donations to send the *Recorder* to Black troops. In this conception, each church—indeed, each pulpit—functioned as an extension of the Book Concern, as a conduit for the *Recorder*. Each single copy purchase and each subscription was an offering, and like all true offerings, they were designed to create a community and a world where "far greater would be our blessings."

From Pine Street to the Nation (and Back Again) 95

Weaver's walk from 619 Pine to 631 Pine that opens this chapter embodied the next steps in building a permanent locus for that print-centered community—a home where members could send their donations, funds for single-copy sales, and subscriptions as well as their letters, stories, poems, marriage announcements, obituaries of family members and friends, and information-wanted ads. In reply, Weaver—and Stanford and Lynch and, later, Tanner—would then send out the *Recorder* and wait none too long for the weekly cycle to start again.

{ 4 }

"Their Friends at Home with Papers": *Recorder* Subscriptions and Subscribers

Mrs. Helen Yancy stepped into the African Methodist Episcopal Church at 806 North Center Street in Bloomington, Illinois. She had fifty cents that she planned to give to her pastor William J. Davis for a partial subscription to the *Christian Recorder*. It was late October 1862, so the young spouse of barber Lewis Yancy may have shivered a bit remembering her warmer birthplace in Hopkinsville, Kentucky. But Bloomington probably felt a bit like home now. She'd joined its AME church in the spring of 1859 and at that time placed herself under the pastoral care of Abraham Thomson Hall, a man who, according to Benjamin Tucker Tanner, was "so zealous for God" that he "must preach" (321).[1] A Pennsylvanian who had helped found Quinn Chapel in Chicago, Hall had been ordained an elder in the AME's Indiana Conference by Bishop Daniel Payne. In Tanner's words, Hall was "a man full of energy" and "a dear lover of his race," and he had been a strong steward for the Bloomington church that would eventually pass to Reverend Davis (321).

The Bloomington congregation had begun more than a decade earlier when a small group of perhaps twenty African Americans came together under the leadership of local exhorter P. H. Ward, gained recognition from the AME Church, and was assigned the first of a long list of itinerants, AME stalwart Austin Woodfork. Hall had helped the Bloomington congregation arrange their December 1857 purchase of the building that Yancy entered on that brisk day in late 1862. The structure had been the town's white Congregational Church, but the AME congregation moved it to the Center Street location and made it their own.[2]

Yancy herself had come to Bloomington the autumn before the purchase of the Congregational building. A young woman interested in both religion and education, she taught school for "one quarter" in Bloomington—as part of the number of early Black community efforts to provide education to area children in the face of white exclusionary practices. She probably attended the church's rededication celebration on May 2, 1858, and/or some of the various community events—including a December 14, 1858, festival—that were designed to help the congregation pay for the structure.[3] She would have rejoiced when, according to a letter in the May 18, 1861, *Recorder* from Rev. Frederick Myers (Hall's successor and Davis's predecessor), the Bloomington congregation "succeeded in having the last cent paid" on the debt.

The best estimates suggest that the Bloomington AME congregation had more than fifty members by this point—striking, given that the 1860 federal census tallied only 192 African Americans in the entire city. In the early 1860s, Yancy, who was "a great support to the Gospel," was an active member of what had become the centerpiece of the "Bloomington circuit."[4] Walking into the church in late 1862, Yancy would likely have felt pride in the building but also recognized that, if her church community continued to grow, the physical space would have to grow, too. Historians and archaeologists estimate that even after the building was significantly enlarged in 1871, it was still only about forty feet by sixty feet, with eave lines at or below eighteen feet.[5] (See Figure 4.1 for a later view of the church.) In Reverend Davis's words, Yancy had "numerous friends" in the congregation; many may have called her, as Davis did, "Sister Yancy." The congregation of Yancy's time—like that of the church's next generation, whose traces were studied in a 1992 archeological dig at the church—probably came together at the church not only for worship but for community meetings, educational and community health activities, and potluck suppers.[6]

Notably, the October 1862 congregation included two other women who were also giving Reverend Davis funds for partial subscriptions, and Davis's November 15, 1862, *Recorder* letter duly noted his enclosure of the money. Those two Bloomington women, Martha Ann Wells and Nancy Cooper, surely knew Helen Yancy. Martha Wells—who appears in some records simply as Ann—was, like Yancy, a transplanted Kentuckian. Born c. 1823, she was married to William Wells, who had been enslaved to John F. Henry and who may have settled in Bloomington as early as 1835. At William Wells's manumission in 1841, Henry asserted that he had "sober and industrious habits" and was "able to gain a sufficient livelihood," words recorded in Wells's registration with McLean County as part of the unevenly enforced Illinois "Black laws."[7] William Wells worked as a whitewasher and general laborer and had managed to gather $1,000 in real estate by 1860; by 1870, his real estate was valued at $3,000.[8] Nancy Cooper had been born in Tennessee c. 1825. Her husband's name is not yet known, but by 1862, she appears to already have been widowed. Cooper worked as a laundress and had at least one daughter, whose name appears variously as Emily L., Emily Louisa, Luticia, Lutlia, and Tishus. Cooper, like Wells, must have been "industrious," as she

FIGURE 4.1 *Bloomington's AME Church in the early twentieth century. Courtesy of the McLean County Museum of History, Bloomington, Illinois. While the tower and the church's name at the time of this photograph—Wayman AME Church—wouldn't have been familiar to Helen Yancy, Martha Ann Wells, and Nancy Cooper, the basic structure shown here was the same church building they attended in the 1860s.*

had amassed $2,000 worth of real estate by 1870, growing from a more modest valuation of $150 in the 1865 Illinois state census.[9]

Yancy and Cooper may have renewed their *Recorder* subscriptions, as Davis called Yancy a subscriber in a late 1863 *Recorder* letter and Cooper donated twenty-five cents to the book concern in June of 1869. Wells definitely renewed her subscription—at least twice. Though incorrectly listed as "Mrs. N. A. Wells" in her first *Recorder* acknowledgment, she sent $1.25 for a six-month subscription via A. T. Hall that was acknowledged in the January 30, 1864, *Recorder* (correctly as "Mrs. M. A. Wells") and $2.50 for a full-year subscription via Rev. J. W. Malone, acknowledged in the November 25, 1865, *Recorder* ("Mrs. M. Wells").

These were significant outlays in a wartime economy. The fifty cents each of these three Bloomington women sent initially could have been used to purchase two yards of medium quality cotton flannel, or five pounds of butter, or five dozen eggs; it could instead have purchased a "plain cloth" AME hymnal or two dozen AME catechisms.[10] Totaled, the funds for Martha Wells's subscription and renewals could have purchased an AME hymnal in "fine morocco" binding "with clasp" and *still* left her funds for a half-dozen yards of good cloth. That kind of expenditure is striking when we note that, her husband's real estate holdings aside, the 1860 census credited the family with only $150 of personal assets.[11] Beyond paying the subscription price, these three women were also agreeing to pay postage when they went to the Bloomington post office each week to pick up their paper from a white postal worker; by July of 1863, that postage had risen to twenty cents a year.

They may also have had to deal with discrimination in the post office, as subscribers regularly reported "irregularity" with their mail service.[12] That said, the three Bloomington women were likely better served than, for example, Reconstruction-era subscribers in some areas of the South. In the January 20, 1866, issue, Weaver called "the special attention of the Postmaster General and Congress" to the fact that many post offices in the South received the *Recorder* but told subscribers "there is no such paper there for them. We also hear that some of these postmasters have taken the wrappers off them, read them, and then sold them for waste paper." Subscribers who did not receive papers were told to contact Weaver so that he could "publicly expose" clerks participating in such "nefarious practice." Lynch's February 2, 1867, comments were more blunt: "Remember there are some vile negro-hating, *wishy washy*, well-cultivated moustached, whiskey-loving clerks who think it beneath their 'dignity' to deliver a 'colored newspaper.'" He urged subscribers to "put some influential Radical on their track."

In addition to these financial and public demands, there were a host of other ramifications tied to subscribing that the Bloomington women may have been aware of. As early as the February 2, 1861, issue, Weaver was informing subscribers that if they did "not give express notice to the contrary," they would be considered "as wishing to renew their subscriptions" and would be "responsible" for "all arrearages." Weaver also sometimes, as seen in the August 1 and December 12, 1863, issues, published lists of the names of those who did not pick up (and pay postage on) their papers—a clear public shaming. Further, of course, subscriptions were both requested and praised from the pulpit. The subscriptions of Yancy, Cooper, and Wells were thus both private and public acts—acts of engagement with both local community forces and more national structures.

This chapter studies a number of *Recorder* subscribers like Yancy, Wells, and Cooper—individuals who made these kinds of commitments from churches and towns both smaller and larger and who thus began to create a core community of supporters and (probable) readers for the *Recorder*. Specifically, it builds beyond my 2011 "Remembered (Black) Readers," which studied acknowledgments published in the *Recorder* between November 12, 1864, and November 4, 1865. This chapter instead considers *all* of the extant acknowledgments published in the paper between January 1861 and December 1867. Extant issues from this period yield over 4,300 acknowledgments, a sample more than five times larger than my original.[13] Such acknowledgments generally appeared in lists on either page two or page three of the four-page weekly, though some—like Yancy's—appeared in published letters from ministers or, more rarely, from subscribers themselves. The lists were printed in the *Recorder*'s standard type and often simply headed "Acknowledgments." In addition to names, they often contained honorifics, amounts paid, places of residence, and (more rarely) the names of the agents who sent the funds to the *Recorder*. Most acknowledgments are for *Recorder* subscriptions, though a host of other matters tied to funds submitted to the Book Concern were sometimes dealt with in such listings.[14] Format and completeness of acknowledgments varied over time and especially between editors; Lynch was, for example, much messier in preparing acknowledgments than Weaver. That said, the uses and structure of such acknowledgments remained similar throughout the period. They served as receipts for subscribers and agents—important given the risks in sending funds through the mails—and they served as a kind of reverse dun; that is, rather than insulting or making demands of delinquent subscribers, the lists publicly commended those who practiced the desired behavior of paying for subscriptions in cash and in advance. In a general sense—and sometimes in specific acknowledgments tied to famous subscribers—the lists also implied the paper's reach and power.

Roughly two hundred of these acknowledgments are fully or partially illegible or are so incomplete that tracing them may be impossible. Of the 4,091 legible acknowledgments, 3,396 were marked as for *Recorder* subscriptions—3,385 individual subscriptions and eleven group subscriptions. Beyond these, 180 acknowledgments noted funds covering groups of single-copy sales like those discussed in the last chapter, six were for advertisements, 103 were for donations to the paper and/or the Book Concern, and 406 were for unspecified purposes. Of the 3,385 acknowledgments tied to individual subscriptions—including those of the three Bloomington women who open this chapter—2,545 represent individual first-time subscriptions to the *Recorder*.[15] There were also 840 acknowledgments of renewals (or renewals of renewals) by individuals.

I have been able to identify—and by this I mean gather significant demographic information about an individual—1,109 of the 2,545 individual first-time subscribers (almost 44%).[16] I have also been able to identify individuals who sent in 670 of the 840 renewals (almost 80%). This means that I have been able to identify 1,779 of the 3,385 acknowledgments for individual subscriptions and renewals (over 52%).[17]

After a brief discussion of methodology, much of the chapter focuses on the 1,109 identified individual first-time subscribers—as these were people who made the initial choice to subscribe to the paper—though it does attend, albeit more briefly, to renewals and, at the chapter's end, group subscriptions. The goal is to consider individuals who had the clearest opportunity (via their own interest and backed by their own funds) to read the texts in this key venue for early African American letters. In discussing the acknowledgments, I treat data on location and gender first because such data were often included in acknowledgments *themselves* and so are available for a wide range of both identified and un-identified individuals. I then analyze information on race, age, marital status, parenthood, occupation, real estate valuations, and personal property valuations tied specifically to the 1,109 identified individual first-time subscribers and the 670 identified renewals. Throughout, I balance discussion of broad demographic trends with specific examples of individual subscribers, and I attempt to at least occasionally "drill deeper" into suggestive bits of individual life histories. I do this—and I open the chapter with discussion of the acts of subscription by Yancy, Cooper, and Wells—because, in work heavy with statistics and analysis of larger patterns, I want to remember that each person named in the acknowledgments was an individual who weighed her or his options in the marketplace of American print (and American culture); an individual whose life was shaped by a nexus of print, faith, race, and diverse other factors; and an individual whose life story and multiple community presences can barely be glimpsed by demographic data.

With this in mind, though Yancy, Cooper, and Wells are mentioned again later in the chapter, I now briefly turn to these women's lives after their acts of subscription, in part because the lack of information on these women's lives is illustrative of the difficulties confronted by this chapter and by any attempt to remember the lives of nineteenth-century free African Americans. Martha Ann Wells fades from public view after her subscriptions. She is likely the "Ann Wells" listed with William Wells in the 1870 Bloomington census, though the listing of a seventeen-year-old Francis Wells—not included at all in Martha Ann and William Wells's 1860 listing—is perplexing and suggests the possibility that Martha died and William remarried a woman who also (at least sometimes) used the name Ann. William Wells continued to be active in Bloomington's church; the April 17, 1869, *Recorder* carries part of a letter from the preacher then assigned to the Bloomington circuit that noted William Wells was serving as "the class leader" of the Sabbath School "in the absence of the pastor." The Bloomington *Daily Pantagraph* interviewed William Wells briefly for a January 24, 1873, story on those good old times" in Bloomington before "the introduction of the iron monster" came.[18]

Helen Yancy's story is much sadder. Her obituary, written by the same William J. Davis who sent in her subscription, appeared in the January 2, 1864, *Recorder*. While it is still the most detailed single source on any of these three Black women, this short paragraph presents a host of frustrations. Its tone and diction are that of a minister preaching for conversions: Davis opens the obituary by noting that Yancy "departed this life in full triumph of a living faith in the Sun of Righteousness" and ends by saying "she is gone to join the General Assembly and Church of the first born." He lists "an affectionate husband, a kind mother, sister, stepfather and son, besides numerous friends" without naming any of these individuals; the curious commas make one wonder whether the "son" was her son, her stepson, or even her stepfather's son. Without a marriage record for Yancy, her parents' and sibling's names are lost, and I have recovered no record of a son or stepson. Even Davis himself calls attention to his limited knowledge with an inserted "I think": "Sister Yancy came to Bloomington, I think, in the fall of 1857." Still, his obituary evinces an ethos of caring remembrance. He speaks of how he "often visited sister Yancy during her sickness, and read the word of God, and prayed with her." Davis's paragraph also tells of another, more specific, and deeply painful event: "Sister Yancy also lost a sweet little babe, which departed this life July 25th, 1863, aged 6 months and 11 days." Her name, at least, we know: "Little Mary Jane and her mother have gone up in a golden chariot."[19] This short paragraph embodies both the possibilities and the disappointments in many of the sources used in researching this chapter: they are fragments, painful reminders of how much of the history of individual African Americans we have lost.

Nancy Cooper's memory has survived in fragments, too. After her daughter married barber Richard Blue in Bloomington on May 5, 1870, Nancy Cooper was recorded as living with the pair and their two children in the 1880 census of Bloomington—though she was mislisted as a "boarder." The family remained at their home at 306 S. Madison (now a parking lot) for more than two decades, during which both Cooper and her daughter passed away. Eventually, the home was taken over by one of Nancy Cooper's grandchildren, Belle, and her husband James Claxton. Born April 30, 1872, Belle Blue Claxton knew both her grandmother and the AME Church: the September 17, 1891, *Recorder* reports that "Miss Belle Blue, of Bloomington, read a paper, in which she showed very satisfactorily the use and value of the Illustrated Lesson Leaf" to twenty-six "pastoral and lay delegates" at the sixteenth annual Illinois convention of AME presiding elders. She was a woman of both ability and aspiration who worked for more than two decades as a bookkeeper, stenographer, and secretary for prominent white men in Bloomington and Chicago; she also battled tirelessly (alongside her husband) for civil rights as a member of Bloomington's National Association for the Advancement of Colored People and Bloomington's Colored Citizens Bureau. And she continued to attend services at the same building her grandmother had entered with her *Christian Recorder* subscription back in 1862—which, by then, had been renamed to honor Bishop Alexander Wayman. Buried in Bloomington's Evergreen Memorial Cemetery after she died in 1926, Belle Blue Claxton's life was honored during the 2003 Evergreen Cemetery Discovery Walk. Though her story is attached by a thin thread to this particular narrative, Belle Blue Claxton serves as a reminder of the history we might still recover, a past that includes Black periodical subscribers and readers like those studied here.[20]

As suggested by these three women's stories, various factors tied to the *Recorder*'s practices and to the character of external records complicate any effort to identify those listed in the paper's acknowledgments. Like much of the rest of the *Recorder*, acknowledgments were set in type from handwritten texts submitted by a range of agents (usually, as discussed in the last chapter, ministers), and those texts had often traveled through the mail system, as well as in agents' pockets, satchels, perhaps even bibles. Some agents likely *heard* names rather than seeing them, which surely led to some misspellings (for example, "Beekman" for "Beakman"). *Recorder* acknowledgments also sometimes listed only a first initial and/or an honorific with a last name. The similar sounds of "Mrs." and "Miss" seem to have led to more than one *Recorder* misprint, and, as the first Martha Wells acknowledgment demonstrates, initials could also be misread or misreported. Place listings offer similar difficulties for researchers: in addition to occasional misspellings, town names might be replaced with county names or references to nearby landmarks or post offices; further, some locations have since been renamed.

These concerns, though, pale before the complexities of using government records to identify individual subscribers. To prepare this chapter, I searched for each listed name and a host of variants in indexes of the 1860 and 1870 US federal censuses.[21] For every name located, I examined individual listings on the page images of the original census schedules.[22] In several cases, I also searched indexes for the 1850 federal census (especially in cases of women listed as unmarried in the early 1860s) and the 1880 federal census (most often in researching individuals who lived in slave states and might have been enslaved—and so not named—in the 1860 census). I did similar work with several other record collections available online and at a handful of key repositories.[23] In hopes of compiling a similar data set, whenever possible, rather than relying on these more distant censuses and other records, I used any information found to search the 1860 and 1870 censuses again, thus treating those documents as demographic and informational touchstones. I selected these censuses because of both their proximity to the dates of the study and the similarities in the data they collected. In cases where I was able to locate both 1860 and 1870 federal census listings for a given individual, I worked primarily with the census closest to the individual's subscription date unless that census provided significantly less information than the other possibility. In the final analysis, I used 1860 or 1870 federal census records as the primary data source for researching 995 (89.7%) of the 1,109 individual identified first-time subscribers and 612 (91.3%) of the 670 renewals.[24]

Locating a census record for an individual, however, does not guarantee fully usable information. Federal censuses were completed by white census takers whose unevenness, unease, racist irresponsibility, and/or ineptitude in recording Black people is well known. While they might abbreviate, misspell, or mislabel individuals from all races—and might simply have bad handwriting—census takers disproportionately condemned African Americans to such errors.[25] Some census takers simply ignored (partially or wholly) free Black people's life stories, and, of course, they were instructed *not* to include the names of enslaved people when they filled out the separate 1850 and 1860 federal "slave schedules" of their censuses.

Assistant Marshall J. G. Campbell, the 1860 census taker for Pittsburgh's sixth ward, for example, listed the vast majority of that ward's residents—especially its Black and immigrant residents—with initials only, rendering future–Bishop Benjamin Tucker Tanner as "B. T.," his wife activist Sarah Tanner as "S. E.," and their first son, who would become the famous painter Henry Ossawa Tanner, as "H. O." Tanner. Had he not included middle initials—and he often did not—this family might have been lost among greater Pittsburgh's other Tanner families. Even so, the rest of Campbell's record says little: the occupation space for the elder Tanner, for example, was left blank (825). Assistant Marshall A. B. Buttles, the 1850 census taker for Columbus, Ohio's second ward, marked Frances Watkins—later poet, novelist, and activist Frances Ellen Watkins Harper—as illiterate, even though the specific reason she was in Ohio at that point was to teach at the AME's young Union Seminary (335). AME minister John W. Stevenson was similarly marked as illiterate in Philadelphia's eighth ward in the 1860 census (taken by Assistant Marshall John Magee), even though the December 13, 1867, *Recorder* celebrated him as a notable "colored author" (85).

Even the most diligent and trustworthy census takers might produce erroneous records, and some nineteenth-century African Americans had their own reasons for absenting themselves from—or clouding their representations in—government records. The January 26, 1861, *New York Tribune* reported that restaurateur and oysterman Thomas Downing, referencing Dred Scott, "refused to state the value of his property, on the ground that the Government at Washington did not regard him as a person, and that property could not own property." Antebellum African Americans had to worry about a Fugitive Slave Law that gave them every reason to tell white census takers that they had been born in the North or even Canada, for example; the uneven enforcement of the various Black codes across the North gave some African Americans further reason to keep their cards close. As some of their white counterparts did, some African Americans doctored the amounts of real estate and personal property they reported to nosey (white) government workers; diverse reasons might have led them to similarly embroider ages. Some information in censuses was also based on a census taker's quick visual assessment and/or on perceptions gleaned from neighbors. That the period studied here falls outside of the closest census years also means that, after the 1860 census and before the 1870 census, there were deaths, moves during a period of widespread mobility, name changes, marriages, and adoptions (formal or informal) in some families; as I note below, the problem of a young woman's loss of her surname at marriage can cause significant difficulties searching for unmarried women—especially those who subscribed in, say, 1864 and married in 1868. And, of course, almost all of those African Americans who were enslaved in the early 1860s "appear" only on the separate 1860 slave schedules that list age, sex, and color for each enslaved person, but *not* names; such schedules instead name only the men and women (almost always white) who owned those African American people.

Given these complexities, I was quite conservative in assigning individuals to the "identified" list that generated the majority of the statistics below. Unless, for example, there was only *one* individual with a given name in a specific location that clearly matched the *Recorder* listing or unless other sources narrowed the choices to one individual, that listed name was counted as unidentified.

For all of these issues, though, the sample studied here is large enough to draw conclusions about broad trends and to offer select windows into the lives of several individual subscribers. Arguably, this work also tells us a great deal about the paper's *readers*, though we cannot completely conflate this term with "subscribers." It is possible, for example, that some individuals subscribed out of social pressure or a desire to support their ministers, their local church, the AME Church generally, the AME Book Concern and education efforts, and/or AME political efforts. We must also assume that the subscribers studied here included very different kinds of readers whose acts of reading likely varied over time and were, like all such acts, deeply contextual. Some subscribers may have read the full paper every week in a single setting; others may have selected specific types of texts to read regularly; still others may have varied their reading depending on time and interest. Some may have read the paper aloud to family, friends, or church colleagues; some ministers read selections from the paper from their pulpits; some individuals may have subscribed not so they could read the paper themselves but so family members or even friends could; some subscribers may have passed their copies on to neighbors, friends, or other church members.[26] That said, the most logical and obvious reason for subscribing would have been a desire to read the paper.

I pepper the next several chapters (especially chapter 5) with hints of such reading experiences and responses to texts, but emphasize that I am only setting the groundwork—as the efforts of Elizabeth McHenry do—for what should be a massive and essentially new archival effort to explore the individual experiences of nineteenth-century Black readers. My goal in this chapter is to trace copies of the *Recorder* to individual homes and so to allow us to "visit" those households (however briefly) in order to discern some of the contours of the paper's greater textual community. Further, because this chapter traces subscribers rather than the single-copy sales of the last chapter, it "visits" specific (potential) readers who chose to have the particular types of regular and consistent exposure to the *Recorder* embodied in subscription.

What is initially striking in reading massive numbers of the *Recorder's* acknowledgments is the diversity of locations listed. The left column of Table 4.1

TABLE 4.1 Acknowledgments, First-Time Subscribers, and Renewals by State/Territory

State/Territory	Acknowledgments	First-Time Subscribers	Renewals
Alabama	2	2	0
Arkansas	10	7	0
Arizona	1	1	0
California	28	26	1
Colorado	17	15	2
Connecticut	52	29	11
Delaware	82	28	14
District of Columbia	139	67	14
Florida	9	7	1
Georgia	59	54	0
Illinois	218	140	54
Indiana	248	149	77
Iowa	37	25	5
Kansas	67	41	25
Kentucky	76	51	8
Louisiana	75	64	5
Maine	1	0	0
Maryland	205	116	44
Massachusetts	175	100	39
Michigan	27	19	6
Mississippi	35	24	4
Missouri	124	85	30
Montana	1	1	0
Nevada	11	11	0
New Hampshire	0	0	0
New Jersey	444	255	98
New York	275	118	53
North Carolina	54	53	0
Ohio	506	334	131
Pennsylvania	661	403	146
Rhode Island	155	79	46
South Carolina	160	140	15
Tennessee	19	15	3
Texas	6	2	0
Vermont	1	1	0
Virginia	72	62	4
Wisconsin	1	1	0
Canada West	23	11	4
unidentified	15	9	0
Total	**4,091**	**2,545**	**840**

offers a state-by-state breakdown of the 4,091 total acknowledgments, 4,076 of which list either a location or an individual whose location was traceable.

That 661 of these 4,076 traceable acknowledgments came from the *Recorder*'s home state, Pennsylvania, and represent the largest state presence (16.2%) should be no surprise; that Pennsylvania and New Jersey account for a total of 1,105 of the 4,076 acknowledgments (just over 27%) makes similar sense given the AME's strong presence in the area.[27] On the other hand, New York, with the very different Black denominational and print landscape, accounted for only 275 of the 4,076 traceable acknowledgments (just under 7%), and many of these acknowledgments were tied to the individual efforts of Reverend Henry Davis in New York City. A different facet of denominational differences—but also of the *Recorder*'s wide appeal—can be seen in 23 acknowledgments of subscriptions and contributions from Canada West (just over 0.5%), including several ministers in the British Methodist Episcopal (BME) Church.

The geographic diversity of the remaining two-thirds of the identified locations is more surprising. Ohio—with 506 of the 4,076 traceable acknowledgments (12.4%)—actually ranks second among individual states, and combined acknowledgments from Iowa, Illinois, Indiana, Wisconsin, Michigan, and Ohio total 1,037 acknowledgments—just over a quarter of the 4,076. Other clusters show that the reach of the *Recorder* was even wider. Broader New England—specifically Connecticut, Massachusetts, Maine, Rhode Island, and Vermont—combined to garner 384 acknowledgments (9.4%). The young far West—specifically, locations in what are now Arizona, California, Colorado, Kansas, Montana, and Nevada—had a combined total of 125 acknowledgments (just over 3%).

The District of Columbia, Maryland, and Delaware—all territories thick with the legacy of slavery—combined to total just over 10% of the 4,076 location-specific acknowledgments (426), and border/slave states Kentucky and Missouri account for almost 5% more (200). Eleven (former) Confederate states accounted for 498 acknowledgments—just over 12%—with South Carolina alone listed in 160 acknowledgments, a figure that places it ahead of locations like Delaware and the District of Columbia. While subscriptions from the upper South came in almost as soon as Weaver jumpstarted the paper in 1861, all of the acknowledgments from the deeper South came after the Union began regaining control of territory in the latter part of the Civil War—often immediately after (or even *while*) that control was being established.

The paper seems to have reached subscribers across the rural/urban spectrum, too—though we should recognize that these terms had different resonances in the mid-nineteenth century.[28] Urban centers in some regions were hubs for Book Concern activity. Among slave-holding and, later, former slave-holding states, for example, 101 of Missouri's 124 acknowledgments came from St. Louis, 55 of Kentucky's 76 acknowledgments came from

Louisville, and 49 of Georgia's 59 acknowledgments came from Savannah. Similarly, in the West, 53 of Kansas's 67 acknowledgments came from Leavenworth. In the East, 78 of Massachusetts's 175 acknowledgments came from Boston; 47 more came from New Bedford. But this pattern did not dominate all regions. Only 54 of Illinois's 218 acknowledgments came from Chicago; tiny Chester, Illinois, managed 10 acknowledgments. In Indiana, the comparatively small city of Vincennes had 48 acknowledgments—equal to the total from Indianapolis. The comparatively small Xenia, Ohio's strong AME community (connected to the Black cultural center at Wilberforce) brought in 76 acknowledgments—several more than the 47 garnered by the much larger city of Cleveland and approaching the 104 from the region's Black locus, Cincinnati.[29] Similar patterns can be seen in acknowledgments for first-time subscribers and renewals (combining identified and unidentified names in these groups), as seen in columns three and four of Table 4.1. In free states, the broader lesson is that where the Church and the post reached, the *Recorder* seems to have soon followed.

The locations of the 1,109 identified individual first-time subscribers often echo the larger sample, as seen in the second column of Table 4.2.

Pennsylvania again leads (with 185, 16.7%), and Ohio again comes in second (with 163, 14.7%). Clusters are also often similar: among identified individual first-time subscribers, the far West garners 3.5%; the eastern border areas (DC, Delaware, and Maryland), 7.4%; the (mid)western border areas (Kentucky and Missouri), 5%; the (former) Confederacy, 12.4%; and Canada West, 0.6%. The regions with more significant variation probably have as much to do with the quality and quantity of local records: the cluster of Midwestern states anchored by Ohio, Indiana, and Illinois had communities of free African Americans that were sometimes recorded more accurately than their fellows in other parts of the county. This region makes up just over 30% of the identified individual first-time subscribers. On the other hand, New York, in part because of the difficulties of finding individuals within the sprawling New York City area, comes in with just over 3% of identified individual first-time subscribers. The rural/urban spectrum looks similar among identified individual first-time subscribers, too, though urban areas are more heavily represented in several cases. St. Louis accounts for 26 of Missouri's 34 individual identified first-time subscribers; Louisville, 14 of Kentucky's 22; Savannah, 14 of Georgia's 18; Leavenworth, 12 of Kansas's 16; Boston and New Bedford, 16 and 23, respectively, of Massachusetts's 56. Chicago takes 15 of Illinois's spots—while the rural Chester claims 5. Indianapolis claims 14 of Indiana's 81 spots, with the smaller Vincennes taking 13. Xenia accounts for 26 of Ohio's 163 identified individual first-time subscribers, while Cleveland accounts for only 18, and Cincinnati, 30. As shown in the fourth column of Table 2, renewal locations were relatively consonant, though there were fewer renewals in the period in the far West and South because many residents of these

TABLE 4.2 Identified First-Time Subscriptions, Identified First-Time Subscriber Birthplaces, Identified Renewals, and Birthplaces of Identified Renewal Subscribers

State/Territory	Identified First-Time Subscriptions	Birthplaces of IFT Subscribers	Identified Renewals	Birthplaces of IR Subscribers
Alabama	0	4	0	0
Arkansas	3	0	0	0
Arizona	0	0	0	0
California	15	0	0	0
Colorado	4	0	2	0
Connecticut	14	8	9	3
Delaware	6	31	14	20
District of Columbia	30	31	13	27
Florida	4	0	1	0
Georgia	18	18	0	1
Illinois	71	17	49	7
Indiana	81	41	69	29
Iowa	11	1	5	0
Kansas	16	0	12	0
Kentucky	22	84	6	65
Louisiana	19	10	4	1
Maine	0	1	0	0
Maryland	46	137	38	123
Massachusetts	56	15	28	11
Michigan	9	1	4	2
Mississippi	10	5	4	1
Missouri	34	12	17	7
Montana	0	0	0	0
Nevada	4	0	0	0
New Hampshire	0	2	0	0
New Jersey	108	102	82	60
New York	37	34	40	18
North Carolina	17	57	0	32
Ohio	163	50	106	25
Pennsylvania	185	154	109	109
Rhode Island	47	10	42	11
South Carolina	39	51	9	9
Tennessee	7	21	3	5
Texas	0	0	0	0
Vermont	1	5	0	1
Virginia	23	167	2	91
Wisconsin	0	1	0	0
International	7	9	2	1
Unidentified	2	30	0	11
Total	**1,109**	**1,109**	**670**	**670**

regions did not subscribe until later during the period studied here. Also, because—as discussed below—several renewals came from AME clergy, locations where the Church had long-term presences are better represented.

That the location patterns of first-time identified individual subscribers and renewals are close to those of all acknowledgments makes two data points tied to identified individual first-time subscribers and renewals more striking. Analysis of the birthplaces of identified individual first-time subscribers and renewals as well as comparison of those birthplaces to subscription locations suggests significant mobility among the *Recorder* community.

The third column of Table 2 shows that, in terms of the birthplaces of identified individual first-time subscribers, Pennsylvania, 154 (13.9%), loses the top spot to Virginia, 167 (15.1%). Maryland (137), New Jersey (102), Kentucky (84), North Carolina (57), and South Carolina (51) all rise above Ohio, which, though it steadily ranked second in terms of subscription locations, was the birthplace of only 50 identified individual first-time subscribers (4.5%). Other northern locations finish lower: Rhode Island, home to 47 identified individual first-time subscribers at the time of their subscriptions, was the birthplace of only 10 subscribers. Massachusetts was birthplace to only 15, though it was the subscription location for 56. No identified individual first-time subscribers listed birthplaces in Arkansas, Arizona, California, Colorado, Florida, Kansas, Montana, Nevada, or Texas, and only one each listed birthplaces in Iowa, Michigan, and Wisconsin. Illinois was the location of subscriptions for 71 identified individual first-time subscribers, but birthplace to only 17. These trends are sometimes even more clear among renewals—seen in the fourth column of Table 2. While Virginia, for example, was the location of only two identified renewals, 91 of the total identified renewals came from individuals who had been born there; similarly, while only 38 identified renewals came from Maryland, 123 came from individuals who had been born there. Conversely, while 106 renewals were sent from Ohio, only 25 identified renewals came from individuals born there.

Taken together, these details suggest a large population of subscribers with roots in the slave South. They also mark a significant out-migration. Some of these subscribers were part of the South's free Black population who moved north hoping for more opportunity or simply more safety. Some had been, like Martha Wells's husband, enslaved and manumitted. Some had been enslaved and then self-emancipated, though data on such remains scattered and hard to trace on a large scale. Similarly, these details demonstrate how active some African Americans were in the broader nation's westward expansion: some subscribers' births in Ohio, Indiana, and Illinois place their families' settlement concurrently with those young states' own growth. California subscribers often trace to the Gold Rush, and presences in locations like Colorado, Montana, and Arizona mesh with territorial exploration.

But the story is not always as simple as a subscriber (or a subscriber's family) moving from Virginia to Pennsylvania (or Illinois or California). Taken as a group, the identified individual first-time subscribers were immensely mobile; they moved in a stunning range of ways that encompassed distances both long and short and patterns that both speak to and baffle expectations. Of the 1,109, 596 (53.7%) had census-reported birthplaces that were in different states or territories than their subscription locations; in part because of the heavy presence of itinerant ministers among those who renewed, 421 (62.8%) of the 670 renewals show such a shift. An even higher percentage—difficult to calculate exactly given differing designations in censuses (as well as ministers' uneven reporting of place names)—moved *within* states. While we might assume that distant moves included large cultural shifts, even seemingly more local moves could lead to massive differences in lived experience. Subscriber and writer Lizzie Hart, for example, like Helen Yancy and Martha Wells, was born in Kentucky and moved north with her family. Her new home in Morrow, Ohio, though, was less than thirty-five miles from the Kentucky border, but was free and offered the Harts significant opportunities, including the chance to engage with the large community centered on Black activism, education, and faith at Wilberforce University.

Some moves were undoubtedly influenced by larger forces. Questions of slavery and freedom likely caused moves to the North before the Civil War, and the chance for African Americans to reunite with lost family and/or find new opportunities brought some to the South late in and (especially) after the war. Some moves were undoubtedly grounded in a thicket of individual contexts—such as the number of moves between border towns in New Jersey and Pennsylvania that crossed state lines but totaled only a few miles of travel. Care needs to be taken in ascribing motivation to any of these moves: Reverend Jessie W. Devine's move to Arkansas from a Pittsburgh pulpit, for example, might on the surface read like a pioneering move west (and south). In some ways it was, but the *Recorder* also reported that this one-time "most popular minister" in greater Pittsburgh had "a misfortune which befell him in the Pittsburg [sic] conference" and which removed him from the Church ranks for at least four years.[30] Mobility, in other words, was not necessarily a good thing: some folks had to move.[31] What we can say definitively is that *Recorder* subscribers were both incredibly diverse geographically *and* quite mobile. This combination of geographic range and active movement undoubtedly pushed the *Recorder* to become a meeting place—imagined philosophically but also fully material in the printed pages that passed through the mails and across the nation to the subscribers studied here.

The other demographic issue addressed in a wide number of acknowledgments was the gender of those acknowledged, which was often signaled by gendered first names and honorifics. Among the 4,091 acknowledgments, 3,552 individuals can be identified as male or female. Of these, 2,408 acknowledgments were tied to male individuals (almost 59%), and 1,144 were tied to female individuals (almost 28%). Of the 2,545 acknowledgments from individual first-time subscribers, 1,242 acknowledgments (48.8%) were from men, and 837 (32.9%) were from women. If we narrow further to the 1,109 identified individual first-time subscribers, we find 355 women (32%) and 751 men (67.7%).[32] Of the 840 renewals—a place where the all-male ministry made the biggest impact—246 (29.3%) came from women and 574 (68.3%) came from men. Among the 670 identified renewals, 171 (25.5%) came from women, and 499 (74.5%) came from men.

There are, of course, different ways to read these numbers: if we removed the roughly 163 ministers among the 1,106 individual identified first-time subscribers whose gender can be determined, the remaining sample of 943 breaks down as 355 women (37.6%) and 588 men (62.4%). Similarly, if we remove the 216 renewals that were specifically acknowledged as "Rev." from identified renewals, the remaining sample of 454 includes 171 women (37.7%) and 283 (62.3%) men On the other hand, the single largest *group* subscription, Chaplain Enoch Miller's $275 payment for 110 annual subscriptions for the 25th United States Colored Infantry discussed below, was clearly majority-male, though some of the copies may have found their way into women's hands. I offer these diverse ways of thinking about the gender of those who were acknowledged in the *Recorder* to both recognize that the clear majority of subscribers—and monetary contributors of other types—were men, but also that women were consistently an important presence. Neither the act of subscription nor other possible acts of supporting the paper were marked "male."[33]

If statistics tied to geography and gender show significant diversity among subscribers to the *Recorder*, race, at first glance, seems a much more homogeneous category. One of the most striking data points in my preliminary study of subscribers in late 1864 and 1865 was that almost 99% of the subscribers I was then able to identify were African American. Study of all acknowledgments between 1861 and 1867 reinforces this conclusion, even as it allows us to add nuance. Only 25 of the 4,091 acknowledgments considered here can be tied definitively to white Americans—just over 0.6%; however, this number is perhaps a bit low, given that it includes a number of unidentified acknowledgments. What is more telling is that, of the 1,779 identified individual subscriptions and renewals, only 22 (1.24%) were connected to white individuals—17 of the 1,109 identified individual first-time subscriptions (1.53%) and 5 of the 670 identified renewals (0.75%).

Given the valuable scholarship on the social construction of race and the complexity of race as a category, a word on my terms is in order. Census takers' identification of race could be shaped by a host of factors: available choices in government marking instructions, a census taker's visual judgment (based on diverse social mores and biases), a community or even an individual neighbor's sense of a person's race (sometimes quite separate from skin color), and even, sometimes, a person's own self-identification. Such labeling was complicated by sloppy recording practices and/or damage to the schedule sheets census takers filled out. Digitization has actually complicated this miasma: over 70 of the 1,109 identified individual first-time subscribers, for example, appear in ancestry.com's online indexes as white even though images of schedule sheets show them marked with either an "M" (for "mulatto") or a "B" (for "Black").

A small group of subscribers—perhaps twenty, depending on approaches to counting—moved among different census racial categories and thus fell among the small group of nineteenth-century African Americans who went back and forth over the color line in one way or another, some of whom passed permanently into whiteness. Huntington, New York, resident Charles Bristol, for example, who originally subscribed in January 1862, was listed as "Indian" and as "colored" in different records, and Junius C. Morel, an important teacher and activist in Brooklyn's Black Weeksville neighborhood who subscribed in March 1862, was listed in the 1870 census as "Indian" while other records marked him "Black" or multiracial.[34] These specific shifts remind of the need to expand our understanding of African American senses of and relationships with first peoples, but they also point to the fact that the nuances of race were often destroyed by the crude tools at census takers' disposal (and, often, their even cruder use of such).[35] Allegheny Institute teacher Martin H. Freeman—a graduate of Middlebury College often cited as the first Black professor in the nation—was counted as white in the 1860 census, though his occupation was listed as "teacher C[olored] S[chool]."[36] Alice Carter, the daughter of a Cincinnati steamboat steward, was listed—as were her parents and siblings—as "mulatto" in the 1860 census; in 1870, although she was teaching in Cincinnati's Black schools, she was listed as "white," while the family with whom she boarded was listed as "mulatto."[37] Hostler William Mabines was listed in the 1870 census as "white" and in the 1880 census as "mulatto."[38] A resident of Bloomington, Illinois, he would have known Nancy Cooper and perhaps Martha Wells and Helen Yancy; his initial 1867 subscription was forwarded by Johnston Mitchem, the same AME minister who wrote of William Wells's work as a "class leader." The "race" of these subscribers offers fascinating possibilities for further considering the often-painful dance of racial classification and for specifically thinking about the act of self-identifying as "African Methodist Episcopal," especially given scholar Julius Bailey's sense of AME "race patriotism."

That said, the very small number of *Recorder* subscribers who placed themselves or were placed by others on the "color line" suggests that, for the vast majority of subscribers, race was often a much more fixed functional category. Even though labels tied to African American identities encompassed a wide range of ethnicities, skin colors, genealogies, and social positions, most of the subscribers who were marked as African Americans were so marked throughout their lives, sometimes in numerous and diverse records; the same is true for all of the seventeen identified individual first-time subscribers who were white.

Because they identify some of the limits of the *Recorder* and remind us of the comparatively small number of white activists who went beyond abolitionist speech and action to explore something like Black faith, those white subscribers are worth some brief note before we turn to the much larger Black population of subscribers. *Recorder* editors did recognize some rhetorical power in being able to claim white readers; such work argued for the Church's reach and the paper's quality in ways that echoed the paper's comments on periodical exchange.[39] That power was especially apparent when local minister Nelson Fitzhugh wrote from Natchez, Mississippi—in a letter published in the October 20, 1866, issue—that he "obtained a new subscriber today, a very worthy Confederate friend . . . who has taken a liking to our paper. I brought it to his notice by lending him a copy to read. . . . He says if the paper continues as it now is, he will use his influence to get subscribers." Such a claim not only positioned the *Recorder* as a key agent of reconstruction but also suggested that it could successfully shape the course of the newly reunited union.[40] Thus, the September 1862 subscription of former Vermont Governor Ryland Fletcher was acknowledged as from "Ex-Gov. Fletcher," and the May 1867 subscription of Massachusetts politician and co-namesake of Claflin University William Claflin was acknowledged as from "Lieut. Gov. Claflin." Mason Brayman and Bernard Farrah's October 1864 subscriptions—both through Fitzhugh—were acknowledged as subscriptions from "Brigadier-General Brayman" and "Col. Farrah"; given their Natchez tag, readers of war news may have recognized these key figures from the Vicksburg Campaign and Union efforts in Natchez. Each of these acknowledgments made tacit arguments about the power of the *Recorder*—that it touched important white politicians in New England, Union commanders, and perhaps even a former Confederate.

The "name" white subscribers above—each of whom seems to have sent funds one time—belied the small number of other white people who entered the *Recorder* community. A handful of white subscribers engaged in social causes decided to subscribe. Wealthy Bostonian Frederick W. G. May, who initially subscribed early in January 1862, renewed his subscription three times—a rare move for almost all but Black clergymen. May was from an activist family and circle (he was among Theodore Parker's executors), and he had a long personal engagement with social justice. He was also wealthy enough to not even notice the subscription cost. Alexander Ketchum, who subscribed in April 1865 from Savannah, was an officer over Black troops and had served on the staffs of both Rufus Saxton and Oliver O. Howard. Girard Riley, a committed abolitionist and church activist from Clermont County,

Ohio, left his work as Chaplain to the Ohio 50th to be Captain of Company K of the 6th US Colored Infantry; he subscribed from Camp William Penn in October 1863. William McDonald, a Methodist Episcopal clergyman friendly to the AME Church, subscribed in May of 1867; his subscription, which came at the same time as Claflin's, was probably the result of *Recorder* editor James Lynch's visit to the Methodist Episcopal Church's New England conference meeting.[41]

Other white subscribers left less—and sometimes no—clear traces of the motivation behind their subscriptions. The August 1861 subscription and the April 1862 renewal of J. W. Barker, a dry goods merchant in Pittsburgh, for example, might seem baffling given Barker's prior life as an important politician in the Know-Nothing party in New York City, but then Barker's publication of anti-slavery poetry in the *North Star* and the *Provincial Freeman* seems equally curious.[42] Educators Charles Cushing and Emily Nelson might have subscribed for reasons tied to their focus on teaching, but they seem to have worked only—or at least mainly—with white students. Figures like Iowa farmer's wife Anna Ralley, who subscribed in February 1865, and English immigrant and mill worker Mark Pilkington, who subscribed in September 1866, are even harder to connect to the paper's emphases.

I treat these white readers (and Black readers on the color line) with some specificity in part to explore their presences in the public record but also to point out the other side of that presence. If we know, for example, that only 22 of the 1,779 identified individual first-time subscriptions and renewals were tied to white individuals and if we recognize that other racial categories almost never came into play, this means that 98.76% of identified subscriptions and renewals were tied to African Americans. Even if we remove African Americans on the color line—and I submit that we cannot, in part because at least some self-identified as Black—this number remains quite high. Similarly, when we note the 17 identified individual first-time white subscribers (1.53%), we should recognize the 1,092 identified individual first-time African American subscribers (98.47%); seeing the 5 renewals tied to white individuals (0.75%) should make us remember the 665 renewals tied to African American individuals (99.25%). Put simply, the subscriber base of the *Recorder* was overwhelmingly composed of people who consistently identified and were identified as African Americans.

A set of factors—age, marital status, and family structure—contribute to our thinking about these African American subscribers in dialogue with questions of geography, mobility, gender, and race. Individual subscribers ranged in age from Anna Louisa Williams of Bristol, Pennsylvania, and John W. Beard of Vincennes, Indiana, who were both twelve when they subscribed, to Charles Peters of Lancaster, Ohio, who was eighty-three when he subscribed. However, such extremes were rare. Only 47 individuals among the 1,109 identified individual first-time subscribers (4.2%) were under twenty years of age at the time of their subscription; only seven of those (0.6%) were fifteen years old or younger; only three of those seven sent in a full year's subscription.[43] The lack of young subscribers was likely tied to class issues discussed further below: many African American youths did not have ready access to funds to subscribe. At least one of the three young full-year subscribers had comparatively wealthy parents: Emily Wil[l]son was fifteen when she sent in her subscription from Cleveland; the 1870 census credited her parents with $5,500 in real estate and another $2,000 in personal property. Students of African American print may know this specific family: Wilson's father, Joseph, was the author of the 1841 *Sketches of the Higher Classes of Colored Society in Philadelphia by "A Southerner,"* and, after moving the family from Philadelphia to Cleveland, saw his daughter Josephine wed Blanche K. Bruce.[44] At the other end of the age spectrum, only nine subscribers were seventy years of age or older when they subscribed, and only eighty-year-old George Berry of Alexandria, Virginia, joined Peters as a (reported) octogenarian.

While 30 of the 1,109 have only hazy and incomplete data available on their ages, 220 (19.8%) were in their twenties when they first subscribed; 321 (28.9%), in their thirties; 288 (26%), in their forties; 149 (13.4%), in their fifties; and 54 (4.9%), 60 or over. Considered in slightly different terms, 829 identified individual first-time subscribers (or almost 75%) were between the ages of twenty and forty-nine, inclusive; if we shift these ages to thirty to fifty-nine, inclusive, we find 758 (68.3%). As might be expected—given the number of ministers who renewed, the fact that a subscriber's age was lowest when he or she first subscribed, and the likelihood that age sometimes brought a bit more financial stability—the ages of those who renewed trend older. Only fifteen (2.2%) of identified renewals were tied to individuals under twenty at the date of renewal—and only three of these were tied to individuals who were under fifteen (including one from John Beard and two from Jared Morris). Of the identified renewals, 87 (13%) were tied to individuals in their twenties; 217 (32.4%), in their thirties; 187 (27.9%), in their forties; 116 (17.3%), in their fifties; and 34 (5.1%), sixty or over. For 14 identified renewals, the ages remain unclear. If we look for those between the ages of twenty and forty-nine, inclusive, we find individuals tied to 491 of the identified renewals (73.3%). If we shift this to the ages of thirty to fifty-nine, inclusive, we find 520 (77.6%).

If we recognize marriage as a social expectation for many in this age range, we can also understand the preponderance of married identified individual first-time subscribers and renewals.[45] Of the 1,109 subscribers, 771 (almost 70%) were listed as married in the primary record used for their data; 491 of the identified renewals (73.3%) came from individuals listed as married in the primary record used for their data. Of 464 identified individual first-time subscribers primarily studied using the 1860 census, 303 (just over 65%) were listed as married; of the 364 renewals traced primarily through that census,

248 (68.1%) came from married individuals. Of 536 individual identified first-time subscribers primarily studied using the 1870 census, 410 (over 71%) were listed as married; of the 254 renewals traced through that census, 209 (82.3%) were from married individuals. But even these numbers are low in terms of telling whether subscribers had *ever* been married or *would* ever be married. Of the remaining 338 individual first-time subscribers, for example, I have found evidence that at least 63—or another 5.7%—were widowed; renewals seem to trend similarly.[46]

The majority of identified individual first-time subscriptions and renewals also came from individuals with children. Of the identified individual first-time subscribers, 663 (just shy of 60%) were listed with at least one child; 403 of the identified renewals (just over 60%) came from individuals who had at least one child. Subsets tied to the primary record bases tell a similar story. Of the 464 identified individual first-time subscribers primarily studied using the 1860 census, 253 (almost 55%) had at least one child listed. Of the 536 primarily studied using the 1870 census, 357 (almost 67%) had at least one child. Of the 364 renewals traced primarily through the 1860 census, 216 (59.3%) came from individuals with children. Of the 254 primarily studied using the 1870 census, 155 (61%) came from individuals with at least one child. In all of these groups, the resulting numbers are likely low, as some individuals had grown children who were not listed with them, as individuals (especially traveling ministers) were sometimes listed separately from their families, as infant and child mortality rates were painfully high during the period (remember Mary Jane Yancy), and as divorce and marital separation are not indicated in many of the primary documents utilized. Further, some young couples primarily studied using the 1860 census did have children by 1870; the same was true by 1880 for some couples primarily studied using the 1870 census.

Household configurations varied widely. Among those researched primarily through the 1860 census, 142 (just over 56%) had, like William and Martha Ann Wells, one or two children listed with them; only 42 (17%) had five or more children. There was similar range among those primarily researched through the 1870 census: 191 (53.5%) had one or two children listed, while only 58 (just over 16%) had five or more children. Trends are similar among those who renewed. Many of the families with one or two children were young couples; others, like Martha Ann and William Wells, were middle-aged; still others were elders whose grown children and grandchildren lived with them. A similar range existed for families with multiple children. Patterns do not seem to have been shaped solely by class, occupation, or location. Some young couples lived by themselves; some lived with a set of parents; still others boarded with unrelated (or not obviously related) people. The families with the largest numbers of children hint at yet another arrangement: multigenerational households with several members contributing to the family resources.

Subscriber John Cornell and his wife Mary, for example, had ten children listed in their Georgetown, DC, household in the 1860 federal census. Cornell was a cart man, as were two of his sons. Another son was a blacksmith, and three daughters were seamstresses. Mary "kept house"—a fallback term that barely hints at her diverse work, including caring for the couple's three youngest children, who were all listed as attending school (52).[47]

That said, taken together, statistics relating to age, marital status, and family configuration strongly suggest that the clear majority of *Recorder* subscribers (both first-time subscribers and those who renewed) were adults who had either established or were in the process of establishing their own households during the complex decades before, during, and just after the war—often, if we add in statistics tied to location and mobility, after a move.

Nonetheless, looking at this cluster of statistics with another factor in mind—gender—again highlights the presence of significant subsets of subscribers. Age varies only slightly when compared between women and men, with women trending a bit younger. Among identified individual first-time subscribers, just over 8% of women were under twenty when they subscribed (29/355), while only 2.4% of men (18/751) fell into this category. Of renewals by women, 4.7% (8/171) were from individuals who were under twenty, while only 1.4% (7/499) of renewals by men fell into this category. Similarly, 23.4% (83/355) of women first-time identified subscribers were in their twenties, while only 18.5% (137/751) of men fell into this category. Of renewals by women, 22.2% (38/171) were from individuals in their twenties, while only 9.8% (49/499) of renewals came from men in this category. On the other hand, 15.7% of male first-time subscribers were in their fifties (118/751), while only 8.7% of women fell into this category (31/355). This statistic is even more striking among renewals: 20% (100/499) of renewals by men were made by individuals in their fifties, while only 9.4% (16/171) came from women in this category.[48] Still, all of these percentages are close to the norms described above, and the clustering of ages between twenty and forty-nine at both the point of subscription and the point of renewal—78% of women and 73.5% of men first-time subscribers (277/355 and 552/751, respectively) and 77.8% of renewals by women and 71.7% of renewals by men (133/177 and 358/499, respectively)—runs across the board.

More pronounced differences can be seen in marital status. Of the 751 men among the identified individual first-time subscribers, 583 (77.6%) were married. Among the 286 men primarily researched through the 1860 census, 209 (73.1%) were married, and among the 388 men primarily researched through the 1870 census, 326 (84%) were married. Of the 499 renewals by men, 409 (82%) came from married individuals. Among the 266 renewals tied to men primarily researched through the 1860 census, 203 (76.3%) were from married individuals, and among the 198 renewals tied to men primarily researched through the 1870 census, 176 (88.9%) were from married individuals. On the other hand, among the 355 female individual first-time subscribers, divisions are much more even: 186 (52.4%) were marked married. More specifically, among the 177 women primarily researched through the 1860 census, 93 (52.5%) were marked as married; among the 146 women primarily researched through the 1870 census, 82 (56.2%) were married. Renewals generally reflect this trend, too. Of the 171 renewals by women, 85 (49.7%) came from married individuals. Among the 98 renewals tied to women primarily researched through the 1860 census, 45 (45.9%) were from married women, and among the 59 renewals tied to women primarily researched through the 1870 census, 36 (61%) were from married women. As with general marriage numbers, the true counts would likely be higher, especially given the lack of reporting of widowhood, divorce, and separation—a fact seen in the numbers of women recorded below with children but without spouses. Still, the differences here are stark: the percentage of married male first-time subscribers researched in the 1870 census, for example, is thirteen points *higher* than the norm for married first-time subscribers, and the percentage of married women in the same census is almost fifteen points *lower* than the norm.

The difference in parenthood statistics is not as pronounced between the sexes but is still notable. Of the 355 female identified individual first-time subscribers, 189 (53.2%) had children; that percentage is more than six points below the full sample norm and almost ten points below the percentage for male first-time subscribers (472/751, 62.8%). This division remains similar in both the 1860 and 1870 census groups: in the 1860 group, 50.9% of women had children (89/175), while 57.1% of men had children (164/287); in the 1870 group, 59.6% of women had children (87/146), while 69.1% of men had children (268/388). In all cases, women were well below the full sample norm, and men were consistently above it. Parenthood among those who renewed trended higher, but the men who renewed remain more likely to have had children listed than the women. Of renewals by women, 55.6% (95/171) came from individuals with children, while 63.5% (317/499) of renewals by men came from individuals with children. Among renewals primarily researched through the 1860 census, 55% (54/98) of those tied to women came from individuals with children, while 60.9% (162/266) of those tied to men came from individuals with children. Among renewals primarily researched through the 1870 census, 56.1% (37/66) of those by women came from individuals with children, while 65% (128/197) of those by men came from individuals with children.

Taken together, this analysis suggests that single women made up a notable subscriber group—and that several of those women renewed their subscriptions. "Single women," of course, had varying definitions: women who had not yet been married or might never be married, as well as women who were widowed or separated and not remarried. That said, a more anecdotal statistic is worth note: among women's names listed in the 4,091 acknowledgments, 606 are given honorifics. Of these, 219—or just over

36%—are assigned the title "Miss" instead of the more common gendered marker assigned to both married women and widows, "Mrs." This titling was occasionally important enough that subscribers expressed concern when they were misidentified. Annie M. Smith of Xenia, Ohio, for example, wrote the editor to note that he had "accidentally called me Mrs. A. M. Smith. It should have been Miss."[49] A teacher, Smith may have felt that her job or community position depended on clearly marking her unmarried status. While the *Recorder*'s titling of women was inconsistent—individual ministers varied widely in listing honorifics—these 219 (220, if we count Smith) women titled "Miss" also mark a clear group of unmarried women engaging with the paper.

Speculating on the class positions of *Recorder* subscribers presents significant difficulties, not only because definitions of class and class subgroups have shifted (and are always contextual), but because neither scholars nor laypeople agree on the practical meanings of terms like "working class" or "middle class." The long-held critical and historical belief that Black print was the province of the "Black elite"—people like Joseph Willson, for example—has never been clearly documented and may, simply and erroneously, be tied to misguided assumptions and stereotypes about "disposable" income, a purported lack of Black reading, and class and race generally. It may also be tied to other assumptions that are being steadily disproven (e.g., that barbering was solely an elite trade) or that should be dismissed (e.g., that the ministry meant financial security).[50] We should also remember, as hinted at by work like Monica Miller's *Slaves to Fashion: Black Dandyism and the Styling of Black Diasporic Identity*, that African American (expressions of) class status and class aspiration may have differed significantly from various white versions of such and that they often had great internal diversity, too.

That said, three census items—occupational listings, real estate valuations, and personal property valuations—do demonstrate that *Recorder* subscribers were quite diverse in class position and were often far from the assumed elite status. In considering occupational listings, scholars need to recognize that few census takers reported all jobs in a given household accurately. Many reported only the job of the (usually male) head of the household, and many more reported only the jobs of adult men in the household. A Black male married farmer might carry the title "farmer" or might be listed as "works on farm"; while his spouse and children also likely worked on the farm, they probably carried no occupational listing.[51] If *any* label appeared in the occupation columns of women's census listings, it was often "keeping house," a term that not only elides the diverse internal and external work demanded by keeping a home but also ignores both contributory work tied to a spouse's occupation (such as watching the AME bookstore, which Mary Weaver did) and occasional or regular external work (for example, taking in laundry—as Nancy Cooper probably did when she was married—or sewing).

Such examples remind again of the significant latitude census takers had. Among the 1,109 identified individual first-time subscribers alone, for example, census takers used over 200 different job titles; the renewals add even more to the list. "Farmer," for example, was supplemented by "works on a farm"—which does not carry the suggestion of land ownership that "farmer" might—and also "farm laborer," "farm hand," "farming," and "farms." A woman who took in laundry might not, per the above, have her occupation noted at all (if her husband or father had another occupation) or might be listed as "laundry," "laundress," "washer," "washerwoman," "washwoman," "washes and irons," or "washing." Men in this field might be assigned the gender-neutral terms among these job titles, such as "clothes cleaner," or, like William Bland of Marysville, California, "washman."[52]

For all of this, some individual occupations and groups of occupations stand out. Ministers accounted for 163 identified individual first-time subscribers—not surprising given the responsibilities and activities discussed in the previous chapters. There were 216 identified renewals that came from men who were specifically titled "Rev." in their acknowledgments; another half dozen were from ministers whose title was omitted. The great majority of these men—and they were all men—were AME ministers, though a few were from African Methodist Episcopal Zion, British Methodist Episcopal, Methodist Episcopal, Baptist, and Presbyterian churches. Eight more of the identified first-time subscribers were the wives of ministers; three more renewals came from wives of ministers. The presence of ministers may have been larger: while the censuses were often accurate in terms of labeling full-time ministers, they were much more lax with local elders who performed essential work for individual churches/communities. I have found men who ministered to/in local churches—some who were later ordained as ministers—whose census labels included barber, carpenter, carter, cook, farmer, gardener, laborer, porter, teacher, and whitewasher.[53] These labels remind us that ministers' backgrounds, charges, locations, and class positions varied tremendously. That said, we should also read these numbers as a reminder of their other side: though the *Recorder* was a church paper, it was clearly *not* just a ministers' paper: perhaps five-sixths of its identified first-time subscribers were not in ministers' households, and perhaps three-fifths of renewals came from individuals not in ministers' households.

The next most common job titles were variations of dismissive census takers' default term for working Black men (and many working-class white men), "laborer." Of the identified first-time subscribers, 107 (9.6%) were labeled with this term or echoes like "day laborer" and "common laborer"; 38 renewals (5.7%) came from individuals so labeled. After these significant groups, the occupational landscape becomes much more complex.

Of the identified first-time subscribers, 92 (8.3%) could be categorized broadly as providing personal service; 56 renewals (8.4%) came from individuals so labeled. Some—including a number of women—were labeled as "domestics," "domestic servants," "servants," "at service," and "works out." Others in this category likely carried more prestige and garnered more compensation, for example, a butler, seven gardeners, three janitors, seven stewards (including three who worked on steamboats), and two messengers. Barbering—the occupation of Helen Yancy's husband—could be included in this general category, but I separate this service occupation because it often bled into a business and sometimes carried more prestige; 74 identified individual first time subscriptions (6.7%) and 47 renewals (7%) came from barbers.

The various job titles related to farming were assigned to 74 identified individual first-time subscribers (6.7%); 29 renewals (4.3%) came from farm workers. Of the identified first-time subscribers, 52 (4.7%) worked in skilled building trades—carpenters, masons, plasterers, etc.; 19 renewals (2.8%) came from individuals in these fields. Twenty-four identified first-time subscribers (2.2%) worked in other skilled trades—a basket-maker, four blacksmiths, and a cabinetmaker, for example, as well as coopers, miners, a potter, and a tanner; eight renewals (1.2%) came from individuals working in these fields. Forty-nine of the identified first-time subscribers (4.4%) worked with apparel, though this category can immediately be split—almost in half (23 to 26)—between makers of clothes and cleaners of clothes. Women dominated both of these groups. They held jobs in the former group like dressmaker, mantua-maker, milliner, and needlewoman, as well as the more generic "seamstress," and, in the latter, the lion's share of laundry jobs (like that of Nancy Cooper). Two men in this category were tailors; eight were shoemakers. Renewals came less often from people in these fields—only a dozen (1.8%), with the ten of those coming from laundresses.

Forty-eight identified first-time subscribers (4.3%) worked in jobs tied to food and drink. Of these, 10 were cooks, 8 were waiters, 5 were restaurateurs, and 1 was a caterer. But there were also, for example, 2 bakers (one, Mingo Collett of Wilmington, North Carolina, specializing in cakes), 2 butchers, and 3 confectioners. Twenty-six renewals (3.9%) came from individuals in these fields. Some of this group should also be seen as entrepreneurs—in addition to the above, a fish dealer, grocers, a flour dealer, 2 dealers in ice and ice cream, and even, the *Recorder*'s decided temperance position aside, saloonkeeper Oliver C. Henson of Chicago and barkeeper William Nichols of Washington, DC (whose subscription was forwarded by no less than future-Bishop Henry McNeal Turner).[54] Forty-one identified first-time subscribers (3.7%) had positions tied to transportation—land-based jobs like cabdrivers, carters, coachmen, and hack-drivers, as well as water-based jobs like boatmen, rivermen, and seamen. After the war, a small handful also garnered positions with the growing railroad industry. Twenty-three renewals (3.4%) came from individuals in these fields. A small group also turned such work into businesses, including the successful Cleveland hostler Madison Telly, who was listed in the census simply as "keeps teams" but who had $10,000 in real estate and another $3,000 in personal property.⁵⁵

While food- and transportation-related positions might lead to individual businesses, there were at least 20 other individual first-time subscribers (1.8%) engaged broadly in commerce—ranging from two with the label "huckster" and two more with the label "peddler" to a number of storekeepers, a tobacconist, a lumber merchant, a junk dealer, and a real estate agent.⁵⁶ Ten renewals (1.5%) came from individuals in these fields, which ranged widely in compensation and prestige.

The clusters of professionals that students of African American letters have been led to expect were actually fairly small. Twenty-four identified first-time subscribers (2.2%) were teachers, though this group itself was fairly diverse—ranging across region, gender, and age, and including longtime teachers like agent Mary Still, Martin Freeman, and Junius Morel; young women (perhaps like Helen Yancy) who taught only briefly before marriage removed them from the ranks; and even figures like Aaron Molineaux Hewlett, whose occupation was listed as "gymnast" and who has garnered some scholarly notice as the director of Harvard's gymnasium, as a boxer, and as the father-in-law of Frederick Douglass Jr.⁵⁷ Eighteen renewals (2.7%) came from teachers. Only 14 first-time subscribers (1.3%) were in medical professions—a botanic doctor, a chiropodist, a dentist, a midwife, 2 nurses, 7 physicians (including Ezra Rust Johnson, an important figure in the Black West, as well as poet Joshua McCarter Simpson and activist/attorney John S. Rock), and a "surgeon and dentist" (Joseph Willson). Only one renewal came from a medical professional. There was only one undertaker among the first-time subscribers—Newbern, North Carolina's Richard Tucker. The only subscriber labeled as an attorney in a primary census listing was white: Union General Mason Brayman.

Only 10 identified first-time subscribers (0.9%) held government jobs, and only 8 of these subscribers were African Americans—all listed in the 1870 census in the midst of the post-war broadening of opportunities. Their renewal numbers were also thin: only 4 renewals (0.6%) came from individuals in this category. This group surely held some prominent subscribers—Justice of the Peace James M. Alexander of Helena, Arkansas; members of Georgia's legislature James Porter and Henry McNeal Turner (the future AME Bishop); DC Black school superintendent George F. Cook; and Peter Gibbs, town marshal in Beaufort, South Carolina. Other subscribers held government posts at other times and thus do not have those posts recorded in censuses: South Carolina politician and future AME bishop Richard Cain, future US Senator Hiram Revels, future superintendent of Cincinnati Black schools William Parham, and future South Carolina politician Robert Smalls (listed in the acknowledgments as "the great hero" for his Civil War exploits). But this group of subscribers was quite small.

The striking number of subscribers—almost always married women listed with spouses or unmarried women listed with parents—who were assigned some variant of "keeping house" or had no occupation listed at all also call for some brief discussion in terms of the job listings of the "heads" of these households. Among the 200-plus first-time subscribers so listed,[58] the 8 women married to ministers noted above are actually not the largest category in terms of head-of-household jobs; rather, the 60 individuals living with relatives who were marked with variations of the term "laborer" are the most common in this group. While the relatives' occupations include some jobs not found among those assigned to subscribers themselves—a "private gentleman" (Susan Gaiter's husband John, a Pittsburgh activist) and a feed merchant (Delilah Jones's husband Alfred of Washington, DC)—and while they also include some less common jobs (Ann Spencer's husband James of Indianapolis, another saloonkeeper), the broad patterns above continue. Barbers account for 24 of such head-of-household job listings, for example, and variations of farming account for 22. These patterns are consonant among individuals who renewed: roughly 100 renewals came from individuals who had no occupation listed but lived with someone (usually a relative, especially a husband or father) who did have an occupation listed. Of these, 21 renewals came from individuals whose relative was listed as a barber; 3, a minister; 9, a farmer; and 22, a laborer or some variation of that term. In short, those women listed as "keeping house" and those without occupation labels did not fall into any single, set class position, either.

While the sheer diversity of occupational labels is notable, what is more striking is how deeply the *Recorder* reached into occupations that were definitely or conceivably working class. Census valuations of real estate and personal property seem to agree with this general conclusion.[59] While setting numbers is always difficult, Douglas Bristol marks a net worth of $2,000 as "the standard of affluence" in the upper South at the beginning of the Civil War, and Stephan Thernstom sets the mark for "distinguishing" those in "high white collar positions" of wealth in Boston in the period at "$5000 in real or $1000 in personal property" (79, 315). Comparatively few—though, importantly, *some*—*Recorder* subscribers reached such levels.

Among identified individual first-time subscribers researched primarily through the 1860 census, 31.6% (144/455) had no listing for either real estate or personal property valuations. There were 22.6% (103) more who had no listing for real estate, though they did have listings for personal property. Additionally, 9.9% (45) held real estate valued between $1 and $500; 10.8% (49), between $501 and $1,000; 7.3% (33), between $1,001 and $2,000; 5.7% (26), between $2,001 and $5,000; and 3.5% (16), over $5,000. Among first-time subscribers researched primarily through the 1870 census, 34.3% (185/540) had no listing for either real estate or personal property valuations. Additionally, 14.6% (79) had no listing for real estate, though they did have listings for personal property. There were also 9.1% (49) who held real estate valued between $1 and $500; 14.4% (78), between $501 and $1,000; 10.2% (55), between $1,001 and $2,000; 9.4% (51), between $2,001 and $5,000; and 4.8% (26), over $5,000.[60] Some subscribers clearly had amassed significant real property: activist and lumberman William Whipper (listed with $23,800 in real estate in the 1860 census), AME Bishop Quinn (listed with $20,000 in real estate in the 1870 census), Nelson T. Grant (listed as a "gardener" in Zanesville, Ohio, with $25,000 in real estate in the 1870 census), and so forth. But many had not, and most of those who had holdings had comparatively small valuations. Further, significant real estate valuations did not always mean high personal property valuations. Some individuals who reached the higher levels of real estate valuations were actually listed with very little personal property: Cleveland's George Vosburg was listed with $6,000 in real estate but *no* personal property in the 1860 census, for one extreme example, while New York restaurateur and son of Thomas Downing Peter W. Downing was listed with $9,000 in real estate and *no* personal property in the 1870 census, perhaps adding a postbellum page to his father's earlier protest. Some of this may simply have been careless census takers lumping valuations together, but it emphasizes two other trends that seem present among subscribers. First, for many subscribers who had funds, real estate seems to have been the choice for investing; second, for at least some subscribers with real estate, those holdings may have represented a lifetime of working and saving.[61]

Real estate valuations for those who renewed had a similar spread—though trending slightly higher. Among renewals studied primarily through the 1860 census, 31.4% (111/353) were from individuals who carried no listing for either real estate or personal property. In this same group, 25.8% (91) of renewals came from individuals who had no real estate listed but did have personal property listed. Additionally, 9.6% (34) of renewals came from individuals whose real estate was valued between $1 and $500; 14.4% (51), between $501 and $1,000; 9.9% (35), between $1,001 and $2,000; 6.2% (22), between $2,001 and $5,000; and only 0.6% (2), at more than $5,000. Among renewals studied primarily through the 1870 census, 29.3% (76/259) were from individuals who carried no listing for either real estate or personal property; 18.1% (47) of renewals came from individuals who had no real estate listed but did have personal property listed. There were also 6.6% (17) of renewals that came from individuals whose real estate was valued between $1 and $500; 12% (31), between $501 and $1,000; 7.3% (19), between $1,001 and $2000; 16.6% (43), between $2,001 and $5,000; and 6.6% (17), at more than $5,000.[62]

Valuations for personal property may be less trustworthy, though they do suggest a similar story. Among first-time subscribers researched primarily through the 1860 census, 4.2% (19/455) who held real estate were listed as having no personal property; 28.6% (130), between $1 and $100 in personal property; 18.9% (86), between $101 and $500; 4.2% (19), between $501 and

$1,000; 2.4% (11), between $1,001 and $2,000; and only 1.5% (7), more than $2,000. Among first-time subscribers researched primarily through the 1870 census, 14.8% (80/540) who held real estate were listed as having no personal property; 8.3% (45), between $1 and $100 in personal property; 26.1% (141), between $101 and $500; 7.6% (41), between $501 and $1,000; 2.4% (13), between $1,001 and $2,000; and 3% (16), more than $2,000. What is again striking is the number of subscribers with fairly modest valuations: 47.5% (216) in the 1860 census and 34.4% (186) in the 1870 census had valuations between $1 and $500.[63]

Personal property valuations tied to renewals echo these findings. Among renewals researched primarily through the 1860 census, only 4.2% (15/353) came from individuals with real estate listed but no personal property reported. Additionally, 30% (106) came from individuals with personal property valued between $1 and $100; 28% (99), between $101 and $500; 2% (7), between $501 and $1,000; 1.4% (5), between $1,001 and $2,000; and 1.1% (4), over $2,000. Among renewals researched primarily through the 1870 census, 8.5% (22/259) came from individuals with real estate listed but no personal property reported. Additionally, 11.2% (29) came from individuals with personal property valued between $1 and $100; 31.7% (82), between $101 and $500; 9.7% (25), between $501 and $1,000; 1.9% (5), between $1,001 and $2,000; and 5% (13), over $2,000. That said, some of these numbers are swayed through multiple renewals from well-off individuals—like the white F. W. G. May. What is again striking is the number of renewals tied to individuals with personal property valued at between $1 and $500—58.1% (205/353) of renewals researched through the 1860 census and 42.9% (111/259) tied to the 1870 census.

We should again note the difficulty of drawing any direct correlation between real estate valuations and personal property valuations; the lack of real estate did not necessarily lead to a low personal property valuation. AME minister and sometime print activist Savage Hammond, for example, was listed in the 1860 census with no real estate but $1,000 in personal property; Cincinnati photographer Alexander Thomas (of Ball and Thomas) was listed in the same census with no real estate but $800 in personal property, a figure that may have included professional equipment. Similarly, Reverend J. Sella Martin was listed in the 1870 census with no real estate but $3,000 in personal property, and Cincinnati grocer Thomas E. Knox was listed in the same census with no real estate but $1,000 in personal property.[64] These examples point again to the contextual nature of concepts like "wealth."

If we omitted the large group of soldier-subscribers discussed below and those who remain unidentified, we could posit that the average *Recorder* subscriber was a married Black man in his early forties living in the Northeast, with church ties and children, and likely in the working classes, even if he held property. But in addition to ignoring the gaps in the sample, that conclusion radically oversimplifies the diversity of identified individual subscribers in terms of location, gender, age, familial status, and class. We cannot remove the soldier-subscribers—any more than we can remove the notable subset of single women, or those subscribers from the Midwest (or the South), or AME ministers, or any of the rich range of others who match some—or *none*—of the characteristics of any "average" subscribers we might mark. The diversity of *Recorder* subscribers is one of the most important findings of this study.[65] But as crucial as understanding this diversity is, it is equally important to recognize that almost all of these diverse subscribers were African American. The parameters of the *Recorder*'s community of subscribers were thus wide in many ways, but quite focused in others.

The handful of group subscriptions during the period reinforces these conclusions. All can be placed into two loose categories—subscriptions for large groups of unnamed subscribers and subscriptions for reading rooms.[66] Three of the four groups in the former category—representing perhaps 155 subscribers—were sent by Union Chaplains on behalf of soldiers in all-Black regiments (like those shown in Figure 4.2).[67] The first of these came from Philander Read and was for twenty subscriptions. In the February 18, 1865, *Recorder*, Weaver reported that Read "states that through the Christian

FIGURE 4.2 *William Morris Smith's photograph of Company E, 4th U.S. Colored Infantry, at Fort Lincoln (1865). Courtesy of the Prints and Photographs Division, Library of Congress (LC-B8171-890). While the specific soldiers here are unidentified, the* Recorder *did have readers among the 4th and reported on the regiment's efforts.*

Commission" some of the soldiers in the 76th US Colored Infantry (of which he was chaplain) "obtained some copies of the Recorder; and such was the feeling of anxiety among the soldiers to have a copy of it, [as] the few [copies] secured did not, of course, supply one-twentieth part; therefore, twenty of them at once subscribed." Read (1831–1904), a white Presbyterian minister who had graduated from Amherst and Auburn Theological Seminary, may have grown up abolitionist and/or may have been (further) radicalized from his service in the 75th New York volunteers, which he joined in November 1861. Regardless, he had been with the 76th US Colored Infantry (USCI) since they were the 4th Native Guard Infantry of the Louisiana Volunteers and through their time as the 4th Corps de Afrique, their assault on Port Hudson, and, after that battle, their garrison duty. In his October 2, 1865, Chaplain's report, Read wrote that the soldiers of the 76th—especially the formerly enslaved among them—were hungry to learn and "the most teachable men that I ever saw" (qtd. in Wilson 131).[68] The *Recorder* thus offered such readers not only a chance to become more literate in the traditional sense, but to gain a wider view of Black experiences around the nation. Weaver summed up the value of Read's work: "Brother Read has our most sincere thanks for the above. He is one of the noble few who are doing good to poor down-trodden humanity, by teaching the ignorant, and creating a desire for knowledge. May God bless him, and may he be spared to do much more in the cause."

Rare enough for a white minister of the period, Read nonetheless never reached the level of the deep engagement of Chaplin Enoch K. Miller of the 25th USCI.[69] Born in England in 1840, Miller came to the United States at age four. His family settled in Rochester—one wonders if he saw Frederick Douglass or his various newspapers—and he joined the 108th New York volunteers early in the war. Convalescing after he was severely wounded at Gettysburg, Miller became a Presbyterian minister. By March of 1864, he had accepted a chaplaincy, and he reported to the 25th at Fort Barrancas on August 7, 1864. By all accounts, Miller was rare in his egalitarian sense of cross-racial collaborative work—an example of what Robin Bernstein notes as "thinkable" anti-racism among a small group of the period's white folks.[70] First, of course, there was the fact of Miller's letters to the *Recorder* themselves—more than a half dozen in late 1864 and early 1865 that offered extended discussion of the regiment, including the spiritual and physical health of members, the unit's military work, and also (again with an egalitarian sensibility) the unfairness of the paymaster's infrequent visits. Given that the 25th had been organized out of Philadelphia and had a number of soldiers from the region, Miller's letters must have been anxiously anticipated by many *Recorder* readers; that Miller also took the time to report his unit's deaths (name by individual name) must also have been seen as another important service. His letters to the *Recorder* addressed Weaver as "Brother Weaver," and they were the thoughtful and chatty letters of a colleague. Miller similarly noted, in his March 4, 1865, letter, that members of the 25th were in the midst of "what our brethren at home would call a revival" and that "Bros. Harris and Turner, Co. B, and also Bro. Mills, Co. C, all licensed preachers in the African M. E. Church at home, render us sufficient aid."

A host of sources testify to Miller's devotion to the men of the 25th. Jacob S. Johnson, of Company H, would refer to Miller as "our worthy chaplain" in his February 18, 1865, *Recorder* letter, and Lewis Buchanan, a 2nd Sergeant in Company F, wrote in that same issue of how "our good and kind chaplain is doing all that lies in his power to educate and train the minds of the men."[71] In Miller's own first quarterly chaplain's report—filed November 30, 1864—he spoke of daily hospital visits, a massive number of religious services, ten baptisms, and the establishment of a post school at Fort Pickens for soldiers that met three times each week; his report also asked that a chapel be built for the soldiers. His June 10, 1865, *Recorder* letter described starting "a Sabbath school, to which I invited all of the children in the vicinity of the fort. We have an attendance of sixty children, and a more eager, hungry set of children after knowledge I never saw."[72]

Given all of these activities, it would be plausible to suggest that Miller was using the subscriptions in the same ways as the Christian Commission—that is, passing out papers to those who queued for them. But Miller's *Recorder* letters make it clear that the funds he submitted to Weaver were for specific individuals: his December 24, 1864, letter said that he "circulated a subscription paper" and had "obtained one hundred ten subscribers"; Weaver's January 14, 1865, "Word to Our Brethren and Readers" noted that Miller "has 130 names." The difference between Miller's initial 110, Weaver's 130, and later numbers may be because, per Miller's March 4, 1865, letter, he sent an additional "list of names" because "several of our men wish to supply their friends at home with papers." These numbers caused of some tension: Weaver sent papers to the 25th for several months before Miller sent funds—as the men of the 25th were waiting to be paid by the government for far too long—but Miller complained that those "at home" were not receiving papers (to be) paid for by the soldiers of the 25th. Regardless, Miller expressed $275 for the 110 soldier-subscribers in June of 1865, only a few months before he was sent North with a number of convalescent soldiers to be mustered out that December.

The final soldiers' group subscription came after the war had actually ended: the October 14, 1865, *Recorder* acknowledged $43.50 from Garland H. White, chaplain of the 28th USCI, for eighteen members of his regiment.[73] This subscription had several surface similarities to those above, but also some key differences: the 28th was a western unit, and Garland White was African American. Raised in Indianapolis in late 1863 and early 1864, the 28th saw significant action in Virginia before being ordered, at the war's end, to Corpus Christi, Texas—from which White sent the funds. White had interacted with the *Recorder* before, and readers who saw this acknowledgment might have remembered his letter in the April 22, 1865, *Recorder*, which told a stunning story of how his "regiment was among the first that entered" Richmond. White made a speech to the victorious troops, and soon after was "found" by some of the soldiers and brought to "a group of colored ladies" that included "many broken-hearted mothers looking for their children." The women asked his name, that of his mother, his birthplace, the place of his sale as a small boy (which had been Richmond), and the name of the man who bought him. White answered each of these questions, finally naming Robert Toombs, Georgia's rabidly anti-Black politician who had bought him as a butler and eventually taken him to Washington, DC, where White escaped—first to Canada and then to Ohio. Gesturing to "an aged woman," one of the questioners said to the 28th's Chaplain, "This is your mother, Garland, whom you are now talking to, who has spent twenty years of grief about her son." Speaking the words those who placed "Information Wanted" ads in the *Recorder* must have dreamed of, White wrote, "I cannot express the joy I felt, at this happy meeting. . . . But suffice it to say, that God is on the side of the righteous, and will in due time reward them."

This background—and such a reunion—were far from the lived experiences of men like Read and Miller. White's reasons for encouraging subscriptions may also have been different in some ways, too. White's politics were in some ways distanced from Read's or Miller's: he had been active in the fight to allow African Americans to serve in the military (pushing both state and federal officials) and had recruited for the 28th, but he was actually less supportive of the fight for equal pay than Miller, and his sense of the *Recorder*'s politics waffled.

For all of these differences, these three chaplains and the Black subscribers they represented (to say nothing of those non-subscribers who benefited from borrowing the paper or hearing it read aloud) were certainly an extension of both the *Recorder*'s efforts to use ministers as conduits for subscriptions and Weaver's push to get the paper to Black soldiers through entities like the US Christian Commission. But as much as they tell us about these questions—and about some of the ways the paper moved into the South during and immediately after the war—we should also not overlook the obvious: these subscriptions meant that a significant number of African American soldiers must be counted among the *Recorder*'s readers, even though they do not show up in most of the demographic information above. Because we do not have their names, we cannot know how many of these soldiers continued to subscribe to the *Recorder* (or to engage in other ways with Black print culture) after the war ended. We do know that some of them wrote letters to the *Recorder*—some of which are collected in Edwin Redkey's wonderful *A Grand Army of Black Men* and some of which are discussed in the next chapter. For this and other reasons—such as the *Anglo-African*'s serialization of key Black texts during the war years and the inclusion of a version of William Wells Brown's *Clotel* in James Redpath's "Books for Camp Fires" series for Union soldiers—we need to attend more deeply to the understudied nexus of Black Civil War service and Black print. For now, these subscriptions remind us of how far the *Recorder* community reached and how rapidly it was changing.

The second category of group subscriptions also raises questions that few literary historians have considered: the place of Black print in nineteenth-century libraries. The December 22, 1866, subscription from Lane Seminary might seem a bit of a surprise. The majority-white college that the *Recorder* felt most connected to was Oberlin, the refuge of the "Lane Radicals" who fled Lyman Beecher's Presbyterian stronghold in the wake of a series of debates on slavery and race in 1834 that had left abolitionist activists deeply dismayed at Lane's conservatism.[74] While African Americans would occasionally be admitted to Lane in the later nineteenth century, it was hardly a bastion for Black learning or Black print. The subscription likely came through the intervention of Cincinnati AME minister Henry J. Young. Young was well connected, and when editor James Lynch came to town, he set up meetings at various Black churches to raise funds for the Book Concern.[75] Young was also involved in the planning of an event at Lane: a "poetical reading" by Black poet James Madison Bell "where a most highly cultured white audience were assembled." Young "suggested that Lynch should introduce Mr. Bell, and preside on the occasion, which he did with such. . . . sparkling wit that he was invited to preach on a subsequent evening, at the white Methodist Episcopal Church" where "the white people exhibited considerable interest in the *Christian Recorder*." Lane's subscription came from these interactions; Lynch himself reported the Lane Seminary subscription in an "Editor's Report."[76]

The other two subscriptions by institutions went to locations that students of Black print might find more likely—but institutions of a type almost completely ignored until Elizabeth McHenry's trailblazing *Forgotten Readers*. Both submitted in 1866, they came from the Moral and Mental Improvement Association of Baltimore and the Israel Church Reading Room in Washington, DC. I have found only very limited information on the Baltimore group: they represent one in a long line of literary clubs, debating societies, and educational organizations that were, themselves, a subset of the number of mutual aid and other race-specific entities created to fill the voids created by white America's racist public sphere.[77] The copies from their subscription would have circulated among Association members and perhaps their families, and they likely would have provided fodder for ongoing discussion of the events of the day.

We know more about the Israel Church. An anchor within the District, it was pastored at the time of the subscription by William Hunter, a former army chaplain and a longtime supporter of the *Recorder* and Church print generally. Prior to Hunter's appointment, another *Recorder* ally, Daniel Moore, had been the congregation's pastor; among its lay leaders, Israel counted J. F. Wilkinson, another longtime subscriber and advocate. During the period studied here, this large church hosted Baltimore Conference meetings, national AME Missionary Society meetings, and diverse other events, including a lecture by Fannie Jackson (later Coppin) that was reported in the August 18, 1866, *Recorder*, as well as the Semi-Centenary Celebration of Laymen of the AME Church, reported in the May 12, 1866, *Recorder*. In the midst of the exciting beginnings of Reconstruction, it had connections and sometimes collaborations with the better-known 15th Street Presbyterian, and some of its members undoubtedly knew Elizabeth Keckley, William Slade, and diverse figures in the Lincoln White House. It was buying a new parsonage that even had a room "furnished for the Bishop or Bishops.... when they are with us"—though a February 10, 1866, *Recorder* letter worried that the congregation did not have adequate funds for such. The February 3, 1866, *Recorder* contained a report from the congregation's Sabbath School superintendent, William Hugh[e]s that reported "regular attendance" of between forty-five and fifty children and six teachers—including the pastor and himself. He told *Recorder* readers that the Sabbath School library offered five hundred volumes for the congregation's use. The nexus between the Sabbath School library and the general reading room is unclear, though they may have been one in the same. Regardless, the subscription from Israel AME meant that its congregants had ready access to the *Recorder*—and meant that the paper had a way of advertising itself to likely subscribers.

While again we cannot trace exactly who read the *Recorder* at these locations, we can recognize that the readers may well have mirrored some of the diversity of the African American *Recorder* subscribers studied above. Israel AME had more resources than the Bloomington church that Helen Yancy, Martha Wells, and Nancy Cooper entered in October 1862, but its membership similarly reflected a range of geographic backgrounds (including all-too-recent ties to the slave South, of which DC had long been a part) and socioeconomic positions. Like Yancy, Wells, and Cooper, some of Israel's members were thirsty for education, and so they, too, sought to join the paper's community of print. Their conduits were not so different from the minister-agents who brought so many of the paper's mail subscribers—like Yancy, Wells, and Cooper—into the fold. How and why these diverse individuals might have read the paper is the subject of the next chapter, and the rest of this volume focuses on the texts they may have read—texts crucial to an understanding of the shape of nineteenth-century African American literature and Black print broadly.

But we should pause to remember first that the subscribers here embody realities and possibilities long ignored by American (literary) history: they were a nation-spanning community of Black readers sharing in a weekly paper that was Black-run, largely Black-authored, and designed specifically for Black people.

{ PART II }

"Would Not Such a Narration Be Worth Reading?"

THE *CHRISTIAN RECORDER* AND AFRICAN AMERICAN LITERARY HISTORY

{ 5 }

"We Are in the World": Reading the *Recorder* in the Civil War Era

In mid-September 1864, Lizzie Hart of Morrow, Ohio, made her weekly journey to her local post office to pay postage on her copy of the *Christian Recorder*, the final requirement for owning the material object and the step that allowed her to take it home to read. A daughter of free African Americans—who, like many *Recorder* subscribers, had moved from a slave state (Kentucky) to a free state (Ohio)—Hart had first subscribed to the *Recorder* in April 1863 via the soon-to-be Union chaplain William H. Hunter (he of the Israel Church reading room discussed in the last chapter). She sent funds to renew that subscription at least once. Her reading of the mid-1864 issues—perhaps privately in snatches of free time, perhaps aloud to her family and/or friends, perhaps both—must have been complex and conflicted. She likely thought, for example, of her younger sister Julia, whose obituary had appeared in the May 28, 1864, issue of the *Recorder*. But even in her tremendous and lasting grief, she might have found some solace and perhaps even a bit of empowerment in the paper, as she herself had penned that obituary, paired it with a short elegy, ensured a print remembrance of her sister, and soon after become a regular contributor to the *Recorder*, writing letters on a wide range of both regional and national issues. Reading the September 10, 1864, *Recorder*, Hart would have found not only reminders of her grief, the comfort offered by the paper, and the fact that she had entered the paper's community as a writer; she would have found a concrete and specific response to one of her letters—proof that, via the *Recorder*, the voice of a young, single Black woman in Ohio could be heard by Black soldiers more than six hundred miles away.

Soldiers, young women like Hart, and the diverse other readers of that September 10 issue would certainly have seen the painful dance of grief and solace on every page. The front page featured "Lines on the Death of Brother Grayson Singleton" by "A. B." of Philadelphia, and the third page contained another poem to Singleton by "A. B." Page three also featured "Lines on the Death of Johnny Jordan"—sent from Norfolk, Virginia, and signed with a penname now rendered unreadable in extant copies. The paper also offered an obituary for young Ann Eliza Henson that included four lines of poetry—in the correspondent's words, a "simple but touchingly beautiful little verse" that had been "selected by a sister of the departed." It wouldn't take much effort for Hart to imagine the kind of community of mourning discussed in chapter 7 of this volume, as she, like so many others in the midst of the long war, was already *physically* part of such a community. While neither Julia Hart's death nor these other deaths were "war deaths," they were deaths during wartime, and Lizzie Hart and many readers probably could not help considering the two issues in dialogue. For Hart, the starkest reminder of such links may well have been the turning from page three's war news to page four, where she would have found a piece of juvenile fiction titled "My Sister."

Hart had followed the war news that filled the paper with deep interest, and she had thought often of those African American soldiers. Her reading of the September 10 issue thus likely included attention to the front-page poem sent by "Raymond"—Jacob Anderson Raymond—which addressed its title figure "Slavery" directly in words that could have been Hart's: "Thy chain is breaking now, and on thy brow / Hangs a funeral pall." She may have also read with interest front-page letters from New Orleans and from Morris Island, South Carolina; a page two "information wanted" request from Catherine Jones of West Chester, Pennsylvania, praying for some word of her cousin John Burton (missing from the 14th US Colored Infantry); a detailed page three report on the Union's victory at Fort Morgan on Mobile Bay; and texts that had become commonplace in the paper, letters from Black soldiers. In such reading, she may well have thought about her own May 28, 1864, *Recorder* letter about "the late massacre at Fort Pillow," which told soldiers both to remember that event and to "fight with your whole soul, mind and strength, and die rather than surrender." She may even have thought of her July 30, 1864, *Recorder* letter, which placed righteous "Shame" on "this boasted Republic" for "refusing to pay" Black soldiers "what is just and right, for no other reason than that they are colored men." And she may have found joy in the fact that, just the week before, the paper acknowledged that, as noted in chapter 3, "Miss Lizzie Hart" had sent $1.15 "to send the *Recorder* to a soldier."

But the piece in the September 10, 1864, issue that most likely caught her attention was a letter from a Black soldier signed "T. R."—for Sergeant Theodore Ro(d)gers of Company C of the 26th US Colored Infantry. It told *Recorder* staff and readers that "By chance, your journal happened to come into my sight. I read in it a letter from Miss Lizzie Hart. I also read your editorial in relation to colored people and the colored soldiers, and I must acknowledge that I fully concur with you. All we want is that those at home should take care of our families, and speak cheerful words to us, do their duty as Christians." The letter concluded, "we will do ours as soldiers."[1]

Consider the layers here. Lizzie Hart had read voraciously in (and beyond) the *Recorder*. That reading—not just of the difficulties of Black troops or war news generally but also discussions of broad questions of race, faith, and death—shaped her writing for the *Recorder*. A world away, stationed at Fort Duane (near Beaufort, South Carolina), a Black soldier had read some of those words—and those of editor Weaver—and had been moved to "concur" in print. And now Hart was reading *about* how her work had been read. It must have driven home the sense that she was not only a writer and a reader but also a participant in a textual community.[2] Hovering in the background of such textual circuits were not only the church and print mechanisms discussed in chapters 2 and 3 (especially ministers like Hunter as well as those connected to Rodgers like his unit's chaplain and area agents of the US Christian Commission) but also the textual circuits that were built from and for the subscribers described in the last chapter. Such entities must be at the heart of any consideration of the *Recorder*—a Black-run paper for Black writers *and* readers—and they deeply inform subsequent chapters' consideration of sample texts from the paper. But before we study those texts and their crucial contributions to African American literature and Black print more generally, we first need to consider how the paper and some of the *Recorder* community's subgroups framed the acts of reading and participating in (AME) print culture.

This chapter thus begins to explore how figures like Hart and Rodgers—and the *Recorder* more broadly—talked about reading (and writing) during and after the war years. It first examines some of the paper's sense(s) of ministerial reading, with some emphasis on extending the conception of ministerial agency discussed in chapter 3. In exploring, for example, the paper's repeated calls for ministers to read and to make (selected) print culture available to their congregants, it articulates the goals the *Recorder* tied to readers and reading and thus offers a sense of the structures that enveloped individual texts. The remainder of this chapter focuses on the ways the *Recorder* represented the reading (and the writing flowing from such reading) of two of the diverse groups of *Recorder* readers hinted at in the last chapter and in this chapter's opening, soldiers (like Rodgers) and single women (like Hart). These examples are meant to provoke (rather than to comprehensively cover) questions tied to Black reading in/of the *Recorder* during and just after the Civil War, but I am especially interested in the moves from reading *to* writing that were tied to these groups and to the complex and variable mutuality of the *Recorder*'s print community.[3] The often-uneasy possibilities and practices linking reading and writing set up the book's later consideration of letters, poetry, and a serialized novel in the paper. This chapter argues that myriad contributions to the paper (like Hart's above) linked such reading and writing with faith, patriotism, duty, and agency and thus with specific roles that the *Recorder* argued African American readers should take in both their local communities and the broader nation. Its sense of "wartime" is thus also multilayered, as the *Recorder* was always already engaged in wars against racial prejudice both in itself and as a manifestation of evil (in a world potentially on the edge of apocalypse). Battles for Black education, full (and fully paid) participation in the nation's military, and real citizenship were thus holy, as were battles for Black places in American print culture during and after the Civil War. Battles against divisions in the Church—caused by geographic diffusion but also by a host of other factors—were thus also part and parcel of the larger war to determine the future of the nation.

The history of Black reading has often been a (hi)story of absences and gaps. In some ways, Elizabeth McHenry's title *Forgotten Readers* is too kind. While barriers against nineteenth-century Black reading were real, massive, and, simply put, evil, American culture's "forgetting" that there nonetheless were Black readers, as McHenry and others have eloquently pointed out, has often been willful, purposeful, and centered on oppression. For evidence, we need look no further than the census data on which much of the last chapter is based. Among the 1,109 first-time subscribers, 75 individuals (6.8%) were marked as completely illiterate in their primary census record. Twenty renewals (3%) came from individuals who were similarly marked. Among those "illiterate" subscribers, consider Robert Meacham, who was marked illiterate in the 1870 census listing of Monticello, Florida (307A). Meacham, who subscribed in June of 1866, was not only an AME minister but also a significant presence in the Florida church and a future AME traveling elder. And there is the small matter of his political activity: he helped *write* Florida's new constitution in 1868, fought for provisions guaranteeing free public education, narrowly missed a seat in the US Congress, and was both a state senator and (later) Florida's first Black postmaster.[4]

The simple fact is that, in many census jurisdictions, there was a systemic undercounting of literate African Americans like Meacham. Such undercounting took some effort: in 1870, for example, the census taker had to check both a box that said "cannot read" and a box that said "cannot write" for each individual.[5] Given this, more damning than an individual example like Meacham is the fact that every single member of Meacham's household who was of age was marked illiterate—his wife, his eldest child (a twelve-year-old who was simultaneously marked as attending school), a sixteen-year-old domestic, and twenty-three-year-old Martha D. Sickles, who had been born in New York and whose occupation was listed as "school teacher." Assistant Marshal J. W. Johnson actually marked the boxes for "cannot read" and "cannot write" for each of these people *and* for all but one African American on the entire page of Meacham's listing. That one Black American seems to have been an oversight: *all* African Americans of age listed on the four pages before that page and the four pages after—including three more ministers and a US mail carrier—were all marked "cannot read" and "cannot write."

In being marked illiterate on a federal census, Meacham and these others joined, as discussed earlier, fine company: Reverend John W. Stevenson, whose letter in the December 13, 1867, *Recorder* praised the "colored authors" he thought most worthy of readers' attention, for example, and Frances Ellen Watkins Harper (shown in Figure 5.1), who was marked illiterate in her 1850 census listing even though she was already becoming known as a teacher and poet. In the course of this study, I found diverse *Recorder* subscribers who were marked illiterate and appeared on census pages where *every* African American was so marked, regardless of occupation or schooling. But perhaps most stunning is the story of Robert Van Hauser, who subscribed in 1864 from Coxsackie, New York. His 1850 census listing marks him literate (232B). In a frightening new take on "Forgotten Readers," his 1860 census listing marks him illiterate (498).

FIGURE 5.1 *Frances Ellen Watkins Harper, from William Still's* The Underground Rail Road *(1872). Courtesy of the American Antiquarian Society.*

As AME ministers, Meacham and Stevenson were expected to be highly literate; indeed, they had to be, given how much of the Church had become tied to the written and printed word. For example, though the Afro-Protestant Bible had long had oral incarnations, as the century went on, AME leaders repeatedly emphasized—in a host of Church texts that included sermons, exegetical essays, open letters, and a range of other works—learned, careful reading and detailed knowledge of printed scripture. Part of the AME Church's push for a ministry capable of engaging in reading and writing certainly spoke to combating public discrimination, but, as Frances Foster has argued about Black print in general, the Church's move toward education requirements for its ordained workers had much more to do with the AME's goals for itself and its community. Many in the Church argued that to fully understand and share the Word, individuals needed to be able to read, read about, write, and write about words—their roots, contexts, implications, and powers.[6]

Using the written word was not, however, simply about engaging metaphysical questions; the Church also recognized that its organizational spread depended on having individual ministers who could manage churches, interact with communities (including local print, educational, and governmental entities), and both report back to and be instructed by the Church hierarchy—all in writing. Ministers were also dependent on print for diverse pragmatic matters. The debates over the *Discipline* shared in chapter 2—which represent only a fraction of broader dialogue on this written collection of beliefs, rules, and practices—should also be recognized as debates among interested readers. Those readers knew that they might have to both enforce the letter and spirit of the *Discipline* and have that *Discipline* applied to their own lives and work, as it was also a job description and a contract. The number of notices of deadlines, policy shifts, calendars for traveling elders and bishops, conference business, and a host of other Church events that appeared in the *Recorder* cannot be exaggerated, and, as already noted, these were equaled in number and sometimes surpassed in space allocated by reports from churches across the broad connection. The AME Church was simply too big in terms of geographic dispersion, membership size, *and* goals both physical and metaphysical to have a ministry not fully conversant in—and able to participate in tasks tied to—writing and print.

Still, the battles to establish formal education requirements for the ministry were not easily won. They swirled in the early Church and came to a head at the 1844 General Conference in Pittsburgh, where a group led by a young Daniel Payne put forward "a resolution to institute a course of studies for the education of the ministry" that he thought "would be carried without much opposition" (*History* 168). What followed "was like . . . a fire-brand is cast into a magazine of powder," and, "with the greatest apparent indignation the resolution was voted down by a large and overwhelming majority, and the house adjourned in great excitement" (168). Payne reported decades later that, in the intense night that followed, "the intelligent laity" and many formally educated ministers asserted that "they would withdraw and organize an ecclesiastical establishment that would be in favor of the measure" (169). The next day, Abram D. Lewis—who Wayman called "an eminent local minister of Pittsburgh" and who Payne called "a brother of lofty stature"—requested "reconsideration of the rejected proposition" with "uncommon eloquence and power" and led the fight for its approval "without a dissenting voice" (Wayman 97; Payne *History* 168–169). Aging Bishop Morris Brown—chairing the meeting—appointed a committee of seven (including Payne and Lewis) to draft the "course of studies."

The draft that was presented and approved soon after actually included two such "courses," a two-year plan for exhorters and a four-year plan for ordained ministers. Reading and writing were both key subjects and central modes for both courses. Initiate exhorters were to read closely the Bible, Roswell Chamberlain Smith's *English Grammar*, Samuel Augustus Mitchell's *Geography*, the AME Church *Discipline*, and John Wesley's biblical commentary *Notes on the Bible* in the first year; in the second year they were to read Nathan Bangs's *Original Church of Christ* and *History of the Methodist Episcopal Church*, as well as Richard Watson's *Life of Rev. John Wesley*. Those studying for full ordination were to read Smith's *English Grammar*, Mitchell's *Geography*, William Paley's *Evidences of Divine Revelation*, a history of the Bible, and Thomas Hartwell Horne's *Introduction to the Critical Study and Knowledge of the Holy Scriptures* in the first year; Samuel Simon Schmucker's *Elements of Popular Theology* and *Elements of Mental Philosophy*, Paley's *Natural Theology*, and Watson's *Theological Institutes* in their second year; and Charles Augustus Goodrich's *History of the Church*, Ebenezer Porter's *Lectures on Homiletics and Preaching*, and Jean Henri Merle D'Aubigne's *History of the Reformation* in their third year. In the fourth, they would study the geography and chronology of the Bible "with a review of the above studies."[7] These were hefty lists, composed of difficult texts, some of which were also fairly expensive.[8] Young ministers were to carefully consider these works—grounded in a combination of Protestant approaches (mainly Methodist and Methodist Episcopal but also Lutheran and Congregationalist)—and to meet with more senior colleagues to talk about them. As these lists became codified in the AME *Discipline* (first in an appendix and then in a section of their own), initiates also had to be ready for annual oral or written examination on their content. A May 19, 1866, *Recorder* notice, for example, named the supposedly illiterate John W. Stevenson among "the fourth year's class" who was called to be examined by a committee of four senior pastors.[9]

During the period studied here, Payne (who had become a bishop in 1852) and his allies dominated many areas of Church life; they consistently emphasized a formally educated ministry and, more and more, a formally educated laity, as well. Consider the 1863 Baltimore Conference annual meeting. Late in the Conference, "several local brethren were offered for membership" as ministers, but "The Bishop [Payne] . . . announced that no local preacher could be admitted into the Conference until he had completed the course of study laid down in the appendix of the Discipline. Local brethren looking forward to ordination must not, therefore, expect to be 'carried on the flowery beds of ease.'" As striking as this action is, the weight Payne placed on the Conference's Committee on Education is more telling. The conference took "great care and pains" to name that group, "as it was remarked by the bishop" that "duties more weighty than ever before, would devolve on this committee." The committee thus included three future Bishops (John Mifflin Brown, Alexander Wayman, and Benjamin Tucker Tanner), future *Recorder* editor James Lynch (who wrote the *Recorder* coverage of the meeting), two longtime supporters of Church print (Savage Hammond and Daniel Moore), and Frances Harper's cousin George T. Watkins.

The interactions of Bishop (and former *Recorder* editor) Jabez Pitt Campbell with the Indiana Conferences of 1864 and 1865 echoed such efforts. Soon after his election to a bishopric, he nudged the 1864 Indiana Conference annual meeting into passing a resolution demanding that all of its ministers "write an essay, to be read before the Annual Conference" of 1865. That resolution told Campbell "to write out a list of subjects" and assign one to each minister on a roster that included many who had interacted or would interact with the Bloomington church discussed in the last chapter. The list consisted of twenty-eight topics ranging from A. T. Hall's assignment on "Divinity of the Bible" to Johnston Mitchem's on "Christian Baptism" and from Willis Revels's on "The Existence of God" to Frederick Myers's on "The Doctrine of Repentance." It was published in the January 14, 1865, *Recorder* along with Campbell's assertion that "it is confidently hoped, and indeed it is expected, that, without further notice, every Brother . . . will be prepared," as no "excuse will . . . be received in justification of his neglect."

The *Recorder*'s consistent representation of ministers as readers flowed from these broader Church impulses. James Lynch was a Payne protégé; while not always close to either Payne or Campbell, Weaver agreed completely that the AME ministry needed to be literate in multiple senses of the term and to have rich education in and experience with print practices. Weaver's publication of items like Campbell's list of topic assignments marks how deeply the *Recorder* favored the cause, as did the Book Concern's regular advertisement of several of the titles on the lists for the courses of study. Weaver, Stanford, and Lynch all consistently told ministers that, as in the italicized language of the a September 13, 1862, piece on "The Methodist Ministry," "*more study, higher intellectual training, more instructive preaching are necessary.*" While the course of study was essential—"a very decided indication of a felt intellectual necessity and of a disposition to meet it"—Weaver went so far as to call, again in italics, for "*university, or at least some collegiate education*" for ordained AME ministers.[10]

The *Recorder* did, however, sometimes recognize that the bevy of tasks ministers were called upon to perform could prevent or limit such engagement, as initiate ministers were accepted "on trial" and so often held charges throughout their course of study. It also recognized that many Church members had been denied access to formal education (including alphabetic literacies) by slavery and/or broader racism. As it did with subscription, the paper thus deployed various methods to encourage fuller ministerial education. Campbell, for example, sent a piece specifically titled "Horne's Introduction" that was published in the October 26, 1861, *Recorder* and that describes his own reading of that text: "Our love" for "young men preparing for the ministry" led him "to critically read and review this little book within a few months past. . . . This labor we have performed amidst our other labors, duties, and profound studies, by making it our duty to devote a portion of every day, Sabbaths excepted, when at home, to its performance." Campbell notes this so "that we may encourage the hearts of those who have such duties to perform, and who are ready to faint at the sight of so much labor to be performed before they can pass their examination"; the solution, Campbell wrote, was "patience and perseverance" and "God's help."[11]

John Mifflin Brown's February 9, 1867, piece on the possible union of the AME and African Methodist Episcopal Zion churches is much more blunt in seeing the texts in the course of study—and wide reading beyond—as the coin of the realm: "Any well-informed Methodist," he wrote, "might have had precisely the same view" on linking the churches as Brown did if he or she had "taken the time to read Dr. Bangs' 'Original Church of Christ,' or 'Steven's Church Polity,' 'Bishop Emory's Defense of the Fathers,' 'Powell on Secession,' 'Steven's History of Methodism,' 'Bangs' History of the M. E. Church' (1st and 2d Vol.)."[12]

The supposedly illiterate John W. Stevenson was a deep devotee of both this larger AME sense of an educated ministry and the *Recorder*'s vision of a clergy of active readers. Initially an apothecary, he was admitted to the ministry on trial in 1862, and his early years saw him not only complete the four-year course of study but also, according to Wayman, attend Lincoln University and "a medical college in Philadelphia from which he obtained the degree of M. D." (*Cyclopedia* 154). The *Recorder* went out of its way to praise this "young man, laboring to obtain an education" in a July 22, 1865, item titled "Rev. John W. Stevenson," as education was "in these days . . . so much needed among our people"; the item also lauds Stevenson's lecture on "Man, considered mentally, morally and physically"—a title that could have been taken from Bishop Campbell's 1865 list of topics. By the August 26, 1865, *Recorder* publication of an announcement of a "Grand Union Emancipation Meeting" at Penningtonville, Pennsylvania, Stevenson was already being celebrated as an "eminent speaker" and was expected to share the podium with "Hon. Fred. Douglass." By the December 15, 1866, issue, Stevenson had been chosen to contribute a biographical "Essay on Bishop Allen," and the July 13, 1867, issue contains his letter on "Colored Authors" for "the purpose of calling the attention to the reading public of the rapid increase of authors among our people." In the letter, Stevenson praises his colleague Benjamin Tucker Tanner's new *Apology*, a pamphlet on Lincoln University, I. J. Hill's memoir of his service in the 29th USCT, and James C. Waters's forthcoming *The Follies of Youth, and the Vices of Young Men*. Stevenson's conclusion about African American literature and Black print? "A brighter day is dawning."

It thus seems likely that Stevenson would have read a range of *Recorder* contributions on faith, theology, and Church policy—perhaps especially the nasty exchange between Campbell and Indiana Conference minister Thomas Strother (see chapter 6) or the fights over the place of Bishop Nazrey and the BME (see chapter 2)—as well as pieces on Church history and broader national and international history. Stevenson so strongly embraced both a lettered ministry generally and the *Recorder* as a specific mechanism for such that, as reported in the January 29, 1870, *Recorder*, he was appointed the Book Concern's General Agent.

But it would be a mistake to assume that ministers read only the paper's copious contributions on Church theory and practice—or, rather, it would be a mistake to assume Church theory and practice were insular or narrow concepts that did not address other texts including letters, poetry, and fiction and, indeed, did not address all of African American literature and culture. The rubrics of Church theory and practice included a host of questions tied to everything from politics to aesthetics and from the broad world to the day-to-day activities of individuals and local groups.

It was a letter describing such local efforts at Monticello, Florida, that the supposedly illiterate Robert Meacham sent for publication in the November 10, 1866, *Recorder*. Meacham came to writing and reading from different places than Stevenson had. Enslaved in Florida, Meacham had reportedly been taught to read and write by his white owner/father and even—again reportedly—attended school briefly in his youth. He received his AME charge from Bishop Payne himself (within the South Carolina Conference, then overseeing all of Florida). That posting likely came from the fact that Meacham was already active in Church and community affairs in the region, especially in Tallahassee. There is no evidence that he completed—or even began—the Church's course of study. AME growth in a free South was a development the Conferences of the 1840s could not conceive of, and it necessitated much more flexibility in assigning ministers than Payne would show before 1864 or after the late 1860s. (Indeed, as Jay Case's *Unpredictable Gospel* suggests, tensions between Payne and Turner over issues tied to the South—including this question—became massive in the 1860s.) Meacham came into the AME's formal structure via Charles H. Pearce, a BME defector who returned to the AME Church post-war and successfully jockeyed for the Tallahassee pulpit. Recognizing Meacham's local clout—and likely a potential friend, competitor, or enemy—Pearce encouraged the Church hierarchy to assign Meacham to Monticello in nearby Jefferson County. While Pearce was able to obtain various roles in the Church leadership—working for a time under Bishops John Mifflin Brown and Alexander Wayman—Meacham continued pastoring locally but also turned to state politics. In the late 1860s, according to Meacham's biographer Canter Brown Jr., "church duties were only a small part of Meacham's activities in Jefferson County. He assumed an activist role in counseling freedmen on their relationships with local planters, urging them to work toward obtaining their own homes and farms and advising them to enter into labor contracts with whites only as a last resort" (4–5). Though his life was repeatedly threatened, during "the summer and early fall of 1867 . . . he assisted in registering some 2,300 voters (1,747 were blacks), a total which represented slightly less than 10% of all registered voters in the state" (6).

As both a member in a distant part of the AME "connexion" and a politician with state and even national aspirations and interests, Meacham would likely have found the kinds of local letters he himself wrote to be of significant interest. The next chapter discusses this broad and diverse genre but it is worth noting that such letters allowed readers both comparatives to their own locations/situations and a broader sense of African American and African Methodist Episcopal concerns and actions.[13] Thus, while much of Meacham's November 10, 1866, letter focused on how "our Church is prospering in this land" and specifically on the congregation, Sabbath school, and day school of Monticello, it saw all of this work in national frameworks. Citing his charge from Bishop Payne, it spoke of how Meacham had "been engaged in attending to the Churches around the county" and so could offer a broad sense of work in Florida. It noted the two "good teachers" who had "taken charge of the school" after coming south to Florida: "Mr. Pembroke, from Baltimore, Md.," and the teacher (listed as "illiterate" with the Meacham family in the 1870 census) "Miss Sickles from New York." It concluded with this: "I am beginning to think that we are in the world, as well as other people, and feel that God is with us, and will crown our efforts with the best success."

This sense of being "in the world" must have been liberating and strengthening: it spoke to diverse lives and identities that had simply been out of reach for Meacham and many of his congregants. That said, Meacham may have sometimes bridled at some *Recorder* pieces: Northern correspondents and especially Weaver and Lynch often felt the need to "instruct" their Southern counterparts—especially those newly freed. Weaver's three-part series of "Advice from the Editor"—appearing in the December 9, 16, and 23, 1865, issues—told formerly enslaved people that "we presume that many of you do not and cannot fully comprehend the great change that you have undergone." Writing with the clear assumption that his words would be read aloud to groups and individuals of varying alphabetic literacy, he emphasized that "your enemies will take advantage of this" and that

> Therefore, my dear brother freedmen, in order that you may be better prepared for the great change, we earnestly beseech you to acquire an education. Learn to read and write first, so as to trace your own name on paper. But you may perchance say that you have no time to go to school now because you are poor, have a family, and must work hard to support them. Your excuse is indeed plausible—but you must do as we have done many a time: cut down big trees, plough the ground, cradle wheat and oats, and mow grass, from six o'clock in the morning until six o'clock in the evening, and often later, feed the stock afterwards, and prepare wood for the morning's use . . . [but then work] until ten, eleven, and twelve o'clock at night, pouring over books.

Meacham and his congregants likely had a better sense of freedom than Weaver gave them credit for. Still, Meacham would have agreed on the practical importance of reading—especially given his extensive battles against unfair labor contracts that were often entered into by those who could not actually *read* such contracts or the laws governing them. He would also have agreed with Weaver that "No nation or race of people can prosper without education."[14] He knew—perhaps better than *Recorder* staff—the importance of public language and print in this "new South," and he may have recognized that, if he continued to write for the paper, he would have to adapt and perhaps even challenge the paper's rhetoric to accurately address his own location and to better inform the Church (and the North) about the realities of Monticello, Florida.

For Meacham—as for Stevenson, albeit from different places—the need to become a reading and writing minister was thus tied directly and repeatedly to congregants' local and national needs. For myriad reasons—ranging from helping congregants learn to read contracts and function politically to aiding them in understanding the Word through written and printed words—the paper thus stressed not only reading (and writing) ministers but also ministers ministering to (potential) readers, especially through providing and supporting social locations and institutions tied to literature. The paper repeatedly emphasized providing congregants with reading material, in part because of the deep need for subscribers and for Book Concern customers, but also because, according to a March 25, 1865, piece by James Lynch, editors fully understood that print was an arena from which African Americans were consistently excluded. Thus, Lynch told readers, "we are now called upon to manfully battle against prejudice. . . . We are to battle for our rights to use the

Public Library, to share the privileges of the Historical and Scientific societies, the Academy and the College."

Book and periodical sales were only part of these battles for print engagement. The kinds of reading rooms considered briefly in the last chapter were a subject of *Recorder* discussion almost from the beginning of Weaver's tenure. A January 11, 1862, piece simply called "The Library" recognized that "one of the most perplexing subjects for the [Sabbath School] Superintendent is the management of the SABBATH-SCHOOL LIBRARY"—because of "the degree of responsibility" necessary "in regard to the use of books," as well as their "selection" and "distribution," and the fact that "a poor child" might misplace or damage a book. For all this, the clear expectation was, according to a January 31, 1863, letter from James Tillman of Bensalem, Pennsylvania, that "A Literary Library should be in every church"; Tillman added that, on taking his own charge, he realized that "we should also have our Sabbath School library replenished."[15] It was not uncommon for ministers reporting basic church information to include library holdings, as A. T. Hall did in his May 17, 1862, letter about the AME mission at Keokuk, Iowa: "The Sabbath School is reviving. Last Sabbath we had 45 scholars and 8 teachers. The teachers appear to be interested in their several classes. We have a library of about two hundred volumes." Similarly, Nelson H. Turpin—who had ministered to the congregation connected to teacher and novelist Julia C. Collins in Williamsport, Pennsylvania—bragged in a September 30, 1865, letter from Salem, New Jersey, that "Our school now numbers from sixty to seventy scholars in fair weather" and "we made a purchase of a new library, at a cost of $40." In a more global sense, the (ideologically messy) June 2, 1866, "What Our White Friends Think" quoted from the *Princeton Journal*'s assertion that the AME Church was "well organized and well manned, and has done much, very much, for the moral and religious elevation of the people to whom it is peculiarly called to minister"; the *Journal* specifically noted that the AME Philadelphia Conference had "about 50 Sunday-schools, with over 3,000 scholars, and nearly 12,000 volumes in their libraries."

Sabbath school libraries had a surface emphasis on Church youth, and so did some parts of the *Recorder* discussions of textual engagement, including its attention to family and juvenile literature. An October 12, 1861, piece titled "A Family Paper," for example, argues that "many of our subscribers, heads of families with children"—a group, as discussed in the last chapter, common among subscribers—"say their experience has been that a good family paper for children is equal to five months' schooling." These families reportedly found that even children "improving but little in reading" when at school nonetheless raced for the *Recorder* as "soon as it is announced that the paper has come from the office," causing many a "scuffle to see who shall read it first." It concludes that "There is no family investment that pays so well, that returned to the family so much good for the small outlay." That said, the piece also emphasizes that the "necessity for a good family paper is not limited to children just learning to read. The boy that goes to college, the girl that goes to boarding school should each and every one be supplied with a good newspaper." Then implying heavily that parents could benefit similarly, the article ends, "An experienced teacher once said he could name . . . every member of a class that had been in the habit of reading a newspaper from the quickness of apprehension, and the intelligence of their replies to questions." Within this framework, Sabbath school libraries, like minister-readers, were actually constructed broadly as "family" resources, encouraging not only reading youth but also reading families—and so also reading adults.[16]

Providing print resources meant that ministers and congregants were also urged to involve themselves with freestanding reading rooms and libraries. The October 7, 1865, issue, for example, contains an unsigned letter from Harrisburg that expressed excitement that the Garnet Equal Rights League officers were planning "a reading room . . . where the members of the League can spend an hour or two perusing the papers that are edited by colored men, and others that advocate equality before the law." The March 31, 1866, *Recorder* reports that that reading room was open "every day, from 10 A.M. to 9 ½ P.M. Among its reading matter we notice . . . all the principal magazines . . . and many other literary and miscellaneous periodicals." Further, "many valuable books have been donated to the League . . . Shakespeare's complete works, and the Works of Flavius Josephus." With this in mind, the paper published an August 4, 1866, item titled "A Want" that argues "Philadelphians want a FREE READING ROOM, where young colored men, desiring to pass their leisure moments profitably, may store their minds with information, by reading select works, on History, the varied Sciences, Art, and politics, or by engaging in instructive debate. . . . The progress of the age demands it." Notably, the *Recorder* positions such an institution against "the many drinking and billiard saloons with which our city is infested."[17]

For all of this discussion, the paper was also definitive that a library alone was not enough, and so all three editors of the period actively encouraged the founding (and consistently reported the activities) of diverse AME literary societies, debating clubs, and other social groups like those studied in Elizabeth McHenry's *Forgotten Readers*. The connections that congregants saw—and that the paper encouraged—between these local groups and national issues were often embodied in the very names of the groups: "Aleph" of Washington, DC, reported in the October 24, 1863, *Recorder* that "our young people here have formed a literary club, styled the Douglas[s] Club, after that distinguished lover of humanity, F. Douglas[s]." Subscriber Francis J. Peck told readers of the September 3, 1864, *Recorder* that he "called a meeting of the young people" of his congregation "and organized a literary society" that the twenty new members "unanimously agreed to call . . . the Daniel A. Payne Literary Society of Buffalo."[18] These societies' gatherings encouraged reading and study in part through conversation, but also in part through writing—sometimes with an eye toward publication. Peck's letter, for example, appends "An Address by Henry Cook, before the D. A. Payne Literary Society" that argues that participation in such a the society "will make some of the young ladies, school-teachers, so that they may go South and teach those poor freedmen how to read and write and spell; it will make some of us young men, ministers—some of us, lawyers—and some of us, school-teachers.... Five of the members have gone to war, to aid in putting down this rebellion, and to free our brethren who are in bondage, and no doubt some one of those boys ... may turn out to be the Hannibal of America."

Generations of critics stereotyped such groups as locations for excesses of schoolgirl and schoolboy sentiment.[19] A biased reading of Black periodicals could certainly yield seeming evidence. Consider, for examples, titles and descriptions of the essays of AME literary society in Wilmington, Delaware, reported in the September 19, 1863, *Recorder*—"Autumn" by Mrs. Mary M. Dowman, which "was very chaste and sublime," and "Friendship" by Miss Mary E. Greenwood, "which was a very good exhibition of talent, and a noble effort for the first." This meeting also featured an essay by correspondent and subscriber Frisby J. Cooper on the "Influence of Women," which the *Recorder* actually published in full and which recites the standard roles of mother, sister, teacher, and wife, emphasizing in each how women's influence could shape men—ranging from "the Apostle Paul of old" to Richard Allen and Daniel Payne.[20] But even when such venues served to distribute conservative views on gender, we need to note that they often *did* include both men and women as not just listeners but speakers, did significant work toward further establishing (albeit circumscribed) public roles for Black women, and placed participants in direct dialogue with a public culture that acknowledged, for example, young women teaching in the South. As the texts studied here suggest, individual women both connected to and separate from literary societies also published much more challenging work.[21]

As part of their charge tied to reading, ministers were especially encouraged to foster such societies with the specific recognition that they combined the social and the Social, and this could create some spaces for broadening senses of gender roles (as well as conceptions of class positions). Though the "festival" of the literary society of Philadelphia's Little Wesley discussed in the June 24, 1865, *Recorder*, for example, included "music, Mr. Joseph Freeman presiding at the melodeon, and several popular songs," it also featured to group's president Edward Evans speaking on "The Part the Colored Man Has Taken in the Rebellion, and His Rights as a Citizen." Such connections were just as pronounced in a March 7, 1863, *Recorder* report of a meeting of the "Oswego Gentlemen and Ladies' Literary and Lyceum Association" which, on March 3, 1863, debated the question "Is it the duty of the colored men of the North and South to fight?" Emphasizing the importance of the question—and perhaps tipping his hand as to which side he favored—the reporting pastor, John Leekin, added this postscript:

> Our quiet city was . . . last week, thrown into one of the most intense excitements ever known to the oldest inhabitants. A young contraband, who came home with an officer from the Army of the Potomac, was found in First Street, about 6 o'clock, A. M., in the last struggles of death, having been attacked on the night before, by three Irishmen who have since been arrested and convicted of the foul deed. The boy died on Saturday night at about 10 o'clock. . . . I preached the funeral service. They stabbed him twelve times in and about the head and neck, and left [him] for dead. . . . No cause whatever is given by the murderers, only that "he was a d—n nager [sic] came to take the work from us."

Leekin's letter thus neatly, frighteningly, not only shared the news but also emphasized how literary societies and church newspapers might help people—people at great risk—access and contextualize that news.[22]

Poetry was not far from politics in such constructions, either. Stevenson actually wrote poetry published in the *Recorder*: his October 5, 1861, "Prayer" speaks of "A Pattern still for us to be, / To lead us on to heaven," and his May 14, 1870, "Oh! Be Not the First" considers the difficulties caused by the fact that "We none of us know one another, / And oft into error do fall." If Meacham wrote poetry, it has not yet been found, but, according to his biographer, when he was flirting with a run for the US Congress, he chose to travel for two months in Florida's "heavily black areas in the train of charismatic orator" and poet "Mrs. F. E. W. Harper" (Brown "Where" 15).

This connection is of particular note because it embodies Harper and the *Recorder*'s own weaving of the poetic and the political and, more broadly, the *Recorder*'s recognition that its calls for reading ministers were always calls for Black writers. The Harper/Meacham trip saw Harper both recite her poems and lecture on Black rights, and it led to, among other writings, her essay "Land and Labor"—on two issues that were key concerns for Meacham, too—which was published in the November 19, 1870, *Recorder*. Always frank, Harper used part of that essay to argue that, while she did not "wish it to be understood that I would level all social distinctions," she was certain that "notwithstanding the intense prejudices of the white race, we could have made greater progress in the North had our sympathies been stronger and deeper with each other," as "there had been . . . a disposition among some of our people when they were favored by fortune, to draw the hem of their garments a little too carefully from social contact with others less favored." In this vein, she asserts that "there are colored men in the South whose names neither bard nor historian may ever celebrate in song or story" who "in their way . . . have been doing a needed work towards making freedom a success" through "helping others to get homes of their own and to plant their feet upon the soil."

If he read that essay, Meacham would likely have appreciated what must have seemed a kind of answer to Weaver's "Advice" to the recently freed people of the South. He also might have recognized—as Harper clearly did—that while (white) American print might never "celebrate in song or story" the growing sheaf of Black accomplishments, the *Recorder* could and would. This was yet another factor that made both reading and writing ministers (and lay people) essential. Decades after Payne first pushed for the course of study for AME ministers, leaders of the Church and the *Recorder* and a growing number of AME congregants recognized that ministers needed to be prepared to read such stories (individually and publicly), to integrate them into their preaching and teaching, to write them, and to make them available to their congregants. They, like the *Recorder*, needed to minister *using* print.

A major strategy of such a reading (and writing) ministry was a variation of old-style typology; applications of not simply Biblical stories but specific Bible verses to explain current events, to foretell future events, and to offer "right" responses to both appeared regularly in the *Recorder*. Because the Civil War quickly became the central event of the period, the *Recorder* put great energy in using reading (and writing) to address that nexus of concerns tied to politics, race, region, social theory and practice, faith, and violence. A June 22, 1861, piece titled "War Reading" recognizes that "Every body wants to know everything about the war now," but quickly pivots to "we have just been reading the book of the wars of the Lord, and know of no volume more appropriate to the present crisis." Urging all to "get a Bible," it tells readers to "read immediately Exodus, Joshua, Judges, Samuel, the Kings, and the Chronicles, straight through" as "most of our readers will thus learn a great many things about war, which they never knew before." The Bible, the piece argues, "tells us why war breaks out": "It is always a punishment for sins of the people." It also "will tell you . . . what every person ought to do in war times": "it instructs us to humble ourselves before God for our sins, to confess them to him, to ask his forgiveness for Christ's sake, and to put them away from us." While some Northerners hoped that Southerners might "put away" rebellion, this piece was already imagining a possible Black soldiery, telling readers "If you are called to go and fight against the rebels, go like a man, and pray to God to help you. . . . Gather your comrades to read the Bible and sing the psalms around the camp fire, and tell them that God's blessing gains the day." As it imagined reading ministers, so, too, did the paper conceptualize reading soldiers. Ministers were thus encouraged to aid their congregants in doing and in understanding "war reading," and *Recorder* editors as well as many contributors also took on this mission.[23]

The task took on special urgency with the mid-war entry of African Americans into the US military, an event whose importance to both the war effort and the Black polity has been discussed elsewhere.[24] The complexities of camp life, the distance between soldiers and their homes (and home churches), and the sometimes daily possibility of death amidst the horrors of war all demanded ministry—in part to ensure that Black soldiers and Black folks at home were "right with God." A November 9, 1861, piece titled "Thoughts for the Times" bluntly reminds, "O, how eloquent a preacher is death upon the battle ground! Can any soldier fail to hear him?" Similarly, the September 24, 1864, "An Important Letter on the Death of a Soldier"—sent by John Dawson, a sergeant in the 22nd USCT near Petersburg, Virginia—tells of how a fellow Black soldier "requested the loan of a Testament" and then "devoted the chief part of his time to reading its sacred pages." "About a week ago," the correspondent continues, "he was taken suddenly with fever, and soon lost his presence of mind." He died only days later, "but, in the midst of it all, he would say, 'I read it.' I asked him if it told him of heavenly things. He would gaze upon me with a bright countenance and glad smile, and say: 'Yes, yes, I read it.'"

This recognition motivated the *Recorder*'s calls—discussed earlier—to send the paper to Black soldiers; it similarly motivated much debate on both why and specifically *what* Black soldiers should read, debate that grew more complex when some of those same soldiers began writing to the paper themselves—and so turned themselves into not only an important group of *Recorder* subscribers but also *Recorder* writers. The *Recorder* initially took a page from broader Northern reformers' efforts to shape the reading of soldiers. The US Christian Commission's guidelines, published in, among other issues, the November 26, 1864, *Recorder*, includes this section:

> READING MATTER.
> Send no trash. Soldiers deserve the best. A library is a valuable hygienic appliance. For the able bodied, good publications are mental and spiritual food. For convalescents, lively, interesting books—the monthlies, the pictorials, works of art, science, and literature, as well as those for moral and spiritual culture, such as you would put into the hands of a brother recovering.
> STATIONARY IS MUCH NEEDED—paper, envelopes, and pencils.[25]

David Hovde, whose studies of the USCC and soldiers' reading are among the most detailed and valuable, reminds us that, beyond the multiple possibilities of dying suggested above, soldiers experienced "long periods . . . of boredom, homesickness, and despondency" that "threatened to make army life intolerable"—especially "during the winter months" (297). In this vein, the August 31, 1861, *Recorder* piece "Morals of Our Soldiers" told readers that "the field and the camp have never been schools of the domestic and social virtues, but ordinarily the reverse"—indeed, "the promiscuous assembling together in close companionship of such crowds of men, of all descriptions of character, many of them of the worst, tends greatly to the corruption of morals." Hovde cites white author John D. Billings's 1888 *Hardtack and Coffee*, which asserts that "There was no novel so dull, trashy, or sensational as not to find someone so bored with nothing to do that he would not wade through it. The mind was hungry for something, and took husks when it could be nothing better" (298).[26]

The USCC and the AME Church both came from a long tradition that associated idleness with (the potential for) evil, and both evinced strict Protestant worries over the moral damage that "trashy" and "sensational" fiction could do. The *Recorder* was expressing concern over soldiers' reading long before Black troops were allowed to enlist. The August 31, 1861, "Morals of Our Soldiers" mourned that "for want of better reading matter," many soldiers were "reading flimsy publications, obscene books, and the worst species of yellow-covered literature," and so "minds that were once fraught with holy aspirations and gleamed with the halo of heavenly light are now becoming like dingy cloisters, filled with cobwebs and the death-damps of groveling desires. Their religion is dying out for want of spiritual food." Paired with these worries was the concern that such reading could stoke "the evil passions engendered in the heat of the strife, the hatred, the revenge, the thirst for blood" and so "deprave the character of the soldier." As much a model as John Dawson's friend (reading his borrowed testament) was the image of "a Methodist preacher" (presented in a piece titled "Morals") who "was a remarkably sure shot" and who, assuming that each shot would kill, "each time after taking steady aim and firing" would say "And may the Lord have mercy on your soul!"

For both the USCC and the *Recorder*, then, the sense that "a library is a valuable hygienic appliance" was critical.[27] Soldiers, perhaps more than any other group of congregant-readers in the *Recorder*'s mind, needed careful guidance. As a February 28, 1863, *Recorder* item titled "Papers for the Army" asserts, "All admit that it is highly important that soldiers be furnished with good reading." "Good reading" for the *Recorder*, though, did not simply mean the kinds of tracts many religious organizations circulated—what Hovde suggests many soldiers dismissed as "goody-goody" print.[28] The paper viewed its mission and the term "good reading" much more broadly and thus spent significant resources on the genres discussed in the rest of this volume, even to the point of serializing its own (Black-authored, moralistic, and deeply political) novel, *The Curse of Caste*, in 1865. It also served as a valuable link between Black soldiers (like those pictured in Figure 5.2) and their home folks, who regularly shared local news in part simply so that far-off soldiers could read such. Thus, "Papers for the Army" could crow, "We are informed by those who are connected with the army, that no publications are read with so much avidity as religious newspapers." While the sense of soldier-readers as needing massive guidance never left the paper, though, as more and more copies of the *Recorder* became available to Black troops both through entities like the US Christian Commission and through direct subscriptions, more and more soldiers began writing *to* the paper. In the course of their letters, they often rewrote the paper's depictions of Black soldiers and Black soldiers' reading.

FIGURE 5.2 *A group of unidentified African American soldiers with books, possibly in South Carolina, late in the Civil War. Courtesy of the Prints and Photographs Division, Library of Congress (LC-B8184-0061).*

The study of Black soldiers' Civil War letters remains nascent. Edwin S. Redkey's 1992 *A Grand Army of Black Men: Letters from African American Soldiers in the Union Army, 1861–1865* was a breakthrough in collecting and sharing both the topic and significant samples—many drawn from the pages of the *Recorder*—and it worked alongside texts like the skillfully edited collection of the New Bedford *Mercury* letters of James Henry Gooding (a corporal in the famed Massachusetts 54th) that was published in 1991 under the title *On the Altar of Freedom: A Black Soldier's Civil War Letters from the Front*. But scholars who cite such texts are often drawn to how they talk about Black camp and war experiences rather than how they intervene in American print culture. Much work remains in terms of placing them in dialogue with the similarly nascent study of Black war literature or the growing body of literary history and literary criticism that recognizes the importance of correspondence.[29] These gaps mean that scholars still rarely see Black soldiers' letters as rhetorical acts. Keith P. Wilson's 2002 *Campfires of Freedom: The Camp Life of Black Soldiers During the Civil War* is sometimes the exception to this rule; it notes that white officers found "the growing stream of letters emanating from their camps as evidence of the soldiers' developing sense of moral responsibility" and thus argues that "It is perhaps ironic, then, that during their off-duty hours soldiers wrote thousands of protest letters about the behavior of line officers commanding them" (72). While Wilson understands that "letter writing thus became a powerful avenue of redress, an empowering pastime," most scholars leave their analysis at simply observing that irony.[30]

As the war continued, more soldiers' letters placed soldiers as actors who were praying—and demanding—that those at home also act. Even when Henry McNeal Turner spoke of the need for spelling books for basic literacy instruction among some Black soldiers and asserted that "there was never such an anxiety to learn to read and write"—as he did in his October 8, 1864, letter to the paper—he also wrote that every time he entered camp with print, his "quarters are invaded by hundreds of soldiers" shouting for texts. These soldiers were literally taking literacy as they were taking Southern territory, one Union victory at a time. As they became more and more engaged with print, Turner recognized that many were turning to the *Recorder*. As Turner notes in his December 17, 1864 letter, "The Recorder is looked for weekly, as a precious visitor, in this part of our noble army. It is dearly prized by many of our gallant soldiers who, I am happy to say, are trying to prepare for whatever position the future may offer them: likely nothing could have inspired a more eager ambition into the men of my regiment, for literary attainments, than the vast number of Recorders and Anglo[-African]s, which weekly find their way into our different companies."

The September 17, 1864, *Recorder*'s "A Soldier's Entreaty to Those at Home," a long piece by Quartermaster Sergeant James H. Payne—then of the 27th United States Colored Troops—suggests some of the parameters of how soldiers' letters reconstructed the paper's representations of Black military presences and Black soldiers' reading. Letters like Payne's had become a regular *Recorder* feature by the publication of his "Entreaty," and that same September 17, 1864, issue also acknowledged Payne's submission of funds for an individual subscription.[31] Initially, the paper welcomed such letters because they offered news of the war—especially on Black engagement—that was simply unavailable in most other periodicals, and the *Recorder* regularly reminded subscribers at home that the presence of such letters made the paper one of the best ways to have at least some sense of the lives and actions of Black soldiers. As the war continued, such letters became a more and more significant feature, and, in the wake of arguments for equal pay for Black soldiers and horrors like the Fort Pillow Massacre, Black soldiers' letters spoke more often on a wide swath of issues tied to what the nation should look like after emancipation and the hoped-for Union victory. In several pieces both before and after his "Entreaty," Payne—who had been born in Mason County, Kentucky, and was already involved with the AME Church—wrote specifically to those who "sympathize with the poor soldiers in the field," with the express intent of shifting representations surrounding those "poor soldiers."

Payne wanted Black soldiers to be recognized as men who had left home and family at great personal sacrifice "at their country's call, to rescue her from the hand of bloody treason, and to restore the glorious flag of our Union to its former" place—as well as "to carry into effect the Abrahamic Proclamation of 1863." His "Entreaty" asks "our friends at home" to see Black soldiers standing "between them and their enemies, like Aaron of old (Numb. 16:48) ... to stay the plague." He requests not "meat, not bread, nor clothes" nor even "money"; rather, he prays for "a great lot of those heaven-gift books"—especially Bibles and testaments. But even those Bibles and testaments had different resonances in Payne's letters: they were tools for helping actuate lives worth living and life stories worth telling. In this frame, Payne's soldiers were on the edge of not just becoming good readers, but also becoming "authors" of texts worth reading. Payne imagines "some poor soldier who went into the field a wicked and careless sinner" who was moved to cry "from the depth of his soul: 'God be merciful to me, a sinner.'" Payne tells readers that the soldier's cry was not "in vain," for "God ... comforted his heart," and that when he finally fell, "he could say: 'I not only fell a soldier for my country, but, better than all, I am a soldier for Christ.'" Then he adds, "Mr. Editor, would not such a narration be worth reading?"[32]

Payne's title entreaty, though, does not simply ask the paper to include soldiers' stories or ask *Recorder* readers to revise their senses of Black soldiers (from readers to writers); rather, it pushes readers to act. The first action he outlines—consonant with several earlier and later letters—was donating funds for books and periodicals or even sending such materials themselves. Even here, Payne was more blunt than many. His "Entreaty" notes that "some will be apt to say: 'The soldiers have more money to spend for Bibles than I have.' Suppose the minister sent out to preach the word says: 'The people can read it better than I can preach it. Therefore, let them read it.'" His analogy of the unwilling supporter at home as a lazy minister foretells comments in his October 1, 1864, letter: "I know that there are a great many ministers who are at home, some of whom are good for nothing, and will always be so while they sit down and content themselves at home." In kinder but no less direct language, Payne asserts that the AME Church "will not only require an active ministry, but likewise an active membership." It was the folks at home, Payne thus argues, who needed to do as much or more soul searching as Black soldiers; just as Payne emphasized that reading soldiers were historical actors, so, too, did he demand that *Recorder* readers at home had to act.[33]

When Theodore Rodgers wrote to agree with Lizzie Hart and Elisha Weaver's words on Black soldiers, he was working within the same structures: he was offering approval of the ways the pieces he cited "got it right." Remember, Rodgers wrote in his September 10, 1864, letter—published just a week before Payne's "Entreaty"—that "All we want is that those at home should take care of our families, and speak cheerful words to us, [and] do their duty as Christians" and "we will do ours as soldiers."

Payne's sense of those print-centered actions went well beyond Bibles and testaments. His January 14, 1865, letter thanks the Bethel Sabbath School of Hamilton, Ohio, for "a very welcome and cherished gift"—a box that not only held sixty testaments and five bibles but also "21 Sabbath School volumes, 18 magazines, 17 hymn-books, and a few copies of the 'Colored Citizen' of Cincinnati." "May God bless them," Payne writes, "and happily reward them for their Christian deeds." His letter, though, ends not just with thanks, but with another call "for more Testaments, and other good articles of reading matter." "Dear readers," he writes, "having delivered you this information, I hope you will do all that you can to supply our need. That god may bless the churches and Sabbath Schools, and open their eyes and hearts both, to this duty, is my sincere prayer." Here, Black soldiers *were* or would willingly *become* readers: they needed texts rather than needing to be convinced of the value of reading. The "dear readers" at home were the people who needed to "open their eyes and hearts both" to their holy duty. Not surprisingly, the letter was headed "Who Will Do Likewise?"

Other texts, like Payne's November 12, 1864, letter, placed the *Recorder* itself high among needed texts: "Is it not a marvel that such a paper should be found in this land of oppression, where every thing has worked against us? Yet it is a fact. We have one, which is the production of a colored man's genius. May God ever smile upon the editor of the *Christian Recorder*, and find him ample support, while he lives, to do good in the world!"

Many soldiers' letters—including Payne's—came to speak of the paper lovingly. One such letter, published in the December 10, 1864, issue under the heading "A Good Letter from a Soldier," calls the paper "an old friend."[34] This soldier writes of receiving his copy of the *Recorder*, but, as it "was only one" copy, he "tore it into two pieces, and allowed the one-half to one part of the company while I read my part to the balance." He concludes, "They were very eager to see and read it." If these physical acts—reading aloud, even ripping the paper in half so that another could read it aloud to even more soldiers—were not enough, Turner's December 17, 1864 letter essentially suggests that recent *Recorder* texts (which came heavily from soldiers) had reshaped the paper: "When it was first resurrected from its long entombed silence," the *Recorder* "continued for some time to be the organ of pic-nics, fine suppers, Sabbath-school demonstrations, and such other trashy matter, as no well-informed person could be induced to appreciate. But the day of small things was not to be despised: with good reason and effort on its side, it ploughed through every seeming impossibility, and has begun to demand a respect that none dare gainsay. I have lately read several articles with pleasure, that the faulty ones could not mar. Theology, philosophy, science, and all other questions connected with religious literature, are now treated or discussed with a surprising masterliness."

As they were changing the face of the war—Turner, Payne, and a host of others argued—Black soldiers were also changing the face of Black print. While the paper initially focused on ministering to them, by the war's end, it recognized that many Black soldiers were ministerial forces in their own right. Many saw reading and writing as a dialogic circuit, an exchange, a way of drawing connections over miles and circumstances. They reinforced—again and again—the sense that textual engagement would strengthen their participation in a post-war nation.

In her own way, Lizzie Hart was part of this striving to re-see Black soldiers and Black readers, and her lively commentary on Fort Pillow, the disputes over equal pay, and the future roles of Black soldiers all testify to how deeply she hoped that print could aid liberation. But Hart also wrote of the troubles she faced writing for the *Recorder*, as in her December 30, 1865, letter: "Some have sneeringly inquired why I meddle about the rights or wrongs of the braves who have defended the country." She fired back: "Have I not a right to do so? Is not this a free country? Am I not an American woman, born and reared on American soil? Have I not been subject to the oppressive laws of the land? Have I not a right to complain? I earnestly hope, that the day is not far distant, when we, as American men and women, long and wrongfully oppressed, both in the North and South, shall enjoy all the rights of a free and happy land." But sadly, even Hart stopped writing for the paper—this letter seems to be her last *Recorder* publication—as she moved toward courtship and marriage.

The challenges to and complications of women's public speech—oral or written—removed more than Hart's voice from the *Recorder*. The Church leadership and polity had debated women's possible public roles in the AME Church almost since its founding, but even in Jarena Lee's long shadow, the Church would ordain no women until decades after the period studied here. Several single women and some married women did write for the *Recorder*, but fewer were as assertive as Hart. Many were affected by the threads of conservatism often prominent in both the Church and the paper.[35]

The editors were generally more friendly to the idea (and the practice) of women *reading*, in part for the pecuniary reasons outlined in chapters 3 and 4. In this vein, Weaver published a May 4, 1861, item titled "Ladies Should Read Newspapers," suggesting that "If you would qualify" a young woman "for conversation, you must give her something to talk about, give her education with the actual world and its transpiring events." The piece directs the reader "qualifying" a young woman to "urge her to read newspapers and become familiar with the present character and improvements of our race." Tellingly—and not unlike the paper's worried commentary on what soldiers might be reading—this piece positions such reading against or at least beside "the fashionable literature of the day": "Let the gilded annuals and poems on the centre table be kept part of the time covered with journals."

The transition between reading and writing, however, that many Black soldiers made—and the circuits they built—were more difficult for single women to engage in for a host of reasons. Lizzie Hart's participation in the reading-writing-reading process helps us understand how Julia Collins could be given enough time and space for the serialization of *Curse of Caste*, but the comparative rarity of such women writers demands that we consider women who were less prominent and less successful in engaging with the *Recorder*, too.

To hint at the parameters in which these women operated, to mark some of the difficulties they faced, and to suggest the ways that single women readers might both succeed and fail as writers for the *Recorder*, I submit the example of Annie M. Smith, the Black schoolteacher in Xenia, Ohio, who wrote, as mentioned in the last chapter, that Weaver "accidentally called me Mrs. A. M. Smith" when "it should have been Miss." She first subscribed to the *Recorder* in September of 1862, dutifully paying for her subscription and planning to go the post office weekly for the next year, pay postage, and pick up her paper. Whether she renewed in 1863 remains unclear; I have found no extant acknowledgment. She did renew in 1864. Again, I have found no extant acknowledgment; the trace of that renewal is solely in her letter correcting her honorific. Thus, like some Black soldier-writers, Smith actually began writing for the *Recorder* as a writer in part to correct a representation of her that she had read there.

However, the December 3, 1864, letter that offered her correction—"the first time I address your most noble paper"—was much more than a simple clarification. As it was for Black soldier-writers, for Hart, and select others, subscribing to the *Recorder* was arguably a kind of gateway act in their struggles for print presences: it not only brought the paper into their homes—connecting those homes with all sorts of larger polities—but also led to their names appearing in the paper's public acknowledgments. Like other acknowledgments, the acknowledgment for a woman's subscription often included her place of residence (marking her as a citizen of a specific locale) and the amount of capital she traded for the paper (marking her as a citizen in terms of commerce, speaking materially of either class position or of class aspirations). In other words, the acknowledgments acknowledged these women's places in communities *and* their joining of additional communities in the Church and the world of Black print. Because of this—and because she was a teacher, whose job may well have depended on her being "proper" and single—Smith wanted to ensure that her listing in the *Recorder*'s acknowledgments was correct.

But her letter placed her as *both* a reader and a writer—and not simply in wanting to correct her naming as a reader. Intriguingly, much of this first letter focuses on gender and specifically on young women *as* readers—though not always in glowing terms. In an "appeal ... principally to the young ladies," she directly addresses her colleagues—"Young ladies, please listen to me"—and urges them to "lay aside the novel" and "those musings which have a tendency to produce evil" because "our native country is being revolutionized" and "our brave fathers, brothers, and lovers are on the field of strife and bloodshed, fighting for liberty and justice." "It is too frequently the case," she asserts, "that many burn the midnight taper over a senseless love story" or the "details of some heroine." Nonetheless, she clearly did not think all reading to be "unbeneficial reading"; while she calls for "sewing circles" for the needy, she also calls for "those who are educated" to "teach the illiterate."[36] Women—and especially young single women—must "think of those who have recently escaped from bondage" and those still enslaved. They must thus both read and write accordingly. Her letter itself stood, of course, as an example of such appropriate writing, but it also contains another example of the kinds of writing to be encouraged—a report of the organization of the (almost-all-female) Freedmen's Aid Society at Xenia's AME Church, of which Smith had been elected secretary.

Though Smith's letter had the support of both her locally elected office and her "membership" as a *Recorder* subscriber, she was much more hesitant to suggest that she might—at this point—be a correspondent. She ventured only, "perchance it may be that I will fail to write as flowery a piece for publication as those which grace your most valued columns from week to week, but practice makes perfect"—hinting that perhaps she would "practice" more. When she sent another piece (published in the March 4, 1865, *Recorder*), she shifted from the language of "practice" to suggest that she was actually fulfilling a "promise" to "pen a few promiscuous thoughts." Under this warrant of obligation, her text—headed "Astronomy" but still formatted as a letter—and her May 20, 1865, "Xenia Correspondence" edged closer to establishing a place for her as a regular writer. Both stretch beyond her first letter's emphasis on simply reporting location-specific news, and both also have the distinct tenor of a novice trying to prove herself. "Astronomy" makes significant effort to demonstrate wide (but still appropriate) reading in not only the title subject but also mathematics, classics, and religion, and it participates in a subgenre not uncommon in the *Recorder*: science writing that emphasizes "the very many mansions which the Great Architect has prepared." It figures a sample star's distance from the sun, for example, and it ends with a quote (with a translation) from Virgil. Her May 20, 1865, "Xenia Correspondence" opens with a sentence in French and closes with "Notre ami, Annie M. Smith." It mixes reportage of a Xenia event honoring the memory of Abraham Lincoln with religious-political commentary that positions Lincoln as "our modern Moses."

Both of these pieces demonstrate what she asserts could be gained if readers, especially women, would "lay aside the novel." Smith's choice of subject matter falls decidedly within the bounds of the knowledge identified in "Ladies Should Read Newspapers," the expectations of Smith's place as a young teacher, and the *Recorder*'s growing acknowledgment of the importance of well-educated women (in part to teach the newly freed). But these structures also allowed Smith's first real gestures toward the fuller print commentary of women writers like Lizzie Hart (and Edmonia Highgate, discussed in the next chapter). Her post-Lincoln assassination "Xenia Correspondence," tells, for example, of how her "city is draped in mourning. The flags are at half-mast and draped also. Even all nature seems to be shrouded in mourning, and lament the loss of one so great, so noble, and so true." That said, even as she was offering her own opinions and observations, she still limited her role, and this work was fully in line with the paper's varying but often still conservative sense of women's "proper" place(s). The final sections of her "Xenia Correspondence," for example, veer from her thoughts to say "I wish to insert a sermon, delivered by the Rev. Mr. Kendrick, on the 16th of April."[37] That sermon takes the rest of the piece. While Smith's reporting style—and the fact that the sermon follows her own letter—are clear reminders of this young woman's deep engagement with (and production of) print, she does not move toward the assertiveness of Hart, many of the paper's ministerial contributors, or several soldier-writers.

In some ways, Smith's September 30, 1865, "Letter from Xenia, Ohio" shifts these parameters—at least a bit. The "letter" portion is actually quite short: it reports on the proceedings of the Xenia AME Church Aid Society in two brief paragraphs. The remainder of the long piece consists of an essay Smith "was called upon to read" to that group, "she being notified at a previous monthly meeting to prepare." The quick description of the occasion—which functions in many ways as a warrant—thus places her essay's inclusion as simply part of her reporting duties, much like her reporting of Kendrick's sermon. She thus "reports" almost two columns of her own discussion of "Motives to Practical Charity, or, Good Works." The essay itself is relatively conservative in its sense of gender—positioning charity as a "she" but emphasizing distant representativeness rather than women's specific felt experiences, offering limited first-person argument, and making few moves to explore genre or voice. What is striking about this contribution, rather, is its use of a short letter to open the door to the publication of the essay—an essay of such significant size that the September 30, 1865, publication ends "to be continued" and leads to another column-and-a-half in the October 7, 1865, issue.

Smith's October 14, 1865, letter "Progress of Christianity through the Instrumentality of Missions" begins with more positioning to explain her place in print: "Mr. Editor:—I am fearful that I will become annoying to the public, because I write so frequently." Focusing on the Wilberforce Missionary Society and including her transcription of a speech by T. H. Jackson that shares its title with the article heading, this piece is more notable for its Franklinian humility, as two more pieces of her work appear in the *same* issue. Her "Xenia Correspondence" opens "Again amid the bustlings of social enjoyment, I find my pen moving with great rapidity, in consequence of the varied, passing scenes," and her "Notes by the Way" offers an even more direct warrant: "I have not forgotten the relation which I hold with your most valuable and interesting paper." Having three pieces by a single non-editor in a single issue of the *Recorder* was rare; at the very least, it did indeed mark a "relation"—far beyond "practice" or a one-time promise. Smith was looking more and more like a regular correspondent, and, as such, while the Wilberforce report echoes her earlier local summaries, the other two pieces range more widely across genre, voice, subject matter, and approach. Her "Xenia Correspondence" reports on the city's celebration of emancipation, but also quotes from Joseph Rodman Drake's poem "The American Flag," reflects on how she was drawn to compare "life to a river . . . amidst mountain scenery," evaluates John Mercer Langston's address ("he did justice to himself"), and promises to forward a copy of the speech.

Her "Notes by the Way" moves even more deeply toward linking the personal and the political, placing her life in dialogue with what she reports, and drawing connections between the national and the local. She opens by praising the men of the 54th Massachusetts—"gallant heroes," "ornaments of society," and "blessings to their country"—in part to introduce her recognition that "these are progressive times, and we need those who are energetic, and disposed to ascend . . . to lead the van[guard]." This conclusion, in turn, brings her to reflect on education generally and "the school of which I have had charge for the last year" specifically. Because she feels "the grand principles of progression" need to be "infused in the hearts of youth," she is deeply concerned that, even though her school was "progressing finely," many parents were "not interested in the future welfare of their children"—so much so that they demanded diplomas without work or attendance, defended "violators of school regulations," and sometimes sent children to school "to get them out of their sight, because they are so wild that they cannot control them themselves." She urges all of her readers—obviously not just single women now—to metaphorically "go South," where schools for the newly freed were seeing "not only . . . the young but the middle-aged and the gray-haired persons seeking after knowledge, if it be but only to learn to read the Bible." There, she asserts, "every one is eager to gather the precious treasures of books." She tells her readers to "arouse from your lethargic dreams, and study the lessons of progression," so as to live "in the sunlight of knowledge."

Such linkages allowed her to further explore first-person, introspective print spaces in her October 21, 1865, letter headed "An Evening Walk," in which she writes of having a group of "intelligent" friends "in whom we confide" and with whom she could share "a retrospective glance at the past" and "dream[s] of the future." Here, in addition to providing the kinds of texts she thought readers—including single women readers like herself—needed, she speaks of widening the purview of "reading," noting that "observers of nature" could see much on such walks, including, in a complex turn, those "who are destitute," whose "crime may be unpardonable," or who might be in "excruciating and unavoidable pain." The lessons from such "reading" were the same lessons she hoped her own writing would teach readers: "let it be our desire to do good" and "let our evening walk not only terminate in self-enjoyment, but in the enjoyment and pleasure of others."

Her November 25, 1865, "Letter from Xenia" not only moves back to location-specific reporting—this time, of the actions of the Xenia Female Benevolent Society, the members of which she characterizes as "busy bees" "alive to the noblest sentiments of pity and benevolence"—but also marks further growth into a correspondent's role. It ranges across subject, genre, and approach even as it offers news to keep the connection informed of its various parts, and it pairs that news with individualized consideration of pressing questions of faith, especially as they might play out in the "new" world after the end of the Civil War. Though she sees "vices about us," she knows that "life is labor" and that "from the inmost heart of the worker rises *her* God-given force, the sacred celestial life essence, breathed into *her* by Almighty God," which "from *her* inmost heart awakens *her* to all nobleness, to all knowledge, 'self-knowledge,' and much else" (italics mine), Annie M. Smith was finding a print voice rich and complex—from "her inmost heart."

But the nexus of reading and writing was not always ideal for single women; even as Annie Smith began to carve out a place among the *Recorder*'s correspondence, she remained in that print venue only at the editor's whim. Smith's November 25, 1865, letter seems to have been her last. The same issue includes an editor's item that reads, in part, "On the first page will be found a communication from Xenia, Ohio. We see that the same appears in the [Cincinnati] *Colored Citizen* of Nov[ember]. 18th." Weaver quickly moves from observation—in painful irony, an observation based on his reading—to attack: "We mention this fact, because this sage writer sent the same article to two different newspapers, and gave each of us to understand that it was written expressly for us." After quickly and decisively dismissing Smith's knowledge and ability—"this sage writer"—Weaver pivots to ignore her and to focus on "our friend," B. K. Sampson, the editor of the *Citizen*, imploring him to "see that we have not violated any rule of professional etiquette."

All evidence suggests that Weaver's relationship with the *Citizen* was good. He praised the paper regularly, telling readers of the November 26, 1864, *Recorder*, for example, that the paper was "flourishing and progressing finely," in part because it was edited by "our worthy, enterprising, and classical friend, Mr. Sampson." Weaver even suggested that "any person residing in Philadelphia who may wish to subscribe to this worthy paper, can do so by calling at our office." As late as the July 28, 1866, issue, the *Recorder* spoke of Sampson as a friend—noting that he was leaving the *Citizen* to "make a tour in Europe exhibiting a panorama" that "is said to be one of the finest in the country." (Indeed, even Smith's twice-appearing "Letter from Xenia" praises Sampson—reporting that he had "delivered the annual address," "did justice to himself and the audience," and was "most eloquent.") It seems unlikely that Weaver needed to soothe Sampson so publicly. He was also not one to talk about labeling original material, as he was often quite sloppy in crediting material he clipped from other newspapers and included verbatim in the *Recorder*. (The

"Letters from Olympus" discussed in the next chapter, for example, were all lifted from the *Lutheran and Missionary* without any citation whatsoever.)

In short, Weaver overreacted, and that reaction—a snarky description of a young woman (barely nineteen) who had just finished her first year of teaching and was just beginning to write in earnest—may have done some damage. As mentioned in chapter 4, Xenia (to say nothing of nearby Wilberforce) had a notable concentration of subscribers, and those subscribers were men and women who went to church with Smith and who employed her as their schoolteacher. If there were any who took both papers (and there might have been some), they might have noticed the duplicated story—or they might not have. It is much more likely, though, that they noticed Weaver's page two editor's item—titled "Our Letter from Xenia, Ohio," complete with the multiply signifying "our." The dearth of extant issues of the *Colored Citizen* prevents us from knowing the extent of Smith's work there and from knowing whether Sampson issued any response to the twice-appearing piece or to Weaver's attack. What we do know, though, is that Smith published nothing else in the *Recorder*. She may have even stopped subscribing—unless the "Ann M. Smith" noted in a list of late 1866 subscribers represents another mistaken listing by Weaver. She was still teaching in Xenia in 1870, but I have found neither later biographical records nor any evidence of later writing or publication. Her short *Recorder* career ended almost before it had fully begun.[38]

If Smith continued to read the *Recorder*, she would have seen the growing push for reading and writing ministers (and ministers ministering through reading and writing), in part because of the massive efforts to ensure alphabetic literacy for the newly freed people and in part because the AME connection continued to grow, thus making textual communication even more essential. Black Union soldiers' letters would continue to be published into 1866, but by then the US military and Black service were also already morphing. Some Black Civil War soldiers went on to become ministers, teachers, politicians, and local church activists, and they continued to write in their new incarnations. The Black soldier's letter, though, underwent a massive generic shift: eventually, it became one of the modes through which the paper and the Church interacted with the American West, the fallout of the removal of First Peoples from the East, the "Indian wars" against the West's native peoples, and the "closing" of the frontier. What had been a genre that sometimes radically challenged US military policy would lean toward reification of the nation's colonialism. Simultaneously, former soldiers (and many of those who stayed home during the war) used letters to fashion Civil War Black soldiers into icons of nationalism, as part of the kinds of battles Julie Roy Jeffrey studies in *Abolitionists Remember*. Many letters thus invoked Black Civil War service in terms of wider citizenship, engaging with issues ranging from suffrage debates to Black participation in the Grand Army of the Republic and other veterans groups.[39] In both cases, the paper's senses of reading and writing continued to emphasize growing Black participation and to insert the AME Church into the wider American print culture. That said, the individuality within these processes sometimes narrowed—especially after Tanner's entry as editor and specifically after the moves to focus on what Julius Bailey describes as "race patriotism," a sensibility that sometimes limited generic flexibility, authorship, and individual voices in favor of modeling a more specific set of uplift goals.

Women's reading of and writing for the paper—and representations of such—were much more uneven. Had Smith continued reading the *Recorder*, she would have seen other women writers—including some she may have known (e.g., Mary E. Ashe, a Wilberforce student and longtime AME activist discussed briefly in chapter 7). But Smith also would have seen increasingly dismissive words from some ministers and writers (including editors) about "schoolgirl essays" and sometimes about women's speech generally. Such commentary often appeared in the same issues as some of the most important literary writing—and most important women's writing—in the paper, including three serialized novels and several shorter pieces from Frances Ellen Watkins Harper. Women readers would have also seen challenge after challenge to the Church's gender hierarchy shunted aside by Church leaders—from the creation of the position of "stewardess" in 1868 (in answer to increasing calls for women's ordination) to the creation of a stunningly complex set of what Jualynne Dodson calls "parallel structures" for women's church activism with the goal of maintaining male dominance in existing structures (49). Those parallel structures entered the *Recorder* regularly—and sometimes formally, as in the paper's late nineteenth-century exploration of "women's" columns—but much work remained in terms of exploring the paper's sense of what and how women (especially young single women) might read, write, and be.

{ 6 }

"So Let Us Hear from All the Brethren": The *Christian Recorder* and Correspondence

Edmonia Goodelle Highgate rode a borrowed roan through the Louisiana countryside. She joked about the horse in her "On Horse Back—Saddle Dash, No.1" published in the November 3, 1866, *Recorder*: "like everything else here," the horse "was Creole, and I am afraid rather *confederate* in his tendencies; for when I was feeling lost, almost[,] to my surroundings in some meditations of an intensely union cast, he had the bad taste to get into a fence leaping mood." For all her humor, Highgate also knew it was risky for a Black teacher to ride unaccompanied around Lafayette Parish; during the second ride she wrote about in this very piece, "some rebel equestrians ... passed, and fired four times almost in my face." Her witty, faith-centered rejoinder shows the courage only brought forth from real fear: "But who is going to let grape[shot] keep them off horse back or off duty? Hasn't He promised to keep His workers? 'Then to doubt would be disloyal; to falter would be sin.'"[1]

Readers of Highgate's previous contributions to the paper—especially her letters from earlier that year headed "Letter from New Orleans" (March 17, 1866) and "New Orleans Correspondence" (July 7, 1866, and August 18, 1866)—also knew that danger had driven Highgate *to* Lafayette Parish. Running the Frederick Douglass School for African American children in New Orleans, she was caught in the July 30, 1866, rioting in which armed police attacked Black Republicans who were meeting to strengthen post-war African American political participation. In the "saturnalia of blood" that she described in her August 18, 1866, letter, she had done "what she could of wound-dressing until near midnight" on the day of the riots.[2] Later, as the city was put under martial law and African American activists were publicly threatened, friends persuaded her to leave the city and take charge of a similar school for the recently freed people of Vermillionville, just outside Lafayette.

Such tension, though, did not stop Highgate from doing what she did throughout her life: exercising both physical and intellectual mobility in the midst of—indeed, *as* a—duty. The opening of "On Horse Back" asked, "Who that has taught school, the elementary branches year in and year out" doesn't "know what teacher's *ennui* is . . . ? But for my roan, I would break down as a harp unstrung." As soon as her "day-school is out" she would be "on his back, and off on a quick gallop for these grand October woods" to explore and to reflect. Those woods offered her beauty beyond the hard world, something magical that she marked as Transcendental: "I plunged into the thickest of the oak tree forest with its exquisite drapery of gray hanging moss. The old dame must have anticipated some children visitors, for she had swings ready made, formed of thick inter-lapping vine-like branches, reaching from treetop to treetop all through these woods. What delightful order! Oh, if dear Henry D. Thoreau were here, wouldn't he go into a rhapsody! But he is here in spirit."

Stunning for a host of reasons—why were we never taught about the possibility of an African American Transcendentalist (re)envisioning the woods surrounding Walden Pond in dialogue with South Central Louisiana?—Highgate's letters to the *Recorder* open and close this chapter both to foreground the amazing diversity of correspondence published in the *Recorder* and to introduce a range of questions such letters call on us to consider.[3] Specifically, building from the last chapter's understanding of the letter to the editor as a transitional document linking reading and writing, this chapter explores the correspondence published in the *Recorder* as a central mode for defining and redefining community and nation. It articulates the *Recorder*'s paired senses of correspondents as writers of personal letters and public conveyors of news and ideas from specific locations and thus studies how the paper constructed the genre broadly as a varying mix of news report, travelogue, autobiography, sermon, and essay.[4] Such work highlighted the tensions between the paper's goals of building a united community and offering public spaces for individual and individualized African American voices; thus, the paper's letters marked and challenged not only the geographic boundaries of the "connexion" but also its metaphysical spaces.

Given the massive geographic diversity and mobility of the paper's subscribers—and the expanding reach of the Church that such factors embodied—joining the far churches and congregants together through print was, as discussed earlier, one of the *Recorder*'s central assigned functions. Letters from individuals in the AME clergy, the AME laity, and beyond thus regularly filled at least a quarter and often half of the paper's space. As a kind of "Christian recording" that was (theoretically) open to most readers (and subscribers), letters attempted to link diverse individuals and entities spread across thousands of miles and to foster national dialogue on key issues of the day. However, such "recording" was carried out by diverse individuals without, as mentioned in chapter 3 and in the discussion below, consistently clear editorial guidelines or even consistent editorial policies and practices. Even the newsiest pieces of correspondence among the paper's letters were—Highgate's more news-centered letters included—perhaps inherently, often deeply individualistic and thus also a genre about which editors (and some minister-readers in the Church hierarchy) were sometimes deeply ambivalent.

To further explore the *Recorder*'s letters—the vast majority of which remain totally ignored by scholars—this chapter first considers some of the expressions of that ambivalence to begin to articulate common structures, tropes, and themes. Specifically, the first section of the chapter considers some of what the paper said it would *not* publish—even as it actively called for letters—to suggest the contours of the letters submitted and ultimately published. From this base, I study two *Recorder* correspondents who the paper embraced, even as they broke some of the spoken and unspoken editorial rules of correspondence: Daniel P. Adger, whose six letters from Australia were published in 1864, and Highgate, who wrote at least eighteen pieces for the paper between 1865 and 1867, generally in the form of letters. My consideration of Adger's work focuses on what his discussion of (massive) physical mobility offered the *Recorder* community; though Highgate's physical mobility was also a crucial part of her *Recorder* correspondence, my exploration of her work centers instead on her promise and practice of intellectual mobility. Throughout, I begin to envision the possibilities and boundaries of *Recorder* correspondence, a subject that demands much further scholarship in part because it marks the entry of a much wider base of African Americans into the realm of literary letters and a significant shift in early African American literature and print culture.[5]

The *Recorder* called for letters regularly. Potential contributors were told—as in a May 31, 1862, piece titled "Correspondence"—that "we shall look for representatives from all parts of our connexion, stations and circuit . . . so let us hear from all the brethren." An August 23, 1866, editorial asserts, "we are glad to get communications, and though we get more than we publish, we want more, because among so many we get a great deal that is precious." A February 23, 1867, piece, simply called "Write to Us," says

> We earnestly solicit correspondence from all parts of the United States. Let every one who has anything to say, send it on to us. We hope no one will feel backward on account of their church relations, [because] we are not influenced by the denominational idea. We like, and welcome a good communication no matter who it comes from.
>
> Let our ministerial brethren forward every item of interest; now is the time we are making history.

Both of these later pieces, however, also add, per the August 25, 1866, editorial, that "those who write for our paper" should "*get subscribers also*, as nothing puts a correspondent on better terms with the editor and publisher than getting subscribers for the paper." The February 23, 1867, call similarly reminds, "Don't forget in the meantime, to send a cash subscriber, [which] always makes us smile and feel very pleasant towards you."

Such financial hints to potential contributors formed one major base for (potential) rejection. In this vein, editors regularly chastised letter writers for not placing sufficient postage on their submissions: according to the February 13, 1864, "To Our Correspondents," Weaver went "three times a day . . . to the Post Office, and, we regret to say, in many instances we are compelled to pay from three to twelve cents on a single letter. . . . There can be no excuse for such persistent and willful disregard. . . . [I]f correspondents . . . persist in their neglect, they must blame themselves if their articles are not published." These issues were, of course, tied to the larger problem of the continuing lack of adequate financial support from the broader connection discussed in chapters 2 and 3. Writing after taking over from Weaver, Benjamin Tucker Tanner put it bluntly in his August 8, 1868, "Editorial News": "The amount of original matter which each number of the *Recorder* contains is a mere matter of finance. We usually have six or seven columns; we could have fifteen or twenty just as well; if the brethren would only lift the collection ordered."

Turner's "fifteen or twenty" was likely an understatement, as the period saw not only African Americans "making history" but also creating texts about that history (and from within that history) in greater numbers than ever before. Thus, whether or not they financially supported the paper, readers and others did send correspondence. The August 25, 1866, editorial claims that "It is no exaggeration to say that we have on hand a half bushel of communications for the *Christian Recorder*. They come from all parts of the United States. Now we cannot insert them all unless the *Christian Recorder* were as large as a double blanket. Some will feel slighted who got the 'go by.' We are very sorry, but cannot help it."

The paper was rarely this apologetic about what it couldn't—or wouldn't—publish. Editors often—building from their comments on the ways finances limited the size of the paper—criticized the length of potential contributions. Tanner used his same August 8, 1868, column to chastise long-winded contributors: "A brother sends us a letter complaining that we did not publish an eight page communication. Do, my dear brother, be charitable, to yourself, to the editor, and to the reader." In this, he echoed earlier editors, who repeatedly—as in a July 27, 1867 item titled "Too Long"—told contributors that if they wished "their communications to appear in our columns, they must make them short and to the point" and then, more aggressively, asserted that "we cannot and will not consent to occupy our limited space with an indifferently written article, extending through eight or ten sheets of foolscap, and of no earthly interest to anyone." "We aim to do justice to all," contended

Weaver in his August 3, 1867, "Long Letters," but then claimed that he could not publish "these remarkable 'fifteen-sheeters'" from individuals when he considered "the colored population at four millions" who potentially demanded equal space: "we cannot accomplish impossibilities."

Such concerns set broad rules for the *Recorder* community. For example, although the paper allowed pseudonyms—Weaver and his fellows repeatedly reminded potential contributors that even if they were writing under pseudonyms, the paper still needed to know their full names; he even, in a February 11, 1865, "Notice," wrote that "anonymous articles hereafter shall receive no attention whatever at our hands." Editors recognized that linking this kind of public (partial) anonymity with the potentially personal form of the letter opened up massive possibilities for personal attacks. Thus, Weaver appended a caution at the end of a December 17, 1864, piece headed "Harrisburg Correspondence" from "Minnie": "Our correspondents must not be personal; if so, we will not publish." Among other myriad examples of warnings issued to writers from being "too personal," a September 20, 1862, item titled "Not Published" chastises a contributor who used "language too personal in reference to one of our correspondents" and reminds readers that "we cannot indulge in a vicious taste for personal *flings* and feuds . . . not even from our regular correspondents or subscribers." Lynch's February 10, 1866, "To Our Correspondents" emphasizes that such writers should "not blame us for your own persistent carelessness."[6]

Beyond these general parameters—and we might even say complaints—the editors were more hesitant to talk about the specifics of "a good thing." Weaver's April 19, 1862, "Hints of Contributors" asserts that "no editor can ever afford the rejection of a good thing" but also claims that "no author" could afford "the publication of a bad one." Weaver continues, "The only difficulty lies in drawing the line," as "it is the vast range of mediocrity which perplexes." However, rather than offering specifics, this piece was one in a series of vague assertions that there *was* a "line" even as it left the line's coordinates unclear and shifting. Still, editors did occasionally talk about style. An October 18, 1862, item titled "A Word to Young Writers" urges writers, "do not aim to be eloquent. Be sure to have something to write about, and then tell your story with plainness." A March 31, 1866, letter from "Historicus" notes that "none but poor speakers and bad writers strain after fine words. Writing and speaking are to be judged as we judge of people's dress. If we see people in gaudy colors and flashy materials . . . we feel at once the ridiculousness of their positions. If they are homely, with all their straining after such finery, their ugliness is all the more apparent, and we laugh at their vanity; and if they are good-looking, we see at once that they do not need such gewgaws to set them off, and we laugh at their bad taste."[7] The language of "bad taste" and "good things" suggests a heavy emphasis on questions of aesthetics and of morals in editorial decisions, though the paper did consistently assert its democratic impulses. There were clearly specific contributors whose work Weaver always wanted to—or felt he had to—publish, but he did assure potential contributors that there was not any "editorial prejudice against new or obscure contributors," as "every editor is always hungering and thirsting after novelties."

Editors often collapsed good writing and good (hand)writing, as in a January 27, 1866, item titled "Letters Sent for Publication" that says "We are thronged and overrun with letters . . . but, as many of them are so badly written, they cannot appear; it would be impossible for any editor or compositor to decipher the hieroglyphics so faintly discernible on the leaves of some of these communications. Every one who can write a few lines should not be so presumptuous as to think himself qualified to write for publication." "Qualified" writers knew how to write with a clear hand to produce visually readable texts, and they often knew this because of a level of class privilege that allowed fuller access to and practice with alphabetic literacies. They used good paper liberally and demonstrated other socioeconomic markers of the kinds of power alluded to in Weaver's numbered list of "Hints to Contributors" published in the November 5, 1864, issue and discussed in chapter 3.

Weaver's November 12, 1864, "Notice" builds additional groundwork for such sensibilities—criticizing the "certain class among our corresponding brethren who . . . persist in sending us a most wretchedly-penned and unintelligible scrawl!" and asserting that "if they persist in their carelessness, we shall become careless, too, and not publish their letters." "We wish," he concludes, "to receive communications from none but those capable of the task, and whose well-written letters we consider it both a privilege and pleasure to spread before the world."[8] In this vein, Weaver's April 1862 "Hints" counsels readers to "look to the physical aspect of your manuscript" and to self-edit—to "prepare your page so neatly that it shall allure instead of repelling. Use good pens, black ink, nice white paper, and plenty of it. . . . If your document is slovenly, the presumption is that its literary execution is the same." He also hoped that potential contributors would "send your composition in such a shape that it shall not need the slightest literary revision before printing," as "for intellect in the rough there is no market."

That said, even at their most definitive, all of the editors noted exceptions to these broad rules, as well as shifting circumstances and their own power to seem arbitrary—albeit in the name of the Church. When Weaver told potential contributors to avoid "personal *flings* and feuds," he immediately followed this dictate with "unless, indeed, there shall really appear a sufficient cause." Here, as all of the editors did, Weaver fell back on the editor's (personal) powers of evaluation: "whether or not any article shall be admitted, we alone must be the judge, and our decision shall be final." This invocation of editorial privilege was already a long-established tradition in both the Black and white presses, but it was also a move to place the editor at the head of the paper's print community—a move, as mentioned in chapter 2, that was not without political peril, and that, as in chapter 5's discussion of Annie Smith, could nonetheless squelch the aspirations and the voices of the less powerful. When pushed, Weaver pointed to his—and the paper's—central charge embodied in the motto on the paper's masthead throughout the period, "Published by the African Methodist Episcopal Church in the United States for the Dissemination of Religion, Morality, Literature and Science." That phrase "published by" was echoed in the regular page one listing of Weaver as the Book Steward, who published the paper "every Saturday on behalf of the African Methodist Episcopal Church."

Ironically, the hazy contours of the editors' evaluation of correspondence can perhaps be best understood through statements editors made *against*— or, at least, critiquing—correspondence, in part because these represent moments when they were exercising such authority. One series of items—texts Weaver specifically chose for the paper—stand out especially: a set of four faux "letters" Weaver (re)printed in mid-1865. All four tell of the (mythical) town of Olympus, Pennsylvania, and all are signed by "Alexandrina Lucilla Mortimer." Formatted with datelines, salutations, and closing signatures, all echo the personal tone, listing of details from a specific location, and chatty style that many *Recorder* letters exhibited. Savvy readers almost surely knew that they were parodies from the start, as their mockery of small-town letters was incredibly pronounced. Further, Weaver placed each of them on page four—where correspondence rarely appeared—and headed them "Sketches" rather than any of the usual variations of "Correspondence."

These "Letters from Olympus" appear to have been written by white Lutheran Harriet Reynolds Krauth (later Spaeth) for another Philadelphia religious paper. Krauth was the daughter of Charles Porterfield Krauth, a prominent minister and author who edited the weekly *Lutheran and Missionary*, where the "Letters" originally appeared. She would later become a well-known writer of hymns herself, but she cut her teeth writing (often pseudonymously) for her father's paper throughout the 1860s.[9] Among the other texts Weaver copied in whole or in part from the *Lutheran and Missionary* specifically in 1865, at least four—the February 4, 1865, "The Beard;" a set of March 4, 1865, translations of Greek hymns by J. M. Neale; the April 15, 1865, "Fred's Easter Egg," and the October 14, 1865, "A Contribution to the Album of Experience"— were actually cited as being from Charles Krauth's paper. Weaver's reasons for not citing the "Letters from Olympus" remain unknown, but his (potentially strategic) lack of citation makes these texts look and feel even more like general *Recorder* correspondence and so highlights their parodic commentary on such. The "Letters from Olympus" generally appeared in the *Lutheran and Missionary* only a few days before their *Recorder* publication: the June 10, 1865, "Matters and Things," in the June 8, 1865, *Lutheran and Missionary*; the

June 24, 1865, "The Great Sanitary Fair," in the June 22, 1865, *Lutheran and Missionary*; the July 8, 1865, "The Bard of Olympus," in the July 6, 1865, *Lutheran and Missionary*; and the July 29, 1865, "The Fourth of July," in the July 27, 1865, *Lutheran and Missionary*.[10]

Each of the letters lampoons features common to letters that appeared in denominational papers of the period.[11] The first, for example, titled "Matters and Things in Olympus," introduces a "modest authoress" who felt called to become "'the sad historian of the pensive plain,' as Wordsworth so elegantly and appropriately remarks in his 'Eulogy of a County Church Yard.'" After "elegantly" erring on both the author and the title in a well-known reference, the "authoress" presses on to share a very detailed "account of the Concert recently given in our Town Hall" for "the benefit of suffering Guerrillas" featuring both—and seemingly of equal importance—"Miss Anastasia Cherubina Handel Smythe, daughter of our respected towns-man, John Smith, Esq." and a piano "furnished by Ockletree & Crown, of our town, importers of music and instruments." The letter closes with a promise and a request. "Should you wish it," "Alexandrina" wrote, "you may hear from me again. Our quiet town is not utterly destitute of events and persons, interesting even to the careless public." The "authoress," though, was specific that the paper should not name her, but should refer to her as "Periwinkle," which "is my favorite flower, owing to its modest beauty, which, I flatter myself, is a characteristic of me."[12]

Subsequent "letters"—"The Great Sanitary Fair at Olympus," "The Bard of Olympus," and "The Fourth of July at Olympus"—all center on community events and personages like those commonly treated by *Recorder* correspondents. All continue to offer an abundance of minutiae, to name specific Olympians, to veer toward the personal even in the midst of "historical" reporting of the specific location, and to (clumsily) leave out critical details, as when "Alexandrina" writes "I can not give you the result of the [Sanitary] Fair in dollars and cents," though "the Committee on Finance will, no doubt, make out a report at some future day." "Alexandrina" argues that her work nonetheless impresses her fellow Olympians; her second letter tells the editor, "See, now, how you are rewarded. The Post-master of Olympus assures me that the subscriptions to your paper are already doubled in this township, and no less than four of your weekly messengers come to cheer the hearts and elevate the minds of this community."

The news "Alexandrina" delivered was certainly timely: at the Olympian Sanitary Fair, for example, "The refreshment table, which was one of the most important parts of the Fair, contained a fine specimen of sculptured confectionary called 'Emancipation.' Slavery was represented by a colossal image in the form of a very black man, made in chocolate with white peppermint drips for his eyes, lying in the dust, which was brown sugar. Over him, with one foot on his neck, was a white sugar-candy image, dressed in red, white, and blue, and with a sword in his hand."¹³ "Alexandrina" also consistently attempts to assert the value of Olympians' efforts within the wider world, as when she offers a sonnet from "The Bard of Olympus," B. Gordon Gambler. Seemingly unbeknownst to her, the poem plagiarizes all eight lines of one of Percy Shelley's more famous short poems, opening with "Music, when soft voices die, / Vibrates in the memory" but then inserting "When mosquitoes cease to sing, / Poison lingers where they sting." The next quatrain again opens with Shelly—"Odors, when sweet violets sicken, / Live within the sense they quicken"—and closes with Gambler: "Cherry-pie succumbs to fate / And leaves the stones upon the plate." The final quatrain finishes Shelley's poem, which ends "Love itself shall slumber on," but a couplet by Gambler is then tacked on: "And if waking, love's dream ceases, / Break your heart—but save the pieces!"¹⁴

The representation of the correspondent—both as personal letter-writer and as location-specific conveyor of news—as naïve, pompous, parochial, obsessed by details, and ignorant of larger issues embodies a host of the *Recorder*'s worries about non-professional correspondents *using* periodicals to simply gain publication credits and thus making both author and paper into laughingstocks. That many of the jokes about this representative (if "Olympian") correspondent rely on gendered stereotypes also meshes with the *Recorder*'s male editors' uneven approach to women, who were, as discussed in the last chapter, essential to the paper as subscribers and supporters but were nonetheless often targets (and occasionally deliverers) of patronizing lectures about female conduct. Similarly, that many of the jokes were tied to "Alexandrina"'s uneven obsession with local minutiae echoes the editors' recognition that such work could amount to a collection of annoying trifles—Henry McNeal Turner's sense of "pic-nic" reporting—even though that recognition was paired with a pragmatic sense that a certain (shifting and unclear) amount of such was necessary as a service to the AME connection and as a carrot for subscribers (and/or local ministers) hungry for notice. Finally, that "Alexandrina"'s letters regularly turn personal—even as they purport to do a kind of Christian recording—addressed the editors' constant struggle to make the paper representative both in a democratic sense and an ambassadorial/exemplar sense in the face of correspondents with wildly differing backgrounds, talents, and agendas. Weaver did occasionally address such concerns about letters submitted to the paper—and sometimes did so fairly directly—but nowhere in the issues he edited is there as dense and blunt a critique of the difficulties of local letters as in the "Letters from Olympus" reprints. Arguably, their humor—and remember that they were placed on page four along with other "entertaining" texts—allowed massive possibilities for educating (potential) contributors unavailable through other means. Specifically, allowing potential Alexanders and Alexandrinas to laugh at this specific correspondent's failings might alert them to the facts that they could be literary and well informed without being snobbish and pretentious (and wrong), proud of their locality without being fawning, and local and detailed without being trivial.

Lynch was less subtle than Weaver and, indeed, was more prone to occasional outbursts on these questions. The most striking short example appears in a May 26, 1866, column titled "Our Talk with Correspondents" and links arguments about both minutiae and representation:

> TO THE FRIEND who kindly sent us an account of the grand wedding and supper which took place at _____, we would say that we cannot publish his article. His description of the ladies' dresses and laces, etc., was, doubtless, *unique*, but, not being skilled in millinery, mantua making and the choice of dry goods, we fail to appreciate it. We would rather he would write about the status of our people in his town, something of their means, industry, education and religion.

An even more blunt piece came at the moment of his resignation, when he was not only leaving Philadelphia for the deep South but also leaving the Church. The discussion of editorial processes that leads his June 8, 1867, "Valedictory" is worth quoting in full:

> For a little over sixteen months I have held the position which I am now about to leave. Like most important positions in life, this one had its severe trials. (1.) It is necessary to regard the interest of the *entire* Connection; while persons in each part, think that the particular interests of their section are of first importance, and are only best pleased when they are so regarded. (2.) As an educator of the public mind great and true principles must be recognized and advocated, not tamely, but zealously. Men who consult expedience, and look not beyond the present, will strongly urge and insist on a different course. (3.) Ministers and others, feeling at home in their Church Organ, as indeed they should, frequently write page after page about matters that would interest nobody beyond their own neighborhood; such as accounts of exhibitions, concerts, festivals, &c. The names of all the leading participants therein, are generally mentioned in order that they may be encouraged when they behold them in print. The editor finds himself in possession of enough of this kind of matter every week to fill up the entire paper. The kindness of his heart says, "gratify these brethren and friends." His judgment says, "abridge, condense, omit, and make up a paper that will suit the majority of your readers." Not infrequently I have written letters to brethren, explanatory. (4) Sometimes an individual with laudable ambition but questionable judgment, attempts to write on political, philosophical, or moral subjects, for the enlightenment of the people, and closes by saying, "Please excuse the bad writing and spelling."

None of Lynch's "explanatory" letters or manuscript examples of his editorial attempts to "abridge, condense, [and] omit" have yet been recovered.

While all three editors during the period worried over the content and style issues embodied in the "Letters from Olympus" and critiqued directly in Lynch's comments, they did give ministers a bit more latitude than "others." This likely came from a range of factors: the calls discussed in the last chapter for a reading and writing ministry, the special agent relationship in which ministers were placed by both the *Discipline* and the paper's own calls, ministers' roles in gathering "Two-Cent Money" and donations, ministers' potential power at both regional and general conferences, and a level of (gendered) identification with ministerial work—as well as friendships and acquaintances made in editors' own past and ongoing ministry. Thus, for example, Daniel Draper's October 8, 1864, letter actually opens, "I thought, as I am a subscriber for your paper, that it would be no harm to drop you a word to inform you and our friends, through your paper, how things are progressing." A young Baltimore-born minister whose first charge consisted of two yoked churches in Maryland, Draper used his status as a minister and a subscriber to allow him to say that he felt "like the little bark that is driven and tossed upon the angry ocean" and that his "circuit is not the best": at one church, his membership was "small" and almost all "females . . . so situated that they cannot do much in the way of supporting a minister," and at the other, he found a group "also weak, not having a church, but which we would . . . had it not been for the frequent raids of the southern army." While he does not give in to the naming of the names Lynch criticized, he does perhaps exercise "questionable judgment" in "attempts to write on political, philosophical, or moral subjects, for the enlightenment of the people"—attempts that criticize those very people—and he concludes with: "Now, sir, as this is my first attempt as a correspondent to your valuable paper, I hope you will excuse all the errors, for they are not errors of the heart, but of the head."

Similarly, what would seem to have been a hard and fast rule—the oft-repeated call to avoid personal attacks—was regularly broken (and allowed to be broken) by select ministers. The debates surrounding Bishop Nazrey's exodus to Canada represent some of the earliest and fiercest attacks. Payne's "Rejoinder to Bishop Nazrey," which appeared in the April 12, 1862, issue and was a part of an exchange of increasingly nasty public letters between the two bishops in early 1862, tells Nazrey that Payne had "neither the time nor disposition for controversy. My precious moments are more nobly employed in feeding the sheep of the fold with strong meat, and the tender lambs thereof with the sincere milk of the word." Payne refers to the structure of Nazrey's earlier *Recorder* letters on the subject as "1st, The Invective, 2d. The Denials, 3d. The silent Contempt" and accuses Nazrey of being "a *miracle of self contradiction*," of ruling a church "*antagonistic* to ours," of lying about Payne's motives and statements (even though "an honorable man regards his word more than his life"), and of lying about his plans to resign from the AME connection.

Payne's rhetoric pales in comparison to the battle between Rev. Thomas Strother (a Nazrey detractor) and former *Recorder* editor Jabez Pitt Campbell (one of Nazrey's print supporters).[15] After Campbell had answered one of Strother's letters with a February 15, 1862, piece called "A Discovery of Inconsistencies" and Strother had begun a follow-up under a similar heading, Weaver himself tried to calm (or at least balance) the fighters; his March 15, 1862, item headed "Brother Strother" reads "Your reply to Rev. J. P. Campbell will appear next week; and we will say now that we hope that our brethren, on a subject of that kind, will not write us such lengthy pieces." Nonetheless, Strother sent another massive piece published in the March 22, 1862, issue claiming that "while I very highly respect Elder Campbell, I must say here that he has misrepresented me very glaringly" and "it is to be regretted that Elder Campbell has spoken so carelessly . . . and has subjected himself to such glaring ridicule." Campbell shot back in the March 29 issue with "a short rejoinder" to Strother's "long and tedious, dark and gloomy story." Strother's April 5 piece suggests that "Elder Campbell seems to have set himself up for a judge. He seems to be trying to avoid an evil that is behind him." Strother called Campbell's letters "groundless," "insidious," and "headed wrong." While this piece brought Weaver in again—inserting a headnote saying that "we give notice to the author of this article, and to other brethren, that, unless the subjects treated . . . by them, are in the proper position for discussion, we shall suppress all articles that occupy over one sheet of paper, except those coming from the Bishops"—the argument continued. Campbell's April 12, 1862, "Rev. T. Strother and His Cavils about Inconsistencies" is his most biting letter, saying that Strother's last three letters came from a "confused and agitated brain" and consisted of "rambling assertions, contradictions and absurdities," were patently "FALSE," and would only frustrate those "who are *really* versed in the science of logic." For all of Weaver's comments suggesting otherwise, a lengthy reply from Strother that continued to attack Campbell appeared soon after. Weaver seems to have exercised some limited power not in "suppressing" this final swing but in diffusing it: this "Rejoinder" from Strother was divided into two parts, which appeared with a week's gap between them. Following the May 10, 1862, initial portion, the May 24, 1862, conclusion actually begins with a direct address to Weaver: "MR. EDITOR:— I ask the privilege of finishing my rejoinder, as my opponent had three trials in his reply."

Weaver's motivations here remain somewhat opaque, but his decision to allow Campbell and especially Strother to break so many of the rules he set out for contributors more generally was surely shaped by his own complex position in the Nazrey affair. A friend and longtime supporter of Nazrey and a sometime antagonist and (former) friend of Payne, Weaver likely couldn't let it appear that he was favoring Nazrey. Indeed, Campbell devoted a whole paragraph of his April 5, 1862, critique of John Mifflin Brown's *Repository* coverage of the matter specifically to praising Weaver's even-handedness: "Recently, the Editor of the Christian Recorder has done himself much credit in the management of the Episcopal discussion [on Nazrey]; he has acted wisely by giving all parties a hearing through the columns over which he presides. None have a just ground of complaint against him, and by the course he has pursued in the matter, he has lost no friends in number; and if he continues to pursue the same course that he has done during several weeks past we shall certainly know how to vote in the General Conference" on "matters pertaining to the *Recorder*." Campbell's linkage of his approval with his voting was as much threat as praise. But Weaver—who had come up in the Indiana Conference and knew Strother personally—seems to have also weighed Strother's status as an active minister who worked hard for *Recorder* subscriptions and who had a voice in a variety of Church decisions.[16] In short, these men could bend and even break rules that writers like Annie M. Smith couldn't even approach. Some of that flexibility came from their positions (and responsibilities) as ministers—and likely even from the simple fact that, however nastily, Campbell and Strother were debating Church business—but both their excesses and Weaver's repeated need to attempt to rein in those excesses call attention to some of the power differentials that shaped what *Recorder* letters could be and do.

Within these broad and shifting parameters, the *Recorder* editors seem to have evaluated each submission based on a bevy of factors—from handwriting to the location of its writer within church politics, personages, and geography. Thus, plenty of writing like that parodied in the "Olympus" sketches was published throughout the period—as was a good deal of pure invective. When pressed, editors fell back on their capacious mission: advancing the AME—and, more broadly, African American—cause. This mandate addressed issues ranging from the kinds of ministerial writing the paper published to the representation and practice of Black soldiers reading and writing to the more fraught world of women reading and writing that Annie Smith briefly entered. The two figures studied in the rest of this chapter help us further understand the character and exercise of that mandate—as well as it's boundaries. But they also highlight the sense that correspondence began with distance and separation and was largely about reaching across distance, about allaying separation.

A massive amount of the paper's correspondence focused on questions of mobility. This focus isn't surprising given the findings discussed in chapter 4 tied to subscribers' moves around the nation. Such mobility was a clear goal of the Church, as it spoke to expansion, to nation-building, to spreading the Word, and potentially to improving conditions for members' lives and faith practices. It also, though—as rhetoric supporting the *Recorder* from the 1840s on regularly reminded—threatened to diffuse meager Church resources and to separate "the Connexion" too much for good work to be done. To further tease out these questions of correspondence, community, mobility, and print, I thus turn to two correspondents for whom mobility was, if differently defined, equally crucial, Daniel Adger and Edmonia Goodelle Highgate.

"I wish some of my young friends were here," wrote Daniel P. Adger in his first signed letter to the *Recorder*, "as there are some noble chances for them." Published in the May 7, 1864, issue, this language carries echoes of Black press accounts of California published a decade before and presages rhetorics of geographically specific opportunity that would soon (re)enter the Black press in letters from the reconstructing South. For all this similarity—indeed, for all of the letter's similarity to others in the paper, from Adger's opening expression of his "long desire" to write for the paper to his humble claim of "feeble abilities" as an author—Adger's letter had one massive difference. The heading of this May 7, 1864, item "Letter from Australia" clearly marks Adger as one of the paper's most geographically distant contributors. Adger's dance with and revisions of such questions of correspondence illustrate some of the ways the paper shifted "travel writing" as genre and the idea of the letter (and especially the letter from a distant location—again, as a genre) into structures that not only linked AME congregants (and others) over long distances but also offered real potential for a complex politics of uplift.

How Adger became the paper's "Australian Correspondent" is worth consideration before turning to the seven texts covering his journey to and time in Australia.[17] Most scholars of nineteenth-century Black Philadelphia know of Adger's family. Perhaps its most notable member—one of Adger's older brothers and their activist father's namesake—was Robert Mara Adger (1837–1910), a community leader, director of the Philadelphia Building and Loan Association (a critical early Black mortgage company), and Black bibliophile whose relentless collecting saved countless artifacts of Black print culture from oblivion. One of their older sisters, Elizabeth (1842–?), was deeply involved in efforts to desegregate Philadelphia's transit system. And one of Daniel Adger's younger brothers seemed poised to make a major contribution to Black letters before an untimely death: William (1856–1885) became the University of Pennsylvania's first Black graduate in 1883.[18]

These brief descriptions only hint at the character of a family that begs for further study. By the time Daniel Adger was born—in 1843 in South Carolina—his father Robert (1813–1896), who most sources say was born enslaved, had obtained his freedom, and was parenting four children with his wife Mary Ann Morong, who most sources list as Native American. Five years and three more children later—the Adgers would eventually have thirteen children in all—the family left South Carolina for Philadelphia, where Robert Adger worked a variety of jobs, including baking, nursing, and waiting tables in the Old Merchant's Hotel. By the time Daniel was in his early teens, his father had already moved from jobbing into real success as a merchant: the 1860 federal census listed Robert Adger as a "China Storekeeper" with real estate of $5,000 and other assets totaling $2,500; by 1870, he was listed as a "furniture dealer" and was credited with $12,000 in real estate and $6,000 in other assets (37, 287B). His financial success allowed all of the Adger children to attend school well into their teens, first at the Bird School (later the James Forten School, on Sixth above Lombard) and then in a variety of venues, including the Institute for Colored Youth. Not surprisingly, the Adgers set a base for their children's activism in both local and national civil rights struggles. The elder Adger helped found Philadelphia's Banneker Institute, a debating society and community resource of massive importance in the mid-nineteenth century. Daniel R. Biddle—biographer of family friend, Black activist Octavius Catto—says that, at Adger's store at "roughly the geographic center of colored Philadelphia," amidst "furniture, china, silverware, and featherbeds" guarded by "a snarling, chained cur of indeterminate breed," "portraits of Douglass and Garrison lined the walls" and store "shelves creaked with writings about race—the tale of Peter Still's escape from bondage and his reunion with his brother; the Weld and Grimke antislavery tracts and the novel they fueled, *Uncle Tom's Cabin* . . .; pamphlets and petitions from a quarter century of Negro conventions; writings against colonization, the Fugitive Slave Act, and *Dred Scott*" (201). Biddle shares oral history that a centerpiece of the Adger store collection was a banner "that sparked a bloody siege" at the "ill-fated temperance parade of 1842," a banner that "rumor" reported "depicted a Nat Turner or Denmark Vesey breaking free and setting the town ablaze" (201–202).

It is no wonder that, writing from Liverpool in his unsigned August 1, 1863, *Recorder* letter, Daniel Adger was moved to highlight British egalitarianism compared to American racism—saying that he saw "nothing . . . where a gentleman of color was debarred from any privilege of liberty. In all public conveyances he is welcomed. In all places of resort he is not looked at for exclusion on part of his color." It is also no surprise that, growing up among those groaning shelves of African American stories, Daniel Adger was drawn to print.[19] Thus, Adger's May 7, 1864, letter makes it clear that he was "proud" to have "realized . . . a past and long desire to be a writer . . . to the Christian Recorder." But Adger was much more directly connected to the *Recorder* than many readers and hopeful writers: he knew Weaver personally. Indeed, he still celebrated "the ever-memorable and gladsome hour when you came to me and asked me to accept the duty as 'Australian Correspondent' to the Recorder."[20] That acquaintance, his family's prominence, his own education, and the exotica promised by his location and subjects were likely enough to get Adger's work published in the *Recorder*, but Weaver was also aware that Adger had a circle of friends who were potential subscribers: Weaver's August

1, 1863, note on the Liverpool letter actually says that he was "sure" Adger's "host of acquaintances" would "all want to get a copy of the RECORDER so as to keep his article before them. Those who want a copy had better call at No. 619 Pine street, and get one before they are all gone."

To understand why Daniel Adger was traveling to Australia, we need to look to yet another sibling, James, who was three years older. After receiving initial training in barbering, James Adger had traveled first to Britain and then to Australia aboard the *Invincible*; he arrived in Sydney on December 3, 1856. There, he seems to have begun a lifelong—if sporadic—correspondence with his Philadelphia family.[21] Biddle, the only scholar to even briefly note the Adger brothers' time in Australia, says that "an 1850s gold rush had attracted a handful of colored Americans to Australia, where British law made slavery illegal" (185). The possibility of gold or gold-related opportunity may have been deeply attractive, but, as James Adger left the United States in the dark year of 1856, we must primarily figure him among the ranks of African Americans of the middling classes who gave serious consideration to emigration in the face of US racism. Working in his father's store, James Adger must have heard enough about Haiti, Liberia, and Canada to dissuade him from going to these locations; though far from perfect, the opportunities he found in Australia must have been attractive enough, as he stayed there throughout his life and died there on December 12, 1916, in Sydney.[22]

By mid-1863, when Daniel Adger was considering joining his brother, James Adger had become quite successful.[23] In 1864, he moved to a new location (313 George Street), where he advertised "Enameled Slate Baths, Hot and Cold Shower Baths" and hairdressing services.[24] Daniel Adger's May 7, 1864, *Recorder* letter describes his "brother's establishment" as a "first-class hairdressing saloon," centering on "a large, spacious room, handsomely fitted up." Even as it participates in the common *Recorder* practice of lauding (very specifically) successful Black businesspeople, this description also quietly alerts readers to Australia's potential for a different racial hierarchy by noting his brother's white assistant as "an English youth, his journeyman."[25] That same letter explains some of James Adger's success: he was "favored by the Governor and gentry of Sydney."[26] On Daniel Adger's arrival, his brother immediately began to use his connections to find him a situation: "not wishing us both to be barbers" so that "we both could be on a high level," James Adger "spoke to one of his customers, (a squatter or sheep and cattle owner,) to take me as a youth requiring 'Colonial experience.'" The acquaintance agreed to "support me during the term," during which Adger would work as "storekeeper and assistant stockman" at the customer's station southwest of Toowoomba, Queensland.

A reading of Adger's *Recorder* letters suggests that he underestimated how hard living in Australia might be. Even as he apologizes in his May 7, 1864, letter for the fact that "pressing business deterred me from writing earlier than now," he promises both brief "weekly accounts" and a series of sketches including "Eight Weeks in Sydney" and "A Tour to Queensland, and Life on a Sheep Station" as well as "perhaps 'Lost in the Bush,' and 'Life in the Bush of Australia,'" though he admits "I have still to copy them." These other texts never materialized, and Daniel Adger was back in Philadelphia well before 1870, when the federal census listed him as a "cabinetmaker" living, along with eight siblings, with his parents.[27] Nonetheless, his *Recorder* letters in mid-1864 offer striking commentary on the potential for Black mobility: they begin to intertwine a story of Black elevation within a variation of a more standard travel narrative (specifically, a narrative of a sea voyage), and they bring readers on Adger's journey into a world far from the United States. As such, they perform an extreme version of what much *Recorder* correspondence did: they try to link a Black community of print across miles even as they emphasize how far select members of that community might reach both physically and metaphysically.

Adger's May 7, 1864, letter, perhaps in some ways like his earlier letter from Liverpool, set the stage for the five texts that followed, which may be best seen as installments of a single, long "Letter from Australia." The later five texts focus on Adger's voyage on the *Champion of the Seas*, which departed from Liverpool July 6, 1863, and arrived in Melbourne on September 25, 1863, under Captain James Manly Outridge.[28] These installments and their internal sections are all organized chronologically; labels tied to the week of the voyage ("week one," etc.) and to individual dates almost always lead individual sections.[29] Indeed, while often journal-like (albeit with a shifting sense of "journal"), Adger's texts are framed as letters from the *Recorder*'s "Australian correspondent" and so suggest the accommodations the genre might make for massive distance and serialization. Nonetheless, chronology sometimes moves from organizing principle to complete content, as in the June 11 letter's weather-centered notes: "Thursday, 3d September. Very cold, bitter; going along favorably. Friday, 4th September. Not so harsh; wind light in the forenoon on the starboard; sprung up briskly in the afternoon." Occasionally, these entries move toward poetry: "Tuesday, 1st September. Wind astern, with a heavy roll of sea; very cold; going ahead well. The breeze plays a melancholy music in the solemn night, and whistles aloud. Every moment carries us ten miles nearer port." But the lack of such commentary—indeed, *any* commentary—is often frustrating, and at many moments, such entries read like a logbook. What, for example, might Adger have considered on "Tuesday, 28th July" when it was "not so squally" and the ship was "300 miles off the coast of Liberia"—that center of colonization so often debated by African Americans in Philadelphia? Or on "Sunday, 2d August," when the wind was "stiff on the starboard quarter" and "Mr. Kean read prayers, as usual" while the ship was "70 miles off the coast of Africa"?[30]

The moments when Adger moves toward richer narrative are uneven, bordering on the picaresque and distant from the autobiographical promises he'd made—and perhaps demonstrating some of the limitations he (and often the *Recorder*) saw on integrating full personal reflection into public letters. Much of the May 28 installment, for example, focuses on the ritual performances tied to the ship's crossing of the equator, and Adger offers lively detail on "Neptune's procession"—a "half holiday," when a costumed ruler of the sea led drinking, carousing, and a ritual "shaving" of "those of the crew who had not yet previously crossed." Only very late in the piece—and then in a total of two sentences—could readers learn that some members of the crew, having dubbed Adger "their 'bright star,'" wanted to shave *him*, too, but were prevented from doing so by the captain. Though clearly a kind of participant, Adger positioned himself as a distant, almost disinterested observer: "During the disgraceful operation I was on the poop, seated in the starboard life-boat, looking at the process, much to their chagrin and astonishment." Indeed, so complete was his observer status that, rather than offering any move toward interiority beyond the word "disgraceful," Adger focuses solely on the crew's emotions. The threat to his person—and *Recorder* readers must have placed such hints in dialogue with the positions of Black bodies in the United States at that moment—seems too much to describe, too "foreign" to the kind of progress narrative/sea story he begins to tell.

Similarly, much of the opening of the June 4 letter centers on "A boy overboard!" Here, Adger shares fascinating detail on the search and eventual rescue—"anxiety . . . at its height" until the boy was recovered, desperately frightened that "a shark . . . took hold of him." Again, though he regularly deploys first person elsewhere in his letters to report events, he says nothing of his own thoughts about these events beyond his participation in the "three cheers" "given with a hearty will." While his letters attempt to close a larger physical distance than almost all other *Recorder* letters, they emphasize keeping some distance between Adger and his subjects and Adger and his readers. But Adger hews to the letter as genre; while these moments also certainly "read," for example, as sea narrative components, Adger never weaves them into a larger framework beyond the voyage's chronology.[31]

Adger's autobiographical subject thus navigates a curious kind of Black exceptionalism, one in which he is privileged and linked to the elite among the crew and select passengers, but sometimes because he is seen as an exotic and sometimes because of British biases tied to nation. The captain, for example, arranges "the variety of form and face" among the hundreds of passengers "according to their nativity, so that national animosity may be kept at bay during the voyage"; this meant that the "large number . . . of the Irish working classes . . . seeking to better their fortunes" were separated from the "good number of Scotch, both of the middle and lower classes" as well as "some few Germans," "a limited number of Welsh," "parties who are re-emigrating," and the more elite English passengers—especially those in "the first cabin" who included "the eminent English tragedian, together with his lady, Mr. and Mrs. Charles Kean." This separation continued throughout the voyage, with, for example, "Mr. Colgan" assembling "the Roman Catholics midships, where they had suitable devotions, while Mr. Kean again read prayers" in the first class (Protestant) cabins.

Adger—apparently a nation of one—was, per his May 7 letter, "favored by the captain and Mr. Charles Kean": though he paid but $50 for his ticket and was listed as a steerage passenger, he "shared" their first-class accommodations and "dined off the best they had." Adger's accounts of that favor emphasize both Kean and Captain Outridge's egalitarian, if sometimes patronizing, sensibilities about African American identities but also hint that such came simultaneously with/from their disdain for white Americans and the ship's non-English passengers. The internationally known Kean, who, along with his wife, "took a decided liking" to Adger, "congratulated me on my departure from America, and gave me every encouragement in going to Australia under English laws, further remarking: 'Why don't more of the colored people leave for parts where they can have better rights?'" The captain, according to Adger's May 21 letter, praised Adger's choice of Australia because there he "would 'be placed on an equality with the best—and not with those scrubs you see forward,' meaning the Irish and other emigrants in the front part of the ship." This May 21 language repeats, with slight variation, Adger's May 7 account, in which he shared how the captain claimed that in Australia, Adger would "be on an equality with the best, and not with those scrubs you see forward. It is not there as it is in America."[32]

Adger emphasizes his special status in describing the traditional ritual of equatorial "shaving" noted above: only "the kind interference of Mr. Charles Kean, who begged the captain not to allow them to shave me" prevented the crew from "handling me" "for the fun of the thing." Adger's difference from Irish Catholic passengers and "common" crewmen was again in evidence when national and religious tensions increased midway through the voyage. Adger's June 4 letter tells of how the Catholic passengers attempted "to have the Protestant services stopped, by dancing, carousing, and the like"—contributing to a "mutinous spirit" in several quarters of the ship and complicated by the fact that some "sailors were drunk." That "mutinous spirit" culminated in a knife fight, and, "after a good deal of trouble," the mutineers "were mastered, and put in double irons." For their safety, passengers in first class, including Adger, were not "allowed forward" on the ship, though the *Champion* reached Melbourne without further incident. Adger's letters show increasing ire at the Irish, noting that "One O'Conner, an Irish saloon passenger, remarked to an English lady, that, if the captain attempted to put him in irons, he had fifty men ready to rescue him." By the end of the voyage, Adger had come to the conclusion, voiced in the June 11 letter, that "the

Catholics ... seem to be a treacherous set of people." Given the extreme difficulties between Irish-American Catholic immigrants and African Americans in the US North, some of his *Recorder* readers likely embraced his conclusions—which also, conveniently and implicitly, used US Protestant xenophobia and nationalism as a mode for battling anti-Black racism.[33]

What is striking in Adger's self-representation is his simultaneous positioning as a promising young man who has striven to rise above prejudices of race, nation, and class to become an elite traveler and as a figure who sometimes benefits from his British friends' prejudices of nation, class, and religion. His final hints about the "treacherous" Catholic passengers came when he described the voyage's conclusion. At Cape Otway, they received "a glorious welcome"; when the captain left and then returned to the ship "bringing fresh meats, butter and new milk with him" before the passengers' exodus, "the passengers cheered tremendously ... in respect to his kind-hearted principles." The conclusion of the voyage, then, embodies English Protestant superiority: the captain's "kind-hearted principles" are shown as the engine behind "truly affecting" reunions between the first passengers to disembark and their long-separated relatives—stories that must have reminded at least some *Recorder* readers of the paper's "Information Wanted" ads from African Americans praying for reunion with relatives lost through slavery and the Civil War.[34] Here again, Adger positions himself as one of—or perhaps more accurately, a potential apprentice to—these (English) men of "kind-hearted" Protestant practices.

An account of a journey that begins with Adger's recognition (in Liverpool) that there were places in the world where "a gentleman of color" was "welcomed" as a traveler and never "debated from any privilege of liberty" essentially concludes by emphasizing just that, albeit in much more far-flung locations. Similarly, though Adger's exodus to Australia—especially in the midst of the Civil War—could have contained (and brought about) much more in-depth discussion of colonization and emigration, he left such questions essentially untouched. Instead, Adger's letters emphasize not just mobility but the transportability of virtue—and so center on suggesting simply that the Christian exercise of mobility could bring rewards to the Church and to individuals. Adger, like many *Recorder* writers and many in the AME Church, argued for an aristocracy of abilities, manners, and morals rather than color—but he neither plumbed the depths of how manners and abilities (much less, morals) might be tied to class or background nor questioned the fact that he was still arguing for an aristocracy. In this silencing of class difference in arguments for merit, Adger's letters performed a similar sense of (elite) Blackness to that which was hinted at in some of the *Recorder* editors' representations of what good correspondents must do and good correspondence, be.

Adger's letters merited extended space in the paper because, in addition to being of interest to his (paying) Philadelphia connections, they offered information on a portion of the world rarely seen from an African American perspective and a location that offered potential promise for Black futures. Fully in line with the paper's calls, they brought the Black community closer through print, reaching over physical distance to assert metaphysical closeness, a "correspondence" between distant writers and readers' goals and ideals. That promise was the base of Adger's May 7 wish "that some of my young friends were here, as there are some noble chances for them," which continues, "Though their prospect may seem dark and gloomy, yet they should remember that the darkest hours are but the preludes to brighter sunshine, and that trouble or great anxiety is often succeeded by sweeter and more lasting sunshine." Adger's letters from Australia did what the *Recorder* wanted all of its geographically diverse correspondence to do: they suggested ways of broadening the boundaries surrounding African American and specifically Afro-Protestant existence, brought readers along to explore and "visit" those places far from them, and proposed that print could hold together an increasingly diverse and diffuse community.

If Daniel Adger's correspondence from Australia emphasized the power of letters to convey the potential embodied in a kind of Black cosmopolitanism and of geographic (indeed, worldwide) mobility, Edmonia Highgate's letters spoke as much or more to the immense geography of Black intellect and feeling, landscapes white power had tried to fence off.[35] To be sure, Highgate's *Recorder* texts embodied post-war Black geographic and physical mobility—and specifically the mobility offered to select Black women through teaching the newly freed throughout the upper and lower South. They also certainly participated deeply in the "local news" structures of so many *Recorder* letters—including those from women like Annie Smith. But their purview was much, much larger.

Born in 1844 in New York—some sources say Syracuse, and some say Albany—Highgate was the child of Pennsylvanian Charles Highgate and Virginian Hannah Francis Highgate. Charles Highgate was a barber who also, along with his wife, kept a boarding house; both were socially and politically active.[36] Edmonia Highgate grew up in a home where education was valued deeply, where activist ministers Jermain Loguen and Henry Highland Garnet were guests, and where Samuel Ringgold Ward's early Black newspaper the *Impartial Citizen* received both moral and financial support.[37] Loguen was strongly Methodist (waffling between African Methodist Episcopal Zion and AME entities), and the Highgate family was also friendly with white Unitarian (and stalwart abolitionist) Samuel Joseph May, but they attended the deeply abolitionist (and also largely white) Plymouth Congregational Church. Public schools in several parts of the state remained separate and unequal, but Highgate again crossed racial boundaries and attended Syracuse High School. On her graduation in 1861, though, she was denied a teaching job in

Syracuse because of her race and so moved to Montrose, Pennsylvania, and then to Binghamton, New York, to teach.

Two events in the early 1860s changed the family forever. First, in May of 1861, Charles Highgate died suddenly, leaving Hannah to support Edmonia's younger siblings. Second, as the war grew and Northerners gained some sense of the educational needs of the newly freed people of the South, the American Missionary Association (AMA) began hiring formally educated Black women (usually young and single) as teachers. Highgate applied, referencing Samuel Joseph May as well as her old pastor at Plymouth, Oberlin graduate Michael Streiby, who was already becoming a force within the AMA. By the time Daniel Adger's letters from Australia appeared in the *Recorder*, Highgate was already working for the AMA in Norfolk, Virginia—struggling alongside other Black women teachers, including fellow *Recorder* correspondent Sallie Daffin.[38] Highgate's mother and sister Caroline would later teach for the AMA, too, and, all told, five of her siblings would eventually become teachers.

Teaching in Norfolk was immensely difficult, not just physically but also emotionally. Highgate worked with "so many of my people who have spent most of manhood's and womanhood's freshness in slavery"; she experienced "peculiar crushing emotions which, at first, check even my utterance."[39] Struck with what Daffin, in an October 8, 1864, *Recorder* letter, called "a terrible malady, aberration of the mind," Highgate—who Daffin said would be "universally missed"—had to be taken back to Syracuse. While similar events would crush many people, Highgate recovered, seemingly at the moment when she began to see herself as not just a teacher but also a speaker and perhaps a writer. Back in Syracuse, she was invited to address the National Convention of Colored Men held that October. One of only two women to speak—the other was Frances Ellen Watkins Harper—Highgate faced delegates including Frederick Douglass, William Wells Brown, old friend Jermain Loguen, George Boyer Vashon, John Mercer Langston, and *Recorder* editor Elisha Weaver. Highgate "urged the Convention to trust in God and press on."[40] By early 1865, she had returned to fundraising for the AMA, was setting up a school for the newly freed in Maryland, and had published her first two pieces in the *Recorder*: the February 4, 1865, "Salvation Only in Work" and the February 25, 1865, "Waiting for the Cars." Six more pieces would appear in 1865.

Some of these early letters focused on the location-specific reporting that was the mainstay of much of the paper's correspondence. Highgate's April 1, 1865, "A Stray Waif from the Port of Grace," for example, reported on the area around Havre de Grace, offering comment on the local geography (at "the mouth of the Susquehanna"), church work (the "uncommon energy" of Reverend William H. Hopkins), and the history of the local Black community within a national context, including the schoolhouse "burned to the ground by the southern branch of the same clique who burned the colored orphan asylums and churches in New York." That letter also gives the names and occupations of some of the leading Black citizens, describes the "rankest secession sentiment" that existed among some area white people, and points to the signs of a coming spring. In this broad, newsy framework, she also adds material tied to her teaching—a variation of the location-specific correspondence common in letters from women teachers of the newly freed like Sallie Daffin. Here and elsewhere, she successfully negotiated the calls for such correspondence and avoided the dangers outlined in various editors' comments and satirized in the "Letters from Olympus" series.

Highgate's later work did not set aside the impulses to provide news of her location(s) and to enhance the Church connection. Her March 17, 1866, "Letter from New Orleans," for example, even opened with this summary list of her topics: "General impressions—Rev. Turner, of A. M. E. Church—Madam de Mortie, Soule Mansion Orphanage—Governmental Schools—Dr. P. B. Randolph—Exhibition—Schulson Pay basis—Fred. Douglass' School—Mardi Gras—'Mystic Krewe of Comus'—Tribune Editor's Courtesy, &c." She was keenly aware of the responsibilities of a local correspondent—so much so that she ended her July 29, 1865, "A Leaf from the South Bank of the Ohio" by saying that "You have several local correspondents here, so I will not attempt a description of the various fairs that have been held in the city, or of Bishop Campbell's visit here—or you will think me unwittingly snatching from burning embers." Readers tired of what Turner called "pic-nic" reporting must have been pleased by Highgate's focus, restraint, and sense of context.

Highgate was also, however, from the very start of her *Recorder* efforts, revising the basic forms of *Recorder* correspondence to weave in both more and deeper commentary and personal reflection and to nudge at just what the *Recorder* might "record." Though no direct evidence seems extant, it seems likely that she had read texts like the lively Black press letters of James McCune Smith, Philip Bell, and William Wilson—correspondence that moved into a nexus of belles-lettres and political analysis.[41] It is clear—from her February 25, 1865, "Waiting for the Cars," which names them—that Highgate was also familiar with Gail Hamilton and Fanny Fern, two white women writers who notably broadened the sense of correspondence and the "sketch" to do all sorts of social, political, and personal work.[42]

In this vein, the newsy "A Stray Waif" also quotes Whittier and welcomes "beauteous, joyous spring" even as it links violence in the border-South with the famed New York draft riots' racist components. Her March 17, 1866, "Letter from New Orleans" offers a physical description of the school she ran—"the building is of gray stone, and being commodious, is comfortably fitted up"—that morphs into political commentary, as the "flourishing school . . . called after our eloquent champion, Frederick Douglass" was "held in what was formerly a 'slave pen.'" Similarly, her depictions of "the Crescent City" weave together light-hearted, heavily sensory, tourist-style description with in-depth commentary on the "crisis in the educational affairs" and the difficulties of the newly freed people in the city. Such abilities were rare among *Recorder* correspondents—and especially rare among those who traveled as widely and worked for the cause of racial uplift as tirelessly as Highgate did. That her letters could offer such diverse commentary while supplying desperately desired location-specific news—and could even branch into realms usually reserved for correspondence like Adger's—must have been part of the reason that, even as a woman writer for the paper, she was allowed some latitude to play with genre and with the potential of correspondence.[43]

That play with genre was present from almost the outset of Highgate's *Recorder* work, and a chronological reading of her letters suggests that she experimented with integrating various forms of the personal, diverse conceptions of audience (using letters in ways that range from massive public lecture to intimate conversation), and questions of race and art—all in exploration of her own place in the nation and the world, which was complexly marked by her gender, race, class, and regional background. All of this work was deeply shaped by Highgate's engagement with American Transcendentalism, as the "spirit" of Thoreau (who she asserted accompanied her into the Louisiana woods) and other Transcendentalist thinkers was present in her thinking long before her ride through the countryside that opens this chapter.

Even in her second piece for the *Recorder*—the February 25, 1865, "Waiting for the Cars"—she tells readers that "the dignity of existing in the present has been uppermost in my mind for a long time. The moral grandeur of having a heartache as one's companion through life, because of the sacrifices we are daily making for freedom's cause, and the sublime privilege of sounding one's soul depth by laying our all upon the national altar, and, also, of forgetting self, losing person identity, and becoming atomic parts of personified principle, forces our duty in general." The tension between self and movement—intensified by the war and "forcing" her efforts—here becomes part of her local reporting because, as she writes, she was "spending nearly three days in a railroad depot, waiting for trains that were but fifteen miles distant, but which were blocked up in a snow-drift," thus delaying her journey to her new teaching job in Maryland. She recognizes that such "duty" was intimately tied to some of her readers: "As the years of blood-reeking war roll on, the old pain becomes a part of loyal women; and, like toothache, it gets benumbed and dull. We would sadly miss it now; for, some how or other, it gives us a sacred right in those noble forms which lie bleaching on Southern battlefields, with faces turned upward, as if imploring Heaven, but whose souls are marching on in the 'bright land of glory.'" In union with those "daily making" sacrifices "for freedom's cause," she finds an understanding of how "the unseen forces that press upon us from every side, and urge us to make what is termed 'transcendental'—the simple rule for controlling each atomic part of the nation! Being loyal to one's self, is loyalty to the cause of liberty, to the country, and to the Union, whose arch of keystone is *Justice*." But even here, other external forces stop African Americans from becoming fully "transcendental" "atomic parts." The very justice-centered Union she long prayed for had not come; the one that she was left with had failed to make gestures as basic as granting equal pay and treatment for Black soldiers.[44] Pushing at the limits of her nominally news-centered letter, Highgate offers a personal voice (and an account of deeply personal response to national, public events) far more developed than Adger's and far beyond what the *Recorder* asked even ministers to share. Perhaps the combined languages of nationalism and evangelism created space for this work—or perhaps it was simply the richness of Highgate's contributions—but early on, Highgate's letters clearly pushed at the boundaries of what *Recorder* correspondence might be and do.

Reports from these places of the heart and the head—places found where "sounding one's soul depths" ran up against sociopolitical limitations on and denials of personhood—eventually made her explore questions she hoped she would never have to confront and made her broaden the idea of a letter to the *Christian Recorder* as an act of Christian recording even more. Her May 27, 1865, "A Spring Day up the James" opens with a deceptively serene title, suggesting a sightseeing day trip, though that title begins to turn in the piece's opening line: "Dear Recorder:—Bright, joyous April, yet tearful enough to be in sympathy with the national sorrow, will ever be memorable to your scribbler." The national sorrow here carries twinned meaning: coverage of Lincoln's death in "Bright, joyous April" had filled the pages of the *Recorder* and most of the nation's papers—sometimes with the elegies studied in the next chapter—but, in some ways, that assassination also made Lincoln yet another death in a long and painful war whose scale and scope the nation had never seen before. Highgate knew she was not the only American sounding her soul's depths because of such death:

> The recent trophies and grand victories placed us in the king's gallery of delightful enthusiasm; but to how many, many hearts, they brought mourning in their train, because of the sacrifice of the first born or dearest one? How many mothers, wives, and sisters read telegrams or letters saying: "He fell on the field making a desperate charge," or "terribly wounded in five places!" "Oh, Christ of the seven wounds, comfort the hearts of the national mothers whose sons die with faces turned away, and no last word to say!" Our pangs in this freedom birth of America are agonizing, yet we rejoice, for the cost endears the end.

"Dear Recorder" thus reads as not just a simple salutation but as both an expression of deep affection for the paper in a time of (national and personal) need and as a gesture of community, with the *Recorder*'s name as a proxy for all the "dear" ones she addressed through its pages. This dancing between alluding to specifics that some audience members knew and general events that most understood is heavy in the language above. Close readers of the *Recorder*, those who knew the Highgate family, and/or members of Syracuse's Black community might have been struck especially by the image of a "sister" reading of her brother being "terribly wounded in five places!"

Highgate's brother Charles—who the May 20, 1865, *Recorder* called "Charlie Highgate, one of the best boys of Syracuse"—had been allowed to join the majority-white, locally raised New York 185th and, in fighting related to the Appomattox Campaign (that "grand victory"), had been shot five times on March 29, 1865. He died on April 2, and the *Recorder* carried both a brief notice of his death in the May 6, 1865, issue and a longer memorial in the May 20, 1865, issue, just one week before the publication of "A Spring Day up the James."

As "A Spring Day" unfolds, readers learn that Edmonia Highgate's trip up the James—"on a half-fare ticket, owning to the kindness of that most Christlike body, the 'Christian Commission'"—was really a trip into despair, beginning as journey to find her wounded brother among the massive Fifth Corp hospital camps, as, at that point, she did not yet know that he was dead. She brings her audience—her "Dear Recorder"—along for this journey via her letter: "Reader, did you ever go to the front to search for your beloved wounded? If you have, you can sympathize, if not, you can learn how trying it is to spend long hours on government transports, moving slowly and lazily along." Ultimately, those readers could see glimmers amidst "the darkness of that night" of how painful a hospital clerk's words "your brother died of his wounds two weeks ago" could be. "A Spring Day up the James" thus rewrites a nation of "atomic parts" into a community in mourning. In this very different kind of "local reporting," Highgate's authorial "we" becomes very much a "we" of those people—and especially those African American "loyal women"—who had heard or read words like those the clerk had spoken to Highgate, words that caused Highgate to know "how sublime a thought it is to suffer and be strong." Highgate thus also rewrites the genre of the consolation letter (already well known in the military) to explore national grief. And Highgate shifts the newsy letter into the intimateness of personal correspondence, even as she delivers news to a large public.

In some ways, Highgate's articulation of grief mirrors much of the counsel given in the *Recorder*—sometimes in answer to letters to the paper, and sometimes offered *through* such letters. She concludes her letter, for example, with the second-to-last stanza of Elizabeth Barrett Browning's elegy to her own brother Edward, "De Profundis."[45] But much of what precedes that conclusion painfully queries "the afflictions with which thou visitest on thy children." Highgate focuses especially on how "one sweet young wife . . . with kindly hands tried to comfort us" even as she was trying to find her husband, "who she said was wounded, little dreaming of the real truth." The grieving of Highgate and that "young wife" was interrupted by "a large concourse of southern female friends on the boat back to Fortress Monroe, who sneered at the Yankee flag." Thus, even as Highgate challenges the expected senses of audience, of purpose, and of "news" in her letters, she also works to combine a level of personal intimacy—and pain and doubt—with a very public letter. Even as that letter reinforces the concept of a community of faith, its details challenge that conception. This is a very different kind of correspondence than what the *Recorder* called for and received—one that queries how the writer's life and soul correspond to those of her (potential) readers and beyond—as different in its own way as Adger's far-flung reports of African Americans and Australia.

These stunning combinations of the personal and political are again in evidence in later work, especially "On Horse Back—Saddle Dash, No.1." But that piece is also of special note for the ways in which it attempts to weave together Highgate's generic stretching of correspondence, her complex awareness of her audience and self, and her explorations of American Transcendentalism as a mode that could situate African Americans—and especially *Recorder* subscribers—in places of opportunity, albeit using a very different definition of that term than, say, Adger's letters do. Highgate's short essay "Truth," which appears in the October 27, 1866, *Recorder* (a week before "On Horse Back") presages such moves by opening with a quote from Margaret Fuller Ossoli, calling her "one of the most highly gifted human beings that ever existed," and making what seem to be a set of allusions to Emerson's "Circles." Urging readers to "sacrifice everything to truth," it asserts that "the real is enveloped in our own souls. All outside is reflected or shadowed" and that "all else will be swallowed up in the immensity of eternity; but truth has an individuality, which is changeless"; she concludes, "Personal truth would save this nation, and the world."[46]

"On Horse Back" *does* address some standard *Recorder* expectations for location-specific reporting in letters: in addition to the discussions of what might be classed "Louisiana scenery," it shows Highgate passing "through several cotton and cornfields worked on shares" and reports that "the former owners are giving half what the crops yield to the hands in payment. Besides, there is a five per cent tax levied to pay for the school privilege for the children of the hands." Matching the *Recorder*'s growing suspicion about sharecropping and emphasis on Black industry, it also notes that these hands "work all day Sunday of their own accord on land they have rented, so anxious are they to get places of their own." Highgate even reports on the simultaneously mundane and life-shaping fact that "cotton is worth from 40 to 50 cents here."

What is striking is how deep she allows her sense of the local to reach. In an amazing pair of paragraphs that follow her descriptions of Louisiana's scenery and weave in the assertions about the presence of Henry David Thoreau's spirit, she critiques spiritualism, free love, racial essentialism and stereotypes, gender expectations, and fashion:

> Yes, they are "ministering spirits." Thee don't imagine me a modern spiritualist after the "affinity-seeking," "wife and husband leaving" stripe. No, I detest "table rappings and crockery breaking," especially the last, for I have broken so much. But those who are of the same mind do coalesce whether in the spirit or not. Oh, what a cluster of scarlet blossoms! All negroes like red, so push on, pony, I must have those flowers! How I wish my Philadelphia friends had these! Why they are handsomer than either "fuchsia's or bleeding heart." But I have left my botany in the city; so I can't trace their genera.
>
> Oh, how independent one feels in the saddle! One thing, I can't imagine why one needs to wear such long riding skirts. They are so inconvenient when you have to ford streams or dash through briars. Oh, Fashion, will no Emancipation Proclamation free us from thee!

These reflections are filled with an edgy wit that walks up to stereotypes and scoffs, even as those stereotypes threaten her potential to transcend the worldly, to be a Transcendentalist. Highgate's letter suggests her careful weighing of multiple forms of (and needs for) real and full emancipation. These paragraphs simultaneously emphasize Highgate's physicality—embodied in assumptions about race and gender that, in the case of the long riding skirt, literally bound her—in ways that complicate any easy transfer of Thoreauvian principles. Indeed, her reverie with Thoreau's spirit is consistently interrupted by the physical—in part by her "confederate" pony and those threatening "rebel equestrians" in the description that opens this chapter. In relating all of this, she seamlessly utilizes an intimate personal style, as "On Horse Back" reads like a letter from a distant friend, and her praxis emphasizes her letters' (and her own) public places. She similarly calls attention to her (location-specific) distance from her "Philadelphia friends" even as she implies that there are spiritual links between all locations—as if Walden could be transplanted and transformed to offer solace to an overworked and multiply threatened African American woman teaching deep in Louisiana.

In some ways, "On Horse Back" stretches the sense of what correspondence might be and do as far as any *Recorder* text of the period, so it serves as a fitting transition to the later chapters of this volume that discuss the paper's poetry and fiction. But as such, it also suggests some of the limits of the form, of the *Recorder*, and, ultimately, of the material conditions that so shaped Edmonia Highgate's life of the mind and of the heart. Highgate herself—in the July 14, 1866, "Neglected Opportunities"—followed a blistering critique of how "the race needs living, working demonstrations" of how to "make something out of yourself" with this almost Whitman-esque series: "Have I said too much? Is it inelegant? Does it not breathe balm of a thousand flowers?" Seemingly in the frame of Lizzie Hart's last letter—weighing what she could say even as she asserted that she *must* say what her heart told her to say—Highgate was consistently asking what a letter could do. And her testing of these limits echoed her testing of other boundaries—of what a Black woman might do in the moments after the Civil War and Emancipation.

She would struggle with those broader limits for the rest of her short life—and she seems to have stepped away (or been pushed away) from using the *Recorder* to record such work. She did return to New Orleans to teach, and she made some limited progress there until the city's political and educational climate changed. Those changes and the fact that her family was regrouping in Mississippi led her to move there to teach. Her few contributions after "On Horse Back" fit much more easily within the traditional bounds of location-specific news; they are considerably less introspective and generally do not address the rich philosophical tensions seen in her earlier work. Her essential absence from the paper for much of 1867–1869, when she seems to have focused mainly on finding work that would support herself and help her family, also corresponds with the tumult at the paper in 1868. She seems to have hoped to write and speak more—as suggested by her February 1870 speech to the Massachusetts Female Anti-Slavery Society and her correspondence with white activist Gerrit Smith about the possibility of a lecture tour—and she also contemplated taking a position at Mississippi's new AMA college, Tougaloo. All of these opportunities might have given her more room to move—to read, think, write, and speak—than did the massively hard and sometimes risky work of teaching the recently freed people of the deep South. Ultimately, though, we do not yet know why Highgate's stunning correspondence with the *Recorder* stopped.

What we do know, sadly, is that Highgate died young, on October 16, 1870, when she was back for a short time in Syracuse. Her death was not noted in the *Recorder*; her drift from the Church and the paper may explain some of that absence. Local press coverage of her death may explain more: in a lurid pair of items published on October 16 and 17, the Syracuse *Courier* taunted her memory by asserting that her death was the result of the after-effects of a botched abortion that she reportedly sought after she was deserted by John Henry Vosburg, a white, married, part-time poet with whom she had reportedly fallen in love. Scholars have not fully tracked down the truth of these accusations—and may not be able to—but Highgate's brother-in-law Albert T. Morgan wrote to Gerrit Smith that Highgate had been "murdered 'with the world as an accessory.'"[47]

The world has been an accessory to her forgetting, too. The *Courier*'s reports would have been enough to prevent discussion of Highgate in the *Recorder*'s pages if her drift hadn't already done so. The lack of coverage of her later life and death in the *Recorder* is a stark reminder that the print community of the paper, including the communities of mourning so important to the next chapter, although radical in building safe(r) spaces for African Americans who had been wounded by racism, could sometimes be intensely conservative and even reactionary in who they excluded from those spaces. Similarly, that lack reminds us that, while the boundaries of the paper's correspondence reached far and wide not only in terms of physical geography but also the geographies of African American minds and hearts, they could stretch only so far.

{7}

"That Wished Home of Peace": The Personal and the Political in *Christian Recorder* Elegies

The Vashon family mourned. The reason for their unspeakable grief was set out in a few lines in the April 8, 1865, *Recorder*: "Died. VASHON.—In Pittsburg, Pa., on Saturday, March 25th, 1865, of congestion of the brain, Anne Paul, only and beloved daughter of Geo. B. and Susan Paul Vashon, aged 1 year, 5 mos., and 3 days."

In the coming weeks, the paper would be dominated by news of another death—that of Abraham Lincoln. Every column of the April 22, 1865, issue would be separated by thick black lines: a dark sight, a newspaper in mourning clothes. While Lincoln's memory has continued to be writ large in diverse spheres, after her short obituary, young Anne Paul Vashon would (almost) leave the public consciousness—so much so that most biographers of the Vashons do not name her at all, noting only that "the couple had seven children, four of whom survived."[1] This chapter begins to treat the swirl of my parenthetical "almost" as an entry point to some of the poetry that appeared in the *Recorder*—as Anne Paul Vashon's memory *did* reenter American print culture, briefly but powerfully, as the unnamed "our baby-girl" in a poem by her father in the August 26, 1865, *Recorder*. Though that poem, simply titled "In the Cars," has been totally ignored by scholars, it embodies not only her memory but also a critical set of functions performed by the *Recorder*'s poetry and especially its elegies during the Civil War era.

During Elisha Weaver's tenure as the editor and/or publisher of the *Christian Recorder*, the paper published well over six hundred poems.[2] Many of these poems were written specifically for the paper, often by African American authors.[3] Some of these poems—which were often labeled "For the Christian Recorder"—were written by poets like Frances Ellen Watkins Harper and J. Willis Menard, whose works have been or are being recovered.[4] Many were penned by subscribers (and occasionally non-subscribers) in what may well have been their only appearances in print. These poems included many of the expected genres of nineteenth-century public poetry—several varieties of occasional poetry, quasi-romantic and often sentimental lyrics, didactic verse (often loaded with biblical references), shorter narrative verse (often patriotic, sometimes historical), and, often, elegies.

In and of themselves, these poems represent a striking entry by African Americans into print culture. Contrary to much recent anthology work as well as scholarship on Civil War poetry, African American poetry during and after the Civil War went far beyond a handful of poems by a smaller handful of poets—and definitely beyond the (albeit important and amazing) songs of enslaved people.[5] Many critics continue to assert that "it has proved difficult to find poems published during or immediately following the war by black poets—a result, perhaps, of their different preoccupations during the war or of these poems having appeared in journals that were not preserved" (Barrett and Miller, *Words*, xvii). That assertion also continues broader Americanists' inattention to Black periodicals and a common willingness to assume that not finding something allows one to draw conclusions about the (seeming) absence. The *Recorder* alone published a number of poems specifically *about* the war during and immediately after the war.[6] Such poems were a small subset of the much larger number of poems noted above, which we must label broadly "poetry of the Civil War era." As a group, most of these poems, like Vashon's "In the Cars," have received no modern notice, scholarly or otherwise; few have even been reprinted since their original publication.[7]

Fully studying this large corpus—to say nothing of the poems the *Recorder* published after Weaver's exodus from the paper, including key work from Harper and several late nineteenth-century Black poets—would take a book in itself. To set the groundwork for such scholarship, to explore the place of poetry in the Civil War era *Recorder*, and to begin to consider how the *Recorder*'s writers and readers used print (and especially poetry) as part of a central community activity—mourning—this chapter focuses on a set of elegies published during the mid-1860s. It opens with a close, contextual reading of Vashon's poem—a text worth recovering in and of itself—and uses that reading to briefly discuss some of the parameters of subscriber-submitted elegies. It culminates in a comparative reading of community mourning in two sets of elegies—those written, first, about two African Americans close to the *Recorder*, young correspondent Frederick Waugh (who died in February 1866) and Weaver's wife Mary (who died in early March 1864), and, second, *Recorder* poems that should be counted among what Max Cavitch refers to as "countless elegies . . . for Abraham Lincoln" (196). This chapter thus challenges what often remains a prevailing critical sense—even though critics from Keith Leonard to Aldon Neilsen and from Cavitch to Paula Bernat Bennett have battled it skillfully—that Black formalist poetry is reactive rather than proactive, that it primarily takes "white" forms and repurposes them.

Far from arguing for a de-raced sense of form, I want to submit that African Americans shared deeply (albeit complexly and unevenly) in what Cavitch provocatively calls the "American Elegy" and that their engagement reminded readers that, to paraphrase Frederick Douglass, "the truth is . . . we are *here*, and here we are likely to remain." My reading of the elegies that *Recorder* authors wrote to Lincoln, for example, argues that these poems, in both participating in public battles over his memory and claiming Black spaces in the republic's public grieving, didn't so much inhabit a "white" space of elegy as they initiated an ideological fashioning of Lincoln as simultaneously "our president" and "*our* president." The *Recorder*'s Lincoln was mourned by a Black community in some of the ways it would mourn one of its own members—members like Frederick Waugh and Mary Weaver—in, with a nod to Ivy Wilson, a kind of "spectral democracy." But elegy upon elegy, like the massive number of obituaries and eulogies in the paper, populated that democracy—or, perhaps better, reminded readers that that democracy *was* populated—with African Americans' spirits. These texts recorded basic details of the earthly lives of African Americans in a print culture that often forgot or ignored them. In so doing, they also rewrote the sense of sentiment that still dominates many critics' conceptions of African Americans in the nineteenth century—that African Americans were objects of print sentiment rather than agents. The *Recorder* elegies thus simultaneously affirmed that African American mourning could be, first and foremost, for African Americans. Like much of the paper's poetry in general and like the correspondence studied in the last chapter, the *Recorder*'s elegies thus conceived of multiple audiences and functions, and they worked within a broader American print culture while simultaneously carving spaces specifically for African American concerns and conversations. And in this large-scale claiming of poetics of mourning and memory, *Recorder* elegists built crucial groundwork for later African American poets and writers generally.

To sketch this landscape, the chapter offers samples both representative and provocative, but it does not pretend to be comprehensive. Similarly, while the chapter—especially the final discussion of elegies to Lincoln—begins to place the *Recorder*'s poetry within larger frames, its central goal is to recover and consider these poems in their "home" publication and in the hands of that publication's readers. In all of this work, like the rest of this volume, this chapter is thus a beginning rather than an ending.

"In the Cars" appeared in one of the spaces the *Recorder* regularly reserved for poetry, the first column of the first page just under the paper's publication and business information. While several of the *Recorder*'s elegies also appeared there, many more were included in the paper's interior—sometimes even integrated into death notices, obituaries, and eulogies. A host of circumstances could explain why "In the Cars" was placed on the front page—from Vashon's comparative fame to Weaver's own respect for him.[8] The poem thus shared page one with a host of post-war news as well as with Chapter 27 of Julia Collins's *Curse of Caste*.[9] The poem's authorship would likely have been clear to those readers who had seen references to Vashon in this and other Black newspapers over the years, as it was signed "G. B. V., Pittsburgh, Pa."[10] Some readers may even, for example, have known of Vashon's "Vincent Ogé," an epic-fragment that had been published in *Autographs for Freedom* in 1854 and that remains his most discussed poem.[11] Other readers, though, may have been drawn by the poem's title, subject, or placement. Most regular *Recorder* readers would have known that the poem was not a reprint, as it carried the "For the Christian Recorder" heading that marked original contributions to the paper (and that had been the locus of Weaver's anger at Annie Smith).

"In the Cars" is composed of two numbered sections, dated October 2, 1864, and August 11, 1865, respectively. Both sections, as suggested by the title, focus on the travels of a first-person speaker. That speaker, an unnamed father who is an autobiographical representation of Vashon, intertwines dreamlike domestic, Christian, and natural imagery throughout both sections. Both sections have formal similarities, too—especially their use of Italian quatrains. Still, even the poem's visual appearance alerts readers to the painful asymmetry and the movement between the two sections. While the first section is composed of five tight quatrains, the second has nine, and while the second section hints at its subject in its first stanza, that subject doesn't become fully apparent until the section's fifth stanza. In a broader sense, the first section's easy resolution contrasts massively with the second section's struggle. All of these features highlight how the poem transports speaker, characters, and readers from a "before" to an "after," one that leaves the experiences between the listed dates unspoken, perhaps because some of them are ultimately unspeakable.

The poem's first line—"Five fleeting hours, on towards famed Lake Erie"—hints at the speaker's journey, a trip north and then east from Pittsburgh to Syracuse. But though this journey offers a "varied scene," as "Night has dropped her sable screen," the speaker bids "Fancy homeward an excursion take" (2–4). The second and third stanza embody this dream:

> The rocking car no more a car doth seem,
> But dons the shape of a familiar room;
> And in the stead of haziness and gloom,
> There all the stars of my affection gleam.
>
> There sits the dear, fond mother of my boys,
> Who kneel around her—while, with smile and nod,
> Their cousin soothes our latest-sent of God—
> Our baby-girl—the crowning of our joys. (5–12)

The second stanza's transformation of the moving car into a domestic scene—a victory of home over machine, the "stars" over the gloomy night of the train's window—is again emphasized in the fourth stanza, especially in the stunning shift of rhyme from "blare" to "prayer":

> And farther, higher, doth my fancy roam;
> For, silencing the swift wheels' iron blare,
> Three lisping voices blend into one prayer:
> "God bless dear papa! Bring him safely home!" (13–16)

The speaker finally leaves his reverie when he is moved to respond in the fifth stanza—in ways that mark two "fathers" in the poem and that simultaneously join and separate "fathers" and "children":

> And, God bless you, my darlings! Gently fall
> The bliss of slumber on you. While we pray,—
> You at your home, I on my far-off way,—
> God, the All-Father, watches o'er us all. (17–20)

The mother surrounded by her three young sons was Vashon's wife Susan Paul Vashon (see Figure 7.1), and the youths' cousin was likely Georgianna Colder, who lived with the family for decades. The youngest child, "our baby-girl," was the much-loved Anne Paul Vashon, who had been named to honor Susan Paul Vashon's own mother (who she had lost while she was herself still a child). Framing this domestic scene is Vashon himself—a loving (Black) father joining his "far-off" family in prayer and anxiously awaiting the

MRS. SUSAN PAUL SMITH VASHON

FIGURE 7.1 *Susan Paul Vashon, from Hallie Q. Brown's* Homespun Heroines *(1926). Author's Collection.*

moment when he can return home and make that family whole again. Contemporary critics might rush to set this section aside as an example—albeit skillful and, I would assert, honestly touching—of nineteenth-century sentimental verse. However, the biographical base of the "excursion" of Vashon's "Fancy" challenges such easy dismissals.

We need first remember that the very naturalness of the deep familial love so emphasized in Vashon's vision—the very factor that makes this section so sentimental—was something that the broader US culture (print and otherwise) actively denied African Americans. Vashon's vision of Black domesticity, for example, is not simply a Stowe-ian "granting" of sentiment to Black Others (like Eliza or Uncle Tom), not simply a moment of white tears shed for Black folks. What's most radical here is the fact that the (political) assertion of Black sentiment's existence and Black agency in *exercising* sentiment is essentially left unstated; Vashon's speaker simply, powerfully *assumes* that existence and agency. The speaker represents the mutuality of Black sentiment as the everyday, an everyday in which white folks looking in would be the Others, in part because they simply don't matter to—and aren't present in—the poem.[12] The first section of Vashon's poem, as Frances Smith Foster argues about the Black press generally, operates much more "from self-interest, from the desires of African Americans to communicate their experiences and philosophies, to record the words and ideas most precious to their own psychic and spiritual (as well as physical or political) survival, and to create and to preserve their history for themselves and others" than from any reaction to white racism or any need to argue for Black humanity to white people (723). Thus, Vashon's very assumptions mean that simply by its existence, the poem challenges the dominant American print culture. Perhaps most powerfully, the poem's first section locks a representative moment of Anne Paul Vashon's short life in readers' minds: the poem *is* literally an act of survival—the survival of the memory of a beloved Black child.

For those *Recorder* readers who knew Vashon's destination in the first section's journey and for those who gave some thought to the reasons for many of the teacher-poet's travels—and some *Recorder* readers likely did—Vashon's first section destination would have only reaffirmed the powerful interface between everyday Black love and activist politics. On October 2, 1864, Vashon was traveling to the National Convention of Colored Men, the same October 1864 gathering at Syracuse that was addressed by a young Edmonia Highgate.[13] In short, Vashon was traveling to and mentally preparing for a critical meeting at which speaker after speaker—Frederick Douglass, Frances Ellen Watkins Harper, John Mercer Langston, Henry Highland Garnet—emphasized Black personhood as part of "domestic" arguments tied to the coming election and to what a post–Civil War, post-emancipation United States might look like.

Even those who did not know or even speculate about Vashon's specific destination might be alerted to such questions simply by the poem's title, as many *Recorder* readers had found discrimination "in the cars." The January 28, 1865, *Recorder*, for example, published "The Right of Colored People to Ride in the Cars," and the subject was regularly discussed in the paper. Richard Roberson's death—his illness aggravated by the enforcement of discriminatory transit policies, as discussed in chapter 3—might even have been in some readers' minds. The fact that the "cars" taking Vashon to the Syracuse meeting are simultaneously both a site of potential discrimination and the mode of visionary transport to an idealized home underscores the fact that those cars, that convention, the racism surrounding *Recorder* readers, and the love in Vashon's home—a variant of which perhaps graced many homes subscribing to the *Recorder*—were far apart and simultaneously very, very close.

The comfort of the fifth stanza's—and the first section's—final lines is soon removed. The opening of the poem's second section extends the first line of the poem's "five fleeting hours" to the "Ten moons" that "have waxed and waned since" this remembrance "I sung." It thus both marks the second section as retrospective and reminds readers that something must have happened in the intervening months (21). Those "ten moons," the speaker says, were "replete with household joys and grief": "Joys many, and one sorrow, whose relief / Can only be when years this heart have wrung" (22–24).

The speaker is "once more within the cars," albeit not in the physical "turmoil of murky night" (25–26). This is a different kind of night: though the journey in this section also promises to return him to "my wife" and "my three darling boys," his "flooded eyes will dim" (35, 39). Much of the beginning of the section sidesteps the cause of that pain—discussing instead the sun "in all his full-blown summer pride" seeking "fair Juniata as his bride" (29, 32)—even though the section, like the train, can only move toward its ultimate destination: dealing with the loss of "she, our babe, our latest-sent of God! / Alas, alas, our earliest called of Him!" (37–38).

Finally, the speaker cries "Ah, father, wherefore fell thy chastening rod?" and visualizes, in a complex rewriting of the first section's dream, the fact that

> She may not come, with tottering gait, to greet
> Her sire's return; nor e're, with gleeful laugh
> Tender her ready lips, whence he may quaff
> Fell tides of love than nectar far more sweet.
>
> Ah, no, sweet bud, that didst too early bloom,
> The chill March wind hath nipped thy promise fair.
> What power, then, may banish our despair?
> What spell recall thee from the icy tomb? (40–48)

Given the *Recorder*'s sensibilities, Vashon's own deep faith, and nineteenth-century mores, the poem cannot end with such questioning—cannot end with the hoped-for spell.[14]

Vashon's speaker uses perhaps the poem's heaviest iamb (almost a spondee) to turn us toward the expected Christian resolution:

> Not so! Be ours the hope and faith which tell
> That our lost bud blooms 'mong the angel flowers,
> That in another life it will be ours,
> Forevermore with God and us to dwell.
>
> Ours! On, towards home! My wife, my boys, my niece,
> Await me there. Our sainted baby-girl,
> In her new state, fairer than orient pearl,
> Waits for us all in that wished home of peace. (49–56)

The repetition of "our" and "ours" here should give us pause—especially given its stress at the opening of the final stanza. Appearing five times in these two stanzas (along with two usages of "us"), this language is the language of family but also—especially if the poem was read and read aloud by subscribers—the language of community. This communal "home" even expands the linking of the father and the "All-Father" in the first section by joining earthly home and heaven. As much as it demonstrates one earthly father's grief and mourning, it also offers instruction and succor to a broader print community tied to that "All-Father," and it calls to the members of that community who might have had similar experiences and have had children (or other family members like Lizzie Hart's sister and Edmonia Highgate's brother) who needed similar memorialization. While both sections allude to the wait until the father's return, the second section defines the journey "towards home" as both a return to the domestic circle—"my wife, my boys, my niece"—and ultimately as the journey to heaven, a journey that also promises reunion. While the specificity of the final stanza marks this text very much as Vashon's—as a family poem—the larger representations invite the *Recorder*'s African American readers who had lost a child (or, more broadly, a loved one) into that same "home of peace." Again, the poem assumes that this home is a specific location for and of African Americans. That a Black child and a Black father and a Black mother and an extended Black family bring about our understanding of this home extends the poem's radical everydayness to argue for a full sense of Black domesticity—a kind of spectral (democratic) domesticity that demands acknowledgment of earthly striving and suffering even as it asserts heavenly promise.

What is more striking, however, is that even as Vashon affirms the *Recorder*'s constant calls to trust in God in the face of great pain, he only offers such resolution after a kind of rebellion. The poem does move toward "home," but in the midst of the journey, we see a full stanza that, while marked with the language of "not" and "nor," creates and shares the Anne Paul Vashon that her father can only dream of, one who in some ways challenges the "All-Father"'s will. Before the poem arrives at its resolution, if only in a fleeting fantasy, Anne Paul Vashon is shown with "a tottering gait," a "gleeful laugh," and "tides of love" (41, 42, 44). Her father even talks of casting a "spell" to "recall" her from death. The radical political acts of loving a Black child and of remembering a Black child—in the midst of an American print culture that wouldn't even bother to forget her because that would mean acknowledging her in the first place—become part and parcel of the everyday acts of a parent journeying on after losing a child, a parent willing to question the very God at the center of the *Recorder*'s endeavors, and a parent who will struggle for "years" in which "this heart have wrung." "In the Cars" offers a glimmer of remembrance *and* of the possibility that was embodied in young Anne Paul Vashon.[15]

As such, race both matters and doesn't matter in Vashon's poem.[16] It doesn't matter because white folks have no place here; *they* do not matter to the poem. And, simultaneously, Anne Paul Vashon and George Boyer Vashon's race is critical to how and where mourning—and especially mourning through elegy—can take place; it matters "in the cars." It matters deeply.[17] Vashon's "community of mourners" moved out in concentric circles from his own grief ("her sire's return," the kisses "he may quaff") to his family's ("our lost bud") to the *Recorder*'s readers, who, as chapter 4 establishes, were almost completely made up of African Americans. Vashon could have chosen another outlet for the poem—one that was not created by African Americans, one that was not focused on African American life, and one that did not reach almost solely African Americans. Certainly the *Liberator*—which had long connections to both the Pauls and the Vashons—would have taken it, as might a number of (white-run) reform and religious papers. Vashon might even have received a positive response from a more "mainstream" white periodical, which could have removed the contexts of the *Recorder* and a community who actually knew the race of "G.B.V. of Pittsburgh." He chose instead the *Recorder*, a venue and a community he must have felt would best understand and appreciate how his poem, like the community of letters discussed in the last two chapters, fought for spaces of Black grief, remembrance, and hope.

The *Recorder*'s elegists of the period, like people throughout the nation, were at a hinge moment in terms of conceptualizing death. As Jeffrey Steele writes, "by midcentury, the culture of mourning had pervaded every area of life in America," but, according to Drew Gilpin Faust, with the Civil War, "the United States embarked on a new relationship with death" (92, 1). Like the correspondents studied in earlier chapters, part of elegists' function was to provide local news—in this case, deeply sad news—to the paper's readers. In this light, elegies were extensions of the early General Conferences' calls for a periodical that would hold the connection together. Each of the subscribers discussed in chapter 4 might want information garnered from such elegies—especially given subscribers' mobility and potential distance from home folks; given how rare positive white press coverage of Black lives (and deaths) was, each might need the reassurance that they and their families and friends might be remembered in print. Several would also want to ensure that those left behind mourned them properly.

Recorder elegies were thus deeply tied to the practice of faith and to education about that practice. Many were especially concerned with the distinction Faust articulates between "the Good Death" and "the Bad Death." Faust argues that "the concept of the Good Death was central to mid-nineteenth-century America, as it had long been at the core of Christian practice. Dying was an art, and the tradition of *ars moriendi* had provided rules of conduct . . . since at least the fifteenth century: how to give up one's soul 'gladlye and wilfuly'; how to meet the devil's temptations of unbelief, despair, impatience, and worldly attachment; how to pattern one's dying on that of Christ; how to pray" (6). The specificity of Faust's "the" when labeling "The Good Death" reminds us that, to many, all deaths that did not meet such criteria could easily have "bad" results.

Faust recognizes that "perhaps the most distressing aspect of death for many Civil War Americans was that thousands of young men were dying away from home" and so were intrinsically at risk of dying badly (9). This was certainly a central concern in Mrs. E. Morris's October 15, 1864, *Recorder* elegy to Sergeant James W. Davis—son of AME minister and *Recorder* subscriber Henderson Davis—who died at Fort Pickens, Florida, while a member of Company B in the 25th USCT: "No wife was near him when he died, / No friendly voice to cheer" (5–6). But Davis's death was clearly "a Good Death" in Morris's poem because his moral character and actions ensured that, even far from home, he was right with God:

> He fell the country's greatest pride—
> A noble volunteer.
>
> 'Twas hard for one so young and good;
> But God had willed it so:
> He fell, as every soldier should—
> His face turned to the foe. (7–12)

It would be easy to think of the *Recorder*'s elegies (like this one) as doubly instructive: teaching readers to right their souls' condition before death and teaching readers how to mourn appropriately. Certainly Emma A. Tates's "Lines on the Death of John L. Herley" does both. Reverend Daniel Cooper sent in an obituary of Herley that was published in the August 9, 1862, *Recorder*, and he appended the elegy, identifying Tates as Herley's sister. Cooper spoke of how Herley "was brought up by Christian parents—but, like the prodigal son . . . departed from their instruction," felt "the hand of affliction," "return[ed] and repent[ed]," lost his wife, "went into a backsliding state," and finally, in "very much suffering" before "the monster *Death* came," "found pardon." Cooper said his inclusion of the poem was designed, in part, "to encourage our people here to write." Cooper—like countless other eulogists and elegists thus reaffirmed the fact that Vashon's print-centered memorializing impulse was wide and deep in the Church.

Tates's first stanza is a textbook example of Max Cavitch's sense of the elegy as the poem (for the) left behind:

> Death has been here and stole away
> My only brother, John,
> And I'm still mourning here below,
> As one that's left alone. (1–4)[18]

Like Cooper, Tates's autobiographical speaker asserts her function as accurately memorializing her brother's complex life: while he "too soon backslid; / Like Adam, he partook of sin," "like Peter, then, he grieved" (18–20). However, her position was much closer, and her intent, more personal: "One thing I know—that he did pray; I witnessed with my ears" (13–14). She is also moved to memorialize her family's distress—presaging Vashon's family grief and emphasizing Faust's sense that "family was central to the *ars moriendi* tradition" (10). She asks,

> My sisters, don't you feel his loss?
> Oh! father feels it more.
> My *mother*—she can count the cost,
> Upon whose breast he leans.
> She often offered him to God
> In prayer, both night and day,
> That He would his backslidings heal,
> And wash his sins away. (37–44)

Such work emphasizes the impact of sin on an entire family—and, by extension, especially given Cooper's headnote, a community. But it also speaks to lessons learned through death:

> Remember, friends, as we pass by
> The grave of brother John,
> As we are now, so once was he,
> But time with him is o'er. (29–32)

But we need to think of the paper's discussions of how to mourn and how to right the course of a wrongly directed (or undirected) life as more than simply didactic and to see that even their didacticism might not always have been aimed at the assumed audience or the assumed function. The elegy to Sergeant Davis, which contained a clear headnote listing his rank (twice) as well as his unit, reminds all readers that Davis's "Good Death" had come in part because he was "a noble volunteer" (8). Davis's elegy marks a fallen Black soldier as "the country's greatest pride"—"How wondrous his reward!"—and this approach uses nationalism to cross racial lines (7, 14). Further, the lessons taught by Davis's death are different from those of Herley's. Even if the core message of right living and right dying is present, Davis's death was as much or more a lesson in bravery, patriotism, and African Americans' (potential) places in the nation.[19]

In and beyond such lessons, consolation was central. The opening lines of the elegy to Davis—"The loved of many hearts is gone, / The light of many eyes"—are clearly designed to console those left behind, especially the family who could not gather at Davis's deathbed. *Recorder* writers, too, shared in the recognition, again per Faust, that "sudden death" in particular "represented a profound threat to the fundamental assumptions about the correct way to die" (18). In this vein, the assurances of a "Good Death" and a call to heaven— even Vashon's "Not so!"—were crucial. "No tears shall dim her bright black eyes," Samuel C. Frisby wrote in his November 21, 1863, elegy to Rachel Price, the youngest daughter of Henry and Mary Price who died of diphtheria at fifteen months (17). "No sorrow shade her brow," he assured family and community, "Our gentle, precious, loving child, / Is with her Savior now" (18–20). Similarly, James Davis's father Henderson Davis Jr. promised—in an elegy he wrote to Anna Eliza Smith, "infant daughter of Edward and Harriet Smith, aged 3 months and 24 days"—that there was only "one thing so consoling": "We, thy presence soon shall see, / In a world that's free from mourning, / Love! we'll come to live with thee" (9–12).

But because many must have felt the precursor emotions to Vashon's "Not so!" some elegies offer spaces to reflect on the difficulties of giving or receiving *any* consolation. Lizzie Hart's May 28, 1864, elegy to her sister Julia, for example, says bluntly

> I cannot realize your death,
> I wait, I watch, I look for you,
> Sometimes I almost think I hear
> Your cheerful voice within the room. (5–8)

While Hart *knew* that "you are gone where angels dwell," still "sometimes I almost think I hear / Your well-known footstep at the door" (4, 17–18). Perhaps almost as striking as Vashon's battle with resolution, Hart's poem ends by telling how her tears "come again, and wet my cheek" (21). She writes,

"When e're I think of you, / I will plant flowers on your grave," but does not represent that act as an ending (22–23). Rather, she says,

> We'll miss you when the morning dawns,
> At noon we miss you too,
> But oh! when twilight cometh,
> There is none we miss like you. (25–28)

As this grief is not marked with a clear end, so, too, the poem continues to address Hart's sister directly—as if by the force of "you," death could be beaten, transcended through a linguistic spell.

The need for room to explore—and for a poetry that acknowledged—the difficulties of grieving for a child (especially one who much of the world might ignore) were embodied in what initially seems the most didactic among all of the *Recorder* elegies I have surveyed, a poem that seems most to deny such a need, Benjamin Tucker Tanner's "Benny's Gone." The April 18, 1863, issue that includes the poem also carries one of Henry McNeal Turner's regular letters, which notes that "Rev. Benjamin T. Tanner lost his youngest son yesterday evening, and it was remarkable how willingly he gave it up to God, considering that he is a man whose affections appeared to be at all times clustering around his children." Tanner's poem is signed "B. T. T.," and *Recorder* readers who did not recognize this signature from several earlier contributions would surely have connected the initials to the name in Turner's letter. Most would have recognized Tanner as a fast-rising force in the AME Church, and many may have read his *Recorder* essays and letters on theology, church history, national politics, and ministerial praxis.

Tanner's poem—six five-line stanzas—relies on a repetition of the title in the second line of each stanza to set up a variation of consolation in each stanza's third and fourth lines, as in "Benny's gone. / Benny's gone from tears to smiles, / Tears are depressing, smiles refreshing," and "Benny's gone. / Benny's gone, from earth to heaven, / Earth is sad, heaven is glad" (22–24, 2–4). While these lines lack the technique and artistry of Vashon's poem, the end resolution to the young child's death is not dissimilar. What is more striking is the repetition of the poem's first line at the beginning of every stanza, an apostrophe to Tanner's wife Sarah (shown in Figure 7.2), "Sadee, cease thy weeping:" The colon marks this as a frame for the discussion of their child's fate—a frame closed in the first four stanzas by a variation of "Why dost thou weep then, dear" that then progresses to the fifth stanza's "Why weep, why weep, my dear?" and then, finally, in the last line of the poem, to "O cease thy weeping, dear" (20, 25, 30).

Arguably, this frame makes the poem as much about the grieving Sarah Tanner as about young Benny, and the necessity for the frame emphasizes that Sarah Tanner was, indeed, weeping—and may have been asking

FIGURE 7.2 *Sarah Miller Tanner, c. 1897, unidentified photographer. Henry Ossawa Tanner Papers, Archives of American Art, Smithsonian Institution.*

questions similar to Vashon's or hearing the kinds of ghostly reminders of which Hart writes. If we read the poem aloud, Tanner's voice could be didactic—even a command or a patronizing lecture, with a troubling sense of gender politics—or it could be a struggling, pleading husband trying to comfort his inconsolable wife, weeping and weeping. Read alongside Turner's letter, one could even wonder if this minister "whose affections appeared to be at all times clustering around his children" might not have been trying to talk himself into believing his own words. . . . By being so didactic, Tanner again and again emphasizes *why* such didacticism could be necessary and might fail, even for a minister and a minister's wife. That the language "cease thy weeping" most directly echoes God's instruction to Rachel (as she is weeping for her children) makes this moment all the more complex, as it reminds us that Tanner is preaching and praying in multiples ways.[20] In these frames, Tanner's very denials establish and remember Vashon's spells, Hart's ghosts, "Sadee's weeping," and other markers of the struggles in the *Recorder*'s elegies.

All of these gestures emphasized the importance of the individuals who peopled Vashon's concentric circles of grief—different layers of a community of mourners who made a collective effort to remember those who had passed and to aid those still alive. This praxis explains the massive number of elegies in the *Recorder* during the period studied here, but it also places that praxis specifically in an almost-all-Black community, an AME framework, and a set of print venues and practices separate from—even as they functioned in dialogue with—the majority-white "mainstream" of American print, including the tropes and approaches common to (white) American elegies. Considering how Abraham Lincoln—a white man, albeit a very particular white man—came into this Black network of community mourning and specifically into the frameworks for *Recorder* elegies hinted at above thus teaches us about all of these elements and argues more broadly about the places of poetry in the *Recorder*.

Such exploration, however, demands that we first consider a distinction other than race, albeit one that was deeply shaped by the segregated national culture. While only a handful of *Recorder* workers and readers would be recognized as "public" figures by a nation run by a white hierarchy, within the African American nation and especially the AME community there were well-known figures who had "national" reputations within specific bounds marked by race and denomination. The cases of Frederick B. Waugh and especially Mary Weaver offer instructive examples of how these more public AME figures were mourned. Such mourning for public figures by definition offered moments for teaching and learning and meant that such figures still served "public" functions in death and in memorialization, including elegist's typifying and troping of their life stories. But such mourning also acknowledged that these figures were very much private citizens—an oxymoron indeed, given the debates over Black citizenship—and that the grief of their family and friends shared in the complex personal relations that made up the innermost regions of Vashon's concentric circles. *Recorder* elegies to AME public figures found varying balances between these impulses.

Waugh's AME public status was comparatively new, and the troping of his memory focused on his age and potential within and beyond the Church. That troping called for specific action from youth: to be like Waugh. A student at Wilberforce who had just entered Oberlin, Waugh had returned home to Providence, Rhode Island, to visit family when he died on February 21, 1866. He was nineteen. New Bedford minister J. H. Johnson remembered him as "the little hero and young orator" and "a young man of great intellectual talents, and of rare moral and religious attainments." Waugh had authored a well-received *Recorder* poem, "The Song of the Freedman," which appeared in the March 21, 1863, issue and promised "A glorious union we shall have ... where the oppress'd of every land / May enjoy their liberty."[21] Waugh himself was not listed as a subscriber, but his father, John T. Waugh, a waiter in Providence, was acknowledged in the June 29, 1861, issue and renewed at least three times after. After the publication of "The Song of Freedom," the young Frederick sent a number of letters to the paper, and at least seven were published between late 1863 and 1865. Dubbed at times "Our Wilberforce Correspondent," Waugh authored two letters on the catastrophic Wilberforce fire of 1865, and Weaver was moved in a March 3, 1866, *Recorder* memorial to note that his "death has carried sadness to many hearts," as he was "deeply imbued with the Spirit of Christ."

Two elegies to Waugh appeared in the *Recorder*—both in the March 10, 1866, issue. Johnson, a mentor, penned a short quatrain to conclude his longer letter about Waugh. An untitled, group-authored poem that came at the end of a letter from a "Committee" of students at Wilberforce (in response to "the death of our highly esteemed brother and fellow student") is more informative to this study. That committee offered a powerful demonstration of the intellectual hope at the AME's young college, Wilberforce: composed of two young men who would become prominent ministers (John T. Jenifer and Thomas H. Jackson) and two students who are tougher to trace (future minister James E. Carter and Mary J. Philips), the group was chaired by Mary E. Ashe. Ashe was likely the (lead) author of the elegy: she had already had an essay published in the October 14, 1865, *Recorder*, would eventually garner praise for her Wilberforce collegiate graduation address on "Science: The Thought of God," and would enter American print more broadly, albeit under another name. She married Benjamin F. Lee—future *Recorder* editor, Wilberforce President, and AME Bishop—on December 30, 1873. In the late 1880s and early 1890s, she published more than a dozen poems in the *Recorder* alone, and her "Afmerica," parts of which appeared in both the Boston *Negro* and the *Southern Workman* in 1886, was, as one biographer put it, "copied extensively."[22] It is included in Paula Bernat Bennett's groundbreaking 1998 anthology *Nineteenth Century American Women Poets* and has received some modern attention—including in Bennett's 2003 *Poets in the Public Sphere*.

Ashe, then, brought to the elegy for Waugh some real understanding of nineteenth-century poetic conventions and a working sense of Black periodicals and print culture. Her (committee's) elegy to Waugh addresses many of the calls and tropes discussed above, opening "He is gone from this world of sorrow, / From the land of sin he has fled" and praising him profusely: "As a student, no blemish was on him; / As a Christian, he lived by God's grace, / And his class, ah, how tender he led them!" (1–2, 13–15) The poem also balances consolation, continuing pain, and questioning, especially in its last stanza's repeated "methinks":

> Oh, God! Oh God! what makes our sadness?
> Frederick Waugh, where art thou now?
> Methinks I see thee now in gladness.
> Methinks you wear an angel's brow. (21–24)[23]

But Ashe wants to emphasize Waugh's place as a public figure, and she thus moves beyond grieving in public (through print) to calling *for* public grieving. She integrates and even names a much wider community in the poem's second and third stanzas:

> Weep, weep! all ye students of Wilberforce,
> And, ye students of Oberlin, cry:
> Let not a student of either
> Show his or her cheek to be dry.
>
> Oh, God! why has thou bereft us?
> Forgive us for questioning Thee;
> Our Father Almighty, console us,
> Oh! make us as worthy as he. (5–12)

The poem's ongoing dialogue between asking and ordering consolation bridges into asking and ordering forgiveness for questioning God's decision, especially given the first line of the third stanza's allusion to Psalm 22:1 and the better-known Matthew 27:46 (cries to God about anguish and faith made by David and Jesus, respectively). But this battle to mourn appropriately *and* faithfully is framed in terms of not just Waugh's family but specifically named broader circles of community members—students of the all-Black Wilberforce and the majority-white Oberlin. The final two lines of the second stanza in particular—with their careful "either" for Black *and* white college students as well as the "or" for men *and* woman—demand that these communities recognize and be recognized as participants in the mourning of Waugh. This demand is reemphasized in the language of the final resolution the committee sent with the poem: "*Resolved*, That a copy of these resolutions be forwarded to the parents of the deceased, and to the *Christian Recorder*."

The elegy to Waugh does not set aside the concerns of the more "private" elegies discussed above but rather articulates a level of sharing in these concerns among the different circles of mourners, circles invoked in the "to the parents of the deceased, and to the *Christian Recorder*." The repeated "us" here brings these various groups together in a collective, communal mourning and also represents a reaching out to other (potential) mourners. The resolutions especially evince an understanding that the *Recorder* could stitch this Ohio-centered community not only to Waugh's family in Providence—who would receive the resolutions in manuscript—but, through print, to the larger AME community across the nation. Evidence of that larger community can be seen in the March 24, 1866, issue, which included a set of resolutions to Waugh from another group. Remembering Waugh as "a bright star in the literary sky," "our loved and respected companion," and an "eloquent champion" of "our race," the L'Ouverture Literary Assembly, a group of "colored young men of the city of Providence," joined their colleagues from Ohio in communal mourning and a collective attempt to memorialize Waugh.[24] From Ohio to Rhode Island and back again, readers of the *Recorder* mourned Frederick Waugh. The topoi and tropes that allowed such collective grief for an AME public figure were expansions and revisions of those in more personal *Recorder* elegies.

The print response to the death of Mary Weaver in early March 1864 functioned within these frameworks but was larger and more multidimensional—and, of course, happened before both the end of the Civil War and Lincoln's assassination. Her place in the AME public sphere as the wife of a major Church figure—though circumscribed by her gender—was more significant than Waugh's, and so the size of the response is not surprising. In the wake of her death—possibly through complications tied to childbirth—the *Recorder* published a eulogy by J. H. Turpin, a letter of consolation from Henry McNeal Turner, a handful of short items, and at least five elegies: "Lines in Memory of Mrs. Mary C. Weaver" by "Shalom" (a pseudonym used by Benjamin Tucker Tanner) in the March 26, 1864, issue; "Lines on the Death of Mrs. Weaver" by the as-yet unidentified "A. C. W." of Providence, Rhode Island, in the April 2, 1864 issue; "Sacred to the Memory of Mrs. M. C. Weaver" by Sallie [Daffin], then of Norfolk, Virginia, also in the April 2, 1864, issue; "Lines on the Death of Mary C. Weaver" by Susan Paul Vashon in the April 9, 1864, issue; and "On the Death of Mrs. Mary C. Weaver" by Jane E. Thompson in the April 16, 1864, issue.[25] These poems spoke of the larger print community of mourning suggested above but were diverse (and numerous) enough that they also illustrated some divisions within that community, especially in terms of gender and public mourning.

For all this outpouring, we know frustratingly little about Mary Weaver—in large part because of gender and racial discrimination in record creation and preservation. As discussed earlier, her better-known husband was essentially written out of the AME record after his 1868 expulsion from the Book Concern (and his subsequent troubles with Church leaders), but Mary Weaver was *only* ever marginally a part of that record. We know her mother's name, for example, only because of a May 22, 1869, obituary of Louisa Miller that notes that Miller and her unnamed husband "gave to the world Mary C. Weaver." We do not know whether Miller was indeed Mary Weaver's maiden name, and, as discussed in chapter 3, we do not know her birthplace or even her exact birth date, though she was likely about thirty-one when she died. A few might have remembered her brief essay, "The Beauties of Nature," in the January 1860 issue of the *Repository*, which seems to be her only published work found to date.[26] But most *Recorder* readers who did not have personal knowledge of Mary Weaver would have glimpsed her—as contemporary readers must—only briefly in her husband's *Recorder* comments, like those in his September 14, 1861, report of returning home to find "Rev. A. L. Stanford and Mrs. Weaver . . . struggling for life to keep things as near right as possible until we returned." The paper also offered brief notes on the Weavers attending various AME churches together and notices of Mary Weaver's work for the "contrabands," in which she engaged with figures like Jabez Pitt Campbell, the man who would preach her funeral sermon.[27]

But given Elisha Weaver's position in the national Church, his charges (and colleagues) in both the West and the AME center of Philadelphia, the expectations (social and otherwise) of ministers' wives, and Mary Weaver's own inclination to good works, the number of AME Church members and *Recorder* readers who *did* have personal or at least secondhand knowledge of her cannot be underestimated. As Turner's letter notes, "the name of your esteemed consort has often been mentioned as a co-laborer with you, in a manner which did honor to her industry and attainments."

Benjamin Tanner's elegy to Mary Weaver—the first of the extant poems to appear—comes closest to the more public-minded Black poems Cavitch studies in *American Elegy*. While she is named twice in the long poem, even that naming relies more on Christian sensibilities of "Mary" than on any move toward particularity. Indeed, throughout much of the poem, she is an "angel spirit" (used twice, in lines 1 and 11), "dovelike" (again used twice, in lines 19 and 24), "too pure for earth and time," and "meek" like "the stream which hides / Its face, while through dark shades it glides" (15–16). There is little working through grief here—though the speaker says, "Weep, maidens! For the vacant seat"—and the consolation the poem offers focuses on how "amidst a glorious array / of peace and light, she took her way" (33, 30–31) "A. C. W."'s elegy went even further into anonymous typification—never naming Mary Weaver outside of the poem's title, but instead referring to how "The Christian" was now "living through Jesus' love" (6). Here, Weaver's death was more of a lesson than anything else: the poem ends by hoping readers would "Bear in our faithful minds the end, / And keep the prize in view" (14–15). It is as if these poems "mourn" *only* a public "Mrs. Weaver."

While the elegies and resolutions to Waugh marked him as the ideal young/future renaissance (church)man, they leaned toward personalizing and particularizing that public figure. They never reached the level of specificity of Vashon and Hart's poems, but they went far beyond these initial elegies to Mary Weaver, which were all about offering a (sterling) representative of a type, sans individuality. Notably, both the Waugh "type" and this Mary Weaver "type" were tied deeply to the Church's sense of community and especially community development, in which both potential/future ministers and ministers' wives were critical presences. Finally, even in representing death, both were future-centered, both in terms of *ars moriendi* for *Recorder* readers and ultimate heavenly assurance.

That said, "maidens" did "weep" at Mary Weaver's death, and some of the AME women who knew her wrote to the paper. Their elegies do not totally sidestep the structures of Tanner and "A. C. W."'s poems—in part because at least two of the women, Sallie Daffin and Susan Paul Vashon, knew very well the demands on and for church women. Daffin was already teaching in Norfolk, Virginia—her poem was datelined there on March 22, 1864—but she had been schooled in Philadelphia, knew the Weavers, and had already begun several years of reading and writing for the *Recorder*.[28] Vashon's activist work, building from both her and her husband's family ties, was also already broad and deep by 1864.[29] Her identification with Weaver, the mother of two small children when she died, may well have been especially pronounced; when Vashon sent her "Lines on the Death of Mary C. Weaver," her daughter Anne (the child memorialized in "In the Cars") was barely five months old. But even as these poems engage in a kind of departicularization focused especially on marking Mary Weaver as an ideal of a community type, they offer a different—if still consonant—public Mary Weaver with a different set of lessons, and they work in different tones and registers, with some nods to the more personal elegies studied above. They do this through linking diverse frames of "the domestic," emphasizing an extended kinship network of both family and (national) Church family. Notably, the types into which Waugh and Weaver were placed centered on multigenerational continuity and growth; on a more individual, personal scale, the elegies above—including those to Waugh—were also about linking various *existing* families and communities in shared mourning.[30]

As they emphasized a future more perfect, they also—perhaps more so—consistently asserted that the break in this network (caused by death) was temporary. Heavenly assurance became not just a promise of reunion but specifically of broad community reunion. Writing not just as elegists but also as her friends, Mary Weaver's female elegists saw the elegy as a mode of doing both individualized and public grieving, of establishing Mary Weaver as a key public figure and role model, and of expressing their personal love and loss.

Daffin's poem may seem the most departicularized of the elegies by women, if only because it remains non-specific. Still, rather than addressing the "maidens," as Tanner's elegy does, the poem directly addresses Mary Weaver without naming her (beyond the title reference), and it speaks to both her earthly incarnation and her heavenly one: "Thou are gone hence. From all the cares /

of life, thy happy soul is free" (1–2). While not as clearly particular as Hart's direct address and while in a higher register—marked with solemn "thou" and "thee" forms—the repeated direct address turns deeply personal, especially when the poem moves (halfway through) to the "host of hearts" that "thy winning, graceful manner / Drew . . . around thee" (7–8). That "host" is not an unnamed group of (public) "maidens" so much as it is a "we" of family and friends: "In the time of deep distresses, / We will ever fondly cherish, / The example thou hast set us" (10–12). Certainly there is a lesson for those "left behind" here, and certainly Mary Weaver is marked as an "example" for "us." However, the "us" can and does function like Vashon's concentric circles, allowing those with deep personal ties *and* those without to learn from and to find consolation in the midst of "the hour of pain and anguish" (9).

In this, to reach again to Cavitch's important analysis, the poem is not only about "consolation for the deaths of others" but also "fulfillment . . . of a specifically political, shared happiness that 'loss' misnames" (24). Central to these politics is the placement of Mary Weaver as a logical citizen of heaven and the call to readers to become part of the Daffin's "we." This is emphasized in the poem's conclusion, which carries the expected heavenly assurance:

> And when life's short race is ended,
> All our sorrows here are o'er
> By angelic guards attended,
> May we meet on heaven's bright shore. (13–16)

Presaging Stephen J. Ferris's massively reproduced illustration "Washington and Lincoln (Apotheosis)"—remember especially the group of angels looking on from the upper left as the two presidents clasp each other in Lincoln's heavenly ascent—this conclusion sets up a holy reunion for the "we" of family, inner-circle friends, and larger community when "All our sorrow here are o'er." That is, it offers a deeply generalized and typified—even iconic—depiction that remains adaptable to—and still deeply representative of—personal mourning.

This was, of course, a difficult balance to strike. Jane E. Thompson's "On the Death of Mrs. Mary C. Weaver" is illustrative, in part because it carries echoes of Tanner's "Benny's Gone." Thompson opens each of her five stanzas with "Oh! weep not for Mary"—ironically, a much less particular call than Tanner's words to his wife Sarah, though the broad message is often similar. The unnamed "we" are not to "weep" because "she has gone to her rest," "she sleeps in the grave," and so forth; instead, "we" are to "remember the day / When again you shall meet her is not far away, / If believing in Jesus, and trusting his word" (1, 5, 17–19). Weaver herself is depicted with only limited specificity—and, arguably, all details offered support the placement of her life within an idealized type. Such work isn't so much "anonymous"—to use

Cavitch's term—as it is a mode of beginning to adapt generalized tropes and topoi to a specific person. Thompson depicts, for example, how Weaver's eyes would "beam" with "delight" "when her husband was nigh" but also shifts to how they would "sparkle" more—this time, "with holier love"—when she welcomed him "home to the mansions above" (14–15) In short, we do see Weaver as more particular than the "we" or the weeping "you" to whom the poem is addressed.

Susan Vashon similarly moves between the typifying work of identifying Weaver as an ideal minister's wife (and Christian woman) and the individual, albeit still public, work of grieving for a friend. Consider, for example, the differences between her penultimate stanza's discussion of Weaver's calling and the conclusion of her "Lines." In the fourth of her five stanzas, Vashon, well versed in the expectations of wives of Black clergy as well as teachers and the practices of elegy and eulogy, pushes a typified piety and a variation of Tanner's description "meek" by asserting that Weaver "had chosen the ways of virtue and truth" "in her beautiful youth," had "bowed to affliction," and had "kissed" "the hand of a chastening God" (14, 13, 16).[31] Her final stanza, on the other hand, picks up themes from "Benny's Gone" and anticipates Thompson's revisions of such:

> Then cease to repine; let all sighs be suppressed;
> For Mary is happy—dear Mary is blessed;
> Her spirit, too pure to remain longer here,
> Has gone peacefully upward to yonder bright sphere. (17–20)

While such language could, out of context, read as departicularized, I would submit that the "sighs" here are those of Weaver's "friends and her kindred" who are named in the poem's second line; they are "her friends" who "no longer hear / The sound of that voice which to them was so dear" (5–6). Again here, Vashon engages in the adaptation of tropes of public grieving for a public figure to encompass the more private grieving of Mary Weaver's friends: she was a type, but she was also that circle's "dear Mary."

The difficulty of composing elegies to figures with public status within the *Recorder* community (and the larger AME community) was, in part, finding such a balance that would allow public mourning (and mourning for the public's good) alongside more personal mourning (and its extension to far-flung family members and friends). The task of mourning Abraham Lincoln was difficult in a different way because it focused on a figure at the far edge of the outer circles of grief that *Recorder* elegists drew but one massively central to the nation's sense of the Civil War and the period generally. While a few *Recorder* readers had interacted directly with Lincoln, those interactions were often brief at best. The paper had been fairly critical of him during his early years in the White House; remember John Rock's positioning of him as "honest" but not radical enough (see chapter 1), the letters of Black soldiers (and home folks like Lizzie Hart) demanding equal pay, and a host of political pieces in the paper that time and space prevent me from considering here.[32] Later pre-assassination *Recorder* treatments moved toward valorization of select actions, but even this work was fraught with critique and sometimes hotly debated. The paper consistently argued that Lincoln needed to recognize African Americans as part of "his" community—indeed, to make the nation a shared community. The logical extension of this framework—which, of course, no one predicted—was that the paper mourn him in ways similar to how it would mourn a member of its own community, making him simultaneously "our President" and "*our* President."

Recognizing the complexity of Black mourning for public figures *in* public, cognizant of how unwelcoming public spaces (both physical and in print) could be, and in some ways creating his own version of Vashon's radiating circles, editor Elisha Weaver's April 22, 1865, editorial "Our National Sacrifice" claimed, "Our country has lost a patriot.... Humanity has lost a friend, and the colored man one not easily replaced." Weaver's language works hard to place the final group in his list as part of the first two, but simply the need to specify all three groups highlights the separation of "the colored man." This difficult dialectic surrounding Black bodies in the body politic ran throughout the paper's post-assassination discussion of Lincoln. Perhaps with a drop of sarcasm—or maybe hope—Weaver emphasized, for example, that Black Americans were the alpha and the omega of the Lincoln's funeral procession—"first... a detachment of colored troops," followed by a long list of white military and governmental groups, and ending "with a large number of colored men." But such work also emphasized that, again, the procession was not fully integrated.

Recorder elegies to Lincoln negotiated this terrain in different ways, but all borrowed tropes, topoi, and approaches from elegies to (local) public figures like Waugh and Mary Weaver, while dancing much more hesitantly with more personal and particularized elements. Part of this difficulty came not only from Lincoln's whiteness but also from the fact that these poems, the *Recorder*'s first real foray into full mourning for a white public figure, focused on arguably *the* most public figure in American history. Intertwined with these issues was the fact that "Lincoln" was already a text at the heart of national language and in complex flux. At Lincoln's death, Cavitch writes, "popular reaction confirmed him to be not only the self-sacrificing equal of George Washington—another father to his country—but also a Christ-like figure" (225). Some of the difficulty for *Recorder* mourners focused on these terms themselves, as the sense of "father to his country" already invoked the same kinds of feelings that Frederick Douglass would crystallize years later in his famous assertion that African Americans were "at best" only Lincoln's "stepchildren."[33] The paper had also consistently fought for images of Black manhood and womanhood in answer to pro-slavery's paternalistic tropes and was hesitant to put forward any white "parent." Some mourners were also considering the harsh realities that were already becoming clear in the weeks after Lincoln's assassination: as Cavitch notes, "Lincoln's martyrdom helped to enhance his reputation as the 'great emancipator' and his image as 'Father Abraham.' But his death left millions of blacks as they were before: without the consistent, reliable support of the national government" (227). In other words, if God thought Lincoln's work were truly done, then several crucial questions remained unanswered.

The *Recorder* certainly understood that "Lincoln" was a loaded set of rhetorical events, and it regularly attempted to shape those events. It even worked to represent and re-present his image through poetry, as in an unsigned July 30, 1864, poem, "Abraham Lincoln, An Acrostic," which ended:

> C ontention in our land shall cease, God's word resume its mission,
> O rder and peace supremely reign triumphant o'er oppression.
> L iberty, the choicest gift a nation can bestow,
> N o longer sectional, will they its beauties clearly show.

Elegies picked up this idealization of Lincoln, emphasizing what those "left behind" in (his) government could and should do as members of, to use Weaver's community-centered terms, "our country" and "humanity." As in the acrostic, these claims usually spoke much more to hopes for Black civil rights than to any of Lincoln's actual actions or policies.

To date, I have located eight elegiac poems to Lincoln published in the *Recorder*: the unsigned "In Memoriam. Written on Hearing of the Death of President Lincoln," which appeared in the April 22, 1865, *Recorder*; Angeline R. Demby's "Lines, Respectfully Dedicated to . . . Lincoln," April 29, 1865; Samuel B. Williams's "National Sorrow," also April 29, 1865; "W. H. F."'s "National Ode," May 6, 1865; a short quatrain ending Lizzie Hart's May 27, 1865, letter; a poem signed "Peregrinator" titled "President Lincoln. Mighty Champion! Freedom's Son!" that was clipped from the San Francisco *Pacific Appeal* and reprinted in the June 3, 1865, *Recorder*; the last fourteen stanzas of Richard H. Stoddard's long Horatian ode "Abraham Lincoln" that were reprinted in the June 10, 1865, *Recorder*; and a translation of George Freudberg George's "On the News of the Murder of Abraham Lincoln," July 10, 1865.[34]

The diversity of the poems and poets alone is striking. Stoddard was a noted white writer—friend to Hawthorne and arguably jockeying to make his piece the national poem of remembrance—and George was a minor Swedish diplomat. Hart, as noted above, was a single Black woman from Ohio who sent in several contributions during the period. Angeline Demby was also a single Black woman, but she was from Philadelphia—where she worked as a nurse—and sent in a handful of poems during the period.[35] Samuel B. Williams was an AME minister who, in April of 1865, was readying himself for a move to North Carolina, where he would pastor and write for the *Recorder* for several years.[36] In addition to the race, gender, formal training, and location of the poets, the poems were quite diverse in form. Taken together, it is as if the paper wanted to capture the sense of a whole nation (indeed, a world) grieving for Lincoln—a nation of which African Americans like Hart, Demby, and Williams were and should be an integral part.[37]

The variations in the *Recorder*'s elegies for Lincoln—especially those by Black poets, on which I focus below—are fascinating. But in some ways, what's most interesting is that they are clearly *variations* of the paper's other elegies; that is, the elegies for Waugh, Weaver, and Lincoln by *Recorder* writers don't just share the general form but also share in the expression of that form. All center on drawing personal connections to the deceased in language that typifies, all assert kinship and pray for reunion, all emphasize a communal "we," and all see the elegy as an occasion for action. Taken in one direction, this suggests that, for example, Mary Weaver's elegists were making her not just a public figure but a national figure—a radical enough move; taken in another direction, this suggests that Lincoln's elegists were bringing him into the *Recorder* community, that he was to be remembered alongside Waugh and Weaver.

Three sets of issues are most interesting given the above: the Lincoln elegies' use of plural first person, their typification of Lincoln, and their discussion of what "we" must do to reach—to again use Cavitch's words—"a specifically political, shared happiness." The first elegy to Lincoln published in the *Recorder*, "In Memoriam" moves from a singular speaker who "cannot write" because "my heart's too full of grief" to, by the poem's end, a plural first-person who speaks of "the green acacia leaves / We place within the grave, our broken hearts to ease" and of the moment "the trump shall sound" as "a token of our Heavenly Father's love" (1, 15, 16, 18). The poem's speaker here fits neatly within Cavitch's sense of Walt Whitman's "location of lyrical subjectivity in the figure of the elegist," and, of course, the acacia of "In Memoriam" may, for contemporary Americanists, call to mind Whitman's lilacs. But the "we" is doubly communal—referencing both an AME community and a national community—and that "we" even broadens to the generalized (Christian) humanity of the final "our" waiting for the trumpets. "Personal" grief is here, too, albeit not in the form of the direct interpersonal connection so crucial to the more private *Recorder* elegies (and still present in elegies to AME public figures). Rather, individual sadness is purely (and only) participatory in national, Christian sadness.

This kind of plural first-person is even more emphasized in Angeline Demby's elegy in the next issue—simply titled "Lines"—which opens, "We mourn, to learn that we are struck / With such appalling wo[e]" (1–2). This poem even shifts the individual pain of "In Memoriam" to a communal hurt: "We cannot bear this stunning pain" unless God applies a balm to "bleeding hearts" (19, 21). Certainly this "we" represents a charged entry into the white body politic, a national entity. But it also, in some ways like the "we" in the elegies to Mary

Weaver, is multivalent. It suggests not only the "we" groups around Black hearths ("Humanity has lost a friend, and the colored man one not easily replaced") and the Black individuals who might express their mourning through gestures like bringing flora to Lincoln's coffin (albeit acacia instead of Whitman's lilac). It also includes the "we" of the *Recorder*'s readers, who were already moving to consider sociopolitical options in the wake of Lincoln's assassination and, a circle outward, a national "we." W. H. F."'s "National Ode" similarly asks, "Where can we go, but unto Thee, / In this, our dire extremity?" (5–6) Here, as in all of the elegies by *Recorder* writers to Lincoln, there is an element of national prayer—and "national" in both the sense of the nation and the nation within that nation, and praying in both the sense of *for* the nation and *with* the nation.

Even though the "we" of Samuel Williams's "National Sorrow" is not directly stated until line nine of his sixteen-line poem, by that point in the poem, that "we" is clearly tied to the poem's title, as the poem opens, "To-day! The Nation mourns to-day; / For grief has seized on every heart." In the third quatrain, Williams tells of

> How soon our transient joy is changed!
> We now sit mourning in the dust;
> The country now we see deranged,
> And gladness from our hearts is thrust. (9–12)

For Williams, the "we" is the nation that celebrated how "the Union armies drove the foe" from the field (7); it is also the nation that needed to know that "yet the just, Almighty God, / Will work for us, if we but pray" (13–14). Arguably, such moves speak to the doubled "nation" and the doubled prayers discussed above. Even in this most "national" we, however, Williams concludes the poem with a reference that speaks to Protestants familiar with Isaac Watts's hymn "How Awful is Thy Chastening Rod" and specifically to AME readers of Susan Paul Vashon's elegy to Mary Weaver: "We now must feel the chastening rod, / But God will wipe our tears away."[38]

To have these coexisting layers, *Recorder* writers had to assign Lincoln, like Waugh and Weaver, a place in the earth-to-heaven economy. While the initial "I" of "In Memoriam" carries some limited echoes of the struggles over grieving in the most personal of the elegies above, that poem represents Lincoln not as a friend or family member so much as the captain who "took the helm when clouds began to lower, / And from that time to this, has safely steered the bark / O'er many dangerous rocks and shoals" (10–12). Demby marks him as "the true Republican" working until "God shall unto every man / perpetual freedom give" (29, 31–32) These modes move quickly from typifying Lincoln as an ideal leader to speak, like many white elegies, of "martyrdom": Weaver's editorial coverage actually uses that word, and Demby writes of how "the nation mourns a patriot slain!" (6, 17).

The poems that do not name Lincoln—or refer to him only obliquely—do essentially the same work. "W. H. F." refers only to "our noble Leader," and Williams does not name Lincoln directly at all—only referring briefly to his "murderer," the cause of the "national sorrow" (3). While these poems remove the specific person, they leave a "Lincoln" embodying the best republican virtues of the nation; indeed, they mark the attack on Lincoln as an attack on the nation. Such extreme synecdoche is also extreme typification: Lincoln becomes so departicularized as to become something different, but something very, very particular: a (perhaps fanciful) nation that had fought for freedom and civil rights and that would continue to fight for freedom and civil rights. This work is deeply different from the typing of Waugh and Weaver, as it leaves out all traces of the personal—indeed, sometimes even the very possibility that there was a *person* before there was a public ideal. Even here, though, *Recorder* poets use elegy to mark the deceased as an ideal to strive for, a locus of community values, and an agent for (re)linking the community through mourning in all of its phases (ending with both heavenly assurance and calls for earthly action).

The crucial end—enaction of a specific version of Christian virtue—is the area where *Recorder* elegies for Lincoln became some of the most politically active poems in the paper. For "In Memoriam," that work means calling for "the avenging rod throughout the land [to] be borne"—both an important echo and a variation of the language of Job used in both Vashon's elegy to Weaver and Williams's later elegy to Lincoln. Articulating the most radical of radical reconstructions, this call asserts that the South had to pay, in this Biblical frame of reference, for its past sins—a category that included the assassination. Thus, while the final lines of "In Memoriam" include the "we" placing "green acacia leaves . . . our broken hearts to ease," the poem's final image is this: "And when the trump shall sound by archangels above / May it be to thee a token of our Heavenly Father's love" (15–19). Such love might seem a soft sentiment if taken out of context. However, in Job, the chastening and "avenging rod," the heavenly "correction," is an awesome expression of immense power that causes real fear and damage.

Demby is even more direct, finishing her elegy with, "Though we still weep, we will not stand, / with folded hands and mourn— / But, with all friends of Abraham, / We'll trample treason down" (34–36). Surely the "we" is here a call for national action to "trample treason" in a just national vengeance; it is a reaffirmation of the "avenging" and "chastening rod," albeit one actuated through people. For regular readers of the *Recorder*, this language would have looked most like commentary on the need for Black—and white—response to the Fort Pillow massacre. (Author of a short elegiac quatrain to Lincoln, Lizzie Hart herself had, of course, urged Black troops to "Remember Fort Pillow.") It also invoked the action of Julia Ward Howe's "Battle Hymn of the Republic," a crucial, multiply-incarnated text for nineteenth-century

African Americans. The "we," then, again marks not just the nation but also individual Black groups, and most especially the Black readers of the *Recorder*. Elegy becomes a call to arms—one designed to advance, in Cavitch's words, "fulfillment . . . of a specifically political, shared happiness that 'loss' misnames," a "shared happiness" that is dependent upon a specific (re)creation of the nation's sense of values like "freedom" and "justice." This is the radical prayer called for in Williams's recognition that "the just, Almighty God, / Will work for us, if we but pray." And it most certainly describes the actions—both heavenly and earthly—that are called for at the end of "W. H. F."'s "National Ode":

> And now, our noble Leader's dead,
> Raise up a Joshua in his stead,
> To guide our brave victorious band,
> In safety to the Promised Land! (13–16)

The exclamation point finishing the poem calls attention to both the antislavery/Underground Railroad and the Christian/heavenly senses of the poem's last words. Similarly, the "victorious band" encompasses diverse faithful Christians (especially the Union's Black soldiers), and the Civil War is reconfigured as the God-ordained Battle of Jericho, itself a fascinating hint at just what the "trump" in "In Memoriam" might bring about.

For all their differences, these actions were very much expansions of those called for by elegists of Waugh and Weaver. All envisioned an earth made closer to heaven by good works and Christian living, and this construct depended on the growth of young men like Waugh and the praxis of ministers' wives like Weaver but also grew to be articulated as a "reconstructed" nation in which African Americans were treated equally in a range of public settings and were full (and fully recognized as) American citizens. Further, in both their content and the fact of their authorship, the *Recorder* elegies to Lincoln also marked African Americans as men and women who were vested with remembrance not just of Lincoln the person but "Lincoln" the purported embodiment of an ideal nation. Such work not only gave African Americans voice within national mourning but also concretely encouraged African Americans to see themselves a rightful part of national mourning.

The elegies that the *Recorder* reprinted from elsewhere offer instruction on how the paper used reprinting as a mode for furthering such representations. The reprinting of "Peregrinator"'s poem, for example, was likely both a gesture of goodwill to the *Pacific Appeal* (one that in itself asserted a national, bicoastal African American community) built in part on periodical exchange and an echo of the poems described above. Its opening stanzas address the assassination, but in the abstract language of faith and nation rather than detailed personal account. After three stanzas on the "pole-star of Republic's range" having his "Longevity denied by traitors' wild, malignant rage," the poem first turns to the speaker's interface with the broader collective: "But hark! methinks the nation's voices ring / With anger, mingled with contempt" (6, 8, 21–22). That "anger" promises "retributive justice" will "crush the dire infatuated fiends" (23, 24). The next and final stanza, though, makes the connection hinted at so heavily in *Recorder* elegies: "And now, Oh, ye sons of darker hue—most loyal hearts—Droop ye, alarmed, for fear ?" (28–29) "No, no," the speaker calls, "look up to HIM whose spangled lights adorn / Yon vaulted heavens above: / He will surely break a brighter morn." (31–33)

The call for action in the sections of Stoddard's poem that the *Recorder* reprinted was notably tamer than those above: he urged the "sons of darker hue" to "let your tears, indignant fall, / But leave your musket on the wall" as "Your country needs you now / Beside the forge, the plow!" (21–24).[39] He even felt obligated to add this:

> When Justice shall unsheathe her brand
> If Mercy may not stay her hand,
> Nor would we have it so—
> *She* must direct the blow! (25–28)

But even Stoddard's Black "your" figures *owned* muskets—something to which an earlier line noting "bronzed veterans, grim with noble scars" emphasized (18). The potential for Black retribution is here—and strong enough to seem to the white Stoddard to need direction. Arguably, Weaver's reprinting—which notably removes the parenthesis that surrounded the stanza above in Stoddard's original—might actually remind readers of how earlier calls for (righteous) retribution and radical reconstruction suggested that Justice might actually "direct" African American hands to make the blow.

In each of these reprints, Black spaces in the "we" and "you" of national moral action are affirmed and encouraged, albeit with some difference, and these spaces flow directly from Black participation in national mourning. Time prevents full discussion here of the diverse other kinds of *Recorder* texts mourning Lincoln, including scores of letters and, later, initial reports of the majority-Black National Lincoln Monument Association's efforts. However, such efforts often picked up the approaches of the elegies discussed above. Quartermaster Sergeant of the 43rd USCT John Brock, for example, used his May 6 letter to specify a key mourning circle, saying that Lincoln "lives in the thousands of brave soldiers, who still keep step to the music of the Union," as well as "in the hearts of those bereaved wives and children whose husbands, fathers, and brothers have been struck down by the fell hand of rebellion, whose universal cry is that this rebellion must be subdued, and traitors receive their due reward." That "due reward"—which loomed so large even in Stoddard's call that Justice "must direct the blow!"—was spelled out in a May 20, 1865, letter from George Duval of the 26th USCT, which opened by noting that "we all mourn the loss of him" and reported of his unit, "We all swore we would have revenge for our President."

Grieving for Lincoln was thus an extension of some of the kinds of mourning in other *Recorder* elegies that brought such social and emotional work even more fully into national political frameworks—frameworks that included military and other direct, physical action as a part of prayer and struggle. In this, *Recorder* elegies allowed specific and focused Black presences to exist within a wider (print) setting; indeed, they placed Black presences at the center of the *Recorder*'s version of that setting. After July of 1865, there were no more direct elegies to Lincoln—as elegies to specific figures in the paper (and, often, generally) were often *of* the moment, thus their "news" value. But through claiming the right to grieve in specific collective ways for Lincoln, *Recorder* elegists used poetry to assert places in the wider nation.

Given this, a final note on Stoddard's ode suggests how far the personal and political mourning in *Recorder* elegies Lincoln reached. The last reprinted sections of Stoddard's poem retrace Lincoln's funeral train, locating the center of grief in "the awful Car" and "thou Sacred Car, / Bearing our Woe afar!" (4, 8). Only two months later, readers of Vashon's "In the Cars" must have wondered about the ways in which Vashon also located the act of grieving in an "awful Car" even as he rewrote the father in that car as living, Black, and fast-returning to his children, carrying the memory of his family's loss even as he hoped to lead that family to "that wished home of peace." Even as Vashon attempted to ensure a place in a national memory and a national poetics for his beloved daughter, he was affirming that it might be Black poets rather than white Presidents who would understand that communal mourning must lead to communal growth and change.

{ 8 }

Black (Women's) Fortunes and *The Curse of Caste*

When she was able to snatch a moment of free time, Julia Collins readied her carefully written pages for the mail; when she found another few moments, she walked to the post office in Williamsport, Pennsylvania, and paid postage to send her parcel to the *Christian Recorder* office in Philadelphia. Much of Collins's biography remains a mystery: we know almost nothing definitive about her life before 1864 and precious little about the two years before her death in late 1865. However, this scene must have happened again and again in 1864 and 1865 as Collins sent the *Recorder* first essays and then installments of her recently rediscovered serialized novel *The Curse of Caste*.

Whether or not we mark *Curse* as "the first novel by an African American woman"—as the 2006 edition's cover does—what she was doing was audacious by any standard. The *Recorder* had published no extended serialized fiction in its entire existence; indeed, almost all of the shorter serialized fiction it published (and there was not much) consisted of stories specifically for children. While the AME *Repository* had experimented a bit with serialized narrative—Maria Stewart's (likely semi-autobiographical) "The First Stage of Life" is the most notable example—neither that magazine nor *any* early Black church periodical seems to have published anything like a novel.[1]

Prior to the 1860s, extended serialized fiction remained comparatively rare in the Black press in general. When Frederick Douglass decided to devote significant space in his newspaper to reprinting Charles Dickens's *Bleak House*, he took some public abuse from readers who thought the paper's resources could be better used.[2] As this example illustrates, a notable portion of even the small space the Black press devoted to extended fiction went to white authors' work—often that which embodied specific political stances. While Douglass's 1853 serialization of his own novella "The Heroic Slave" is certainly notable, prior to the *Recorder*'s work with Collins—and especially to Frances Ellen Watkins Harper's three serialized *Recorder* novels—the New York City publications related to the Hamilton family represented the most in-depth exploration of serialized Black-authored fiction by the early Black press: the *Anglo-African Magazine*'s 1859 publication of significant portions of Martin Delany's novel of Black revolution, *Blake, or the Huts of America*; the *Weekly Anglo-African*'s 1861–1862 serialization of what appears to have been a revised, full version of *Blake*; and the Redpath-influenced *Weekly Anglo-African*'s 1860–1861 serialization of a revised version of William Wells Brown's 1853 novel *Clotel* under the title *Miralda; or, the Beautiful Quadroon*.[3]

The dearth of women's fiction among such ventures should give pause. Part of the debate over the "firstness" of *Curse* hinges on how we label of Harriet Wilson's 1859 *Our Nig*, which Henry Louis Gates sees as an "autobiographical novel" and William L. Andrews calls a "novelized autobiography."[4] Part also hinges on the place of *The Bondwoman's Narrative*, a novelistic manuscript signed "Hannah Crafts" and published for the first time in 2002. The end of 2013 saw *New York Times* assertions that "Hannah Crafts" had been discovered and was, indeed, a formerly enslaved woman. Still, even if we overturn assertions about *The Bondwoman's Narrative* like those in Andrews and Kachun's introduction to *Curse*—that "no one has effectively confirmed the racial or gender identify of the author" of *Bondwoman's Narrative* (xxxviii)—we have yet to fully explore the status of *Bondwoman's Narrative* as a manuscript and *not* a published text.[5] I won't weigh in on these debates here, but the simple fact of their existence marks just how rare African American women's extended fiction in any print venue was during the period. Ultimately, *Curse*'s "first-ness" is less important than its "early-ness," its extreme rarity among the already rare.

Collins's choice of venue and the *Recorder*'s decision to publish her novel thus both demand some exploration. We have no direct statement on why Collins chose to write a novel, though it is likely she envisioned her novel as being specifically *for* the *Recorder*—both because her race and gender radically circumscribed her publishing options and because she had already established a working relationship with the paper and its editor. The flowering of diverse approaches to the different genres discussed in the previous chapters may have specifically opened Collins's mind to the possibilities of asking the paper to publish a novel. Collins also clearly knew that the issues explored in *Curse* demanded an extended form, and, as both a teacher and an active reader, she may have understood the limits of using nonfiction in these ways (e.g., veering into the polemical) or the "goody" literature so disdained by some soldiers.

If our sense of Collins's choices remains speculative, we can make stronger guesses about why the *Recorder* welcomed her novel. Of course, when Weaver resurrected the paper in 1861, he offered no suggestion that he would be open to such work. In fact, an item that the May 4, 1861, *Recorder* reprinted from the *Presbyterian Herald* suggests just the opposite—calling attention "to one of the great sins of the Church—that is religious novels" and worrying that "the time is fast approaching when our youth will read no religious books except [if] they are written in that style." Telling of "a young man" introduced to religious novels through "attending a Sabbath School," the piece's unnamed author reports that "by this means he formed a taste for reading such books . . . until he became a confirmed novel reader" who was unwilling to read faith-centered texts that had not "put on the garb of novels."

However, as this volume demonstrates, the paper and especially Elisha Weaver's editorial sensibilities grew and diversified, in part because of the paper's contributors and subscribers. While that widening was not always easy or complete—remember Annie Smith—by 1865, the *Recorder* embraced a much richer range of voices and content. The arguments over what soldiers should read and what soldiers *were* reading (see chapter 5) likely provided a heavy nudge toward at least occasionally publishing the kinds of (religious) fiction that caused the paper worry in 1861. The growth of Sabbath School libraries that was widely discussed in the paper may have had similar effects. Soldiers and some Sabbath School teachers did not want only tracts; many relished wider faith-centered literature that was interesting and connected to their world. Weaver grew to understand what Henry McNeal Turner would state directly when Turner plugged Frances Ellen Watkins Harper's *Sowing and Reaping* in the July 13, 1876, *Recorder*: that a "thoroughly religious" "tale" might aid readers in interacting with their faith and might attract subscribers to religious periodicals.[6] All of these factors would have shaped decisions about the content and language of the paper's February 18, 1865, announcement under the heading "Something New and Good for Our Readers": "Mrs. Julia C. Collins, now of Williamsport, Pennsylvania, proposes to write a narrative on the Curse of Caste, through the columns of *The Recorder*, and as we go to press we have received the commencement, the first chapter, which will appear next week."

This chapter offers the first close reading of *Curse of Caste* to emphasize the communities of readers and the commitments suggested in Weaver's announcement; it studies both the ways the novel fit the *Recorder*'s expectations ("good") and pushed to expand those expectations (in diverse senses of "new"). To begin to think about Collins's relationship to such readers and to the *Recorder*, this chapter opens with an exploration of Collins's place in the AME community. It then reads the novel through the lenses offered by Juno Hays, a character previous critics have dismissed as minor and "stock." It asserts that such a reading offers a rich sense of the contours of Collins's negotiation with the *Recorder*'s boundaries and goals, and it specifically suggests that understanding Juno can help us better consider the novel's central questions, reread key characters like Lina and protagonist Claire Neville, and rethink the novel's wide geographic range and sense of Black places.

A brief summary of the novel can both highlight such questions and hint at why scholars have deemphasized Juno. Young Claire Neville initially seems to be a beautiful white orphan. Raised in the North by a kindly Black nurse (Juno), Claire finishes her education at the novel's opening and accepts a position as a governess for the rich Tracy family of New Orleans. As she travels to and then joins the family at their plantation outside of the city, the novel reaches back in time to begin to tell the complex tale of her parentage—a tale completely denied to Claire.

Years before, the Tracy family's scion Richard fell in love with the beautiful Lina. Lina (like Claire) had been raised to think she was white; educated in a convent school in Canada, she met Richard as she was returning to her recently deceased father's home not far from the Tracy plantation. Her "return," however, culminated in her sale at open auction, as her (half-) brother and sister revealed on Lina's arrival at the family plantation that she was actually the daughter of their debt-ridden slave-owner father and an enslaved woman. Ironically, Lina was sold to Richard's father, Colonel Tracy, though Richard convinced his friend Manville to purchase her from Colonel Tracy and thus enable Richard to take her north. After taking her to Connecticut and connecting with his father's estranged sister (and his own loving aunt) Laura Hays, Richard then married Lina. After their marriage, when Laura's husband Alfred Hays was charged with a church in the West, Richard and Lina settled into the Hays's beautiful Rose Cottage in domestic bliss. After six months, Richard returned to New Orleans to attempt to explain his love and his marriage to his family—not knowing that Lina was pregnant. Though he promised to keep in touch with Lina through letters, that promise was destroyed when his father (Colonel Tracy) shot him in a fit of rage and then his "friend" Manville secretly burned Richard's last letter to Lina. Convinced that Richard had forsaken her, Lina died soon after Claire's birth. Manville traveled North, told Juno that Richard had left for Europe, and arranged to move Claire and Juno to a different location; when Richard returned months later, he assumed both Lina and Claire dead and left the country.

Diverse characters in the novel know fragments of this story—though none as much as Juno, who feels compelled to keep her secrets because of her love for Lina, Richard, and Claire, even as she sees Claire on a collision course with the Tracys. Indeed, the longer Claire stays with the Tracys, the more they themselves see a family resemblance.[7] Tensions rise as Claire and the Tracys gradually discover the truth, Manville confesses on his deathbed, the good Count Sayvord (visiting the Tracys from Europe) falls in love with Claire, Claire grows ill with "brain fever" and seems on the brink of madness, and Richard finds out that Claire is alive and races from abroad to find her (86). The resolution of the novel, however, remains a mystery, as Collins died before the final installment(s) could be sent to the *Recorder*—one (more) reason why *Curse* was never published in book form before the twenty-first century and a reminder that critics have to work with an unfinished (or, at least, incomplete) artifact.

Enough of the novel is extant, though, to recognize that, far from what modern readers assume the dominant story possibility for Claire (the tale of a "tragic mulatta"), *Curse* mixes tropes of sentimental fiction with a sense of Reconstruction's possibilities.[8] It thus pays real attention to moral choices, using the sensational to teach the kinds of values regularly advanced in the *Recorder*—ranging from the need for Protestant faith structures to the ways the nation needed to make places for (at least select) African Americans in a reconstructed "family."[9]

While the mixed-race Claire undoubtedly resembled select *Recorder* subscribers, few critics have spoken to how the vast majority of *Recorder* subscribers and readers figured into this equation, to how the free character most clearly and consistently marked as African American (Juno) functions in the novel, or to how the novel addresses the power and places of visibly Black people (especially women).[10]

All of these factors make a fuller sense of Collins's place vis-à-vis the *Recorder* and its community all the more important to reading the novel.[11] Weaver's announcement, for example, suggests that he put real thought into publishing *Curse*: he had received a proposal, likely considered it with some care, and had at least the novel's first chapter in hand well before its publication. But beyond reviewing the proposal and chapter, Weaver was probably also relying on two things: his knowledge of Collins's writing and his sense of her place within the AME community. The first was garnered at least in part through six of Collins's essays that he had accepted for the paper—some in the form of letters, all written in dialogue with the generic considerations described in chapter 6, and all shared by Andrews and Kachun: "Mental Improvement," published in the April 16, 1864, *Recorder*; "School Teaching," May 7, 1864; "Intelligent Women," June 4, 1864; "A Letter from Oswego: Originality of Ideas," December 10, 1864; "Life is Earnest," January 7, 1865; "Memory and Imagination," January 28, 1865. These essays show a nimble mind, a clear style, reasonably wide reading (with references to Byron, Longfellow, Shakespeare, and the Bible, for example), and a vision of uplift through faith consonant with much of the *Recorder*.

What is most striking, though, is the essays' clear and consistent emphasis on education and growth—from the very first sentence of "Mental Improvement": "It is a faulty and indolent humility that makes some of our people sit still and learn *nothing*, because they cannot learn everything" (121). Collins emphasizes a cross-racial equality of natural potential: "Destitute alike of knowledge, the children of the white race have, in this respect, no advantage over the black; both have everything to learn" (121). Collins's careful recognition that there were other "respects" in which white children had clear (material and political) advantages presages *Curse*'s arguments about race and "caste," but it also sets up her hope (in "Intelligent Women") that "the time is coming, with great strides, when the black man will have only to assert his equality with the white, to have it fully and cordially awarded to him" (124–125). Collins's un-gendered "people" and "children" led her to open such considerations up to women, as she was worried over "*naturally* intelligent young girls" who "never spend one hour in trying to improve or cultivate their minds" (125). She asserts, as "one who is closely allied with you by caste and misfortune," that such (Black) women, like Black men, needed to "improve your time," and she promises that "you will never have cause to regret your choice" (126).

Lest we assume Collins was advancing a radical sense of women's rights, we need remember that "Intelligent Women" argues that "it is a woman's province to make home happy, to be man's companion . . . to be mother, and instructor of his children; and this is what every woman should prepare herself to become" (125). In some ways, Collins's work functions like that of better-studied white women: it uses the language of domesticity to carve public/print roles for women but maintains some limits. Collins, for example, places the roles of mother and teacher especially close, as seen in the opening claim in "School Teaching" that "two qualifications" "indispensible" for teachers were "tact and patience," both of which Collins marked as the traits of an ideal mother (123). Arguably, she would have represented her own writing—including *Curse*—as an extension of these education-centered roles.

Weaver had long shown himself open to some such broadening of women's roles: well before the *Recorder* begin publishing texts by diverse women, he'd printed a range of women's writing in the *Repository*; as noted earlier, his own spouse had even published an essay there.[12] Collins's essays may well have been more comfortable for him than the more charged political writing of Lizzie Hart or the deeply introspective (and so differently political) work of Edmonia Highgate—and he was certainly supportive of the ways even these works spoke of and practiced women's domestic (in multiple senses of that word) Christian missions. In short, Collins's construction of gender may have danced with the Church's sometimes-conservative leanings, the paper's broad base of female supporters and readers, and the need for Black women who were publicly engaged and active in ways Weaver could countenance.[13]

Andrews and Kachun's landmark work sketches out how at least part of Williamsport's small Black community—only 170 Black residents in 1860 and only 602 in 1870 (xxv)—seems to have embraced both Collins and these sensibilities. They cite AME lay leader and community activist Enoch Gilchrist's April 16, 1864, *Recorder* letter—appearing in the same issue as Collins's first essay—that reports the re-opening of the town's small Black school "by Mrs. Julia C. Collins" (xxi). They also, crucially, share the December 16,

1865, *Recorder* letter from AME minister John Spriggs reporting that, on November 25, 1865, "Mrs. Julia C. Collins, the wife of Stephen C. Collins, departed this life after a short, but severe attack of consumption. . . . Mrs. Collins will not only be missed by her bereaved husband and motherless children, but by the public generally, as she was one of the writers for the Christian Recorder." Spriggs's letter not only places Collins in Williamsport (as a wife and mother and as a writer) but also identifies her husband. Andrews and Kachun speculate on deeper connections to Williamsport: while unable to prove a definite tie, they note that "according to the 1860 federal census, the only African American 'Julia' living in Lycoming County . . . was a literate seventeen year old 'mulatto' named Julia Green, who was living in the Williamsport household of Enoch Gilchrist" (xxvii).

In this work, Andrews and Kachun rightly locate the AME's formal church presence in Williamsport immediately pre-*Curse* in the appointment of Nelson Turpin (who held the Hollidaysburg circuit before Spriggs).[14] Andrews and Kachun assert that while Turpin may have helped expand the Church and the *Recorder*'s presences in the area, he was a fairly conservative force on gender issues. They remind readers that Black evangelist Amanda Berry Smith would later find Turpin to be a "fierce" minister who she was "afraid of," even though Smith spoke of visiting Turpin's spouse Amanda often (lix). Nonetheless, Andrews and Kachun also note two short *Recorder* pieces published by Amanda Turpin during the couple's year in and around Williamsport—a suggestion that the Turpins' sense of the AME Church and gender might have been broader. That said, they assert that Amanda Turpin's views on women were as conservative as her husband's and that her work advanced "an even more subservient role for women" than Collins's texts (xxv).

In part because of genealogist Reginald Pitts's substantial post-2006 research on both Gilchrist and Stephen Collins and in part because Andrews and Kachun are perhaps a bit too quick to dismiss the Turpins, all of these figures demand further consideration as we explore Collins's Williamsport and AME base. Whether Julia Collins was Gilchrist's stepdaughter or not, for example, Pitts sensibly recognizes that, in part given Gilchrist's *Recorder* letter and his long involvement in the community, Collins would have interacted with him closely.[15] Expanding on Andrews and Kachun's work, Pitts demonstrates that Gilchrist would have exposed Collins to a range of activism. In addition to working with the Underground Railroad, Gilchrist was a member of the local "Loyal League," a pro-Lincoln group. Pitts has also more fully documented Gilchrist's long ties to the AME Church in Williamsport as well as, following up on Andrews and Kachun's recognition that Gilchrist became a *Recorder* agent in 1865, his deep interests in reading and learning. In short, Gilchrist was a model of community-centered AME activism—one close to Julia Collins.

Pitts's study of Stephen Collins demonstrates a different but still consonant set of connections to Black Williamsport and, more broadly, African American concerns central to the *Recorder*. It also offers a situational rationale for Collins's turn to public writing. Tracing Stephen Collins through diverse records, Pitts has determined that he is listed in some records by his given name and in some, as "Simon C. Collins." More importantly, as Andrews and Kachun suggest, Stephen Collins does indeed seem to have served in the Civil War. Pitts has gathered evidence that he was, first, a personal servant to Captain Charles H. Wombaugh of Company K of the 86th New York between November 23, 1861, and October 20, 1862, and then, from either late 1862 or early 1863 until May 23, 1863, a personal servant to Captain Frank T. Wilson of Company I of the 131st Pennsylvania and Colonel Peter H. Allabach, commander of the 131st. When African Americans were allowed into the Union army, he served as a soldier himself until October 7, 1865. Pitts reports that Collins was mustered into Company I of the 6th US Colored Infantry, rose to the rank of sergeant, fought in Virginia and North Carolina, seems to have been wounded, was discharged several months after the War's end, later filed for a military pension, and worked actively with the Grand Army of the Republic.[16]

FIGURE 8.1 *"Reading the Emancipation Proclamation," by Henry Walker Herrick (1864). Courtesy of the American Antiquarian Society.*

Stephen Collins's Civil War service would undoubtedly have been a shaping force in the composition and publication of *Curse*. That service and specifically the absences from home it caused may have actuated or demanded Collins's return to teaching, and such circumstances also created a reason for the community to support a married woman's teaching at a time when such was comparatively rare. For much of the war, Julia Collins was essentially a single parent, likely in some economic need.[17] Teaching was likely a way to supplement whatever monies (if any) Stephen Collins sent home, one that might have allowed some options in terms of childcare—and, of course, Collins's essays suggest that her writing flowed from her teaching. Stephen Collins's service may have also expanded Julia Collins's sense of the nation and of her potential audiences. If Julia and Stephen Collins corresponded while Stephen Collins was with the Union army, Julia Collins would have heard firsthand, for example, about some of the efforts of Black soldiers and (formerly) enslaved people, perhaps including those tied to reading and education discussed earlier. (Certainly she knew something of how crucial a text like the Emancipation Proclamation was to enslaved people, as shown in Figure 8.1) Such correspondence would have been a powerful complement to the kinds of texts Julia Collins would have read in the *Recorder* on not just Black soldiers (and their reading) but also on the newly freed people of the South and the Black (women) teachers working with them. While some critics have wondered why *Curse* does not address the Civil War directly, it is certainly plausible that Collins was thinking of Black soldiers—including her own husband—as she penned her novel. Similarly, while we do not know how Stephen Collins or Enoch Gilchrist felt about public or activist women, their decisions situated Julia Collins in a place that offered both knowledge of public action and possibilities (perhaps even necessities) for women to take such action. It is clear, in this swirl of circumstances, that she spent significant time considering the praxis of womanhood across the nation—including both the societal limits and potential surrounding young Black women.

Amanda Turpin may actually have been considering similar questions in somewhat similar circumstances, even though Andrews and Kachun mark her *Recorder* pieces as conservative, "short and unremarkable" (xxv). They may be correct that Nelson Turpin could be "a hard man to deal with," and Amanda Turpin's first *Recorder* piece—the August 6, 1864, "The Character of a Wife"—seems definite in its support of a gendered hierarchy, especially in its assertion that a wife should make "it her business to serve and her pleasure to oblige her husband" (lix). That said, Nelson Turpin's sometimes "fierce" demeanor was paired with some education and some recognition of the importance of women to the Church.[18] As a minister's wife, Amanda Turpin would have had to practice some of the more public versions of womanhood. As they did for Mary Weaver, the roles of wife and mother would, under the broad rubric of helpmeet, have called on her to lead and/or participate in a variety of church functions before, after, and sometimes even during worship services. As Collins's writing may have initially grown from her work as a mother and a teacher, Turpin's may have grown from these more public activities. Nor was this the only similarity between the two women. Nelson Turpin also traveled often, sometimes for extended periods.[19] In short, Amanda Turpin—like Julia Collins—may have been more independent and more interested in women's self-sufficiency than previously thought. Her essays actually address such issues directly.

Turpin's August 20, 1864, "Female Influence" wonders aloud, for example, about "the marked influence . . . exercised . . . by the female over the opposite sex" and about why "strong men—men of intellect, power, and talent, should be influenced or persuaded by the female to abandon one project or scheme, and repair to another." Turpin asserts that "the female must have been created for some greater and more eminent position than she has yet attained." She claims that "both the learned and unlearned women exercise a great influence"; indeed, she even suggests that "when we consider the influence she wields in society, we are almost persuaded to speak in behalf of women's rights." Turpin claims that "There is nothing the female undertakes, no matter how difficult, that she does not by some means perform." She concludes that "there is a great field of labor opening" and says "therefore, let us rally to a post of duty, and help to burst open the dark prison-doors of ignorance, that the light of intelligence, mental and moral improvement, may break forth and shine into the minds of our once down-trodden and oppressed but now freed race." She thus does *not*, as Andrews and Kachun claim, consistently "support an even more subservient role for women" than that found in Collins's early essays (xxv). Certainly Amanda Turpin was no radical—and the fact that this piece follows only two weeks after "The Character of a Wife" reminds us that Turpin's calls for "appropriate" female influence were governed by some sense of separate spheres. Still, Turpin pushed for recognition of a wider—and growing ("a great field of labor opening")—sphere of influence.

My point here is not simply to recover a fuller sense of Amanda Turpin's (or the Turpins') sense(s) of gender in general. Andrews and Kachun rightly submit that the two women could have been anything from friends to rivals to enemies even as they acknowledge that they definitely knew each other. What is more important is that the widening sense of gender roles in the *Recorder*—in works by writers from Lizzie Hart to Edmonia Highgate to Annie Smith—had echoes (albeit with variance) in Collins's Williamsport; further, this widening sense attended to diverse women—not just the handful of folks who looked physically or demographically like Claire Neville. As sure as Collins must have seen her husband Stephen and his fellow soldiers among the possible readers of *Curse*, so must she have seen Amanda Turpin and other AME women in and around Williamsport. Given the fact that *Recorder* readers were already well aware of plans (and initial forays) to help educate the enslaved people of the South post-emancipation, many *Recorder* readers may have read Turpin's "post of duty" as something like the roles held by, for example, Sallie Daffin and, later, Edmonia Highgate. But Turpin's "great field" could certainly be conceived in general racial terms—a possibility for Black education writ large—and she might have seen local implications of such, as she, like Collins, was involved in area schools. Certainly when the *Recorder* talked of women's roles, duties, and possibilities, it did not limit itself to young women like Claire. Rather, it regularly addressed (and even heard from) Black women closer to the working classes, labeled and living as Black, and thinking about the "great fields" in both their own localities and the whole post–Civil War nation.

I submit that, although layered in the trappings of a sentimental treatment of a mixed-race character, *Curse* functions in deep dialogue with the stories about the "great field" opening to Black women that appeared in almost every issue of the *Recorder* in the mid-1860s. In this, I agree with most scholars of *Curse* that womanhood (and girlhood) are critical concerns of the novel, but I submit that we have focused too heavily on *Curse*'s protagonist. If we are to understand the young governess Claire Neville, we need to also study the first Black "governess" introduced in the novel, Juno Hays. If we want a full sense of race in the novel—of the "curse of caste"—we need to closely consider the novel's first and most prominently named Black character. And if we want to probe the nexus of gender, race, faith, love, and reconstruction so central to *Curse*, we need to closely read the Black character who addresses that nexus most fully and most prophetically.

Discussion of Juno in the scholarship on *Curse* has been brief. For example, Jean Lee Cole says that Juno "is relegated to a passive role," "simply a receptacle for knowledge"—and that Collins sometimes resists quoting her directly and so "clearly demonstrates her discomfort with representing another black woman's voice, in speech patterns or accents that were not her own" (736–737). Several critics link Juno to the novel's (often silent) enslaved characters without clearly articulating the basis for this linkage. And even though Jennifer Greeson gives Juno a bit more emphasis, her sense is that Juno is a "stock character" (773). I assert that Juno is both the center of much of the book's tension and a key actor in events tied to the novel's plot and themes. These facts grow more evident as the novel continues, culminating in the book's detailed attention to Juno's practices (and powers) of fortune-telling and dream interpretation and her articulation of the central problem of the novel. In this, Juno is thus key to thinking about the novel's sense of Black women and its reach to key groups of both *Recorder* subscribers and potential subscribers.

Juno's introduction in the novel called for both a caring response and a level of identification from *Recorder* readers. Claire mentions her in the very first chapter as her "old beloved nurse," and the next reference makes Juno the first character clearly labeled as African American in the novel even as it marks her with a rhetoric of care—"Juno, an old colored nurse, had taken care of" Claire for "as long as she could remember" (5, 8). Collins's author-like narrator even calls attention to both Juno's entry into the story and her importance: "Now that we have introduced Juno to our readers, she will appear, from time to time, with the other characters who play an important part in the following narrative" (10). That narrator also assures us of how critical Juno is to Claire, noting, in describing Claire's move South, that "the parting, between the faithful old nurse and the child she had watched ever so long, was touching in the extreme" (10).

Arguably, by this point in the novel, Juno is already central among the characters who, as Tomeiko Carter puts it, serve as the story's "spiritual and moral barometer" (720). But as the backstory unfolds, we also learn that, in helping Richard and Lina from the very start of their marriage, Juno quickly proved "an efficient hand" and an anchoring presence—often "quietly knitting 'neath the shade of the lofty tamarack trees" while "the mingled voices of Richard and Lina" could "be heard, freighting the fragrant air with melody" (26–27). When Richard decided to go South to challenge his "angry father," it was Juno who Richard charged with "regularly attend[ing] the village post-office, every day . . . to bring the letters" from him ("which would be anxiously waited for by the lonely little wife") and Juno who Richard "playfully importuned . . . to bring the rose to his lady love's cheek ere his return" (28).

Still, Carter's choice of the word "barometer" ironically calls attention to just how much pressure surrounds Juno. Even her name would have carried multiple resonances for some Black readers of the *Recorder*. One of the first times the name "Juno" appeared in the *Recorder* was in an exam question (on Virgil's *Aeneid*) shared in a May 3, 1862, *Recorder* report on Philadelphia's all-Black Institute for Colored Youth. The novel's invocation of that name points to Black engagement with Greco-Roman classics and Black pride in educational endeavors. But even as Juno's name invokes the warrior wife of Jupiter (and so the mother of Vulcan and Mars), it also suggests slave-owners' longstanding "joke" of assigning enslaved men and women names of legendary greatness (Caesar, Apollo, etc.). The classical Juno's ties to the protection of homes were similarly counterbalanced by the fact that hers was a "pagan" name in a Christian paper.

Readers' racial identification with Juno might also have been a minefield. Juno is, after all, *not* the novel's heroine and not the main character; she is, in fact, immediately separated from the protagonist by the signifier "colored." Some of the *Recorder*'s readers might have wanted—across lines of gender and (seemingly, initially) race—to see themselves more in Claire Neville; some might have picked up the novel's sometimes heavy-handed suggestions about Claire's "tropical loveliness"—her "darkly beautiful" air, "eyes of midnight blackness," and "wealth of purple black hair" (3). But even if they saw Claire as a figure of racial ambiguity and potential Blackness—like, perhaps, the woman in the Bustill family hair care advertisements discussed in chapter 3—she likely resonated differently with various Black readers. Some of those readers may have simply sighed at yet another piece of sentimental fiction where the loyal Black caregiver hovered in the background behind the pretty white girl. Indeed, the position Juno potentially occupies vis-à-vis the "white" and "clear" Claire carries resonances of "Mammy" stereotypes, the Aunt Chloe of *Uncle Tom's Cabin*, and/or the generations of enslaved Black women forced to care for white children even as their own children were separated from them or simply stolen from them. How many of the Black service workers among the *Recorder*'s subscribers, for example, worked for white employers less fair and kind than Richard Tracy, and how many served children less loving than Claire? If readers' identification with Claire Neville was fraught with the complexities and lies of racial identification that permeate the novel's world, their identification with Juno was fraught with both stereotypes and truths of racism in American print and beyond.[20]

Readers looking for Juno's own history would have had to dig through the novel for the bits mentioned in the extensive discussion of Claire's family, arguably much like Black readers would have had to dig through American print to find the fragmented records of their own histories—but also arguably much harder for readers of the serialization than of the contemporary book. As the novel's complex genealogy unfolds, while Juno's birth and youth remain shrouded, we learn that her early years were tied to Colonel Tracy and his sister Laura's unmarried aunt, with whom Laura "had always resided in the North" (16). The narrative asserts that John Tracy, the father of Colonel Tracy and Laura and the brother of this "old maiden aunt," was "a Connecticut man" who "had emigrated to Louisiana"—so the strong suggestion is that Juno's home place was Connecticut (16–17).[21] Juno thus seems freeborn or freed young—as Connecticut passed its first version of a gradual emancipation law in 1784, as there were only a few dozen people in Connecticut still officially enslaved by 1830, and as full abolition (though *not* full rights for African Americans) came to the state in 1848, when there were officially six Connecticut slaves.[22] That said, her early years seem to have taken place in a liminal zone between slavery and freedom—perhaps a kind of indentured servitude turning into a long-term informal agreement. The language of Juno's entry into Laura and Alfred Hays's family (the elderly Miss Tracy comes to live with them "taking Juno with her") and the implication that Juno takes or is "given" their last name is countered by the agency implied in the language of Juno's later entry into Richard and Lina's home—at which her "services . . . were secured." Further, Juno's care for Claire is activated not just by Manville's support but primarily by a promise she made at Lina's request on Lina's deathbed (30, 26). And later in the book—after Claire has gone to live in the South—it is clear that Juno is, like the majority of *Recorder* readers, a free African American living in the North.

Juno's limited agency and her power to make select choices are crucial to both the novel's plot and themes but nonetheless suggest even more tension. Juno's early appearances in the novel are deeply tied to secrets—from the first reference, in which Claire is "confident" that Juno "knows all" even though she "can prevail upon her to impart nothing" (5). Juno's role as the novel's keeper of secrets is emphasized when she implicitly admits that she *does* know the secrets of Claire's parentage and prophecies that Claire "will see great sorrow, and will often wish you had taken poor old Juno's advice, and never gone to be a governess in that proud [Tracy] family" (9). It is Juno who gives Claire her mother's ring—inscribed "R. T. to L."—and Juno who holds back the ironically named "dark mystery" that "surrounded her father" (10, 14). If these suggestions aren't enough, in chapter 8, after readers know that "Richard Tracy and the beautiful quadroon, Lina, were united for life," the narrator directly tells of Lina's "long talk" with Juno in which "she told Juno all the reader already knows, together with other facts which it is not our purpose at present to disclose" (32). In short, Juno knows more than any character in the novel and keeps (almost) all of it secret.

That secret-keeping is at least partially her choice. It is Juno who decides to raise Claire as white (remember how sporadic Manville's visits are), Juno who decides to withhold the full history of her parentage, Juno who decides not to keep Claire from going to the Tracy family, and Juno who places Claire one step closer to making her own discoveries by passing on Lina's ring—telling Claire "I have something to give you" (10). Juno's care for and use of the secrets she holds should give some pause. Some critics read Juno's silences as passive, but I submit that she keeps her secrets under significant pressure. Claire repeatedly tries to convince Juno to tell her what she knows, and Juno's worries over Claire's plans to go South to the Tracy family yield "loud . . . remonstrances" and fearful "excitement without bounds" (9). When Claire interrupts Juno's vague (and "loud") warnings with "Who and what is Richard? And what is he to me?" Juno "could not be induced to say another word about Richard" (9). Juno wants very much to tell Claire everything—in order to protect her—but has made a commitment to keep her secrets and tries desperately to stay true to her word; she is tormented and tells Claire "I will never cease to pray for you, darling" (10). In this, Juno is not the sometimes-coy narrator who offhandedly mentions "other facts which it is not our purpose at present to disclose" (32). Late in the novel, we see that Juno keeps her secrets out of her love for Lina and Richard and especially out of her reading of her promise to Lina.

Both Juno's moral stance and the fact that she knows "all the reader already knows" (and more) suggest further calls for *Recorder* readers to identify with her, even as the novel begins to show just how much potential damage seeps from keeping these secrets. As the novel moves toward conclusion, Juno becomes the character who almost everyone has to come to seeking knowledge, and this oracle-like positioning is paired with growing discussion of Juno's own powers of prophecy. In a novel whose very first chapter invokes prophecy—Claire's friend Ella says that "all will be made clear" and asserts that her words are "prophetic" (6)—Juno becomes the book's central seer, one who reaches deeply into the seemingly pagan practices of interpreting dreams and fortune telling and who foretells some of the novel's most crucial events.

One would expect that the interpretation of dreams, signs, and the like would have no place in a character like Juno or a publication founded as the organ—the "recorder"—of the African Methodist Episcopal Church; indeed, later in the nineteenth century, the *Recorder* regularly attacked such "pagan" practices. However, the *Recorder*'s sense of fortune and fortune telling in the 1860s was actually much more complex—in part because of the *Recorder*'s varying representations of "fortune" and in part because of its multivocal ambivalence toward alternative spiritualities at a moment when the Church was trying to reach out to a much wider group of potential members, including both the newly freed and the much smaller number of previously free African Americans in the South.

Some brief context helps show how Collins's novel functions within broader debates about the place of alternate versions of Christianity in the paper—including those that valued African and hybrid African/American folk traditions. This work, in turn, suggests the ways in which Juno ultimately comes to embody a kind of fortune telling that is symbiotic with some Christian domestic spaces and "Christian recording." For many early African American writers, editors, and readers, the broader term "fortune" was a locus of conflicting conceptions of agency and materiality that ranged from divine providence to "fickle" luck, from wealth defined monetarily to wealth defined spiritually, from the future of visionaries and prophets to the future of fortune tellers and humbugs. These conceptions were inflected by the ways in which the remnants and revisions of African-ness met various senses of American-ness—and so by the ways in which Americans defined and were defined by race, history, and place. Most of the *Recorder*'s multiple usages of the term and the concept attempted to revise the acquisitive senses of "fortune" into evangelizing devices; that is, *Recorder* authors argued that Christian values of industry, self-denial, and humility led to and were thus prophetic of intertwined material and spiritual prosperity. The *Recorder* was much more troubled, though, when "Lady Fortune"—a term occasionally invoked—actually demonstrated some power or veered from Protestant structures.

That conflict had roots in popular representations of Black fortune-tellers and conjurers—often Black women like Juno—that had circulated since before the beginnings of the American republic. Such constructions often (sometimes by design) attempted to separate Blackness from Christianity, domesticity, and public agency, as in transatlantic representations of West Indian Obi, which led to an 1800 novel and widely performed plays about Three-Fingered Jack, and in Chloe Russel's *The Complete Fortune Teller*, which marks the supposed-author as "the Black witch" in the book's front matter.[23] Chronologically closer to *Curse*, Mortimer Thompson—writing as "Philander Doesticks"—devoted a full chapter in his 1858 *Witches of New York* to a pair of "culled" seers named Mr. and Mrs. Grommer. Amidst racist jokes about demonic blackness and skin color, Thompson attacks Mrs. Grommer's domesticity, Mr. Grommer's industry, and the Grommers' class aspirations, as well as Mr. Grommer's attempts to avoid the "peculiar negro dialect" (305, 317, 320).[24]

The *Recorder* was also deeply worried about the rise of Spiritualism—a movement, which, in both theory and practice, questioned some Protestant values, was often linked to the occult, sometimes veered toward fortune telling and conjure, and drew interest from African Americans ranging from Harriet Jacobs to Harriet Wilson. In over a dozen anti-Spiritualist articles published in the 1860s, various *Recorder* authors condemned communication with spirits through rappings, dream interpretation, and other venues as foolish in both the material sense (because buying into scams damaged wealth potential) and the spiritual sense (because pagan activities were inherently evil). While most of these pieces were more aggressive than Edmonia Highgate's earlier-mentioned jokes about spirits breaking crockery, they were uniform in dismissing any possibility of "truth" garnered through Spiritualism and were sometimes fearful of the dangers such practices opened up.[25]

The *Recorder*'s sense of fortune telling as a threatening scam is best demonstrated in "The Fortune Teller," a two-part short story published anonymously in the October 10 and 17 issues in 1863. Supposedly taken "from the Posthumous Records of a London Clergyman," this narrative relates how a (white) young woman—named, of all things, Julia—expresses "her unqualified disbelief" at a fortune teller who is alternately referred to as "the prophetess," "the pythonness," and "a very dirty old woman." As her revenge, the fortune teller prophecies that Julia's impending marriage will never happen, that she will reject food and friends, and, finally, that she will "lose her wits." All of this comes to pass—*not* because the fortune-teller is real, but because Julia is "weak" and "silly" and believes the prophesy: at the beginning of the penultimate sequence, the story's participant-narrator *pays* the fortune teller to come to Julia's sickbed, recant, and prophecy a good life (demonstrating to readers that she is a fraud). Simply seeing her, though, frightens the weak-willed Julia into madness.

At odds with this approach, other pieces in the *Recorder* suggest that some readers wanted a broader sense of Christianity—one that valued or at least accepted select "folk" spiritual practices. A much gentler version of divination can be seen in the April 23, 1864, children's story "Grandmother's Fortune-Telling," which was copied from the *Methodist* and offers readers a kindly grandmother who catches one of her grandchildren telling the fortunes of two others. To the children's surprise, the *grandmother* then offers to tell their fortunes. In a conversion of "fortune telling" as a concept, she asserts that she does "not approve of common fortune-telling" and proceeds to tell "fortunes" tied to Christian agency and choice. If Lizzie, for example, "will use her eyes and mind well, in getting a good education, . . . employ her . . . fingers in useful work . . . and strive to love and obey God every day, she will be very likely to have a long, healthful life . . . and [be] beloved and respected." Lest readers doubt the wide applicability of such "fortunes," the story ends with the claim that such efforts can be "applied just as well to children whose eyes and hair"—and presumably skin—are "of any other color." If this is an anti-fortune-telling piece, it is one that invites those interested in fortune telling into the Protestant fold, much as the AMEC was trying to invite groups like the "contraband" and the newly freed into its specific section of that fold throughout the 1860s.[26]

Occasionally, the *Recorder* even allowed some variations of spiritualism and seemingly pagan divination more direct support—or, at least, tolerance—in its pages. Amid the several ads for holistic medicine like those discussed in chapter 3, a note from Dr. H. S. Phillips, a "practical magnetic physician" of Philadelphia, announced that "Madam Julian, a remarkable (and only public colored) Clairvoyant and Trance-Medium" would aid his practice. Phillips reports that this "granddaughter of . . . a Chief of a tribe of Kanaka Indians," "has been a seer from early childhood." The ad's conclusion asserts both that "those . . . unable to pay will be treated free of charge on Thursday of each week" and that "cleanliness in person" would be "required" of visitors. This fortune teller, linked to modern medicine, cleanliness, and charity, seems much less threatening than the "pythonness" of "The Fortune Teller" or even the table rappers of Spiritualism. The account of Madam Julian appeared in the July 15, 1865, *Recorder*—more than halfway through *Curse*'s serialization and less than a month before the scenes that focus most on Juno's divination.

Juno thus sits both literally and figuratively among the complex matrix of representations of Black seers in and beyond the *Recorder*, even as she is placed in squarely Christian domestic spaces, and, in the face of some gendered *Recorder* attacks on "Lady Fortune," spaces of some female agency. Juno's first prophecy in *Curse*—"Dear child, I fear you will see great sorrow"— leads to her promise to Claire that "I will never cease to pray for you, darling, and . . . I hope you may be happy" (10). Similarly, Juno's foreboding that Richard's trip to New Orleans will lead to "some trouble"—paired with the narrator's assertion that "Juno always had her 'suspicions' and the remarkable part of it is, they were nearly always right"—happens in Richard and Lina's idyllic Rose Cottage, a setting described as a domestic "dream of happiness" (30, 27).

It is within these frames that Juno's crucial acts of divination late in the novel take place. Both of those acts also circle events that demonstrate Juno's important role in the novel, as both are tied to visits by key characters—Claire's schoolmistress (and Richard's mother's old friend) Miss Ellwood and then Richard Tracy himself.[27] Both visits are catalysts in the novel. Juno dictates her narrative of Claire's parentage to Miss Ellwood—finally releasing her central secrets because she is sure (because of a dream) that "Claire is in trouble" (89). Miss Ellwood sends the transcription to Colonel Tracy in hopes of warming his heart. Juno's later conversation with Richard confirms Manville's evil and convinces Richard to reconcile with his father and find Claire. Both moments thus advance not only the plot but also the potential for happy resolution.

The setting of these events—conceived broadly—is worth discussion, as it extends and revises the domestic bliss of Rose Cottage. At this point in the novel, Juno lives in "a neat little cottage" of her own that is "almost embowered in green trees and trailing vines"; its "neatly arranged" exterior sets the stage for a "cozy kitchen . . . suggestive of neatness and comfort" (88). The "baskets of newly washed muslins" in that "cozy kitchen" may be Juno's own or may mark a new occupation shared with a number of *Recorder* readers, that of skilled laundress (88). Entering this scene, the narrator tells us that, after Claire went South, Juno "had taken herself a husband. Martin Ray was a worthy, industrious man, with an unlimited confidence in his wife's opinion" (89). Many *Recorder* readers may have noted, in addition to this description, that Ray shared his surname with Reverend Charles Ray, a moral powerhouse in African America. Regardless, none of the trauma surrounding Lina visits this "darker" version of Rose Cottage; of Juno and Martin, the narrator simply says "they lived happily and quietly together" (89). Collins sprinkles examples of perfect Black domesticity throughout the rest of the section: Martin and Juno talk on their "pleasant, vine-wreathed porch"; after predicting Richard's visit, Juno does "a thorough sweeping and dusting"; and once Richard and company arrive, they leave only "after doing justice to Juno's spring-pullets," which she prepares especially for them (90, 100, 102).

This setting emphasizes that Juno is neither the "pythonness" of the *Recorder*'s "Fortune Teller" nor even the grandmother who does "not approve of common fortune telling." Rather, her skills at divination are part and parcel of her industrious, ideal Black home and are, indeed, part of her new family setting. While the text makes much of the fact that the critical visits are foretold by dreams prior to Miss Ellwood's visit, Juno's husband Martin is actually active in Juno's augury—he suggests that her dream "that Squire Farley's barn burned" could be read as "signifying hasty news," and he has a "good long talk" with Juno that ends only after he himself "had interpreted Juno's dreams for the fiftieth time" (89–90). Juno pairs these efforts by her "worthy, industrious" husband with her own more notable powers, and her sense that Claire is in trouble makes her advance both a plan and another prediction: that Martin must seek out Miss Ellwood and "that Master Richard *will come*" (89). As if to emphasize how deeply domestic such dream interpretation and divination are, Juno tells much of this in soliloquy as she does laundry—with narratorial comments on her perfectly done white shirts both before and after her augury. This fortune teller is certainly not a "very dirty old woman."

As much as the domestic setting of Juno's divination is emphasized, though, so is the fact that what she does *is* divination. Building from all of the earlier discussion of her "suspicions," her definitive proof that Richard is coming—following her dream—is that "the rooster crowed before the door three times this morning"; her definitive pronouncement to Martin that Richard's visit will happen is told, as if reading the leaves, after "looking thoughtfully into her tea-cup" (100). Martin is especially convinced of her magic: "If his wife had said, 'Martin, the moon will fall to-morrow night,' he would have believed it quite possible" (100). None of this language implies the attacks (or even the more mild mockery of Highgate's crockery comments) that some *Recorder* comments on folk practices did.

Still, these features might be seen as making her dream-work quaint, minor heresy with a basically Christian intent, safe and—if not quite grandmotherly—far from Obi, Black witches, and Doesticks's Mrs. Grommer. Certainly some of Collins's ambivalence about Juno's class (writ largely) reinforces this. At one point in the midst of these prophecies, the narrator parenthetically addresses her as "Unsophisticated Juno," and when Richard finally comes, the narrator says Juno tells of Lina's trials "in simple but eloquent words" (89, 101). These moves may edge toward patronizing, and, of course, Juno does carry some of the "stock character" traits noted above.

But Juno and her prophecies are accorded more power in the narrative. When she convinces Martin to kill the pullets after "looking thoughtfully into her tea-cup," for example, she speaks "in low impressive tones" that might well befit her classical namesake (100).[28] Juno's predictions take a serious toll on her, too; after learning from Miss Ellwood that her predictions of trouble for Claire have come true, "she had been sad and silent" for days, "frequently indulging in long crying spells" (99). Part of this power comes from Juno's amazing accuracy. The narrator not only tells us that Juno's "suspicions" are "nearly always right" but also repeatedly shows such; everything she predicts in the novel is accurate. Even Juno reminds readers of her accuracy: near the end of this sequence, when Martin returns to find Richard Tracy in their cottage, he is "met at the door by the triumphant Juno who exclaimed, 'Martin, Martin, he has come. Master Richard has come!'" (101) So powerful is the revelation that Martin "could only gaze upon his wife as one in a dream" (101).[29]

In this frame, it is worth noting again that Juno's dreams and prophecies are repeatedly linked to Christian practice. If she is an oracle, she is simultaneously a kind of Christian recorder herself. Almost all of her critical prophecies are paired with oral links to (an Afro-Protestant) God, as if she is recording each as heaven-sent. Again, after issuing her first prophecy in the novel, Juno tells Claire, "I will never cease to pray for you" (10). The results of her first dream prophecy—Miss Ellwood's visit to scribe her story—could be seen as causing a concrete act of Christian recording by Claire's "dear preceptress," who writes down Juno's words (7). When Miss Ellwood returns with Richard Tracy—fulfilling another of Juno's prophecies—Juno greets them with "God be praised!" and then, reduced to sobbing, can initially only "fervently ejaculate: 'Thank the Lord! Thank the Lord!'" (100–101). But then she speaks words that confirm her agency in keeping the secrets surrounding Claire, offer another suggestion of divination, and emphasize Christian commitment: "I never believed the wrong was in *you*, Master Richard. I always thought and said you would come. I never told Claire who her father was, because I wanted her to respect you; but, *thank God*, it will be made all right" (101; second italics mine).

We should thus revisit Jennifer Greeson's suggestion that Juno's "act of critical reading" offers "Collins's overarching moral" because Juno "reaches beyond the triangle of characters to identify a caste-riven society as the ultimate source of tragedy" (774). Greeson is absolutely right, and Juno's most direct "reach" comes when she says "I always thought it best that Claire should never know she was tainted with black blood. But I must say this child don't see the difference,—don't see why black blood ain't just as good as white any day!" (89). Greeson understands that Juno here asserts that "fighting the erroneous assumption" of racial "tainting" is the only solution that "will save Claire from living out a repetition of her mother's fate" (774).

But the layers here are thicker. The fact that Juno's "solution" is embedded in prophecy—she makes the statement above while laundering the shirts and soliloquizing on her dream of Squire Farley's barn—reminds us of her augury; here, the words of the oracle promise to "lift" the title curse. The magic is not complete and does not immediately change everything. Juno's "this child" language is as complexly doubled as her name, both ringing of the "dis chile" so common in minstrelsy and directly invoking Juno as a child of God. But Juno holds immense power—remember again how Juno's "suspicions" are always true—and that power is simultaneously Christian and "folk," centered on a deep and wide sense of Black domesticity and augury, and linked to a mass of *Recorder* subscribers even as it reaches to wider ranges.

Locating Juno as one of the book's most crucial agents and, simultaneously, as the first and most directly labeled African American character calls on us to rethink much of the work on the novel to date because, on another level, Greeson's claims do not go far enough. The problem of the novel is not just the "caste-riven society." Rather, it is how white people shaped and shape that society; that is, it sees agents beyond any vague "curse." Racism here is a failure of white people; Juno rises above such foolishness by asserting that "this child don't see the difference" in innate value between white ancestry and/or skin color and Black.[30] This is the message that Juno delivers repeatedly—from her love of Claire to her final release of her secrets, when, notably, she tells two of the novel's most liberal white characters just how deeply prejudice has damaged the extended Tracy family and the nation. Juno's prophecies and analysis speak truth to even "friendly" power.

In this vein, I close with brief speculative work on Lina, Claire, and, less so, Miss Ellwood before considering the "place" Juno occupies at the novel's (near) conclusion and the importance of that place to this study. Claire's mother Lina, of course, is different from Juno in myriad ways: educated, even initially pampered, as opposed to Juno's youth in servitude; "beautiful" and "singularly attractive" in part because of "that dark brownish skin which we observe in the Spaniard and half-breed Indians" as opposed to Juno's generally unspoken and essentially unevaluated Blackness; somewhat traveled (to Canada and back to New Orleans) instead of rooted (Juno remains in Connecticut throughout); passionate, "sensitive," and "excitable" instead of steady; willing to marry a white man rather than staying single and then marrying a Black man; enslaved (albeit momentarily) instead of free (18–19, 28). If both seem stock characters in this comparison—Lina as the "tragic mulatta" and Juno as the "comforting mammy"—we need remember that both are more complex and that these trappings of "stock" are part of what allows Collins to begin to rewrite sentimental expectations.

Key among their differences, Juno is able to articulate the central problem of the novel (and the novel's world)—racism—and to work in small ways to fix it. Lina's realization of her Blackness leads her instead to the edge of madness: remember, for example, how she swoons when Colonel Tracy buys her and how the sense of the threat to her multiplies when readers consider that she does not own her own body and is in the New Orleans of "fancy girls." Lina's fear—fully grounded in horrific reality—leads her to misjudge Richard and to assume that he will turn out like many of the book's white people and cast her aside because of her caste. This means that her happy marriage must be brief and ultimately tragic. Juno falls into none of these traps and instead uses her knowledge to try to protect Lina and then Claire—and to build a life for herself.

These differences, however, only emphasize the deeper values Lina and Juno share—a recognition that leads Lina to confide in Juno in a moment that leaves Juno "striving to keep back the tears that would fall in spite of all effort to restrain them" (32). It also leads Lina to give Juno the token embodying Lina and Richard's love, the ring Juno later gives to Claire. Most importantly, this recognition causes the dying Lina to choose Juno as Claire's caregiver—her most definitive choice in the novel: "Be faithful to my child, Juno; never forsake her, and, as you may be faithful to her, my Father in heaven will reward you" (35). This decision places Juno as (almost) a stand-in for Lina, and Collins tells us quite early—in the second chapter—that Juno has been Claire's central caregiver for most of her life: "Juno, an old colored nurse, had taken care of her as long as she could remember.... They lived thus together, Juno and the lovely little girl, until Claire had reached her twelfth year" (9). Manville's "last visit" leads to Claire being placed at "L—Seminary" under Miss Ellwood's tutelage for six more years, but even during this time, it is clear that Juno represents the home to which Claire returns and that Juno remains her anchor (9).

Juno thus walks a complex line—in some ways a parent, in some ways not. In either construction, the love between Juno and Claire is deep and lasting: when Claire visits before going South, "Juno was delighted to see her dear child," the two share many tears, and "the parting, between the faithful old nurse and the child she had watched over so long, was touching in the extreme" (9–10). The balancing of the possessive "her dear child" with Collins's regular tagging of Juno with a title ("nurse") and a race ("colored") acts in many ways like other strategies in the novel: it brings Claire to the edges of Blackness but then inserts a separation. This placement also means that, if the central problem of the novel's world denies Claire her (Black) mother, a Black woman nonetheless mothers her. In a powerful answer to the shattering of Black families embodied in the *Recorder*'s "Information Wanted" ads, Collins hints at a more communal sense of childrearing, a sense based on a promise and love; even as Collins's use of Lina and Juno as foils demonstrates how dangerous white racism can be, it also reaffirms the power of the Black Christian domestic.

Juno's middling state between parent and (immensely important) servant places her in dialogue with Miss Ellwood and Claire in another way essentially ignored by critics. The cloudiness of her mothering role emphasizes that Juno is the book's first Black governess and is thus linked deeply to Miss Ellwood—a link reemphasized by Juno and Miss Ellwood's collaboration building from Juno's prophecy late in the novel.[31] When Miss Ellwood visits Juno's cottage, Juno "ushered the good lady" in and "placed the rocking chair for her greater comfort"; Miss Ellwood tells Juno to "sit down here, by my side" and sets to writing down Juno's remembrance (90–91). While the initial inclination might simply be to place Miss Ellwood (or Claire) and Juno as foils, a better approach is thus to study how Claire's work as a governess represents a melding of Juno and Miss Ellwood's efforts and values. Like the written narrative that will tell the Tracys in New Orleans what they need to know of Claire (and of the evils of their racism), Claire's own development is a result of Juno and Miss Ellwood's shared work.

While Claire's actual work as a governess is deemphasized in the novel, we do learn that "Claire was warmly attached to her pupils" and that "they improved rapidly under her gentle tuition" (54). While some of this "gentle tuition" undoubtedly builds from Miss Ellwood's schooling, the language here most echoes what we know of Juno's relation to Claire. Especially telling is the end of this paragraph in the novel, which tells of how "Mrs. Tracy loved" Claire "with an almost material affection" and the Tracy family (save the wicked sister Isabelle) grew to love her as "almost" family, language that also resonates with the careful dance of Juno's (almost-)mothering of Claire (54).

The central act of Claire's charges also echoes lessons that must have been taught to Claire in Juno's home; notably, that act also centers on the preparing and sharing of food (so central to Juno's welcoming of Richard) and includes a prominent and kind Black presence. At the edge of falling deep into her own illness in the midst of caring for Mrs. Tracy, Claire chooses to skip dinner, leading little Nellie Tracy—in a chapter titled "Little Nellie's First Sorrow"—to spill "great tears . . . over her round cheeks" and then at the dinner table, to lose her "fortitude": with "one glance at the vacant chair" usually occupied by Claire, she "sobbed aloud" and told the gathered family that Claire must eat (75). Belle mocks her, causing her to leave the table and "go out on the verandah, where she . . . sat looking very disconsolate" (76). Jim, one of the people the Tracys enslave, however, "had been a quiet, though not an uninterested spectator of the scene at the table, and the result was that he soon appeared by Nellie's side bearing a small tray, on which was a slice of delicately browned toast, a cup of fragrant tea, and several choice delicacies, very neatly arranged. 'Miss Nellie,' said he, 'let us take Miss Neville her supper'" (76). The learning Nellie shows (and gains) here—rooted in domesticity and love, embodied in the sharing of food, and aided by a Black presence—is deeply consonant with what Juno seems to have taught Claire in her youth.[32] From what little we see, Claire is an immensely successful teacher.

Gabrielle Foreman's essay on *Curse* is perhaps the first to closely examine Collins's own work as a teacher, though Kachun and Andrews do critical setup work. Rightly calling Collins's teaching "a daring venture into the public professional realm," Foreman uses this venture to explore the "preceptress" Miss Ellwood's power in the text—"an independent model whose orbit moves largely outside of the Colonel's patriarchal pull and influence" (713). She thus recognizes the novel's representation of just how crucial education is "in Black—and Black female—liberation" (713). We cannot know why Julia Collins did not write directly about the "great field" opening to Black teachers of the North (with whom Claire has several similarities) and to the newly freed people in the South—or of the war that created that field.[33] She may have been hesitant to write a story whose ending had not yet been fully decided, hesitant to write a "news" novel, or even hesitant to stray too far from the kinds of positive Black characters that edged closest to the mainstream of American print. Foreman's astute suggestion that Miss Ellwood and Claire address diverse issues swirling around Black women going South to teach the newly freed people there reminds us that the novel does often talk to its world, albeit at a slant—as that slant seems to offer more opportunity to advance both Collins's critiques of the nation and her calls for a rapprochement that is sentimental but nonetheless honest and fair about the damages of racism.

It would seem a significant stretch to suggest an ending that allowed Claire room to grow into a free Black Northern teacher of Southern children after the Civil War—though perhaps no more a stretch than the 2006 editors' presentation of two possible endings to the novel.[34] Certainly such a figure would appear in *Recorder* fiction as early as Frances Harper's first serialized novel (the 1869 *Minnie's Sacrifice*), and similar characters populate a handful of other novels published in the years after the Civil War. Collins would have had to do some chronological gymnastics—given that the war doesn't feature in the last published chapters of *Curse*; she would likely have had to open a final chapter or chapters with phrasing like "seven years later" and glossed the war that had filled so many of the *Recorder*'s columns.

On the other hand, we do not have to completely fantasize about such an ending. By the time we learn of Claire's success as a governess, we already know that her family tree mingles Black and white Americans and that, legally in the novel's world, she is Black.[35] Indeed, she *is* a free Black Northern teacher of Southern children. What is missing and what may or may not have been added in Collins's never-published and perhaps never-written conclusion is a move to teach (formerly) enslaved people—though we do know that the people the Tracys enslave are fascinated by Claire and we know, as well, that newly freed people did receive copies of the *Recorder* that contained *Curse* chapters.[36] Claire and Collins are thus much closer to Black teachers like Sallie Daffin and Edmonia Highgate than even previous scholars have suggested, and Claire is specifically capable of such closeness in part because Miss Ellwood *and* Juno prepared her for it.

The geographic range Claire shares with these Black teachers also contributes to the novel's massive landscape—a landscape that includes not only Claire's Connecticut and the New Orleans countryside but also, albeit briefly, the Canada of Lina's (safe) convent school and the France of both Count Sayvord and, for a time, Richard Tracy—leading to the chapter titles like the July 22, 1865, "Across the Atlantic" and the July 29, 1865, "This Side of the Atlantic." Even this quick listing of various settings says little about the wide "travels" via print that are also part of the novel—like those embodied in the volume of British poet Tennyson that is gifted to Claire by Sayvord and that speaks of both his affections and a kind of transatlanticism still understudied. However, this range makes the fact that Juno stays in one small area all the more striking.

I submit that Juno's rootedness facilitates much of the mobility of many of the book's characters and themes. The homes that Juno makes serve as nexuses for such travel. Rose Cottage is the beginning point in Alfred and Laura Hays's exodus from Connecticut (and the novel) to the West, the place where the homeless Lina finds a home, and the place from which Manville moves Juno and Claire—thus setting Richard's nomadic grief in full motion. Juno's own "neat little cottage" is not only the place of prophecy but also the meeting place of Miss Ellwood and Juno (and, via letters, the Tracy family and Juno), as well as where Richard "meets" much of the truth about his daughter. As critical as the Tracy home is to the destructive events in the novel—ranging from the shooting of Richard to the illness of Claire—Juno's homes are equally essential to the possibilities for domestic ideals moving throughout the novel's world.

Her homes are also places where texts and memories matter, even though Juno's alphabetic literacy is never established (and may be limited, given Miss Ellwood's scribing). Rose Cottage is the site of Richard's letters from New Orleans—disrupted when Manville burns the last of those letters before it is sent. Rose Cottage is also the first home to the "little rosewood box" that contains Lina and Richard's wedding ring—the rosewood box that Juno carries to her own "neat little cottage" and produces for Miss Ellwood in order to share "the letters and little ornaments" as well as "the certificate of the marriage of Richard and Lina" (10, 91). After Miss Ellwood writes Juno's remembrance down—making Juno's home the central site of Christian recording in the novel—she packages these items with her letter to send on to the Tracy family, as if recognizing that the remnants of Richard and Lina's domestic love may now find flower in the South. Juno's rosewood box is a repository—like Juno herself—of the novel's key memories, and it is Juno's home that allows these memories (textual and otherwise) to both stay safe and, in the end, travel.

It is thus a mistake to assume, as some critics have, that, after Richard's visit, Juno "is, for the purposes of the story, discarded—left with her husband on their isolated farm to live out their lives" (Cole 737). Given the lack of a conclusion to the novel, we have no idea whether Collins would have revisited Juno and Martin after the last published chapters.[37] Rather, Juno's home—the home of a free African American couple—is the launching point for what the characters "with hopeful hearts" suggest may be a loving reunion of Richard and Claire and a healing of the Tracy family (102). Demographically close to many homes that held copies of the *Recorder* and morally close to what the *Recorder* hoped Black homes could be at the war's end, Juno's cottage embodies, to use Collins's description of Martin Ray, "worthy, industrious" domestic ideals. Those ideals were not far from many embodied in Collins's essays, Amanda Turpin's *Recorder* letters, Stephen Collins's Civil War service, and Enoch Gilchrist's activism. They were far from perfect; even as they stretched some limitations placed on Black women, for example, they reinforced and accepted others. But they did emphasize the potential for a

Black community—joined in part by print—that would finally link the North and the South in freedom and Afro-Protestant values. Juno's homemaking concretizes that potential not only by creating a safe space for the formerly enslaved Lina and a cradle for the governess/teacher Claire but also by serving as an exemplar of Black domesticity—even as (and perhaps *because*) Juno's homes are sites of fortune telling, folk practices, and a wide sense of the possibilities of Afro-Protestantism and are embodied in a novel rather than in a genre more common to the paper.

I end this volume by considering Juno's (free Black) homes intentionally. I make this choice not simply because both the physical and metaphysical spaces they mark are critical to *Curse of Caste*—though they are, as a center for Claire's development, a geographic and spiritual nexus of the novel's plot and themes, and a site of the novel's sense of Black potential in freedom, and an argument about what the post–Civil War United States should look like.

Nor do I make this choice because Juno's homes, the homes they embodied and encouraged, or the *Recorder* homes that read about them were metaphorically or literally that far from the Lincoln White House of this book's introductory chapter. As chapter 1 and especially chapter 4 demonstrate, the AME's weekly newspaper had a stunning geographic and philosophic reach; it had even entered the South as soon as such was physically possible—through copies in Black soldiers' packs, copies carried by Northern teachers, and copies received by subscribers among the newly freed African Americans there. The journey to Washington was much easier: an installment of *Curse* could certainly have entered the national house in the pocket of William Slade or the bag of Elizabeth Keckley, to cite just two possibilities, and both of those figures would have been familiar with the questions of Black homes Collins engaged. The *Recorder* had created a community of print joined by loose but functional senses of faith, identity, and possibility—a community that stretched beyond physical location, that relied on the pages of the paper for a common meeting place, and that reached for the national, even in unexpected places.

I don't even conclude with Juno's homes because they challenge a sense of the Lincoln White House as the centerpiece of the Civil War period—or out of any desire to idealize a specific type (or denomination) of Black homes. In this, it is worth pausing to once more complicate our sense of key locations, events, and foci by revisiting the orbits of the two figures who open this volume—though to consider a date a few years after their White House meeting, April 14, 1865. Most students of American history know this as the date when Booth shot Lincoln, an event that deeply shaped the nation's moves into Reconstruction and led to a representational battle over how to remember the (first) martyred president. (Chapter 7, of course, touches on this battle, which has been studied in texts ranging from Kirk Savage's *Standing Solider, Kneeling Slave* to Julie Roy Jeffrey's *Abolitionists Remember.* That struggle reached into the largest Black churches and the smallest Black classrooms, in part because of African America's recognition that it wasn't just about legacies but about duties and national futures.)

Bishop Payne (seen in Figure 8.2) was not terribly far from the White House on April 14, 1865; he was attending the Baltimore AME annual conference. He likely followed the news from Washington as quickly as it came in. Distance and media bias may, however, have kept immediate knowledge of another April 14, 1865, event central to his life from reaching him quickly. Young Frederick Waugh (of chapter 6), then a student at Wilberforce, summarized that more distant event in an April 29, 1865, letter to the *Recorder*. His words might have been about the jubilation at the war's end days earlier and the explosive moment of Lincoln's assassination: "We enjoyed the celebration very much" but then "our joy ceased, and, in its stead, was anguish."

But Waugh was writing about was the fact that, on the same night as Lincoln was shot, as students and faculty were off-campus celebrating Lee's surrender, Wilberforce was destroyed by fire. "We hastened home," Waugh writes—using that last word to link AME education with a nexus of political and personal domestic ideals—"only to see our beautiful building in lurid flames." Then he essentially assumed that his community of *Recorder* readers must share his ideals: "You can better imagine our feelings than we can describe them." Though Waugh claimed that "the library, most of the furniture, and many seats of our large chapel, together with doors, blinds and sashes, were saved," later reports would assess the damage much more heavily—saying the college's main building was, in the words of Daniel Payne's *Recollections*, "reduced to smoldering ruins" (154). Some of the library collection

FIGURE 8.2 *Eliza J. Payne and Daniel A. Payne, from* Proceedings of the Quarto Centennial Conference of the African M. E. Church of South Carolina *(1890). Courtesy of the State Archives of Florida.*

was indeed destroyed, including significant print and manuscript materials ranging from Martin Delany's papers to back runs of AME periodicals like the *Recorder*. Waugh had noted that "all of the students sustained some loss" and "some lost all, excepting what they had on." It would be months before the institution would be able to see the damage fully: many students left, many more did not come the year after the fire, and the head of the women's department "never returned," because, per an 1881 account by Payne, her "nervous system was so affected by the catastrophe, that for twelve months she was unfit for labor" (*Biography* 115).

The *Recorder* reported that the April 14 fire was the result of arson but did not comment further on the perpetrator(s). Certainly the initial suggestion was that the fire was the result of anti-Black sentiment in the wake of Appomattox; Payne remembered more than one "enemy" of the college saying "I wish lightening from heaven would burn down Wilberforce" (114). But Payne himself would later speak in more depth on the arsonists in ways that stop any move toward easy conclusions. His 1881 *Biography of Daniel Smith* notes that the fire was set by "two obstreperous female students" who "were detained on the grounds" instead of being allowed to attend the Union celebrations "by way of punishments for acts of disobedience" (114–115).[38]

As tempting as it is to read Frederick Waugh's love of Wilberforce as an ideal linking of Black education and Black homes, so is it also possible to read the arson at Wilberforce as tied to the difficulties "obstreperous" young Black women could face. The *Recorder* seized on Waugh's version of events and, for literally years after the fire, carried reports on the rebuilding of Wilberforce, as well as requests for funds from a host of AME leaders (including Payne) and acknowledgments of contributions. It was a heroic effort to rebuild a massively valuable institution—even if it had been born of complicated and conflicted circumstances.

The coverage of the Wilberforce fire and its aftermath is a reminder that studying the Black press cannot give us all that has been lost, stolen, suppressed, or forgotten, but it is also incontrovertible evidence that if we do *not* study the Black press, we cut out massive and important pieces of our past. April 14, 1865, was not just the day Booth shot Lincoln. More than one complex and conflicted home faced trauma that night in the wake of war, slavery, and oppression. None of these (or myriad more) complex, intertwined stories of African American—nay, *American*—life in the Civil War era can be told without real attention to the facts, ideas, and practices surrounding Black locations, Black texts, and Black people's lived experiences. *This* is why I end with Juno's home. Such Black homes—from Juno's fictional homes to the real Black homes that saw the novel's composition, editing, and reception—should be a locus of our study of early African American print, the growth of African American literature, and American literature and history writ broadly.

Such homes need not be monolithically constructed, need not be assumed to hold the deep sentiment(alism) of Juno's homes, and need not be idealized. The data presented in chapter 4 begin to demonstrate just how diverse one community of such homes was—even as the discussions in that chapter and this book broadly call on us to study how the *Recorder* fought to expand its demographic reach and struggled with its philosophic and aesthetic boundaries. Like the *Recorder* itself—as this volume begins to show—the power and, indeed, the blessings of those homes did not mean that they were perfect or even ideal entities. In their diversity, though, such homes were the sites dreamed of in soldiers' letters, and they were the sites from which some Black women began to enter print. They were the sites of celebrations of emancipation and the Union victory, and they were the sites of Black mourning for figures from Abraham Lincoln to Anne Paul Vashon. They were sites of wonder and fear tied to war and Reconstruction in both the North and the South. Periodicals like the *Recorder* offered spaces for critical cultural work tied to such Black homes, including chances for those homes to engage with American print when much of the rest of the nation and its print culture offered only hatred or dismissal.

The *Christian Recorder* certainly, in Payne's words to Lincoln, showed what "the A. M. E. Church was doing to improve the character and condition of our people in the republic"—though the multiple resonances of Payne's "our" should now stand in stark relief (147–148). The *Christian Recorder* shared and became part of the lived experiences of individual African Americans across the nation, including the events in and representations of Black homes both like and *not* like Juno's—and Waugh's and even William Slade's and Elizabeth Keckley's, both so close to the Lincoln White House. It shared so much of what African Americans wanted known and remembered, so many of their hopes and fears, so many of their prayers for (to use George Boyer Vashon's words) "that wished home of peace," and so much of their desire to use language and print to "record" for each other and for all who came after.

{ NOTES }

Chapter 1

1. Quarles talks about the meeting in *Lincoln and the Negro* (1962); see 103–106. He cites Payne's *Recollections*. Manisha Sinha's 2008 "Allies for Emancipation?: Lincoln and Black Abolitionists" also notes the meeting and cites Quarles (181–182).

2. On these general issues, see Burlingame. *The Lincoln Log*, a project of the Abraham Lincoln Association, the Illinois Historic Preservation Agency, and the Abraham Lincoln Presidential Library and Museum (available free and online at www.thelincolnlog.org), attempts to reconstruct a "daily chronology of the life of Abraham Lincoln." It builds from *Lincoln Day-by-Day: A Chronology* (1960) but remains—and may always remain—incomplete. Payne's meeting was added to the *Log* in the course of researching this volume.

3. See Burlingame 334–345.

4. Such listings range from George Washington Young's sixty-nine enslaved people (valued in total at $17,711.85) to Sarah T. Simpson's one enslaved person, Ellen Worthy, who was valued at $284.70. See pages 36 and 48 of the *Letter*, respectively. Though available through the Internet Archive, the *Letter* remains unstudied. For an introduction to questions surrounding enslaved people in the District during this time, see Elizabeth Clark-Lewis's edited collection *First Freed: Washington, D.C. in the Emancipation Era* (2002) and Kate Masur's *An Example for All the Land: Emancipation and the Struggle over Equality in Washington, D. C.* (2010). See also Glenn David Brasher's *The Peninsula Campaign and the Necessity of Emancipation* (2012).

5. See especially Wood's *The Horrible Gift of Freedom: Atlantic Slavery and the Representation of Emancipation* (2010); though Wood focuses on visual culture, his insights can be applied broadly to many American constructions of slavery and emancipation.

6. Indeed, Burlingame argues that Lincoln "delayed signing the bill in order to allow Kentucky Congressman Charles Wickliffe time to remove two sick slaves who, in the president's view, 'would not have benefitted from freedom'" (344).

7. Lincoln himself seems to have left no extant documentation of the meeting. Payne notes two others present at the meeting—Lincoln allies Carl Shurz and Elihu Washburne. I have yet to find extant documents tied to these figures that comment on the meeting. Two primary accounts of the meeting are known: one, noted above, appears in Payne's 1888 *Recollections of Seventy Years*; the other was likely fed to a *Christian Recorder* correspondent by Payne and appeared in the April 26, 1862, issue under the heading "District of Columbia Correspondence." (An editorial "Interesting Items" in the same issue called special attention to this piece.) The *Recorder* correspondence shares Payne's prayer "that God would stand behind the Government at Washington, as he stood behind the throne of David" and notes that Lincoln assured "the Bishop of his reliance on Divine Providence." It says that "the Bishop left the White House most favorably impressed" but does

not mention Payne's gift of Black print. The 1888 account shows Payne handing the *Repository* and the *Recorder* to Lincoln. It also engages heavily in the liberation historiography common to late nineteenth-century African American texts and in the broader Lincoln hagiography of the period; for background, see John Ernest, *Liberation Historiography: African American Writers and the Challenge of History, 1794–1861* (2004); Laura Maffly-Kipp, *Setting Down the Sacred Past: African American Race Histories* (2010); Stephen G. Hall, *A Faithful Account of the Race: African American Historical Writing in Nineteenth-Century America* (2009); Julius Baily, *Race Patriotism: Protest and Print Culture in the AME Church* (2012); David Blight, *Race and Reunion: The Civil War in American Memory* (2001); Julie Roy Jeffrey, *Abolitionists Remember: Antislavery Autobiographers and the Unfinished Work of Emancipation* (2008). Within this framework, the account concludes with Payne's sense that "President Lincoln received and conversed with me as though I had been one of his intimate acquaintances or one of his friendly neighbors. I left him with a profound sense of his real greatness and of his fitness to rule a nation composed of almost all the races on the face of the globe" (148). Such memorializing of Lincoln was crucial to Payne's ongoing political struggles, as it created a Lincoln who embodied the sense of equality so desperately needed post-Reconstruction.

8. Lincoln's reading and sometime lack thereof continue to interest scholars; see, for example, Robert Bray's *Reading with Lincoln* (2010). Burlingame notes Lincoln aide John Hay's comment that President Lincoln "scarcely ever looked into a newspaper" but also cites a number of moments where Lincoln sought out and read periodicals carefully (287–289).

9. I use the language "begins to tell" to emphasize that study of Black periodicals in general and the *Recorder* in specific remains nascent. Mitch Kachun's "Interrogating the Silences: Julia C. Collins, 19th-Century Black Readers and Writers, and the *Christian Recorder*" and Chanta Haywood's "Constructing Childhood: The *Christian Recorder* and Literature for Black Children, 1854–1865" offer short introductions to the early *Recorder*, as does Jean Lee Cole's immensely valuable recovery of Henry McNeal Turner's *Recorder* Civil War columns, *Freedom's Witness: The Civil War Correspondence of Henry McNeal Turner* (2013). That said, these works are more concerned with introducing specific texts and/or concerns than with treating the *Recorder* broadly. Mitch Kachun's "The Making of a Public Biography: Richard Allen and the AME Church" is also valuable on several of these issues. Gilbert Anthony Williams's pioneering *The Christian Recorder, Newspaper of the African Methodist Episcopal Church: History of a Forum for Ideas, 1854–1902* (1996) is the only modern, book-length study of the paper, but its title dates are unfortunately misleading, as it says very little about the period before Benjamin Tucker Tanner was appointed editor in 1868. Julius Bailey's work on the *Recorder* is perhaps the strongest to date. His *Around the Family Altar: Domesticity in the African Methodist Episcopal Church, 1865–1900* (2005) explores the paper, but generally uses it as a source rather than an object of study and is also thin on the pre-1868 period. His lively *Race Patriotism: Protest and Print Culture in the AME Church* (2012) does more work on AME print as a subject, but also says very little about the *Recorder* pre-1868. Stephen W. Angell and Anthony B. Pinn's landmark collection *Social Protest Thought in the African Methodist Episcopal Church, 1862–1939* (2000) offers a fascinating collection of AME periodical writing, but includes comparatively little from the *Recorder*—favoring instead the later *AME Church Review*—and offers only a very brief introduction. I argue for the importance of the *Recorder* before

Tanner's entry, a period in which Elisha Weaver was the dominant figure. I further argue that post-Weaver nineteenth-century church historians and editors essentially wrote him out of the *Recorder*'s story—thus explaining some of the absence of not only Weaver but also many events between 1860 and 1868 from contemporary scholarship. Work on the Black press in the nineteenth century (cited below) is deeply uneven—but *is* uniformly brief—in discussion of the *Recorder*.

10. Such acknowledgments are discussed in more depth in chapters 3 and 4. My estimate is conservative and based on the following acknowledgments: January 19, 1862, $5 (Lynch); January 25, 1862, $5 (Lynch) and $5 (Moore); March 1, 1862, $1 (Lynch); March 15, 1862, $5 (Moore); March 29, 1862, $1 (Lynch). We should also note the December 21, 1861 acknowledgments for $3 (Moore) and $3.30 (Rev. David Smith). All of these were listed as "for papers," shorthand for funds covering single copy sales. The single copy price noted in the January 4, 1862, *Recorder* was five cents; prior to this, the paper was sold for either four cents a copy or five cents, depending on the agent and various other circumstances.

11. Totals by agent during the period are instructive here. Lynch sent a total of $23 "for papers"; Daniel Moore, $29.97; Smith, $3.30; Rhodes, $2; Handy, $2; Charles O. Moore, $37.75; Simms, $40.50. The grand total of $138.52 would mean at least 2,770 single copy sales at the higher price of five cents each ($138.50)—though the two-cent remainder here reminds us that some of these sales were likely at the lower rate of four cents per copy. Also, as discussed in more depth in chapter 3, Moore and Simms received some commission from their sales, so their copy sales numbers were likely higher than the listed amounts suggest, as they would have held back such commissions.

12. For comments about subscriptions and single copy sales in the District, see the August 31, 1861, March 29, 1862, and October 24, 1862 issues. Both single copy sales and subscriptions from the District increased significantly after 1864 and especially after Lincoln's April 1865 assassination. By March 17, 1866, then-editor James Lynch and then-publisher Elisha Weaver could also announce that, though not "supersed[ing] or effect[ing] . . . any of our stationed ministers in Washington, D.C.," "the *Christian Recorder* can be obtained every week at Davis' Hotel, 212 K st., Washington, D. C."

13. See Mary Lincoln to Elizabeth Todd Grimsley, September 29, 1861—in Turner and Turner, *Mary Todd Lincoln: Her Life and Letters*—where she wrote a favorite cousin that Keckley was "a very remarkable woman" (106). More generally, see Catherine Clinton's *Mrs. Lincoln* (2009) and especially Jennifer Fleishner's *Mrs. Lincoln and Mrs. Keckly: The Remarkable Story of the Friendship between a First Lady and a Former Slave* (2003).

14. A September 8, 1866, item noted that "The name of Mrs. Lizzie Keekley [*sic*], Washington, D. C., was omitted" mistakenly from an earlier list of acknowledgments.

15. The first mention of Keckley in the paper seems to be in Henry McNeal Turner's September 13, 1862, letter, which both Accessible Archives's and Cole's transcriptions of the *Recorder* erroneously render as "Trekly" from a hard-to-read copy. Problems with spelling her name continued in subsequent *Recorder* pieces. Boston minister Leonard Grimes marked Keckley's visit to his church in a November 29, 1862, *Recorder* letter and noted her "highly interesting" statements "from one fresh from the spot, and bearing upon their face the impress of truth and earnestness"—though the piece misspelled her name as "Keckler." Keckley's ties to the AME Church continued after she joined the Fifteenth Street Presbyterian Church: she worked with Wilberforce for a time, and Quarles, for example, notes her 1868 donation of one of Mary Lincoln's dresses from the Second

Inaugural "along with the cloak and bonnet she wore at Ford's Theatre" to Wilberforce College to use in their fundraising efforts after the massive fire of 1865 (248).

16. Many accounts of Slade rely on John E. Washington, *They Knew Lincoln* (1942), 105–117. He is unfortunately not well represented in more recent scholarship and is absent from works like the *African American National Biography*.

17. In addition to Masur's piece in the *New York Times*, see also Masur's "A Filmmaker's Imagination, and a Historian's" in the *Chronicle of Higher Education*; the *Atlantic*'s roundtable on the film at http://www.theatlantic.com/entertainment/category/lincoln-roundtable/; and Manisha Sinha's "Lincoln Again" at the History Workshop Online at http://www.historyworkshop.org.uk/lincoln-again/.

18. Among more recent important works on the AME Church and/or key figures in the Church, see Clarence E. Walker, *A Rock in a Weary Land: The African Methodist Episcopal Church During the Civil War and Reconstruction* (1982); William Seraile, *Voice of Dissent: Theophilus Gould Stewart (1843–1924) and Black America* (1991); Stephen Angell, *Bishop Henry McNeal Turner and African American Religion in the South* (1992); James T. Campbell, *Songs of Zion: The African Methodist Episcopal Church in the United States and South Africa* (1995); Seraile, *Fire in His Heart: Benjamin Tucker Tanner and the AME Church* (1998); Lawrence S. Little, *Disciples of Liberty: The African Methodist Episcopal Church in the Age of Imperialism, 1884–1916* (2000); Jualynne E. Dodson, *Engendering Church: Women, Power, and the AME Church* (2002); Richard S. Newman, *Freedom's Prophet: Bishop Richard Allen, the AME Church, and the Founding Fathers* (2009). Such work should be read in the context of broader studies of Black faith practices, including C. Eric Lincoln and Lawrence H. Mamiya, *The Black Church in the African American Experience* (1990); Theophus Smith, *Conjuring Culture: Biblical Formations of Black America* (1994); Albert Raboteau, *Slave Religion: The "Invisible Institution" in the Antebellum South* (1979); Eddie Glaude, *Exodus! Religion, Race, and Nation in Early 19th Century Black America* (2000); Allen Dwight Callahan, *The Talking Book: African Americans and the Bible* (2006); Cedric May, *Evangelism and the Black Atlantic, 1760–1835* (2008); Christopher Z. Hobson, *The Mount of Vision: African American Prophetic Tradition, 1800–1950* (2012). Pamela E. Klassen's "Robes of Womanhood" represents some of the exciting work building from these studies.

19. Foster and Haywood's 1995 call appeared in their "Christian Recordings: Afro-Protestantism, Its Press, and the Production of African American Literature"; Foster's 2005 "A Narrative of the Interesting Origins and (Somewhat) Surprising Development of African American Print Culture" echoes, updates, and expands that work. Among important recent studies of nineteenth-century Black literature vis-à-vis Black faith—many of which notably extend Black feminist scholarship and often focus on Black women—see Joycelyn Moody, *Sentimental Confessions: Spiritual Narratives of Nineteenth-Century African American Women* (2003); Chanta Haywood, *Prophesying Daughters: Black Women Preachers and the Word, 1823–1913* (2003); Yolanda Pierce, *"Hell without Fires": Slavery, Christianity, and the Antebellum Spiritual Narrative* (2005); Katherine Clay Bassard, *Spiritual Interrogations: Culture, Gender, and Community in Early African American Women's Writing* (1999) and *Transforming Scriptures: African American Women Writers and the Bible* (2010). While not only about Black faith, Carla Peterson's 1995 *"Doers of the Word": African American Women Speakers and Writers in the North (1830–1880)* is also critical.

20. If we recover key texts and general readers cannot access them, we have failed. The *Documenting the American South* project—and, for African Americanists, the "North American Slave Narratives" section, created under the leadership of William Andrews—available in searchable form at http://docsouth.unc.edu/index.html is a beacon in providing free online access to a broad general public. The later *Black Periodical Literature Project* focuses on literary texts from the Black press but is quite difficult to access. We need also remember that individual articles sliced out of Black periodicals and presented separately—in the mode of both the *Black Abolitionist Papers* (albeit with fine annotations) and the *Black Periodical Literature Project*—are only fragments and can only tell us small bits of the story of the stunning world of Black experiences. Such individual pieces of periodical content were always presented on specific periodical pages in specific issues, and, more broadly, in specific periodicals—contexts often lost or ignored by compilations.

21. I. Garland Penn's *The Afro-American Press, and Its Editors* (1891) is a crucial ancestor of research on the Black press. Early scholarship also includes Martin E. Dann, ed., *The Black Press, 1827–1890* (1971); Roland E. Woseley, *The Black Press USA* (1971); Abby Arthur Johnson and Ronald Maberry Johnson, *Propaganda and Aesthetics: The Literary Politics of Afro-American Magazines in the Twentieth Century* (1979); Bernell Tripp, *Origins of the Black Press, New York, 1827–1847* (1992); Frankie Hutton's strong *The Early Black Press in America, 1827–1860* (1993); Armistead S. Pride and Clint C. Wilson II, *A History of the Black Press* (1997). Important historical-bibliographic efforts include Penelope Bullock, *The Afro-American Periodical Press, 1838–1909* (1981), and James P. Danky, ed., *African American Newspapers and Periodicals: A National Bibliography* (1998). See also Todd Vogel, ed., *The Black Press: New Literary and Historical Essays* (2001); Elizabeth McHenry, *Forgotten Readers: Recovering the Lost History of African American Literary Societies* (2002); Jacqueline Bacon, *Freedom's Journal: The First African American Newspaper* (2007); Jeannine Marie DeLombard, "African American Cultures of Print" in *A History of the Book in America: Volume 3, The Industrial Book, 1840–1880* (2007); Eric Gardner, *Unexpected Places* (2009); and Lara Langer Cohen and Jordan Stein, eds., *Early African American Print Culture* (2012). Frances Smith Foster, more than any other scholar, has pushed literary critics and historians to consider Black periodicals; see especially her "A Narrative of the Interesting Origins" and, with Haywood, "Christian Recordings." She also created a germinal anthology, *Love and Marriage in Early African America* (2008), that draws from a wide range of periodicals and shares sources referenced in her *'Til Death or Distance Do Us Part: Love and Marriage in Early African America* (2010). This work extends her earlier efforts to recover Black women's texts; see, e.g., *Written by Herself: Literary Production by African American Women, 1746–1892* (1993).

22. On this last, see especially Heather Andrea Williams's elegant *Help Me to Find My People: The African American Search for Family Lost in Slavery* (2012).

23. I offered an earlier version of this argument in *Unexpected Places*, 6–10. Simply the fact that a fine 2008 collection subtitled "New Perspectives on Early African American Literature" is titled *Beyond Douglass* should serve as a reminder of the power of a single figure—indeed, a single text—in the canon of nineteenth-century (African) American literature.

24. For two examples of finding texts that many have assumed lost, see Julie McCown and Cedric May's recent rediscovery of a Jupiter Hammon manuscript poem as well as my own rediscovery of a "missing" chapter of Frances Ellen Watkins Harper's serialized

Recorder novel *Sowing and Reaping*. Among a growing number of recent recoveries, see also Robert Levine and Ivy Wilson's collection of James Monroe Whitfield's poetry, Wilson's volume of Albery Allson Whitman's poetry, Cole's volume on Henry McNeal Turner, Lois Brown's edition of Susan Paul's *Memoir of James Jackson*, Julie Winch's editions of volumes by Cyprian Clamorgan and Joseph Willson, and John Stauffer's collection of works by James McCune Smith. That said, we also need to recognize the academy's sadly uneven acceptance of recovered African American literature, as few of these texts are taught widely, and, as John Ernest argues in his "Artless Stories, Simple Facts," many modern editions of key early African American works have suffered from inadequate introductions and editorial apparatus. On Kenneth Warren's 2011 book—alluded to above—and the discussions following, see clusters in the *Los Angeles Review of Books*, *PMLA*, and *African American Review*—especially, in the latter, John Ernest's "Canals and Rivers." While some of the response has rightly questioned the reasons for and consequences of setting an end date of "African American literature" as a rubric, fewer questions have been raised about the book's assertion of a start date—c. 1896—for African American literature.

25. Loughran summarizes:

> Numerous scholarly accounts ... follow Anderson in presuming a coherent and connected print culture as the crucial apparatus that successfully knits together dispersed North American communities from the colonial period forward. Print serves, in such analyses, as the central and centralizing agent in the processes of American nation formation. *The Republic in Print* takes a different view. It challenges this account as ahistorical, a postindustrial fantasy of preindustrial print's efficacy as a cross-regional agent. . . . I argue instead that there was no "nationalized" print public sphere in the years just before and just after the Revolution, but rather a proliferating variety of local and regional reading publics scattered across a vast and diverse geographic space. (xviii–xix)

While Loughran herself is careful to speak of "nation" rather than Anderson's "communities," many Americanists have collapsed the two. Similarly, while Loughran is careful to couch her initial argument above "in the years just before and just after the Revolution," to suggest that such fragmentation shifted between the 1830s and the 1850s, and to pick specific moments/events for her analysis, later scholars have been much more willing to apply her model to a much wider range of texts and events. This may be, in part, a result of Loughran's sweeping, century-long narrative and subtitle.

This volume leans toward Loughran's arguments, as she rightly asserts that we must consider "the historically specific ways that both artifacts and affect circulated under the still emerging relations of early industrial North American (nation) production" and because she recognizes that Anderson relies on a "fantasy about the ability of print to erase local differences and to install, in their place, a formal homogeneity, whether in fact or in feeling" (9, 14). Key post-Anderson/pre-Loughran works on some of these issues include Cathy Davidson, *Revolution and the Word: The Rise of the Novel in America* (1986); Michael Warner, *Letters of the Republic: Publication and the Public Sphere in Eighteenth-Century America* (1990); Partha Chatterjee, *The Nation and Its Fragments: Colonial and Postcolonial Histories* (1993); and Christopher Looby, *Voicing America: Language, Literary Form, and the Origins of the United States* (1996). For samples of post-Loughran work, see

Matthew P. Brown, "The Tiger's Leap and the Dog's Paw: Method, Matter, and Meaning in the History of the Book"; Carolyn Eastman, *A Nation of Speechifiers: Making an American Public after the Revolution* (2009); Carolyn Levander, "Sutton Griggs and the Borderlands of Empire"; Chris Apap, "'Let no man of us budge one step': David Walker and the Rhetoric of African American Emplacement."

Space prevents me from fully examining recent work on trans-Atlantic, trans-national, hemispheric, and diasporic Black print identities, some of which—like Ifeoma Nwankwo's *Black Cosmopolitanism* (2005)—I find useful. I do, though, continue to find "nation" an especially valuable category for analysis, as many of the authors, editors, readers, and other figures tied to the *Recorder* thought of themselves—and fought for positions—specifically as citizens of the United States and as members of a nation-state even as they were members of an oppressed "nation" within that nation-state. This does not mean I see "nation" as given or fixed—indeed, much of the *Recorder*'s work was tied to shifting constructions of (the) nation. Koritha Mitchell's discussion of "full citizenship" in her *Living with Lynching: African American Lynching Plays, Performance, and Citizenship, 1890–1930* (2011) is useful here, as, while she recognizes deep fallacies in simplistic senses of "citizen" and "nation"—senses that depend as much on who is "out" as on who is "in" without ever confronting such questions—she also sees concrete political and social value in the rhetorics of and individuals' positioning as "citizens."

26. Similarly, what began as a small mission and a few unofficial churches founded by AME congregants in California in the 1850s grew into demands for a full Church commitment to the state (and to the West) and eventually to the formation of the California Conference in 1865. To illustrate how much stretching of the Church's sense of itself was involved here, I note that early California efforts were nominally supervised by the AME's Indiana Conference—then its furthest-West body. See Case, *An Unpredictable Gospel*, for one reading of the AME Church's post-war expansion in the South.

27. Building from Jacques Ranciere's "signature notion of the equality of intelligences," Pratt critiques taking "for granted the superiority of the current critic's knowledge when measured against the knowledge generated in the past," even as he notes "the peril of any form of identification" with the past "that could be taken as sentimental" (155, 157). Pratt posits that "if Ranciere is right . . . all of these reservations around mediation, identification, and empirical details should be understood as . . . the predictable attempt of a mandarin intellectual to guard against his fundamental equality with a past capable of speaking directly to him" (157).

28. Also of note is Pratt's sense that "past historical actors are tethered to the present," as "our practice of recognition" is not a debt owed "to who they were but to who they are still becoming" (159–160).

29. The strongest moments of Jackson's piece are when he pushes for conversation between the two fields, though he unfortunately sometimes attends much more to the absences of "book history" in African American literary study than to the absences of African American texts (and figures) from book history. Early moves to explore the potential dialogues between the fields like Jordan Stein and Lara Langer Cohen's groundbreaking collection *Early African American Print Culture* (2012) and their follow-up seminar, which was given as part of the American Antiquarian Society's Summer Seminar in the History of the Book program, have generated both great excitement and strong critique. (For an example of the latter, see Gabrielle Foreman's important "A Riff, A Call, and A

Response" and the cluster of responses in *Legacy* following its publication.) I think, too, that as much as book historians might have to teach some African Americanists about a whole set of issues, they need to recognize the complexity of, for example, studying books and periodicals as circulating objects in a culture in which the *authors* of those books and periodicals were also often treated as circulating objects. (One thinks of both Frederick Douglass and Harriet Jacobs's accounts of how they themselves were purchased and then freed by well-meaning supporters in part to enable them to write—and to speak—to broad publics.) Similarly, we cannot assume that graduate training in American literature and/or book history represents any kind of real or just engagement with African Americanist inquiry. I am daily reminded of John Ernest's recognition, shared at the opening of *Chaotic Justice*, that "I have had many occasions for realizing anew that I did not know nearly enough about the literary and cultural history on which, according to my doctorate and professional experience, I was supposed to be an expert" (1). Historians of the book and print have much to learn from African American studies, too.

30. Recovering the periodical portion of early Black print culture, for example, is only part of what must be much broader efforts. Richard Newman, Patrick Rael, and Phillip Lapsansky's *Pamphlets of Protest: An Anthology of Early African American Protest Literature, 1790–1860* (2001) has already stirred some interest in pamphlets. Attention to Black manuscript culture and visual culture is much more nascent. With the exception of a handful of texts like McHenry's stunning *Forgotten Readers*, attention to African American readers and reading has been even thinner. I cite Pawley's approach specifically because it is consciously designed to offer "a window onto the acts of reading and writing by nonelite groups" (73); see especially her "Beyond Market Models and Resistance: Organizations as a Middle Layer in the History of Reading."

31. Here I mean "sampling" of both texts and genres. My emphasis on letters, poetry, and extended fiction in chapters 6, 7, and 8, respectively, should not dissuade scholars from much-needed examination of other genres and sets of genres, such as, for example, material in the paper designed for children.

Chapter 2

1. For a primer on Lane, see Hanses. Michele Valerie Ronnick has done rich work on other early Black classicists—especially William Sanders Scarborough.

2. See, e.g., March 9, 1882, *Recorder*.

3. Tanner did not rise to a bishopric until 1888. In 1884, Daniel Payne and Alexander Wayman were the Church's senior bishops. As both had already written Church histories, there were clearly figures beyond Tanner who could have fielded Lane's inquiry.

4. While the *Magazine* was scheduled as a monthly, it took three years to publish its first twelve issues. Penelope Bullock's discussion of its content and mission remains the best available; see 39–43 and 228–229. The thematic of loss in Tanner's comments had already entered his broader response when he admitted, of the printed conference minutes, "how far back these go we are unable to say." Contemporary scholars will find painful irony in Tanner's assertion that "without any very great effort we think a full copy of" the AME magazine of the late 1850s and early 1860s *The Repository of Religion and Literature* "could be obtained," as the *Repository* remains one of the early Black periodicals that has received the least attention and is among the least accessible.

5. Newman's valuable *Freedom's Prophet* provides more detail and can be read usefully alongside older Church histories like those Tanner cites as well as recent scholarship that focuses on or includes other denominations—like Craig D. Townsend's *Faith in Their Own Color: Black Episcopalians in Antebellum New York City* (2005) and David E. Swift's *Black Prophets of Justice: Activist Clergy before the Civil War* (1989).

6. Campbell, *Songs*, 38–42 gives a succinct summary of Payne's desires for and efforts toward a more educated ministry and laity; see also Owens 49–53 for a sampling of the diverse other discussions of the AME's shifting sensibilities on education in the Church's early years. Payne's *History* and his *Recollections* treat these issues in depth, although, of course, from Payne's perspective.

7. See Jean Marie Lutes's "Beyond the Bounds of the Book."

8. See *Writing with Scissors: American Scrapbooks from the Civil War to the Harlem Renaissance*.

9. Even the best intentions by individuals hoping to save copies of the *Recorder* could fail painfully: in preparing his response to Lane, Tanner might have remembered James H. A. Johnson's August 30, 1877, *Recorder* piece "Blasted Hopes," which tells of how Johnson took in a young man "to school him" only to have him pilfer and destroy much of Johnson's collection of personal diaries, speeches, pamphlets, and Black newspapers including "back files of the CHRISTIAN RECORDER."

10. While a full historiography is beyond the scope of this study, we might note that limited access to already limited archives can lead to multigenerational errors. Penn's *The Afro-American Press and Its Editors* (1891), for example, doesn't even name Weaver as one of the *Recorder*'s editors, likely because Penn had no access to many issues from the period and relied heavily on post-bellum Church histories like the germinal work of Payne and Wayman, which radically deemphasize Weaver's work.

11. Accessible Archives' version is full text and searchable, but transcription quality is uneven. Transcriptions and searching capabilities in the *Black Abolitionist Papers* are stronger, but this project includes much less of the paper. Given these concerns, all quotations from the *Recorder* in this book are drawn from direct examination of the microfilmed *Recorder*.

12. Noliwe Rooks's discovery of lost periodicals at Fisk (*Ladies Pages* 3) is a reminder of such issues and possibilities. Foster notes that she found the final missing chapter of the 1888–1889 Frances Ellen Watkins Harper novel *Trial and Triumph* at Drew (xxvii). The uncovering of a larger collection of paper *Recorder* issues at Drew than previously known—and the subsequent cataloging of those issues for the first time—represents yet another call to look and then look again for what (we think) we have lost.

13. Post-1860 and pre-1869 issues of the paper that were likely published but are missing from the Campbell collection and derivatives include those of January 12, 1861; June 6, 1863; June 13, 1863; June 20, 1863; June 27, 1863; July 4, 1863; July 11, 1863; November 19, 1864; March 11, 1865; May 13, 1865; December 1, 1866; March 30, 1867; and June 27, 1868. Issues of the paper in this period that are only partially extant on the Campbell film and its derivatives include those of June 14, 1862; July 26, 1862; August 23, 1862; December 13, 1862; December 20, 1862; January 17, 1863; February 7, 1863; February 28, 1863; September 26, 1863; October 31, 1863; November 28, 1863; December 5, 1863; December 19, 1863; February 6, 1864; March 5, 1864; March 19, 1864; April 23, 1864; August 13, 1864; October 22, 1864; October 29, 1864; November 5, 1864; December 24, 1864; January 21, 1865; January 28, 1865;

February 11, 1865; June 17, 1865; January 13, 1866; April 14, 1866; August 11, 1866; October 6, 1866; March 2, 1867; April 13, 1867; May 11, 1867; April 18, 1868; August 1, 1868; and November 28, 1868. Such partial issues generally consist of pages three and four, though some include, instead, pages one and two.

14. Weaver opened 1861 with a "new series," dropping Campbell's numbering and labeling his first issue—seemingly no longer extant—volume 1, number 1. The rest of the 1861 issues are numbered correctly, ending with 1.51. The January 4, 1862, issue is numbered 2.1 and whole number 52. Though some 1862 issues are extant in only partial form, all are accounted for in terms of numbering. The December 27, 1862, issue is correctly numbered 2.52, though its whole number was mistakenly given as 104 (as 51 + 52 = 103). As the December 13, 1862, and December 20, 1862, issues are partials missing their first two pages, it is difficult to tell where this error began (though the December 6, 1862, issue's whole number is correct.) The January 3, 1863, issue is numbered 3.1 with the incorrect whole number 105. The January 10, 1863, issue is numbered 3.2 and the corrected whole number 105 (thus sharing this whole number with the January 3 issue). As per note 13 above, six 1863 issues are missing, but the July 18, 1863, issue is correctly numbered 3.29, whole number 132—confirming that while the above-noted June and July 1863 issues may not be extant, they *were* published. While some issues between late 1863 and 1867 are extant only in partial form or are missing, all are accounted for in terms of numbering. The final issue of 1863 (December 26) is correctly numbered 3.52, whole number 155. The first issue of 1864 (January 2) is numbered 4.1, whole number 156. The April 9 issue has an incorrect whole number—171, which should be 170—and this error persists in whole numbers for the rest of 1864. The final issue of 1864 (December 31) is numbered 4.52 (correct), whole number 209 (which should be 208). The initial issue of 1865 (January 7) corrects the whole number error and is numbered 5.1, whole number 209 (thus sharing this whole number with the December 31, 1864, issue). The February 18, 1865, issue, which should have been whole number 215, is mislabeled 216, and this error persists for the rest of 1865 and the beginning of 1866. The January 27, 1866, issue's whole number (264) corrects this error (and so shares the whole number with the January 20, 1866, issue). Also, the March 18, 1865, issue is misnumbered 5.12; it was actually 5.11. (The April 1, 1865, issue, which is numbered 5.13, corrects this error by carrying the same number as the March 25, 1865, issue.) The final 1866 issue (December 29) is correctly numbered 6.52, whole number 312, and the first issue of 1867 (January 5) is numbered 7.1, whole number 313. The last 1867 issue (December 28) was numbered 7.52, whole number 364, and the first issue of 1868 (January 4) was numbered 8.1, whole number 365. No issues after February 8, 1868 (8.6, whole number 370), up to March 28, 1868, are extant, and the April 4, 1868, issue is available only in partial/damaged form. The April 11, 1868, issue is numbered 8.9, whole number 372; this confusing numbering (it should be either 8.8, 372 or 8.9, 373) suggests that only one or perhaps two issues were published during the gap. Issues for April 18, April 25, and May 2, 1868, seem to have come out roughly on time, but the numbering of the May 2, 1868, issue (8.12, whole number 375, continuing the April 11, 1868, error in numbering) and of the May 16, 1868, issue (8.13, whole number 376)—as well as the lack of an extant issue between—suggest that no issue was published on May 9, 1868. The June 20, 1868, issue—the first extant issue from new editor Tanner—is listed only as whole number 377, though Tanner's later continuance of the numbering above would also mean it was 8.14. All of this strongly suggests that the paper did not appear at all on May 23, May 30,

June 6, or June 13, 1868. After Tanner took over, at least two more issues seem to have been missed before the final issue of the year (December 26), which is numbered 8.39, whole number 402 (continuing the April 11, 1868, error). Because of these issues, my citations in this book list issue dates rather than numbers.

15. Accessible Archives' description of its *Recorder* holdings is thus similarly wrong; it promises the *Christian Recorder* "complete from 1861 through December 1902, excluding 1892" with no mention of the significant number of missing issues cited here or of the later issues cited in Frances Smith Foster's edition of Frances Harper's serialized *Recorder* novels (from 1869, 1876, and 1877—five missing and eight partial). It is also worth noting that issues for *all* of 1871 and 1879 seem to be missing from Accessible Archives, even though some 1871 issues, for example, are in the Campbell run and the subsequent film.

16. One does not need to accept all of Nicholson Baker's controversial *Double Fold: Libraries and the Assault on Paper* (2001) to see, as did Karin Wittenborg at the "Do We Want to Keep Our Newspapers?" Conference (available on the Association of Research Libraries page responding to Baker at http://www.arl.org/preserv/presresources/Nicolas_Baker.shtml), that preservation efforts "have not done a very good job in the past, thus suffering the loss of some critical titles" and that "in our zeal to tackle preservation and space problems we often have given short shrift to the experience of the newspaper artifact. And many newspaper microfilming projects did not have adequate quality control." Wittenborg's approach *seems* sensible and measured: "We do not have the resources to save every single newspaper in its original form. There are parallels to architectural preservation, where it is routinely accepted that not all buildings are worth saving. Likewise, some newspapers are not worth saving. They will have little or no value to scholars. The challenge will be to get scholars and librarians together to make these tough choices." This approach is echoed in ARL documents like the 2009 "Safeguarding Collections at the Dawn of the 21st Century: Describing Roles & Measuring Contemporary Preservation Activities in ARL Libraries," available at http://www.arl.org/bm~doc/safeguarding-collections.pdf. However, Wittenborg's comments never speak to potential biases shaping "these tough choices." We know that generations of "scholars and librarians," sometimes systematically and sometimes unconsciously, found many African American texts to be "not worth saving." I have also located no discussion on de-accessioning items based on the use of incorrect cataloging data—an issue that is also pressing, given the above.

17. My discussion here draws on extensive reading of AME *Discipline* volumes, the early Church histories cited above, the *Recorder*, and more recent work ranging from Newman's biography of Richard Allen to Campbell's *Songs of Zion* to Dodson's *Engendering Church*. Owens's *Formation of the African Methodist Episcopal Church* explores some of the rhetorical and (albeit less so) theological questions involved in these structures.

18. Throughout the 1850s, for example, the Indiana Conference had charge of most of the American Midwest and West—including California. The shift to a separate California Conference reflected the AMEC's changing sense of the American West, revised governance practice to emphasize local connection and local presence even more, and seems to have made existing conferences think even more about their boundaries and charges.

19. General Conferences, for example, were the sole site for elections for bishops and for discussion of broad church levies—one of which, the "Two-Cent Money" (a two-cent annual tax on each church member) was set up in 1844 to provide crucial funding for the young Book Concern.

20. General Conferences, for example, were national, representative groups joined in large part by print (ranging from the *Discipline* to newspaper announcements of meetings), and they functioned both as communities of the moment (in and of themselves) and links to a much broader collection of physical congregations.

21. Green (c. 1815–1878) later split with the AME Church and moved to Ontario. While there, he started the *True Royalist and Weekly Intelligencer* (1860–1861), a short-lived BME newspaper that exchanged with the *Recorder*; see March 9, 1861, *Recorder*. By then, he had published a collection of short texts, *A Treatise on the Episcopacy of the African M. E. Church; Duty of Parents and Churches to Baptized Children; An Examination of the Mother Church* (1845); as well as *The Life of Rev. Dandridge F. Davis* (1850; available online as part of the *Documenting the American South* project) and a pamphlet advocating Black emigration to Canada, *A Discourse for the Times, on Our Condition as It Is and Might Be* (1853). After the Civil War, Green returned to the United States and the AME—serving charges in the deep South, sending letters to the *Recorder*, and co-authoring *A Brief Account of the Re-Organization of the BME Church* (1872) before dying in Mississippi.

22. While even Green said that Hogarth was "a first class business man," Hogarth had never been able to get more than 250 of the 900 subscriptions he estimated were needed for the *Magazine* to break even.

23. See Payne *History* 219–220. His coverage is summarized in Smith *History* 19–20 and Handy *Scraps* 181–182 and forms the basis of most scholarship. Others remembered the events differently; John T. Jennifer, for example, writing for the May 27, 1875, *Recorder*, credited Bishop Quinn with pushing this initiative through the General Conference. The other source that mentions such a committee is J. C. Embry's "Address . . . Delivered at the Dedicatory Jubilee in Bethel Church," which appeared in the May 11, 1893, *Recorder*. The "Address" shares otherwise-unknown information but is also filled with errors—making its conclusions difficult to evaluate. It says "Thos. Lawrence, Byrd Parker, and others, were appointed [to] a committee to purchase the 'Mystery Press.' But in all this high procedure we find no account of any money being raised or appropriated, and so the paper they were to buy remains a mystery to the present day."

24. The words are Haywood's (418) but could come from diverse sources. While her linkage between AME Church print and "Afrocentric and politically charged" ideas is in some ways too totalizing, her placing of the *Recorder* in dialogue with its radical roots is wise and accurate.

25. The extant issues are from April 16, 1845, and December 16, 1845. Levine's *Martin R. Delany: A Documentary Reader* contains the best discussion of *The Mystery* and collects texts from extant issues as well as *Mystery* texts that were reprinted by the *Liberator* and the *Palladium of Liberty*.

26. The *North Star* version of the "Farewell" is reprinted in Levine 38–40; for an introduction to Delany's initial work with Douglass, see Levine 27–28.

27. A letter in AME minister Levin Tilmon's oft-ignored *A Brief Miscellaneous Narrative of the More Early Part of the Life of L. Tilmon* (1853) confirms several issues of the

Herald published in 1848. Tilmon (1807–1863) reprints a letter he wrote to Green that opens, "Dear Brother,—I have just received the first, second and third numbers of the 'Christian Herald,' which I hail with pleasure, as a welcome messenger." (Tilmon dates the letter October 27, 1848, which suggests that either his date is wrong or that the October 31 initial issue date in Green's March 1, 1877, *Recorder* letter is an error.)

28. The rare later *Recorder* subscribers who remembered the *Herald* in writing usually commented on its "failure" and "the embarrassed state of the Book Concern"; these words, for example, are from Mrs. E. A. Jackson's March 10, 1862, speech at a meeting in Vincennes, Indiana, reported in a letter from her husband, William, that was published in the March 22, 1862, *Recorder*. See also Rachel A. Smith's letter in the April 9, 1864, *Recorder*. A time capsule placed in the cornerstone of Macedonia AME in Camden, New Jersey, in 1850—opened in 1883 and reported on in the June 28, 1883, *Recorder*—also included "a copy of the Christian Herald of the A.M.E. Church Rev. A.R. Green, editor, with Revs. M.M. Clark and John M. Brown, corresponding editors. Quite a difference in present RECORDER."

29. Both Payne's quote and Clark's "Prospectus of the Christian Recorder" appear in Payne, *History*, 219 and 278. Even as late as an August 27, 1891, *Recorder* piece, T. M. D. Ward—then a bishop—said that Green's "struggle" was "very vigorous."

30. On Clark (c. 1794–1874), see my *Unexpected Places* 62–66 and Joseph R. Wood, *The Moral of Molliston Madison Clark* (1990).

31. Copies of issues seventeen and nineteen are missing from or damaged in the Campbell run. Issue 18 was dated August 17, 1854; issue 20 was dated September 16, 1854; issue 21 was dated October 2, 1854; and issue 22 was dated October 18, 1854. Publication quickly became more sporadic—with issue 23 not coming out until November 17, 1854, and issue 26 (the next fully extant issue in the Campbell run) not coming out until February 1, 1855. With that issue, Campbell addressed "those who subscribed in 1852" to Clark's paper, saying that "this is the 26th and last issue to which they are entitled."

32. Campbell included several pieces on education and sections devoted to "Our Children" that carried texts studied in Chanta Haywood's "Constructing Childhood."

33. This slight inaccuracy—Campbell published 23 issues—shows the danger in using reports of conferences quoted in Church histories written decades later. This may have been Campbell's original error, may have been an error in conference records, may have been Payne's error, or may even have been an error of C. S. Smith, who helped with Payne's *History*.

34. Elisha Weaver later claimed that the idea came from the Indiana Conference Literary Society—and specifically from him. He also suggested that Payne and Molliston Clark were unable to set up publishing for the magazine and so that the task fell specifically to him. See the September 27, 1862, *Recorder*.

35. Basic information can be found in Bullock 43–49 and 268–269; Foster's "A Narrative"; *Unexpected Places* 54–91.

36. Bullock takes Weaver at his word on these numbers, even though some of the math in Weaver's *Repository* reports does not add up (44).

37. During the Conference, a committee proposed that Nazrey join the British Methodist Episcopal Church and resign his AME bishopric—a move that garnered a formal protest from Nazrey supporters (446). Delegates also spent significant time debating changes to the AME *Discipline*, boundary disputes between the various regional conferences, and

a battle between Payne and Richard Bridges (a minister who appealed Payne's ruling that he had improperly ordained a deacon).

38. This claim complicates Mary Weaver's listing in the 1860 federal census of Philadelphia, which marks her age as 27 (and so her birthdate as c. 1833) but her birthplace as Pennsylvania (592). Mary Weaver is probably the Mary Miller—age 17, race "mulatto," born Virginia—listed with the Charles and Louisa Miller family in Pittsburgh's sixth ward in 1850 (401). The Miller obituary, though, also places Weaver's birthplace as Pennsylvania.

39. Mary Weaver was mourned widely in and beyond the AME Church; as late as March 1, 1877, a *Recorder* item would say, "All know how the wife of Elisha Weaver sacrificed her life in her devotion to the Concern."

40. A February 2, 1867, note in the *Recorder* confirms that though "many" of Weaver's "Western friends" had been led "to suppose that he had led a *widow* to the hymeneal altar," "Mrs. Martha Statia" was "the mother of the bride."

41. According to the 1870 Census, Elisha Weaver, his two children from his first marriage, Martha (Statia) Weaver, and their daughter Martha lived with the elder Martha Statia in Newark in 1870 (408). After Weaver's death, Martha (Statia) Weaver married Edward Jackson. Their 1880 Newark census listing includes the younger Martha Weaver—with the surname Jackson—as well as the elder Martha Statia, then a 72-year-old widow (389C).

42. See Will 17075G in Essex County Will Book 2: 146. When Sarah Hedden died on August 27, 1871—reported in the August 28, 1871, *Newark Daily Journal*—her funeral was held at a different church. Her will was proved September 29, 1871 (17331G, R: 179). The accompanying inventory, which was never done for her husband, listed her entire estate as being worth $3,509.83, but consisted mainly of loans to various relatives.

43. The precariousness of Stanford's entry is further suggested in a letter from "S. M." of Mount Holly, New Jersey, on the very same page as the "List." It argues that while "the Conference has seen fit to make a change in the editorial department," "we hope this will make no change in the paper." Stanford (1830–1883) was, like Weaver, seen as an up-and-coming minister. Though his term as *Recorder* editor was comparatively brief, after some successes in both Philadelphia and in various Southern locations (from Savannah to Denton, Maryland), where he helped start AME churches after the end of the Civil War, Stanford was called on to be the AME Book Steward in 1869. Kenneth C. Barnes's *Journey of Hope: The Back to African Movement in Arkansas in the Late 1800s* calls Stanford "a flamboyant man of questionable character" and writes that "in early 1872, allegations surfaced that he had embezzled money, left his wife, and disappeared in the company of a young woman who clerked in his office" (17); among other sources, those allegations were reported in the January 27, 1872, *Recorder*. Stanford turned up in Mississippi and then moved to Arkansas, where he was elected to the State Senate in 1876 and became deeply involved with the Liberia Exodus Arkansas Colony group. Bishop TMD Ward reinstated Stanford in the AME Church just before Stanford left for Liberia. See also Seraile, *Fire*, 28–30.

44. See *Unexpected Places* 77–83.

45. This is also a moment when Weaver hints that his wife, Mary, who had contributed to the *Repository*, may have carried some of the editorial weight when he was away. On this, also see the December 14, 1861; January 3, 1863; and May 9, 1863, issues. The last

contains text from the annual examination of the senior class at the Institute for Colored Youth and ends with, "The Greek questions have been omitted by the printer—this and other mistakes our readers will overlook—Mr. Weaver was out of town." Neither Weaver nor Stanford noted employing assistants at this point, and, while a handful of AME ministers might have filled in, Weaver never acknowledged such.

46. Stanford's statement, not published until January 11, 1862, says, hefty with the language of "whereas" and "therefore," that "the General Book Steward informed said Committee, that the change effected in the editorial department of said Book Concern, i.e., in separating the Editor and the General Book Steward, had been, and still continues to be, detrimental to the financial interests of the *Christian Recorder*; causing many who believed as he did, i.e., that the duties of the Editor and General Book Steward should be combined in the person of one, to cease their subscription for the paper." Stanford thus chose "withdrawal" "for the future welfare of this much needed organ in our Church."

47. Weaver was protective of his title during the period: when the New York *Independent* mistakenly called Payne the editor of the *Recorder*, Weaver took to the February 1, 1862, *Recorder* to "respectfully" refer "the *Independent* to the heading of *this* paper for the desired correction."

48. See, e.g., the March 26, 1864, "The Book Concern of the AME Church."

49. John Turner was also elected Book Steward to the West, but the position never materialized.

50. The Philadelphia Conference's claims on the Book Concern continued to be debated throughout the period. A last-minute motion at the 1864 General Conference tried to affirm those claims, but that motion was tabled. See also June 11, 1864, *Recorder*.

51. See Fishel.

52. At the time Lynch was assigned the double charge, Bishop Wayman appointed Theodore Gould as the "Traveling Agent for the Book Concern"—an act that would further limit Lynch's traveling.

53. Lynch moved to Mississippi soon after, where he became active in Republican politics, began a monthly publication, worked for the Freedmen's Bureau, and won election as Mississippi's Secretary of State. He continued to be engaged with the ME-North Church and remained an important Black leader in the state until his untimely death in 1872.

54. A correspondent who signed himself/herself "Hannibal," for example, used his/her January 18, 1868, "The Future of the AME Church: The Episcopacy" to say that, among all the candidates, "I will only mention one—a man who has served the Church long and faithfully in important positions, and who had been of incalculable value in advancing her interests . . . has wonderfully succeeded beyond all human expectations . . . [and] done more than any other living man for the Church. . . . Such a man is the Rev. ELISHA WEAVER."

55. See notes above. Wright 352 notes a fire in the *Recorder* offices, but I have found no other mention of such.

56. The same report notes that, for reasons unstated, "Rev. A. T. Hall of the Indiana Conference, was appointed to assist the editor of the *Christian Recorder*." I have found no evidence of what this "assistance" was to consist of or that it ever came to pass. See also Smith *History* 552–557, which reproduces some of Weaver's *Recorder* reporting of parts of the General Conference without citation.

Chapter 3

1. At least one of the Weavers' children was also likely born there. See *McElroy's* 1863 Philadelphia directory, 789.

2. My comments are based on examination of two images of 631 Pine—an engraving from the early 1870s on a collage of AME Bishops held by the Library of Congress (Figure 2.6) and a photograph from Charles Frederick White's 1912 *Who's Who in Philadelphia: A Collection of Thirty Biographical Sketches of Philadelphia Colored People* (online in the NYPL/Schomburg Digital Gallery). I have also examined several city maps (with Bromley's 1885 *Atlas of the City of Philadelphia* being most helpful; see the Greater Philadelphia GeoHistory Network at http://www.philageohistory.org/geohistory/), studied more recent images in the Philadelphia Historical Commission Files (see http://www.philadelphiabuildings.org/pab/index.cfm), and visually examined the current exteriors.

3. Charlotte Harding is listed as keeping a boardinghouse at 631 Pine in the 1863, 1864, and 1865 *McElroy's* Philadelphia directories (323, 306, 296). The 1863 directory marks her as "(c)," but the others do not signify her race. The 1866 *McElroy's* has a similar listing (310) but also lists a Robert Spencer, "saloon" (693).

4. It is difficult to tell what Weaver paid in rent for 619 Pine, though he reported a total of $67.09 for "house rent" between June and December 1860 as well as payments that seem to run about $20 each month at the beginning of 1861 in financial statements published in the May 31, 1862, through July 19, 1862, issues of the *Recorder*. On previous locations, see *McElroy's* 1856, 86 and 726; *McElroy's* 1857, 92; *McElroy's* 1858, 95; *McElroy's* 1859, 99; *McElroy's* 1860, 132.

5. Three post-2000 sales of the property were all above the $1 million mark.

6. During Weaver's later tenure, there were not many boarders, and they were generally widows with children. These women often had connections to the community downstairs and/or the AME Church; Hannah F. Highgate, for example, the mother of correspondent Edmonia Highgate (cf. chapter 6), was listed there in the 1867 *McElroy's* directory (637). From 1860 until 1868, Weaver continued to use his small housing allowance to keep a home in the upper floors of 619 Pine. See *McElroy's* 1862, 702; *McElroy's* 1863, 789; *McElroy's* 1864, 781; *McElroy's* 1865, 706; *McElroy's* 1866, 768; *McElroy's* 1867, 1939; *McElroy's* 1868, 1598, which lists him as "editor, 631 Pine, and h[ome]. 619 Pine." Weaver's September 28, 1867, note says that "We had the pleasure of uniting Mr. John Ballard and Mary Elizabeth Gibbs in the bonds of holy wedlock, on the 21st inst, both of Philadelphia. The ceremony took place at our residents [*sic*], No. 619 Pine Street, in this city."

7. Other photographs were likely also sometimes available. A June 1, 1867, note, for example, pushed a photograph of that year's Philadelphia annual conference even harder: "Let every member and friend of the AME Church procure a copy."

8. Estimations here and elsewhere rely heavily on the 1885 *Atlas*.

9. In June/July 1860, for example, he was storing 3,000 copies of the just-printed minutes of the General Conference, for which, per his May 31, 1862, report, he had paid $104. Weaver bought "one ton of coal for Store" in January 1861.

10. In a similar vein, a February 8, 1862, ad for a "very neat three-story House to let" similarly sent inquiries to "No. 619 Pine Street."

11. While Lynch was perhaps not present long enough to consider his own business ventures, soon after Benjamin Tucker Tanner took over, he was similarly using 631 Pine Street as the base of both his own book sales and arrangements for his speaking services,

which included, per a February 26, 1870, item, "three Lectures, which he proposes to deliver to the advantage of Churches and Associations."

12. See February 25, 1865; July 14, 1866; January 26, 1867; and July 18, 1868, issues.

13. Tanner was the first *Recorder* editor to integrate printing into the Book Concern's home in Philadelphia; by a March 2, 1876, piece, he could brag that the Concern—mainly the *Recorder*—employed "six colored printers" as well as "a clerk, a salesman, and a mailman." I have not been able to identify Tanner's foreman. An August 15, 1868, letter from William Stiles, a member of "our connexion," seems to suggest that he was working at James B. Rodgers's Philadelphia print shop, though I have found little else about him.

14. There has been some limited discussion, for example, of William Wells Brown (who worked briefly with abolitionist printer Elijah Lovejoy), print workers like New Bern, North Carolina's Andrew Dickinson (see, e.g., *Price of Liberty* 165–166), and a handful of nineteenth- and late-eighteenth-century figures involved in print work, but the field remains a massive absence in both "book history" and African American literary history.

15. Clark's father had been a successful barber who hoped to place his son in the skilled trades, so Clark was apprenticed to learn stereotyping. He worked for two years learning about the process and printing more generally, but his (rare) white employer left for California in the Gold Rush. Unable to find work among other white printers—or even another printer willing to finish his training—Clark turned to barbering and then to teaching, though he remained a print activist for all of his life, editing his own weekly for a time, assisting with *Frederick Douglass's Paper*, and writing for diverse Black print venues, including the *Recorder*. See Harz and Gerber.

16. On Weaver's interest, see the December 13, 1862, "How the Boys Made A Newspaper," which shows fictional boys Robert Mervin and Clarence Morris learning about typesetting (including sorting type and using composing sticks) and starting their own newspaper.

17. On Lewis Douglass, see Yacovone, who notes that Douglass was eventually admitted after considerable public nastiness. Benjamin Roberts's namesake son (1838–1897) was also a printer. Peter Clark's son Herbert—much younger than Lewis Douglass—might represent a next step; he became notable as a teenager for his engagement with amateur journalism in the 1880s (including printing his own paper, *Le Bijou*, an issue of which—from the American Antiquarian Society's unparalleled collection—is online at http://www.americanantiquarian.org/Exhibitions/Inpursuit/case10/case10_10.htm). See Cohen; Harrison, *Career and Reminiscences*, 66, 295, 319.

18. Remember Weaver's difficulties in getting an assistant as well as the 1867 appointment of Lynch to both a church and the editorship. Chapter 2 treats the power dynamics of these events, but they were also attempts at cost saving. The four-year income statements of the Book Concern in Wright are a bit suspect, but they do hint at the Concern's post-war growth: Campbell reported $6,449.57 for 1856–1860; Weaver, $7,410.26 for 1860–1864 and $29,149.86 for 1864–1868; Woodlin, Stanford, and Tanner, $25,275.47 for 1868–1872; and William Hunter, $41,368.69 for 1872–1876, the point when Tanner began printing in-house in earnest (372).

19. See *McElroy's* 1870, 1484; *McElroy's* 1871, 1377; *McElroy's* 1872, 1282; *McElroy's* 1873, 1265; *McElroy's* 1874, 1289; *McElroy's* 1876, 1472; and *McElroy's* 1877, 1422.

20. See the May 31, 1862, *Recorder*, which refers to the *Twelfth General Conference of the African M. E. Church* proceedings, "Wm. S. Young of Philadelphia, printer"; see copy at

the New-York Historical Society Library. Weaver occasionally worked with other printers. James H. Bryson of Philadelphia, for example, printed the 1860 *Doctrines and Discipline*; see copy at the Library Company of Philadelphia. Young, though, did the bulk of the AME work in the early 1860s.

21. See the February 23, 1861, *Recorder* for a sample ad for the bookstore and the January 19, 1861, *Recorder* for a sample ad for the print shop. Both types of ads were likely part of Young's arrangement to print for the Concern.

22. See *McElroy's* 1861, 1100; *McElroy's* 1862, 794 and 802; *McElroy's* 1863, 835, 884, and 892; *McElroy's* 1864, 828; *McElroy's* 1865, 744.

23. The group was responding to the death of AME minister Richard Roberson, a friend of Weaver's who died after an illness complicated by "being compelled, on a dark and stormy night, to occupy the platform" after "his exclusion from a Frankford car" because of his race. The *Recorder* covered Roberson's death in great detail, Weaver began a serialized biography, and diverse African Americans protested this latest example of the damages of racism.

24. Rodgers continued Young's work with periodicals like the *Christian Instructor*, noting in this ad, for example, that he had "permission to refer to the Presbyterian Publication Committee." Rodgers also did printing for the US Christian Commission, whose relationship with the *Recorder* is noted below.

25. John Blakely was a printer who worked for Young. See *McElroy's* 1861, 73.

26. Tanner echoed that homage in the September 4, 1869, *Recorder*, saying "Let no reader of the RECORDER ask, who is Jas. B. Rogers? Let them look at the Hymn Books and Disciplines they have been using for a number of years—let them look at the RECORDER, and on them all the name of the benevolent hearted printer will appear. He was our fast friend while living, let us cherish his memory when dead." (This piece centered on reporting the death of Rodgers's teenage daughter Anna, and its very presence testifies to the regard in which Tanner held Rodgers.) Rodgers's firm continued after his death for several years and also continued to do at least some business with the AME Church. That said, AME imprints from the 1870s increasingly note both publication and printing by the AME Book Concern or, as in the 1875 Samuel Schieffelin reprint *Milk for Babes*, the "Bookrooms of the African Methodist Episcopal Church."

27. See notes in the July 5, 1862, and October 10, 1863, issues.

28. Also notable, the fourth item implicitly invokes the potential to lose pages, and Weaver's twelfth item foreshadows "A Blunder": "Never write a private letter to the editor on the printer's copy, but always on a second sheet."

29. For example, "7. Punctuate the manuscript as it should be printed. . . . 9. Take special pains with every letter in proper names. 10. Review every word, to be sure that none is unintelligible."

30. Stanford's July 20, 1861, editorial asks to have copy "by Tuesday night, so that we may have more time to prepare"; he adds, noting his "double charge," that "as my field of labor is twofold, I am compelled to work by this system: while Monday, Tuesday, and Wednesday, I may look for the welfare of the paper . . . the remaining part of each week I must necessarily devote to the prosperity of the church of which I have charge."

31. A March 9, 1867, "Apology" for "many aggravated blunders" says, for example, in curious passive, "our sheet was unavoidably the victim of careless proof reading."

32. See April 22, 1865, "Cairo Correspondence" as well as items on several dates headed "Crowded Out."

33. Wright's measurements are close to those of extant copies I have examined. As with all of the cataloging of the *Recorder*, the 300-field of most MARC records—reserved for physical descriptions—is usually blank, incomplete, and/or erroneous. A handful of MARC records for Campbell's *Recorder* list "40cm"—close to the sixteen-and-a-half-inch height Wright cites. I have found no catalog record for Weaver's version that has a complete, correct 300-field. Weaver's sheet may seem quite large, but a number of papers of the period were similar in size; in the early 1850s, *Frederick Douglass' Paper*, for example, was only slightly smaller than Weaver's *Recorder*. The first entry for the *Recorder* in *Rowell's*, the standard directory of newspapers, appeared in 1869 and noted that the paper was four pages and "28x42"—in terms of the full-spread measurements used in that source, meaning each page was twenty-eight inches high by twenty-one inches wide (98). Notably, this listing was made roughly a year after Tanner had taken over. He kept this size for a short period, but was experimenting with other sizes and structures by the early 1870s—shifting, per *Rowell's* and other sources (including my own examination of extant copies)—to a four-page paper that was thirteen inches wide by twenty-one inches high in 1870, a smaller four-page paper in 1871 and 1872, and a larger (twenty-two inches wide by thirty inches high) eight-page paper in 1873. See *Rowell's* 1870, 733; *Rowell's* 1871, 137; *Rowell's*, 1872, 159; *Rowell's* 1873, 190.

34. This, too, was a component of community-building. See John Nerone's assertion that in such community newspapers, "the flow of content is channeled into familiar forms, constructing a meaningful representation of the social" (232).

35. In this usage of the front page, the *Recorder* seems to have been ahead of some of its fellows, who continued to place such "news" in their paper's interior pages (Nerone 244). It is also worth noting that the *Recorder*'s look and feel spoke to what Nerone describes as a sense of "a dense page, characterized by thin columns, small type, and little white space," a design "style that signaled prestige, embodied by the *New York Times*." (242). On Turner's letters, see Cole's edition.

36. Weaver published a brief notice in the December 9, 1865, issue wishing "success" to "our two young friends, Thomas H. Boling and C. J. Houston" who "are no longer in the employ of the A. M. E. Book Concern." Both men were African American (like all of the Book Concern clerks I have identified) and truly "young"; Boling graduated from the Institute for Colored Youth in 1864. The pair left at the end of 1865 to form Houston and Boling, "Dealers in Flour, Starch, Soaps, &c." Boling became an important member of Philadelphia's Black community, though less is known about Houston. Among Weaver's later clerks, little is known of Isaiah Mayhew, but William C. Banton, who had ties both to the local community and the AME Church, stayed on under Tanner. Banton may have begun working with the Concern as early as 1865; by Tanner's 1867 *Apology* he was listed as "Chief Clerk" (205). By the October 3, 1868, issue, Tanner noted that "By reason of the frequent absence of the Editor, our Clerk, Bro. Wm. C. Banton, fills the 'Sanctum' with no little credit to himself and the Church. In view of this fact we have ordered the printer to nail to the mast head . . . his name as Assistant Editor."

37. The February 18 text titled "A Blunder, and Who Made It" includes a nasty letter from Gardiner, who was actually a longtime *Recorder* supporter, as well as a blunt rejoinder

from Weaver, who contended that "it is bad enough to put up with such murdered English, but it is next to an insult to be charged with errors the writers themselves make."

38. Lynch's March 17, 1866, editorial asserts that "the expenses of the Book Concern are not increased an iota by the addition of an editor, as the establishment will require less employees in the way of clerks &c."

39. Even Lynch—who would later leave so much for Weaver to do—noted in the April 28, 1866, issue that "we put into the hands of our printer on Friday a number of 'Communications' with the request that he would fill up the Editorial Columns with them, if we failed to write from the" Baltimore Conference.

40. Henry McNeal Turner wrote a July 26, 1877, *Recorder* piece noting that each weekly issue cost $154. Though the paper was larger at that time—and circulation may have been, too—all of the printing and production was done in-house.

41. The opening annual subscription rate in 1861 was $2. Weaver's April 27, 1861, "Our Paper" called on community groups to help save the Recorder from financial problems, saying, for example, that he was losing "some twenty-five or thirty dollars from the Baltimore district, on account of all communication being cut off, the bridges having been burned, etc." and asserting that, "if our sisters in other places would unite together like the Philadelphia sisters . . . and give social entertainments for the support of our paper, we would very soon have a small capital on hand."

42. Consider, for example, this March 14, 1863, language: "Brethren, we are standing in great need of money, *just now*, in order to carry on this great work. Will not the brethren send us in aid? Our need is great and pressing. . . . We know the times are hard, brethren, and we dislike to press this subject upon your attention, but necessity compels us."

43. In this, Weaver was participating in the common practice that some American editors turned into an art form; see Jackson 162–173.

44. A November 9 follow-up ends with "Save yourselves, we beseech you, from having your names published in the *Christian Recorder*." I have located no such list.

45. Students of abolition and temperance movements will recognize the fundraising mode here.

46. The reach of Black periodicals into the hands of Black soldiers begs for further study.

47. Within this frame, one later individual donation seems more curious: the November 24, 1866, *Recorder* acknowledges the "generous" donation of $25 to the AME Union Fair by "the distinguished tragedian and faithful renderer of the renowned Bard of Avon," Edwin Booth, brother of Lincoln assassin John Wilkes Booth. Booth, who had significant Philadelphia ties and was a partner in the Walnut Street Theater during the period studied here, likely knew of the *Recorder*. Whether his gesture was tied to interest in aiding Black readers or to recuperating a reputation massively tarnished by his brother's acts remains open to question, however, and the range between Hart and Booth's donations begs for further attention.

48. Weaver, for example, made calls for funds to send the paper to specific groups (like soldiers)—per the above—and specifically praised donors who answered those calls.

49. These terms had stayed roughly the same since Weaver restarted the paper. See, for example, the January 19, 1861, issue, whose only difference is a $1.50 charge for a single month.

50. Some of the type is hard to read.

51. Some of the Book Concern's ads for books did address questions of race and politics much more directly, as in the January 2, 1864, ad headed "Books for Our Times," which includes, for example, descriptions of Wendell Phillips's *Speeches, Lectures, and Letters*, William Wells Brown's *The Black Man*, *The Public Life of Capt. John Brown*, and *Toussaint L'Overture*, which was endorsed by William Lloyd Garrison.

52. The February 25, 1865, issue, for example, features a letter from William Still on an upcoming lecture by Frances Ellen Watkins Harper that ends by noting that tickets for the event could be purchased at the AME Book Depository; Weaver himself also called "special attention to the notice of the lecture to be given by Mrs. Harper, which may be found in another part of our paper" and repeated that tickets could be purchased "at our office."

53. Some of these advertisers—Longfellow, Spellman, and the Bustills, for example—took such endorsement even further and wrote for the Black press; indeed, Spellman became an important figure in the Black press in his own right.

54. That the Bustill ad offers to *buy* hair—and that such "Black" hair might have been sold for use by white customers—crosses these boundaries even more.

55. Nerone notes this development in US advertising (247–248). Compare Weaver's comments on Brown's "cure" with his February 9, 1861, puff piece for "our highly esteemed friend" Francis Champion's clothing store in Brooklyn: "We hope you will give him a call. He has not only subscribed for the paper, but has given us a card for one year. He is not afraid of his shadow."

56. Of course, Black barbers had long doubled as dentists, apothecaries, and patent medicine creators and vendors, too, and several saw some value in what is now (but wasn't always) identified as alternative medicine. Such "fringe" medical work often opened doors for African Americans barred from mainstream medical practice.

57. Lynch's December 22, 1866, "Marriage Notices" similarly says "when we marry any person, we generally ask them if they wish to have their marriages published, and if so they give us the money to pay for their publication."

58. Heather Andrea Williams's *Help Me to Find My People: The African American Search for Family Lost in Slavery* is an elegant, provocative discussion of the broader phenomena surrounding the ads, but much work on their place in print culture remains.

59. Later, per the January 22, 1885, issue, these ads were singled out for different treatment: "We make no charge of publishing these notices from SUBSCRIBERS" but "those not subscribers must send a year or six months subscription, with notice, to insure insertion."

60. Note, for example, Lynch's July 9, 1866, excitement that *The Nationalist* of Mobile, Alabama, had listed the new agent for the *Recorder* in the area and said the *Recorder* "is one of the few of our weekly exchanges that we invariably read."

61. The most pronounced example of this was the July 14, 1866, assertion that "Our General Book Steward is about [to cut] off some of our subscribers who have not paid any thing for their paper for two or three years." An October 23, 1869, *Recorder* piece asserted that "there is more than $3,000 due from subscribers."

62. Weaver also issued a "Notice" in the December 28, 1861, *Recorder* that, "To avoid any unpleasant words or confusion that *might* possibly arise from an improper understanding or misconstruction of our terms of subscriptions," he was reminding "our patrons that the price of the paper is Two Dollars, independent of the carrier's fee."

63. How many carriers the *Recorder* employed over the years is unclear, though all seem to have been African Americans. In early 1861, James Wiggins and William T. Jones delivered the paper. Late in 1861, Abraham Field, a longtime steward at Mother Bethel, began delivering papers; he was referred to as "our city carrier" in a January 23, 1864, item. Several other items, though, referred to "carriers" in the plural—including the February 14, 1863, offer to have the paper's carriers distribute handbills and other items for a fee.

64. While *Harper's New Monthly Magazine*—and then others—shifted from subscription-based models to distribution through "a host of intermediaries, including periodical depots, book stores, and street vendors" (Jackson 174), many venues were closed to Black periodicals.

65. Weaver, for example, wrote in his February 9, 1861, "Visit to New York" that he "easily disposed" of 212 copies and "could have sold 400 just as easily," but such reports are rare.

66. That said, there were successful agents in Pennsylvania, Maryland, and especially the District of Columbia. Among agents of note, William S. Walker, who Weaver's February 21, 1863, piece called a "very active young man," served the Frankford, Pennsylvania, area in 1863 and 1864 and was acknowledged nineteen times for a total of $25.55 in single-copy sales. Laura Simms, who Henry McNeal Turner's August 27, 1864, letter calls "a lady of splendid literary attainments" and "an indefatigable advocate of educational development," served Washington, DC, in 1863 and 1864 and was acknowledged seven times for a total of $40.50 in single-copy sales. Many non-ministerial agents named later in the paper were Southerners living in areas where the AME did not yet have a firm or consistent ministerial presence. Weaver thus took space in a number of issues in late 1865 and early 1866 to specifically name George Fairweather of New Orleans, Armstead Saxon of Mobile, and Nelson Fitzhugh of Natchez.

67. David M. Hovde's work represents the best consideration to date of the USCC's engagement in American print culture during the Civil War.

68. A February 18, 1865, item about Philander Read, the Chaplain of the 76th US Colored Infantry, then at Port Hudson, Louisiana, noted, for example, that twenty men in his unit subscribed after seeing copies of the *Recorder* "through the Christian Commission"—in part because there was a "feeling of anxiety among the soldiers to have a copy of it," suggesting that there were not enough to go around.

69. As the margin of profit was very small, some agents sent their own version of duns to the editors when they had problems with packets of papers, as when S. M. Giles wrote in the November 21, 1863, *Recorder* that he sent $2.20 "about six weeks ago" for "the number of papers I received" but had not yet received "a package . . . to my address."

70. Weaver's usage here of the term "weekly subscribers" is uncommon and cloudy—and thus might simply signify weekly single-copy purchasers.

71. See Nord, Gutjahr, and Brown on evangelical publishers' work—though none of these scholars says much about African American texts. Jackson's discussion of broader trends is especially useful, though his treatment of the Black press is also brief.

72. Her zeal led her from teaching free African Americans in antebellum Philadelphia to teaching for the American Missionary Association in South Carolina, and then to helping a community anchored by Black war veterans in Jacksonville, Florida, where she finally settled.

73. Some of these notes are cryptic; thus my language "roughly." Lay agents outside of Philadelphia did also sometimes send subscriptions: the above-noted Sergeant Payne,

for example, secured and was acknowledged for eighteen first-time subscriptions from the Wilmington, North Carolina, area in August of 1865; Mrs. Eliza J. Taylor sent eleven subscriptions from Columbus, Ohio, in 1865; Miss Mary J. C. Anderson, five first-time subscriptions from the Darlington, Maryland, area in September of 1864; author Julia C. Collins, one subscription in February 1865; and Weaver's mother-in-law Martha Statia, one subscription from Newark in July 1867. Weaver regularly deployed material incentives when he had such available to encourage subscription procurement—promising in the February 8, 1862, issue, for example, to send anyone who secured ten cash subscriptions a copy of British author Julia Pardoe's *The Adopted Heir*. The January 23, 1864, issue offered a "prize" for twenty-five cash subscriptions: either *Toussaint L'Overture* or Wendell Phillips's *Speeches and Lectures* and the *Recorder* for a year. The December 14, 1867, issue offered, for fifty cash subscriptions, "a beautiful copy" of Tanner's *Apology* and a year of the *Recorder* as well as a variety of lesser prizes for smaller numbers of subscriptions.

Chapter 4

1. On Hall, see especially Tanner 319–321 and Wright 103. A rare photograph in which a white-bearded Hall looks levelly at readers of Richard R. Wright's 1916 *Centennial Encyclopedia of the African Methodist Episcopal Church* suggests that he had a sense of humor, too. He had apprenticed to a barber before coming West, so he had probably talked shop with Yancy's husband in some of the diverse interactions an itinerant minister would have had as part of his consideration of how to serve each congregation and congregant placed in his charge.

2. Thanks to Jack Muirhead for sharing materials and expertise related to Bloomington's nineteenth-century African American community. On the roots of the congregation and the 1857 church purchase, see Cabak, Groover, and Wagers as well as the December 3 and December 8, 1857, Bloomington *Daily Pantagraph*. Prior to moving that building, the AME congregation first moved the smaller frame structure in which they had been meeting to an adjacent space for use, according to most sources, as a parsonage.

3. On Yancy, see January 2, 1864, *Recorder*. On Black education in Bloomington, see Cabak, Groover, and Wagers. On church events, see the May 1, 1858, and December 13, 1858, Bloomington *Daily Pantagraph*.

4. The charge also included what Rev. W. S. Lankford referred to as a "small society" of "willing, working people" in Decatur; see December 10, 1864, *Recorder*.

5. W. S. Lankford's letter in the December 10, 1864, *Recorder* notes "quite a nice church edifice" but, perhaps contrary to claims that the original frame building was serving as a parsonage, that there was "no house for the accommodation of the minister and his family." He asked—or perhaps demanded—a parsonage, and reported that that project was completed in October 1864. Pastor Johnston Mitchem's June 28, 1867, *Recorder* letter noted that the church building "has been raised, and we are to have a brick basement story added." Cabak, Groover, and Wagers briefly discuss the 1871 renovations, which were shown off when the 1872 AME Illinois Conference was hosted at Bloomington. The August 2, 1880, Bloomington *Daily Pantagraph* notes further renovations, and archaeologists Cabak, Groover, and Wagers have documented more renovations between 1907 and 1909, including the addition of a 55-foot bell tower that is arguably the building's most striking feature.

6. While attention has rightly been paid to archaeologists' findings at a handful of plantations, with the exception of New York's African Burial Ground and select other sites, less attention has been paid to free African Americans in the North in the Civil War era. Cabak, Groover, and Wagers's study—resulting from the 1992 dig at the church—is a model.

7. Court Record Book 2: 203–204 (ex parte). See Stephen Middleton's *The Black Laws* on Illinois's regulation of free African Americans. Martha and William Wells seem to have married in late 1842, but tracing Martha Wells is a bit difficult. See marriage record for William Wells and Ann Davis noted in McLean County Records (roll 9 B 52) as well as federal census records for 1860 Bloomington (506) and 1870 Bloomington (105A).

8. The Wells's daughter Charlotte, born in Illinois c. 1844, would go on to marry Albert Waller in a ceremony conducted by Davis at the Bloomington church on July 10, 1863; the wedding was briefly noted in the August 8, 1863, *Recorder*, suggesting that the couple had given Davis the requisite twenty-five-cent insertion fee.

9. On Cooper, see 1865 Illinois state census of Bloomington (2182: 22), 1870 federal census of Bloomington (215A), 1880 federal census of Bloomington (205D); June 19, 1869, *Recorder*. Her daughter would marry a prominent barber in Bloomington, Richard Blue, in May 1870.

10. Book prices are from the November 1, 1862, *Recorder*. For non-paper goods, see Ethel D. Hoover's "Retail Prices after 1850." The prices Hoover lists for flannel are from Bloomington; butter and egg prices are from the somewhat comparable town of Canton, Ohio.

11. Of the three Bloomington women, Wells may have been in the strongest financial position. Cooper, perhaps incorrectly, was listed in 1870 with no assets beyond her real estate. The Yancys had no reported real estate when Helen Yancy subscribed—not uncommon for a young couple—and were credited with $300 in other assets in the 1860 census (731). Later, the Bloomington church would make significant contributions to AME print culture: *Recorder* subscriptions there rose, engagement with the Book Concern increased, and, in the basement of the church, Rev. Charles Spencer Smith produced important Sabbath School texts in the 1880s. Still, only sixteen extant acknowledgments in the *Recorder* between 1861 and 1867 are from Bloomington. Most of these are tied to the ministers appointed to the charge, though some reflect the kinds of collections Nancy Cooper (and William Wells) later participated in.

12. See, for example, the February 13, 1864, *Recorder*.

13. Work for this chapter began with gathering lists of acknowledgments from the Campbell microfilm. Part of the decision to emphasize film over online versions was influenced by the recognition of significant, if occasional, errors in transcription in the Accessible Archives collection, as well as the sad discovery that they have transcribed very few of the 1864 acknowledgments at all, even though images and much of the text of that year are included.

14. My numbers in this chapter do not, for example, include acknowledgments for non-Book Concern purposes, for example, funds collected to aid Bishop Jabez P. Campbell on a trip West.

15. My terminology is in some ways inexact, as by "first-time subscriptions" I mean first appearance in an extant issue in the period of the study. Individuals who subscribed before 1861, for example, are thus assigned this term at the moment of their first published

and extant post-1860 subscription acknowledgment. Similarly, subscribers first acknowledged in an issue no longer extant and whose renewal (or renewal of a renewal, etc.) was acknowledged in an extant issue would have that renewal included under my category "first-time subscription." This becomes more complex because not all acknowledgments were for full annual subscriptions. Of the 1,109 identified individual first-time subscribers discussed later in this chapter, for example, 521 were acknowledged for less than $2, the lowest subscription price of the period; of these, 432 were likely six-month subscriptions. Of the larger group of individual first-time subscribers, perhaps 1,145 of 2,545 sent less than $2—though just over 100 were listed without any amount. These factors also shape my usage of the term "renewal." Some renewals were for a second six-month period, and a few individuals listed multiple times may have been essentially making multiple payments over a smaller time period. (I discuss such in more depth below.) My decision to use these terms in these specific ways centers on subscriber agency: a first-time subscription, whether for six months or for a year, represented a decision by the subscriber to join the *Recorder* community; similarly, a renewal, whether for six more months or another year, represented an additional choice to stay with the *Recorder*. This approach also seems sensible given the fact that, per the last chapter, it was sometimes tougher to get *off* of the subscription rolls than one might think—as Lynch and Weaver's threat to "cut off the two- and three-year-olds" in the July 14, 1866, issue demonstrates.

16. In a tiny handful of cases, I have counted subscriptions in this "identified" category that trace to a definite *household* but that could have been generated by two individuals—a husband and wife with the same first initial, for example, or a father and son with the same first name. This is the reason that totals below occasionally fall a bit short of 1,109: if the father and son in the latter example, for example were married and unmarried, respectively, marital status for this acknowledgment name was marked "unknown" even if their race was "known," for example, because both were African American.

17. There are simply not enough studies like this one to state what such percentages should be. Akiyo Ito's appendix to his study of subscribers to the first American edition of Olaudah Equiano's narrative lists 123 names (some of these individuals bought more than one copy; thus, this list accounts for 336 copies of the book). However, Ito definitively identifies only 28 and narrows 6 more names to 2 or 3 individuals; these 34 individuals represent just under 28% of the 123 names on the subscription list. Richard Newman's study of a list of Philadelphia's Bethel AME voters in an 1828 Church referendum—included in his biography of Richard Allen—positively identifies 27 of the 84 "yes" voters who signed their names in balloting—or just over 32% (228–229). Even David Paul Nord's landmark "Republican Literature" study in the 1790 *New York Magazine*, which uses city directories published within two years of acts of subscription to locate subscribers who were all white, often established, and living in a small geographic range identifies only 265 of 370 subscribers, or just under 72%. Based on my work preparing "Remembered (Black) Readers" and then examining this volume's much larger sample, I set targets I hoped would guarantee some sense of the diversity of subscribers—working for an identification rate of at least 40% among first-time subscribers, an identification rate of at least 60% among renewals (under the assumption that the act of renewal suggested financial and perhaps geographic stability, thus making individuals renewing easier to trace), and an

overall identification rate of at least 50%. I also worked for some evenness from year to year, per the following chart:

	All	F-T Sub	ID F-T Sub	Renewals	ID Renewals
1861	372	243	145	43	35
1862	459	263	156	104	78
1863	565	325	121	154	116
1864	770	464	178	162	130
1865	729	549	232	123	101
1866	645	391	160	158	130
1867	551	310	117	96	80
Total	4,091	2,545	1,109	840	670

Because some of the non-subscription acknowledgments are easier to trace than subscription acknowledgments, figures for identified entities in the whole legible sample—2,296 of 4,091 (just over 56%)—are slightly higher than for subscriptions alone.

18. Further information on the family is sparse. Complicating matters, a William Wells and a Mary E. Wells were married in Bloomington April 30, 1867, though the wedding was performed by William J. Rutledge, a white minister in Bloomington's (white) Methodist Church.

19. I have not yet found further information on Lewis Yancy.

20. On Belle Blue Claxton, see July 20, 1926, *Pantagraph* (obituary) and resources at mchistory.org.

21. I used ancestry.com as well as the less-reliable, less-complete paper indexes from Accelerated Indexing Systems. Variants searched included Soundex- and truncation-based possibilities as well as last-name free variants when unique first names and locations made such possible. Such searching is tied as much to art, perseverance, and luck (or lack thereof) as to science. Context is also a crucial factor: an individual with the surname Gould, for example, can be much harder to trace in the area surrounding Gouldtown, New Jersey, than an individual with the surname Smith and a rare first name in New York City.

22. While ancestry.com's transcription is often strong, it, too, is imperfect. My guiding principle here—as in all my research—was to examine original documents or direct images of such whenever possible.

23. I worked, for example, with select New England vital records at ancestry.com and at the NEGHS website; available state censuses (especially for 1855 and 1865); several states' marriage records; online, microform, and paper city directories; online, microform, and paper church histories; and diverse individual record sets that offered likely possibilities for researching select figures. In a handful of cases, I also worked with Canadian records, especially the 1861 and 1871 Canadian censuses.

24. Primary data sources for the 1,109 identified first-time subscribers include the 1850 federal census (21), the 1860 federal census (455), the 1861 Canadian census (1), the 1870 federal census (540), the 1871 Canadian census (4), the 1880 federal census (57), and various other sources (31). Primary data sources for the 670 identified renewals include the 1850 federal census (10), the 1860 federal census (353), the 1870 federal census (259), the 1871 Canadian census (3), the 1880 federal census (39), and various other sources (9).

25. See Martha A. Sandweiss's *Passing Strange* 1–3 and 212–215 for especially thoughtful discussion of such.

26. On some of the diverse possible *acts* of reading, see Leah Price, "Reading: The State of the Discipline"; David S. Miall, "Empirical Approaches to Studying Literary Readers"; Barbara Sicherman's "Ideologies and Practices of Reading"; and especially the work of David Paul Nord, Ronald Zboray, and Mary Saracino Zboray, though few of these trailblazing scholars' works treat Black readers in depth. My comments here also rely on the understanding, according to Jeannine DeLombard, that the Black press offered "a literacy that was both private *and* communal in nature" and was centered on foundations of text-sharing (361).

27. As discussed in the last chapter, only a very small number of acknowledgments came directly from Philadelphia, where the paper could be delivered to a city doorstep. If we could track these "City Subscribers," Pennsylvania's numbers would, of course, be stronger.

28. In the context of central Illinois, where Yancy, Cooper, and Wells lived, Bloomington was a growing city; compared to Boston or Brooklyn in the period—much less to any contemporary city—it was a small frontier town.

29. We should also note that some "city" subscribers were from surrounding areas and may have *lived* in more rural circumstances; I located subscribers from St. Louis, Louisville, Savannah, Leavenworth, Indianapolis, and Cincinnati, for example, whose occupations were listed as "farmer."

30. See the September 14, 1867, and January 27, 1876, *Recorder*.

31. That said, we should also note that being *able* to move was often still a better condition than that of the millions of enslaved African Americans who could not move by their own choice.

32. The gender of three individual first-time subscribers remains unknown because they fall under the category of identified households but not individuals, as discussed above.

33. The types of records used for this study do not, unfortunately, alert us to individuals' sexualities, an area often difficult to trace in the nineteenth century. Also, I use the term "gender" above rather than "sex," as I am addressing a public sense of whether, given the contexts of identity labels in this period, individuals were (performing ideas of) male or female. Information on how individuals studied here performed within or beyond these gender labels is also exceedingly difficult to trace.

34. See 1860 Huntington, New York, 355, and 1870 Brooklyn, New York, 123A.

35. See Britt Rusert, "Types of Mankind" for recent work in this area.

36. See 1860 Allegheny City, Pennsylvania, 958. In addition to being tallied at the bottom of the census sheet as white, Freeman and his family carry no racial markings next to their names—signifying whiteness, as white census takers assumed such was the default identity for an American. A mentee of Martin Delany, Freeman identified so strongly with the African diaspora that he emigrated to Liberia in 1864 and spent much of later his life there. See Irvine.

37. See 1860 Springfield, Ohio, 289; 1870 Cincinnati, Ohio, 280A.

38. See 1870 Bloomington, Illinois, 201B; 1880 Bloomington, Illinois, 188A.

39. The paper's editors, especially Weaver, also recognized that white philanthropists might aid the paper's continually weak finances. His "Appeal" at the end of the paper's

first year—published in the December 28, 1861, issue—addresses "the Citizens of Philadelphia, and especially . . . our White Friends, in behalf of the Christian Recorder," sharing an "appeal to your generosity to contribute a New Year's gift to the amount of two, three, five, or ten dollars" to keep the paper "in the field." Weaver also expressed his worry in a July 13, 1861, piece that a man pretending to be an agent of the paper had fraudulently collected donations and subscriptions from "our white friends" in New York. Still, his claim in the March 9, 1861, issue that "so many of our white friends" were "coming to our office, nearly every day, and subscribing" was probably more wishful thinking and promotion than reality.

40. Fitzhugh named the "Confederate" as K. A. Buell. He may have been speaking of a Kilbourne Ambrose Buell who farmed in Adams County, Mississippi. Fitzhugh noted that Buell would "pay the subscription the next time he comes to town," but such was never acknowledged in the paper. Indeed, Buell's name appears nowhere else in the extant *Recorder*, and Fitzhugh said nothing more about "Confederate" subscribers.

41. That conference asked Lynch to speak, considered reports on the newly freed people of the South, and discussed African Americans in some depth. Lynch reported in the April 20, 1867, issue that, after the meeting, he preached by invitation for McDonald's Boston congregation. "I felt much at home," Lynch wrote, "and felt it a great privilege to enjoy a few moments with a man of so large a heart and eminent wisdom as Dr. McDonald. . . . I have learned something of that great force at work in the M.E. Church to expel caste, which may be triumphant. I think I succeeded in vindicating our own church against some unjust aspersions cast upon her." White subscriber John Birge Doolittle may have had some similar connections, though I have not located such. When he subscribed in December 1863—tagged in his acknowledgment, "Yale Theological Seminary"—he was a divinity student who had interrupted his studies to become the Chaplain of the (white) 15th Connecticut Volunteers. Sergeant Sheldon Thorpe's 1893 history of the unit remembered Doolittle as a "plain, unostentatious speaker, earnest, sympathetic, and sincere" who quickly earned soldiers' "unlimited confidence and respect"; Thorpe added that he was "a big-hearted man" (74, 83).

42. See July 29, 1854, *Provincial Freeman* ("The Tempest on Galilee") and August 10, 1849, North Star, which reprints Barker's "The Fugitive's Wife" from the Dover (NH) *Morning Star*. The latter poem references Henry "Box" Brown. On Barker, see Anbinder.

43. Beard and Williams did not, though Beard did renew his subscription. The youngest full-year subscriber was thirteen-year-old Ann E. Gross of Baltimore.

44. Julie Winch's 2000 edition of this work, under the title *The Elite of Our People: Joseph Willson's Sketches of Black Upper-Class Life in Antebellum Philadelphia*, does massive recovery work on both the text and this fascinating family. On Emily Wilson, see especially 65, 68, 70–71, and 73; on Josephine's marriage, see 68–71.

45. In this, we should remember the *Recorder*'s regular marriage announcements. Paired with the paper's common usage of the honorifics "Miss" and "Mrs.," such texts highlight the importance of marital status in the Church's thinking, especially about women.

46. Censuses did not consistently mark widowhood until 1880, though individual census takers occasionally did. (Even then, though, for example, second and subsequent marriages were almost never marked differently than first marriages.) Use of other records, including death records and obituaries, accounts for most of this evidence.

Renewals are tougher to track, given the significant number of itinerant ministers in that sample, as these men were sometimes listed at whatever site they were visiting when the census taker came, often as boarders even if they had families elsewhere.

47. Subscriber Edward Miller and wife Leah also had ten children listed with them in their 1870 Haddonfield, New Jersey, home. Younger than the Cornells had been in 1860, they had six children attending school as well as two family elders living with them (174A).

48. The oldest woman first-time subscriber was more than a decade younger than the oldest man, and the oldest woman to renew was almost a decade younger than the oldest man.

49. See December 3, 1864, *Recorder*. Weaver probably confused her with the married Ann M. Smith of Cincinnati, who had subscribed just two months earlier.

50. On the diverse class positions occupied by Black barbers see Douglas W. Bristol Jr.'s *Knights of the Razor*; on the ministry, see below.

51. Of all the farmers' wives in the study, only one, Tamar Singleton—spouse of Beaufort, South Carolina, subscriber and farmer Primos Singleton—is marked as a "farm laborer"; see 1870 St. Helena, South Carolina, 407B. Such issues are similar across both censuses.

52. 1860 Marysville, California, 922. Notably, Bland's wife Julie was, in a rare move toward gender equity in labeling, listed as a "washerwoman."

53. As further evidence of the cloudiness of occupational labels tied to ministry, the *Recorder* itself was uneven in referring to local leaders—sometimes calling them "Reverend" even when they were not ordained.

54. See 1860 Chicago (Ward 4) 781 and 1860 Washington (Ward 14) 499. The Nichols acknowledgment in the June 28, 1862, *Recorder* carries "per Rev. H. M. Turner."

55. 1870 Cleveland, Ohio, 156A.

56. The real estate agent was Mark Rene DeMortie, brother of speaker and philanthropist Louisa DeMortie and an activist in his own right, who subscribed from Boston before removing to Chicago with his new wife, Cordelia Downing, daughter of wealthy Black activist George Downing. See Yacovone, "De Mortie"; 1870 Chicago (Ward 3) 278B.

57. See 1860 Cambridge (Ward 1) 73. Hewlett's middle name is sometimes spelled "Molyneaux."

58. A handful of occupation listings are unreadable.

59. Many households do not carry listings for real or personal property in the censuses used, and so my conclusions here are more tentative. Further, some individuals (the Downings, at some points, for example) probably chose not to report such information, some census taker errors are again likely in such information, and the range between estimating the value of an individual's property and taking the individual's *word* for its worth was never addressed in instructions to census takers. Personal property is also a hazy category, as it could include anything from tools to cash and from furniture to books—so valuations may not be especially trustworthy.

60. The remaining subscribers in these groups had no individual listed real or personal estate, but lived in households—with parents, for example—that did carry listings. The real estate held by the heads of these households had a similar spread in terms of valuation. First-time subscribers researched through other sources do not have trustworthy comparable data, as, for example, the 1880 census lists no such valuations.

61. We should also note that several of those subscribers who had the largest real estate valuations were white: Colonel Farrah, for example, had holdings valued at $15,000 in the 1860 census; General Brayman, $87,000 in the 1860 census; F. W. G. May, $60,000 in the 1870 census; Ryland Fletcher, $100,000 in the 1870 census, and perhaps the wealthiest subscriber, William Claflin, $100,000 in the 1870 census. See, respectively, 1860 St. Ferdinand (St. Louis), Missouri, 1098; 1860 Springfield, Illinois, 150; 1870 Boston (Ward 16) 559A; 1870 Cavendish, Vermont, 305A; 1870 Newton, Massachusetts, 105A.

62. Again, the remaining subscribers in these groups had no individual listed real or personal property, but lived in households—with parents, for example—that did carry listings. The real estate held by the heads of these households had a similar spread in terms of valuation.

63. As with real estate valuations, select white subscribers also occupied some of the slots at the top of the personal property valuations—General Brayman's $49,000 in the 1860 census as well as F. W. G. May's $30,000 in the 1870 census and especially William Claflin's $500,000 in the 1870 census.

64. For Hammond, see 1860 Baltimore (Ward 12) 144. For Thomas, see 1860 Cincinnati (Ward 1) 142. For Martin, see 1870 Washington, DC (Ward 2), 275A. For Knox, see 1870 Cincinnati (Ward 14), 285A. Even in some of the cases when personal property was well above real estate valuation, some individuals had substantial real estate. Mississippi's Nelson Fitzhugh was listed in 1860 as a free African American with $3,000 in real estate and $9,000 in personal property, for example, and Ezra Johnson of New Bedford was listed in 1870 with $3,000 in real estate but $23,000 in personal property. See, respectively, 1860 Natchez 42 and 1870 New Bedford (Ward 3) 129A.

65. Such oversimplification would also ignore, as discussed above, the fact that subscribers could serve as conduits for other readers—a fact that the *Recorder* was aware of; see, for example, the December 30, 1865, "Letter from Sister Habersham" (from Maria Ann Habersham), which reports that Habersham's neighbor "Dr. Lawrence" told Habersham that his wife borrowed the paper "from Miss Fitzhugh" every week "and . . . read it."

66. In "Remembered (Black) Readers," I initially added another category—subscriptions from agencies outside of the AME hierarchy—in which I placed acknowledgments for funds from the US Christian Commission (two, for $5 each, in December 1864) and the New York-based African Civilization Society (two, for $10 each, in February 1865). These *could* still represent subscriptions, according to my original assertions, with each $2.50 submitted paying for an individual annual subscription. That said, based on exhaustive analysis of the much larger sample of acknowledgments (and further rereading of the paper), I now lean more toward thinking that these acknowledgments were payments toward bundles of single copies—thus, my discussion of them in the last chapter rather than in this chapter. The acknowledgments placed as "group subscriptions" here are specifically labeled as being for such.

67. The fourth, from Rev. G. W. Brodie, an AME minister charged with a church in Raleigh, North Carolina, came soon after the war. He submitted $19.25 for a group of subscribers from his congregation. I do not consider this subscription in depth here—it may simply be a lumped-together collection of individuals—but it is worth noting that, though he did not name the subscribers, Brodie was still participating in the responsibilities Weaver so stressed.

68. See Read's military record and W. C. Montague, *Biographical Record . . . of Amherst* (1881).

69. See esp. Larry Wesley Pearce, "Enoch K. Miller and the Freedmen's Bureau."

70. Bernstein's comments focus on a different set of texts and images, but her larger point applies here.

71. Buchanan also noted that he himself was "a Virginian, and gained his liberty by a trip on the *Under Ground* Rail Road, April 1st, 1848."

72. Miller would continue such efforts after the war—working with the American Missionary Association and then as the Freedmen's Bureau's Assistant Superintendent of Education for Arkansas in 1867 and 1868. He shifted denominations to Episcopalianism soon after but continued in the ministry until his death in 1903.

73. White's October 21 letter (dated September 19) says that he sent "$56 of what is due you for the *Recorder*," but no acknowledgment (or other text) specifies the relationship of this $56 to the $43.50 actually acknowledged—which would not have been quite all of the amount for eighteen subscriptions. White's language with this note—"I have done all I can"—suggests some tension in collecting the funds.

74. Oberlin never, though, attracted the attention in the *Recorder* that the AME's own college, Wilberforce, claimed.

75. Young likely had a hand in J. P. Ball's photographing of Lynch, which Young reported in a November 24, 1866, letter to the *Recorder* led to several photographs "to be sold for the benefit of the *Recorder*"; the photographs "went like hot cakes, and . . . may be seen adorning the parlours of many of our best citizens." I have not been able to locate an extant example of one of these photographs.

76. Whether the Lane seminarians read the paper is open to debate, and I have found no evidence of a renewal—or of what happened to Lane's copies when the physical campus was closed and the institution was folded into McCormick Theological Seminary. Weaver did report that readers at another white institution read the *Recorder*, though: while never listed in the acknowledgments, Philadelphia's Mercantile Library apparently had a subscription. Weaver's December 30, 1865, year-end message reported that the copies of the *Recorder* there were "quite extensively read, by rich and poor, friend and foe"; indeed, Weaver reported, "We never go into the library but we see some one perusing its columns."

77. See Ernest, *A Nation within a Nation*.

Chapter 5

1. The first scholarly consideration of Hart and key biographical information on Ro(d)gers appears in my *Unexpected Places* 152-161. For Hart's extant contributions to the *Recorder*, see my "'Yours for the Cause': The *Christian Recorder* Writings of Lizzie Hart."

2. Hart might even have recognized the possibility of Rodgers and/or others reading her words aloud to groups. If she read the December 10, 1864, issue closely, for example, she would have seen that Rodgers actually served as a kind of reader/scribe for part of his unit: editor Weaver reported that "we have received a note from Sergeant Theo. Rodgers" of the 26th US Colored Infantry, "Co. C, which states, that any persons having friends in said regiment, can hear from them by writing to him, enclosing a stamp, at Fort Duane, near Beaufort, S. C."

3. Of course, what the paper *said* about reading and what (and how) folks actually read probably did not always correlate directly. Hopefully, later work will test the representativeness of the individuals selected here and broaden our sense of the parameters for individual reading. African Americanists continue to pray for records of individual reading

experiences—which are exceedingly rare but do exist. See Zboray and Zboray's *Literary Dollars and Social Sense* and McHenry for examples.

4. On Meacham, see especially Canter Brown Jr.'s work.

5. A number of other subscribers were marked as "cannot write" but were not marked as "cannot read." Given the separation of these two skill sets in both instruction and practice in the period, it is difficult to tell how many of these were victims of miscounting and how many could, indeed, read but not write in ways that met a given census taker's demands.

6. See chapter 2, chapter 3, and especially this chapter's later discussion of moves within the Church—especially tied to Daniel Payne—toward specific types of print literacies (within the Church's broader emphasis on education).

7. These lists are reconstructed for more abbreviated versions in sources like Payne *History* 169–170 and Handy 162. I have not been able to definitively determine which history of the Bible first-year minister initiates were told to read; their third-year list also includes an "Ecclesiastical History" that may be Bede's. The lists were revised and expanded a number of times later in the nineteenth century.

8. The July 20, 1861, *Recorder* ad for the Book Concern priced, for example, a two-volume set of Watson's *Theological Institutes* at $4.50.

9. That said, enforcement was sometimes uneven. Henry McNeal Turner's 1885 *Genius and Theory of Methodist Polity*, for example, notes that ministers attending conferences could "interrogate" any candidate "in the course of studies laid down in the Discipline, require him to preach before them, read, write, calculate, and answer all questions touching his conversion, sanctification, call to the ministry, as well as those that affect his life and character" (64–65). Richard Wright's later *Centennial Encyclopedia*, on the other hand, says that, the course "if conscientiously pursued would make strong men," but "unfortunately, it is not enforced in most of the conferences" (304).

10. He added that, while the plan suggested in some quarters for "the training of our ministerial candidates under the care and in the families of our older preachers" had "paternal simplicity and prudence," "*the school and the church should always go together*" (italics original).

11. Campbell also assures readers that "The book is brought down, intentionally, to the capacity of those who have not enjoyed many literary advantages." With this in mind—and worried about "our article becoming lengthy"—Campbell refrains "from our intention to give our dear young brethren a synopsis," instead deciding to "earnestly entreat them to study it, and afterwards make one for themselves." Campbell's August 31, 1861, article on Lowrey's *Positive Theology*, which had been recently added to the first-year studies expected by the Philadelphia Conference, contained similar tone and content.

12. Though just outside of the period of this study, also notable are Tanner's repeated 1868 ads for "Our Minister's Library"—and mark the multivalence of "our"—which included twenty-five volumes "comprising 11,450 nearly printed pages" of "Evangelical literature," "admirable treatises on the evidences of Christianity," "sterling Christian memoirs," and "D'Aubigne's history of the Reformation"—all for $20.

13. The headings and content of W. S. Lankford's July 6, 1867, letter, for example, emphasize the ways location-specific and church-specific correspondence could broaden to address such topics. Lankford—who would briefly minister to some of the Bloomington, Illinois, *Recorder* subscribers introduced in the last chapter—was then in Indianapolis, and he

wrote of the "Political World," the "Education of Colored Children," the "Literary and Church Aid Societies," the local "Union Sunday School Picnic," "A New Thing under the Sun" (a pair of upcoming lectures by Frederick Douglass), and, finally, his own chapel, "Our Zion." Many of these sections reported on specific events in (and details of) Black life in Indianapolis, but many—and especially his discussion of Black suffrage in the "Political World"—drew conscious comparisons to information about other locations he had garnered through reading. Indeed, the local was consistently connected to the national even in the naming of names—with addresses at the "Union Sunday School Picnic" leading immediately to the announcement of Douglass's speaking engagement. While Lankford's letter planned "to inform your numerous readers of the signs of the times in the capital of the Hoosier State," it worked in dialogue with correspondence from a host of other locations.

14. Weaver's good intentions were, of course, paired with a call to subscribe to the paper: "By this means, dear brother freedmen, you will know how to act in the premises; and you can generally look to the Christian Recorder for cheering words of encouragement and sound advice. We hope that those of you who can read will subscribe for the Recorder, (DON'T BORROW IT,) so that you may thus receive our warning ere it be too late. Every one of you should take the paper regularly."

15. In this vein, a November 10, 1866, piece describing prizes for an upcoming AME Union Fair, included an item "of great importance to Sabbath Schools, viz. a new library register, which should be in every Sabbath School in the country."

16. Children's literature in the *Recorder* and the Black press generally demands massive study. I have begun such work re: the *Recorder* building from Haywood's "Constructing Childhood," but I have found that many texts previously assumed to be Black-authored were, in fact, reprints from white periodicals. Anna Mae Duane and Kate Capshaw's forthcoming collection on early African American children's literature should do much to move discussion forward.

17. The paper's extensive coverage of Philadelphia's Institute for Colored Youth also demands further study—as does the Institute itself—but we should note that part of this coverage regularly addressed the Institute's library, as in the October 8, 1864, publication of the Institute's annual report: "our little Library has reached the number of 2,084 carefully selected volumes. Its use is not confined to the pupils of the Institute, but it is thrown open to their friends and others, who avail themselves also of the works of reference in the Reading-room. Seventy-eight volumes have been added by purchase during the year, including eighteen volumes of the American Encyclopedia, which were procured by private subscription. . . . Three thousand nine hundred and thirty-five volumes have been loaned since last report."

18. In a similar strain, students at the Ashmun Institute in Oxford, Pennsylvania, organized the "Garnet Lyceum," in honor of Henry Highland Garnet.

19. Church leaders contributed to such. The July 24, 1890, *Recorder*, for example, carried an item titled "That Essay 'By a Young Lady'" that suggests "those persons who admired the essay and advised it be sent for publication"—usually, it seems, local ministers—"as a rule have not examined it as to originality, orthography, or construction. . . . Not infrequently" such an essay "is found to possess very little excellence" by the editors. The piece concludes that "these brethren fail to remember that just the same programme is being carried out at two thousand churches. Hence, essays on the same subject may be sent here by a hundred misses with equal claims."

20. Using recent work on sentiment to explore the ways the very performance of these positions may have highlighted their problems (and opened possibilities) is beyond my scope here—though such consideration might be of value, as Cooper had to first admit the "great and most potent is the influence of women," and he spent a fascinating amount of time on women who used their influence for evil (like Queen Mary) or violence (like Jael, wife of Heber, who killed her husband by driving a tent nail through his head).

21. Indeed, even the meeting on which Cooper reported featured a "warmly contested" debate over "Which has the greatest influence in the community, the pulpit or the press?"

22. The October 24, 1864, letter from "Aleph" similarly paired a note on the Douglass Literary Society with the fact that "the ladies (Heaven bless them) have long since organized a Soldiers' Aid Society."

23. That said, Weaver's editorials just before and just after the Civil War began mixed patriotism with some skepticism. As they emphasized the ways the war would need to reshape African American lives and, of course, abolish slavery, they were sometimes critical about both Lincoln's approach to the war and the larger nation's sense of the goals of the war. For a sampling, see the April 20, 1861, "War! War! War!" the April 27, 1861, "Better than Peace," the April 27, 1861, "The Star Spangled Banner and the Duty of Colored Americans to that Flag," and the June 8, 1861, "Prayer for the Government."

24. African Americans and African Americanists did their best to ensure that the impact of Black soldiers on the Civil War never totally left the broader American consciousness, though such issues were downplayed for decades. Still, after critical generalist efforts like James M. McPherson's *The Negro's Civil War*, scholarship on Black engagement with the war and the military has grown much more diverse and nuanced only in the last few decades.

25. This material also appears in the USCC's 1863 *Fact, Principles, and Progress* (7) and is quoted in David Hovde, "The US Christian Commission," 299.

26. In addition to Hovde, see David Kaser's *Books and Libraries in Camp and Battle* (1984) on soldiers' reading, though its discussion of African Americans is brief.

27. See Hovde, "The Library is a Valuable Hygienic Appliance."

28. The *Recorder* itself flirted with this distinction when it printed a lone piece titled "Sulphuric Literature" clipped from the *New York Observer* that in turn quoted from the Unitarian *Inquirer* that "the works circulated among the soldiers must not be all religious works of the approved orthodox pattern. If they are, they will call them goody books, and take them as they do the pills of the surgeon." While the *Observer* was troubled by this "ridicule of the work in which Christians are engaged," it did foreground a debate over what was "good" reading for soldiers. Chaplain James A. Dawson's February 27, 1864, *Recorder* letter defended "goody" books and was fairly extreme in what constituted "good reading matter"—objecting to periodicals that "puff Laura Keene and her ilk" or told of the "chief magistrate of the nation and his family" seeing *She Stoops to Conquer* and made "the Washington theatre and similar places" of "more account than sound morality." Dawson also objected to a recent number of *The Atlantic Monthly*, whose opening sentence urged "whoever would learn to think naturally, clearly, logically, and to express himself intelligently and earnestly" should spend "his days and nights" with William Shakespeare. Dawson was less than specific about what soldiers should read, but he clearly leaned toward tract literature, Bibles, and hymnals. That said, several others—evinced in the rest of this volume—saw "good reading" much more capaciously.

29. On the first, see especially Jennifer James's 2007 *A Freedom Bought with Blood*; on the second, see, for example, Elizabeth Hewitt's 2005 *Correspondence and American Literature, 1770–1865*. The 2013 publication of *Freedom's Witness: The Civil War Correspondence of Henry McNeal Turner*—which collects texts of massive importance previously hard to access—reminds us of how much crucial recovery work remains.

30. Examples in such discussions are often limited to manuscript culture (rather than print culture broadly) and say little about how such letters intervened in larger, public representational battles. Wilson usefully notes that "because Southern laws had kept slaves illiterate, letter writing took on a special meaning for black soldiers" and "became a visible symbol of the soldiers' new liberated status. Letter writing became part of the ritual of defining personal identity. The letter itself was a document of entitlement. . . . Even the signature scrawled on the last page underlined his freedom" (71). The limited discussion to date, like much of the scholarship on Black soldiers, also heavily emphasizes only formerly enslaved soldiers. Many Black soldiers from the North had had more time in freedom, sometimes had significant alphabetic literacy, and sometimes were capable of much more than a basic signature. While the power of literacy instruction for formerly enslaved soldiers cannot be underestimated, it is *not* the only story that needs to be told about Black soldiers' reading and writing.

31. He later renewed twice during the period studied here.

32. This may have made longtime readers of the paper remember one of Payne's earliest letters—in the April 2, 1864, *Recorder*—that told of "quite a number of talented young men" in his unit, men who "went forward with undaunted bravery" and men "whose intelligence, I dare say, is seldom equaled by any race" but who were sadly "lacking" the "love of Christ."

33. Payne took his critique of ministers to the point of making active suggestions for how they might secure more subscriptions to the *Recorder* even as he asserted that he himself would do "all I can in co-operation . . . to raise the desired number of subscribers."

34. The letter's signature is hard to read, but appears to be "Sergeant H. S. B." or "Sergeant H. S. H.," in Company B of the 3rd USCT. If it is the latter, the letter was likely from Henry S. Herman.

35. Consider a poem that ran the same year Hart began contributing (specifically in the January 16, 1864, issue). The protagonist of "Knitting the Socks," a "lively old lady," knit socks for the troops because "she cannot shoulder a musket, / Nor ride with the cavalry crew." While the poet told readers "Don't sneer at the labors of women" as "Her heart may be larger and braver / Than he who is tallest of all," the protagonist spends time thinking and praying but *not* reading or writing, much less fighting. Her hands, it seems, are better suited for needles and yarn than pen, paper, or musket. That said—and this complication is emblematic of the messiness of the paper's sense of gender—the poem was reportedly "found in a bundle of socks, sent by a 'Lively Old Lady,' in Amherst, New Hampshire, to the United States Hospital, corner of Broad and Cherry streets, Philadelphia." No mention is made of its author, though the fact that the "Lively Old Lady" sent it suggests she could be the author.

36. Marking another public role for Black women, she asks "those who are strongly constituted" to "go into hospitals." See also chapter 8's discussion of the *Recorder*'s sometimes conflicted sense of novels.

37. Smith shares that Kendrick was white, but an "uncompromising anti-slavery man, and true friend of our unfortunate race"; his sermon places Lincoln as a Moses

figure and ends by asserting that "He declares liberty to all men, irrespective of color or caste."

38. I have found no evidence of Smith knowing Hart or even knowing of her, though their geographic proximity makes this a possibility.

39. The ways the *Recorder* linked (and sometimes didn't link) the American West and the questions of Black citizenship demand further study. The paper's treatment of West Pointer Henry Ossian Flipper might serve as an initial point of investigation.

Chapter 6

1. Highgate's quote slightly revises the final lines of Frederick William Faber's hymn "The Right Must Win."

2. While I take issue with several of its conclusions, James G. Hollandsworth Jr.'s *An Absolute Massacre* (2001) is the fullest consideration of the riot.

3. My discussion of Highgate in this chapter focuses on her work as a "correspondent." For more on her biography and her engagement with American Transcendentalism, see my "'Each Atomic Part': Edmonia Goodelle Highgate's African American Transcendentalism." Additional work needs to be done on both her life and her writing—including fuller recovery of her extant texts, discussion of her senses of gender and race, and consideration of her own (and her representations of) mobility and education. Indeed, that a Highgate *Recorder* piece titled "Neglected Opportunities" was rediscovered only after the publication of "'Each Atomic Part'" emphasizes how early we are in the process of recovering and understanding this figure. For additional biographical work on Highgate, see Dorothy Sterling's *We Are Your Sisters* and the work of Ronald Butchart.

4. Though its opening looks more essay-ish, I treat "On Horse Back," for example, as a piece of correspondence not only because of Highgate's regular letters to the paper and the titling of her as a "correspondent" but also because, though the piece lacks a standard salutation, it meets many other expectations of the genre of the letter—especially in its closing: "Oh! It is time for my night school. Believe me, *Votre Amie des Chevauz [sic]*. Oct. 13th, Vermillionville, Lafayette Parish, La." That said, part of my argument here is that letters, essays, and other texts from "correspondents" cross-pollinated each other, so we need a capacious definition of correspondence when thinking about the *Recorder* and the nineteenth-century press in general. And, of course, almost all of these texts were sent by mail, so in that regard, they began as correspondence.

5. My work here inherently calls on scholars to much more deeply consider letters in Black papers like the *Colored American* and Frederick Douglass's various newspapers—work that has already begun by select scholars studying figures like William Wilson, James McCune Smith, and Philip Bell.

6. That said, even "Not Published" demonstrates that editors treated different correspondents who broke the same rule differently. While Weaver used "Not Published" to tell "Cerberus" of Washington, DC, that his "too personal" language made his/her contribution unpublishable, in the very same piece, Weaver told a correspondent "from Terre Haute"—likely Reverend Thomas Strother, who had a history of combative letters in the paper—that he would send "a note apprizing him of the cause" of his last contribution's "not appearing."

7. For "Historicus" and sometimes for the *Recorder*, this bridged into discussions, as the clothing references suggest, of "Black dandyism"; cf. Miller, *Slaves to Fashion*. "His-

toricus" also argues that some African Americans "straining" after fine words end up sounding like ["]an old colored man I used to know in the South, whose favorite form of greeting his friends was in these words: [']How does your corporasity seem to surgashate upon your nocturnal luminaries?['"] That is, he argues that those who "strain after fine words" sound like minstrels.

8. As late as his August 3, 1867, "Long Letters," Weaver was still asserting that "We have received some letters ... that are about as difficult to decipher as the traditional Gordian knot was to untie. If writers have been aiming to enshroud their meaning in mysterious characters, they have succeeded.... If brethren will not take the trouble to write plain, we cannot take the trouble to decipher their ambiguous communications."

9. Weaver had given positive notice to the elder Krauth as early as 1862, when he devoted almost two full columns of the front page of the March 1, 1862, issue praising Krauth's lecture on "Washington: His Life, Character, and Opinions"; the very next month, in the April 26, 1862, issue, Weaver included a letter addressed to Krauth by J. W. Hassler under the heading "Letter from a Lutheran Chaplain."

10. I have found no other "Letters from Olympus" in the *Lutheran and Missionary* during 1865. In his two-volume biography of Charles Krauth, Adolph Spaeth—Harriet's husband—claims that Harriet authored additional Olympus letters that were published in the 1870s and that share settings, character names, stylistic features, and, most importantly, the pseudonym "Alexandrina Lucilla Mortimer" (2: 215–217).

11. Broader, cross-cultural study of such issues is desperately needed. Beginnings of such work can be found in efforts by David Paul Nord and Candy Gunther Brown, but there has been little discussion of, for example, Black newspapers clipping (and so recontextualizing) items from white newspapers during the period.

12. The next letter chides the editor for publishing "Alexandrina"'s full name and causing this response: "If I appear on the streets of my native town, the rising generation, who are so many mirrors of the adult mind, immediately shout, 'There she goes!' and then hurra in the most flattering manner."

13. The refreshment table received almost as much attention as the speech of "Hon. J. Ludovico Joens [sic]," which was unavoidably shortened when "one of the benches gave way"—an "accident" in which "no limbs were broken, except one of the arms of the chair." The *Recorder* did not comment on the senses of race and racism embodied in such humor.

14. Gambler's plagiarism is hinted at heavily in the five paragraphs preceding the poem, which note that "I cannot deny that Mr. Gambler occasionally invades the rights of property possessed by his brother poets." Still, "Alexandrina" claims that the poem—which embodies the poet's "finest existence" at "the heights of Nothing and Nowhere"—must be original: "If it is not his, whose is it?"

15. Campbell also took to the April 5, 1862, *Recorder* to defend Nazrey from attacks in the (pro-Payne) *Repository of Religion and Literature*, then under editor John Mifflin Brown.

16. Strother continued to send contentious correspondence on a variety of other subjects for much of the period, and Weaver and other editors published such, albeit with some groans. Weaver, for example, headed a September 27, 1862, piece from Strother that spoke strongly against colonization (a topic on which Weaver also seems to have strived for balance, though he was generally anti-colonization) with this: "NOTICE. —We are not responsible for this article in any sense; the author alone will be. —ED."

17. Prior to Adger's May 7, 1864, letter—his first published work from Australia—the paper carried an unsigned August 1, 1863, letter from Liverpool that an editor's note identifies as Adger's. The May 7, 1864, letter was followed by material under the same "Letter from Australia" heading in the May 14, 21, and 28 issues, and the June 4 and 11 issues. Adger also—years later—shared a sample of "native" poetry from "out Antipodes" in the April 23, 1870, issue.

18. In addition to James Spady's entry on the Robert Mara Adger in Appiah and Gates's *Africana*, see esp. Wendy Ball and Tony Martin's *Rare Afro-American: A Reconstruction of the Adger Library*. Adger's collection became a base for the Elbert Collection at Wellesley College. See also the June 30, 1866, *Recorder* report on Elizabeth Adger.

19. The Adgers were city residents and so not likely to be listed in the *Recorder*'s acknowledgments columns even if they were regular "city subscribers." No subscription acknowledgment has yet surfaced, but Daniel Adger's comments suggest that he was a longtime reader of the paper.

20. While Adger's unsigned August 1, 1863, letter is addressed "To the Editor," his May 7, 1864, letter shifts to the more familiar "Mr. Weaver." Weaver refers to him as "our friend" in his attribution of the unsigned August 1, 1863, letter and as "our young and worthy friend" in a February 20, 1864, acknowledgment of Adger's gift of several newspapers from Australia. The Adgers' connection to Weaver dated back at least to mid-1860, when Weaver purchased a "show-case" for the *Recorder* and Book Concern's offices from Robert Adger; see chapter 3. Though the family was not directly and consistently associated with the AME Church—most seem to have been Episcopalians—the *Recorder* carried, for example, a laudatory obituary for Daniel's younger brother, Civil War sailor Joseph R. Adger, in the January 30, 1864, issue.

21. The correspondence has not been found, but the Sydney *Morning Herald* noted the deaths of Joseph Adger, John George Adger, William Adger, and the elder Robert Adger in the April 21, 1864; August 27, 1885; November 20, 1885; and December 10, 1896, issues, respectively. James Adger was the only likely source of—or reason for publishing—such information.

22. See the December 13, 1916, Sydney *Morning Herald*.

23. He took to the columns of the August 30, 1861, Sydney *Morning Herald* to announce that:

JAMES H. ADGER (late assistant to Mr. E. Deeper for five years) begs respectfully to inform his friends and the public generally, that he will commence business on his own account in those rooms, so elegantly furnished by Mr. McMahon, on the first floor over his shop, which is now undergoing complete alterations and improvements, and will be re-opened on Wednesday, September 4th, when he trusts that, with strict attention to directions and cleanliness, to obtain a share of that patronage, which it has always been his earnest endeavor to merit. A separate room for ladies and children. James H. Adger, hairdresser, 410 George Street.

Dubbed "Central Hair-Cutting and Champooing," Adger's business was popular enough that he announced in the August 13, 1862, *Morning Herald* that he had "secured the services of the most competent assistant available."

24. See, for example, September 1, 1864, *Empire*. Like many of the more elite Black barbers in the United States, Adger also had a significant side business selling hair tonic during this period.

25. Notably, Adger, who identified himself with British colonizers, says nothing in these letters about Australia's native peoples—whose long oppression is well known.

26. Sir John Young (1807–1876) was appointed governor on January 18, 1861. His tenure was rocky, but he held on to his appointment until December 1867 and later became governor-general of Canada. The *Australian Dictionary of Biography* notes that he was known not only as "a gentleman & a scholar" but also for always being "clean-shaven, with long side-burns," a note that would likely bring James Adger some pride.

27. In addition to the difficulties of "Life on a Sheep Station," Adger's return may also have been influenced by his brother's later financial troubles. James Adger seems to have been forced into bankruptcy proceedings in early 1866 by hungry creditors: the February 9, 1866, Sydney *Empire* notes that "Adger, Sydney, hairdresser and perfumer" was assessed in the Insolvency Court as owing just over £458 but having, in total assets, just over £450. The March 1 and April 13, 1866, issues of the *Morning Herald* note his failure to attend court, and a December 17, 1870, *Matiland Mercury and Hunter River General Advertiser* item lists him as "now out of business." The bankruptcy proceedings seem to have carried on, with some morphing, for several more years; see, for example, the March 28, 1888, *Morning Herald*. That said, with some exceptions, Adger continued to live and work in Sydney for the rest of his life. Sydney city directories of the 1870s list him fairly steadily back on George Street—at 328—and those published between 1883 and his death label him a "dermatologist," first at 131 Elizabeth Street and later at various sites on Castlereagh Street.

28. Four hundred sixty-nine other passengers—many of whom were Irish and English citizens—joined Adger on the tenth voyage of this "spectacular and graceful clipper." See Fraser 13 and 15.

29. The May 14 installment depicts weeks one and two; the May 21 installment, weeks three and four; the May 28 installment, week five (after additional coverage on week four); the June 4 installment, weeks six and seven; the June 11 installment, weeks eight, nine, and twelve (their arrival at Melbourne). Adger includes no details about weeks ten and eleven.

30. See May 28 letter for these examples. Adger was interested in and equipped to comment on these questions, as evidenced by a list of books that Adger's May 7 letter asks Weaver to send ("at a low[er] per centage than cost"), likely for him to sell: "'A Pilgrimage to My Motherland,' by Robert Campbell, 'Liberia Offering,' 'Touissaint l'Overture,' [sic] 'Father Geffrand,' and many others of distinguished negroes, and any pertaining to Liberia, Africa, and St. Domingo, written by colored men, or of Hayti. "

31. Some of my reading here is influenced by Hester Blum's *A View from the Mast-Head* (2008).

32. In the May 7 letter, Adger describes an extended conversation with the captain early in the voyage in which the captain asked to hear of his background and education and to see a sample of his handwriting. The captain told Adger "Your demeanor convinced me that you possessed no little culture, as your conduct and manners have been very good." He encouraged Adger to explore the possibility of accompanying the Keans on the Australian tour or returning to England with him, for, the captain tells Adger, "I had a young lad, just like you, from the West Indies; but, poor fellow! I lost him."

33. For a corollary, see Helen Jun's *Black Orientalism*, which considers African American engagement with "the Orient" and Asian American immigrant issues later in the century.

34. Adger's own account of his reunion with his brother in his May 7, 1864, letter, while brief, depersonalized, and a bit uncomfortable, likely strengthened such connections.

35. Highgate's rediscovered *Recorder* texts include the following pieces signed "E. Goodelle H.": "Salvation Only in Work," February 4, 1865; "Waiting for the Cars," February 25, 1865; "A Stray Waif from the Port of Grace," April 1, 1865; "Congojoco," May 20, 1865, and May 27, 1865 (with the missing first chapter likely appearing in the missing pages of the May 13, 1865, issue); "A Spring Day up the James," May 27, 1865; "A Leaf from the South Bank of the Ohio," July 29, 1865; "Neglected Opportunities," July 14, 1866; "New Orleans Correspondence," August 18, 1866; "On Horse Back—Saddle Dash, No. 1," November 3, 1866; and "New Orleans Correspondence," March 16, 1867. Other work appeared under the name "E. Goodelle Highgate": "Rainy-Day Ink Drops," September 30, 1865; "Letter from New Orleans," March 17, 1866; "New Orleans Correspondence," July 7, 1866; "Truth," October 27, 1866; "Letter from New Orleans—The Late Madame Louise De Mortie," November 16, 1867; "The Work in Mississippi," January 16, 1869. The October 19, 1867, "Letter from New Orleans" appeared under the byline "E. G. Highgate."

36. The Highgates' engagement in Albany in the late 1840s augers for this city as Edmonia Highgate's birthplace; the family moved to Syracuse c. 1850 but may have lived there earlier. See my "Each Atomic Part" for further biographical information.

37. Charles Highgate also knew George Boyer Vashon and Frederick Douglass.

38. On Daffin, who also wrote lively letters for the *Recorder*, see my *Unexpected Places*, esp. 139–152.

39. Highgate to George Whipple, June 1, 1864, AMA Collection.

40. The full speech has not yet been found and does not seem to have been spectacular—perhaps expectedly, given Highgate's youth, inexperience, and potential nervousness at the venue. Still, she did garner brief praise from Douglass.

41. For useful commentary on this tradition and on Smith's letters in particular, see Stauffer. Such texts need much more study.

42. On Fern, see, for example, Joyce Warren's *Fanny Fern*. Gail Hamilton was Mary Abigail Dodge's preferred penname.

43. We should also note that Highgate's three-part serialized short story "Congojoco"— of which we have only the last two of three installments—represents a generic broadening for the *Recorder*, as it appeared in the same period as Collins's *Curse of Caste*. These seem to be the first two works of extended fiction to appear on the paper's front page; generally, fiction—almost always in the form of tales for youth and/or family audiences and often reprinted—was relegated to the paper's final page.

44. She also writes, for example, that a soldier who is "merely" a "colored Second Lieutenant will not take Richmond. He must have promotion to any and all the line officer ranks; nor must he stop there."

45. I praise Thee while my days go on,
   I love Thee while my days go on,
   Through dark and death, through fire and frost,
   With emptied arms and treasures lost,
   I thank Thee while my days go on.

46. I do not treat "Truth" or "Neglected Opportunities" in depth here, as they are Highgate's most essay-like contributions. "Truth," for example, sets aside almost all of the

formal and visual conventions of the letter—it has no salutation, no signature, and so forth, and it actually appears under the heading "Miscellaneous" rather than "Correspondence." For a fuller reading of "Truth," see my "Each Atomic Part."

47. Morgan's 21 October 21, 1870, letter to Smith is quoted in Sterling, *We Are Your Sisters*, 304.

Chapter 7

1. Both the 1900 and 1910 federal censuses list Susan Paul Vashon as having had seven children, four of whom were alive. The four surviving children were John Boyer (September 1859—April 8, 1924, never married), Frank (1861—October 11, 1926, married Emma Prestina Story), George (April 1863—July 26, 1938, married Fannie Brooks), and Emma (August 8, 1866—November 13, 1932, married Andrew J. Gossin). The quote is drawn from Thornell, 295, which offers one of the richest pictures of the Vashon family over several generations. Other sources say much less about the Vashon descendants.

2. An exact count is, at this time, impossible given the number of partial and missing issues. Further, some poems clearly stood alone, while others were quoted in prose pieces. Finally, especially in 1865, when the *Recorder* offered a small section headed "Hymns" or "Hymnological," the paper regularly published lyrics to hymns by a variety of authors—with some preference for Charles Wesley—that in some ways functioned as poems.

3. The paper also published verse by well-known white abolitionists like John Greenleaf Whittier and Harriet Beecher Stowe, as well as poems by white authors that caught an editorial eye; this was especially the case with some of the poems in the "family" sections of the paper. The poetry of Lydia M. Reno (1831–?), a white farmer's daughter from Rochester, Pennsylvania, who published *Early Buds* (1853) as well as diverse periodical verse, is an example of such work. The paper regularly clipped poems from other periodicals—sometimes reprinting them with authors' names and/or citations and sometimes not.

4. Harper has been treated extensively, though there is still much work to be done. In addition to Jackson's "Frances Ellen Watkins Harper," see esp. work by Foster. J. Willis Menard has received some attention in part because of his political activity. His 1879 collection *Lays from Summer Lands* was republished in 2002 by the University of Tampa Press, edited by Larry Eugene Rivers, Richard Mathews, and Canter Brown Jr.

5. In terms of anthologies, see e.g., Faith Barrett and Christianne Miller's 2005 *"Words for the Hour": A New Anthology of Civil War Poetry*, which informs Barrett's 2012 *To Fight Aloud Is Very Brave: American Poetry and the Civil War*. Among recent exciting work on Civil War poetry—albeit work that also sometimes continues to deemphasize Black letters—see Michael Cohen, "Contraband Singing: Poems and Songs in Circulation during the Civil War"; Eliza Richards, "Correspondent Lines: Poetry, Journalism, and the US Civil War"; and Vanessa Steinroetter's "'Reading the List': Casualty Lists and Civil War Poetry." Much of the study of early Black poetry has offered similarly limited consideration of Black poetry during the Civil War—especially poetry specifically about the war; see, for example, Joan Sherman's trail-blazing anthologies *Invisible Poets* and *African American Poetry of the Nineteenth Century* as well as the more recent *Voices beyond Bondage*, edited by Fidel Louis and Erika DeSimone.

6. Samples of these include Frederick B. Waugh, "The Song of the Freedman," March 21, 1863, *Recorder*; Solomon G. Brown, "The New York Riot," August 22, 1863; a collection

of short poems by "the children and youth of the freedmen, at Arlington Heights," Virginia, submitted by J. R. Johnson, December 26, 1863; Mrs. E. Morris, "Obituary" for James Davis (a Sergeant in the 25th USCT), October 15, 1864; Jacob Anderson Raymond, "The Fifty-Fourth Massachusetts," March 1865; Isaac Langley, "As We Let Rip!!" (datelined the USS Richmond, Mobile Bay), April 8, 1865; Raymond, "The Soldier's Wife," November 4, 1865. The paper also reprinted war poetry, including some on Black subjects, like Elsie Ellis's "Ennobled Bondmen, Written on Reading That the Colored Troops Were the First to Enter Richmond," which was noted as from "*Exchange*" in the August 19, 1865, *Recorder*.

7. See my "African American Women's Poetry in the *Christian Recorder*, 1855–1865: A Bio-Bibliography with Sample Poems." While not addressing the *Recorder*, the more recent digital edition "'Will not these days be by thy poets sung': Poems of the *Anglo-African* and *National Anti-Slavery Standard*, 1863–1864," by Elizabeth Lorang and R. J. Weir, is especially notable in the broader quest to recover Black Civil War era poetry.

8. While rarely recognized as a "major" author, Vashon has never fully left discussions of Black letters. The March 17, 1866, *Recorder* said his "reputation as a man of talent and letters is so widely known that no commendation of ours is necessary." Levstik provides a brief introduction; see also Sherman.

9. "Mrs. Butterworth's Revelation," in which we learn of Lina's dying words—and, of Claire, that, in stark counterpoint to Anne Paul Vashon, "the child *did not* die" (95).

10. Vashon's "A Life-Day" would carry an identical signature line when it appeared in the March 17, 1866, issue, and that issue also contained a contents list that identified that text as "Poem by G. B. Vashon." Because it is one of the poems that contemporary African Americanists may know, we should note that though "A Life-Day" is generally listed as appearing in Daniel Payne's 1866 *The Semi-Centenary and the Retrospection of the African Methodist Episcopal Church* (which the *Recorder* later—ff.1872–1874—used as a premium for those who successfully solicited subscribers), the poem's first appearance was actually in the *Recorder*. The paper noted that the *Semi-Centenary* "will be ready" soon in its March 31, 1866, issue and that a copy had just arrived—with time only for "a glance"—in the April 21, 1866 issue, weeks after the *Recorder*'s publication of "A Life-Day." Also of note, Joan Sherman dates the composition of "A Life-Day" to 1864—seemingly based on its headnote; the *Recorder*'s version of this headnote seems to list 1854, though the print on the extant copy is hard to read.

11. On "Vincent Ogé," see, for example, Brawley 83–87.

12. My thinking here is deeply influenced by the work of scholar/artists like Audre Lorde and Toni Morrison, especially their efforts to recognize African American—and especially African American women's—self-preservation, self-care, family preservation, and family care as radical political acts.

13. See chapter 6. Vashon served on the body's Committee on Rules, was named Corresponding Secretary, and, of course, heard Edmonia Highgate's speech.

14. We need look no further than the back page of this very issue for confirmation of the *Recorder*'s approach to dealing with trauma. That page contains a brief anonymous poem titled "Trust in God" that opens by quoting 1 Peter 5:7, "Casting all your care upon him; for he careth for you."

15. In this and a host of other ways, "In the Cars" certainly bears out the recognition in Cavitch's landmark work that "elegies are poems about being left behind . . . poems, too,

that are themselves left behind, as literary and material legacies" (1). However, "In the Cars" does not function like those African American elegies that Cavitch places within a tradition of the "genealogical isolate"; does not "perform threatened continuity as a form of identity," and does not emphasize "departicularization of the mourned"—a strategy Cavitch rightly asserts is crucial to many elegies across race (186, 185). Indeed, "In the Cars" actually creates spaces between a "departicularization"—Anne Paul Vashon is never named—and a deep particularization that aggressively denies any genealogical isolation: the painful specificity of the constantly present (and absent) relation embodied in "our baby-girl."

16. In some ways, this poem is consonant with Cavitch's assertion—when speaking about what he thinks may be "the earliest extant American elegy by a black author for a black subject"—that "the exhortation not to grieve, the assurance of the departed's happiness in Heaven, the promise of posthumous reunion—these conventions of European-American elegy seem to transcend racial difference" (184).

17. Cavitch's general sense that many Black elegies contribute "to the impression of a collective endeavor—of a community of mourners" is on target, though just who would be a member of that community is open to debate (196). Cavitch's work is especially exciting because it begins to articulate frameworks for Black agency in and through print, to explore Black periodicals, and to recognize that the African American writers he studies were both part of and separate from the larger, white-dominated American print culture. In this, it seems a logical next step from Jeffrey Steele's "The Gender and Racial Politics of Mourning," which moved to mark some Black agency and participation, albeit in, for example, Frederick Douglass's "capacity to mourn the effects of slavery" as both object and subject—even though Steele heavily emphasized the work of African Americans and white women "to exploit the middle-class demand for sentimental pathos by expanding the group of suffering victims" (99, 98).

18. See Cavitch's opening to *American Elegy*: "Elegies are poems about being left behind. They are poems, too, that are themselves left behind, as literary and even material legacies. Their heritage helps constitute the 'work' (both process and artifact) of mourning—a form of psychic labor that is fundamental to the work of culture" (1).

19. In this, the poem works in dialogue with the multifunctional lists of casualties from Black units, like the massive list in James Lynch's "Letter from the South," which takes up more than two columns of the front page of the December 31, 1864, *Recorder* and includes names of dead and wounded from the 54th and 55th Massachusetts, as well as the 32nd, 35th, and 102nd USCT regiments. For connections between white poetry and casualty lists, see Steinroetter.

20. See Jeremiah 31:16. I thank Jodie Gardner for this observation.

21. Waugh was on Elisha Weaver's mind at least as early as December 14, 1861, when Weaver wrote about a visit to New Bedford and specifically about meeting a boy named "Frederick Waugh" who had impressed him with his oratory and faith. While a December 28, 1861, correction noted that the boy was actually Elijah Webb, clearly Waugh had entered both the consciousness of Weaver and the *Recorder*.

22. Scruggs 278. Born in 1851 to free parents in Alabama (Simon and Adelia Ashe) who moved to Ohio in 1860 in part for their children's schooling, Ashe lived until the 1930s. Among the four others with whom she graduated from Wilberforce's collegiate branch in 1873 were Hallie Quinn Brown, Julia A. Shorter, and one of Martin Delany's sons. Ashe's

"Ode to the Class of '73" was set to music and performed at the graduation—at which Benjamin Tucker Tanner, Henry McNeal Turner, and Richard Cain received honorary doctorates; see the July 10, 1873, *Recorder*. See Mossell 81–85 and Scruggs 277–279 for the most detailed early biographical treatments. See Yellin 267–268 for the fullest bibliography to date, though this list is incomplete.

23. The end of the first stanza also embodies this balancing act in its struggle between asking and ordering God to "console his dear mother, / For her last loving child is dead."

24. The Providence group's resolutions even echo the tenor of Ashe's poem, noting, for example, that "while we attempt not to question the inscrutable designs of Providence ... we deeply deplore the recent disposition of His wisdom, so severely realized in our late bereavement." The group's name calls attention to Black (inter)nationalism vis-à-vis these issues.

25. I say "at least five elegies" because the March 19 issue, which may have contained notice of Weaver's death and/or other elegies, is only partially extant (pages three and four in the Campbell run). The March 12 issue says nothing about her death. Weaver had published a note "To Our Many Inquiring Friends" in the February 20 issue that said "Mrs. Weaver is at death's door, and, from appearances, ere this shall have reached all of our patrons, it is thought that she will be with the angels in heaven." The dates of the funeral service and publications above suggest that she lived into March. On Tanner's use of the pseudonym see the May 12, 1866, *Recorder*.

26. The essay (23–26) addresses its title subjects in fairly standard ways and suggests that Mary Weaver certainly had the requisite knowledge and ability to not only write but also occasionally stand in for her husband and edit. Notably, the piece appears next to a selection from Frances Ellen Watkins Harper.

27. See, e.g., January 18, 1862, September 27, 1862, and April 16, 1864, issues.

28. On Daffin, see *Unexpected Places* 137–152.

29. On Susan Paul Vashon, in addition to the sources noted above, see Gardner, "Susan Paul Smith Vashon."

30. A significant portion of Cavitch's arguments about Black elegies focuses on the conception of the African American as a "genealogical isolate"; his chapter on Black elegies is even titled "Mourning of the Disprized." Recognizing the destruction of families common in slavery, Cavitch argues that "elegy sometimes helped to restore a sense of the severed affiliations from which blacks suffered disproportionately" (180). Cavitch's careful "sometimes" and "disproportionately" are well taken here, as the *Recorder* put forth great energy to do this work in texts like the "Information Wanted" ads. I argue that elegies like those described above, however, represent a very different strand—poems that depicted African Americans who were far from genealogical isolates, sometimes from mere fact, sometimes in attempts to articulate Black places in domestic ideals, and often in a combination of both.

31. Indeed, such work echoed Vashon's early assertions that Weaver had died "the Good Death"—that she had been "calm 'mid her pain" and died with "a sweet placid smile" on "her fair face" (9, 11).

32. We desperately need a book-length study of representations of Lincoln in the Black press.

33. See Douglass *Autobiographies* 917–918 for this speech, which Cavitch considers and which has been a centerpiece in tracing Black senses of Lincoln.

34. I say "elegiac poems" here to highlight the fact that, for example, Hart's is only a quatrain and is arguably part of her letter and that the Stoddard excerpt represents less

than a quarter of his long poem, which was originally published in pamphlet form (1865). I suspect that "W. H. F." was actually "W. H. S."—the initials used at times by regular contributor and subscriber William H. Stevenson—but there are two other *Recorder* texts signed "W. H. F." ("Repine Not" in the June 29, 1861, issue and "The Sons of God" in the May 24, 1862, issue), and I cannot definitively determine authorship.

35. On Demby, see my "African American Women's Poetry," esp. 821, 823–834. As she was likely a city subscriber, I have found no record of her subscription, though she was clearly a *Recorder* reader between 1864 and 1866.

36. See April 22, 1865, April 7, 1866, and May 5, 1866, issues, for example. The head note to Williams's April 7, 1866, letter noted that he was "always working for the *Recorder*," and it was clear that he was a subscriber, though I have not yet found record of such.

37. "W. H. F." and "Peregrinator" were likely African American, given the race of the vast majority of authors and readers of the papers in question. The unsigned "In Memoriam" would seem to be by an African American, too, for similar reasons; like "W. H. F."'s poem, it is specifically labeled "For the Christian Recorder." Indeed, given its Philadelphia dateline and its early publication date, it might even have been written by Weaver.

38. See Job 5:17, "Behold, happy is the man whom God correcteth; therefore despise not thou the chastening of the Almighty." The image was a common one throughout the period, but its echo in both Vashon and Williams' poems shows how *Recorder* elegies could speak to broader US trends and topoi while simultaneously talking among themselves.

39. Line numbers correspond to the *Recorder* publication rather than the full pamphlet poem.

Chapter 8

1. On Stewart, see my "Two Texts on Children and Christian Education by Maria W. Stewart." The *Repository* remains massive understudied.

2. See, for example, James Dawes's letter in the August 27, 1852, *Frederick Douglass's Paper* that concluded, "Could not the space occupied by Dickens's 'Bleak House' be better occupied?" On the serialization more generally, see McHenry 124–126 and Daniel Hack's "Close Reading at a Distance." Douglass also serialized white Syracuse activist Joseph R. Johnson's temperance tale "Uncle William's Pulpit" in the second half of 1852.

3. The Hamilton family's ventures demand much more study. Beyond the decidedly mixed critical work on *Blake*, see R. J. Weir and Elizabeth Lorang's wonderful "'Will not these days be by thy poets sung': Poems of the *Anglo-African* and *National Anti-Slavery Standard*, 1863–1864" for background. Christopher Mulvey's work on *Clotel* represents a key consideration of its *Miralda* incarnation; see, for basic information, his "Liberating an African American Text."

4. In addition to Andrews and Kachun's discussion in their introduction to *Curse*, see Dinita Smith's "A Slave Story is Rediscovered" as well as Robert Levine's useful "The Early African American Novel" and the brief discussion in Gates and R. J. Ellis's introduction to their 2011 edition of *Our Nig* (xxvi). Of note, there is actually a section in the Wikipedia entry for *Our Nig* titled "Competition for 'First Novel.'"

5. Levine addresses this issue briefly, but the race to place *The Bondwoman's Narrative* in African American literary studies (and courses) before the identity of its author was definitively determined has meant that this collateral gap in our thinking has received almost no attention. This absence is complicated by the dearth of discussion of African

American manuscript culture and unpublished writing generally. Karen Sanchez-Eppler's work on manuscripts offers one useful set of approaches that begins to address such questions.

6. In addition to Frances Smith Foster's edition of Harper's three *Recorder* novels, see my "A 'New' Chapter from Frances Ellen Watkins Harper's *Sowing and Reaping*."

7. The people enslaved by the Tracys seem to know more, as "at almost every step" Claire "encountered the curious gaze of the negroes, who looked wonderingly at her" (11). Nonetheless, we hear only a tiny bit of their voices on this question.

8. Andrews and Kachun skillfully dismantle a set of misguided assumptions about the dominance of this type and point to a number of mixed-race characters who break with it. See xl-liii.

9. Most critics to date have suggested that the Tracy family is analogous to the nation at the end of the Civil War.

10. Early studies of *Curse* have looked at the novel vis-à-vis, for example, the Civil War, attacks on African American families and family structures, seduction plots, sentimental fiction, and intertextuality—often with emphasis on the book's conceptions of gender and education. Jean Lee Cole, Edlie Wong, and Gabrielle Foreman, for example, albeit in different ways, have usefully traced the book's senses of kinship and have alerted contemporary students to the potential linkages between the novel and the paper's "Information Wanted" ads. Foreman adds the important recognition that "If, in this text, recuperating family provides the key for healing a past riven by enslavement and war, then education provides the bridge for creating empowered Black citizens in a new era" (714). More recently, Sarah Schuetze has explored the novel's treatment of the figure of the invalid and "the disease of racism" that permeates the book. In each of these cases—as in the studies by critics like Colleen O'Brien and Jennifer Rae Greeson that emphasize Collins's intertextual play with other nineteenth-century literature—scholars have often edged around the ties readers might have felt to the novel and especially around Juno.

11. The recovery of Collins's novel has actually demonstrated more awareness of its venue than many similar projects, and Andrews and Kachun's excellent work offers strong lessons for such scholarship. In that spirit, we must both reexamine the artifacts they brought forward and search for more.

12. See Dodson for discussion of women's roles in the AME Church during this period.

13. The number of Black women teachers from the North who went to teach in the South—beginning even before the war's end—would likely have been especially prominent in *Recorder* readers' minds given the writings of Highgate and of figures like Sallie Daffin. On the former, see chapter 6; on the latter, see *Unexpected Places*, esp. 137–152.

14. They also mark the presence of the *Recorder* within Collins's Williamsport group—even as they cite a February 13, 1864, *Recorder* letter sent by Turpin claiming that "I find only one copy of the *Recorder*" in Williamsport.

15. Pitts has not yet found a "smoking gun" to connect Julia Collins to the Julia Green of the 1860 census (e.g., a marriage license for Julia and Stephen Collins). He *has* been able to prove that Julia Green was indeed Enoch Gilchrist's stepdaughter; specifically, he found records of Gilchrist's marriage to the widowed Anna Lockwood Green in the early 1850s and of Anna Green Gilchrist's children's names, including her daughter Julia.

16. Pitts's work on Stephen Collins's long and varied life—including his death on May 12, 1917, in Atlantic City, New Jersey—is admirable, as has been his kindness in sharing his

findings with me. Key among sources Pitts cites are the military pension record of "Simon C. Collins," various census records, and reports of the Williamsport and other GAR groups.

17. Economics and caregiving demands may also explain some of her movement in late 1864 and early 1865, when she traveled to (and may have lived in) either or both Oswego, New York, and Owego, New York, which are listed in the datelines of her last three essays for the *Recorder*. Pitts argues that the "children" referred to in Spriggs's notice of Collins's death were Annie Collins, who was likely born in late 1862, and Stephen Collins's daughter from his first marriage, Sarah C. ("Sadie") Collins, who had been born in 1858.

18. Andrews and Kachun recognize the likelihood that Nelson Turpin "seems to have supported his wife's submissions to the *Recorder*" (lix). Further, the "trustees and ladies" of Williamsport's AME Church bought him a new suit, per Gilchrist's April 16, 1864, *Recorder* letter—in which Gilchrist referred to him as "our revered and beloved pastor."

19. His April 22, 1865, *Recorder* letter notes, for example, that because his "duties have called me from one end of the circuit to the other, I have frequently been compelled to walk from sixteen to twenty miles, over the worst kind of roads, and during the severest weather, on account of not being able to meet the stage."

20. I mean neither to suggest that all readers always first or even primarily identify with characters of the same race and/or gender nor to assume that *Recorder* readers followed such reading patterns. I do, though, in the tradition of several media critics in the twentieth century and beyond, recognize both that readers/viewers belonging to oppressed groups sometimes yearn for heroines and heroes in various media who "look" like them, and I submit that the *Recorder* offered one of the richest "safe spaces" for exploring Black characters, given the dearth of such spaces in the broader nineteenth-century American print culture.

21. Juno was "about twelve years old" when Colonel Tracy and Nellie Thornton wed—and thus perhaps thirteen when Richard was born—and was then living with Laura Tracy Hays's maiden aunt (29–30, 17). We also learn that Juno only met Colonel Tracy once, when he came to argue against Laura's marriage to Rev. Hays.

22. On this subject, older works on New England slavery like Lorenzo Green's *Negro in Colonial New England* should be read in dialogue with more recent studies like Joanne Pope Melish's *Disowning Slavery*.

23. For more on Russel, see "*The Complete Fortune Teller and Dream Book*: An Antebellum Text 'By Chloe Russel, A Woman of Colour.'"

24. Thompson's connections to the print cultures of New York City (he wrote regularly for the *Tribune*) and Philadelphia (the well-known firm of T.B. Peterson published *Witches*) along with his reputation as a humorist meant that the book achieved both sales and notice. Also of note, 1859 saw, in addition to another edition of *Witches* from the New York firm of Rudd and Carleton, the publication of E. D. E. N. Southworth's *The Hidden Hand* in serial form in the *New York Ledger*; this immensely popular novel features a minor (but nonetheless important) Black character "old Hat" who is referred to as a "witch."

25. The *Recorder* was often more strident in these positions than other Black newspapers of the period; the *Pacific Appeal*, for example, even published some material on spirit conversations held by Black spiritualist Shadrach Howard in 1864. Like the complex questions of Black faiths and popular (white) representations of Black augury noted above, the intersections of African American practices and spiritualism desperately need study.

26. This should also be figured in dialogue with both AME debates over education (and specifically an educated ministry) as well as over the Church's expansion into the South, including its sometimes uneasy relationship with formerly enslaved people, which figured massively in arguments over, for example, the ordination of Southern ministers by figures like Henry McNeal Turner (sometimes over the objections of figures like Daniel Payne and, later, Wesley Gaines). See Case, *Unpredictable*, 159–206, for a primer on these questions; see also Angell, Campbell, and Seraile.

27. These characters' recognitions that they must consult Juno to solve the mysteries surrounding Claire echo no less a figure than Colonel Tracy, who tells Claire "It will be necessary to see Juno in the course of our investigation" (66).

28. Some readers were clearly familiar with Virgil, who was, for example, noted no less than seventeen times in the *Recorder* between 1861 and 1865.

29. The "one" in Martin's words is delightfully unclear—offering possibilities for Martin *or* Juno being in that dream. If it is the former, Juno's powers essentially draw her husband into the dream world; if it is the latter, Juno herself joins with that world.

30. Note yet another resonance of "child" here: even "children" know better. It is also worth pointing out, given Sarah Schuetze's reading of the ways racism sickens characters in the book, that Juno is perhaps the healthiest and most vigorous figure in *Curse*.

31. This linkage is reinforced by Claire's delirious "ravings" near the novel's end: "sometimes of Juno, and her northern home. Sometimes . . . plaintively for Miss Ellwood" (87).

32. It bears mention that Claire does not evince any of Juno's fortune telling power, but that she does have "a sort of mesmeric influence over Mrs. Tracy" and consistently uses this ability—which spiritualists would have recognized—to care for her invalid charge, who is really her paternal grandmother (74).

33. It should be noted that while diverse other factors provide evidence of the dating of Hannah Crafts's manuscript novel *The Bondwoman's Narrative*, that text's lack of discussion of the Civil War is thus not as conclusive an absence as literary historians have argued. *Curse* never mentions the war directly even though the war was still raging as *Curse*'s serialization began and even though simple math suggests that the war would have taken place within the (later) lifetimes of many of *Curse*'s characters—if not in the landscape of the novel's concluding moments.

34. I remain troubled by the speculative "happy" and "tragic" endings included in the 2006 edition, which is otherwise a wonderful model of scholarship—in part because they rely much more heavily on novels of the 1850s and much less on the texts published in the *Recorder* in the 1860s and in part because they simply seem to shut down critical possibilities rather than opening them up. The novel is incomplete; we must study it as such.

35. Another component of Claire's legal status has remained curiously absent in the criticism of the novel and, indeed, is curiously absent in the novel itself. Soon after Lina's purchase by Colonel Tracy, we see Richard with "fixed resolution" leave the house "accompanied by Manville" and then, "a few hours later," Manville returning to talk with the Colonel, after which he "departed with the document in his pocket, which pronounced him lawful owner of the young quadroon" Lina (24). Nothing more is said of her status. Given Manville's behavior in the novel, it seems questionable that he would have acted solely and faithfully as Richard's agent here, and so the possibility exists that he owned Lina and, given partus sequitur ventrem, thus also owned Claire. (If this is the case, as he

dies without heirs, the novel leaves Claire's status in limbo.) If we read Manville's "document"—followed quickly by Richard and Lina's marriage—as the engine of Richard's own purchase of Lina by proxy, it seems equally strange that we learn nothing of her emancipation. While Lina and especially Claire's long residence in the North would, in some locations, have given them, pre–Dred Scott, good grounds for a freedom suit, Claire would be at risk of reenslavement by the Tracys if something happened to Richard as, in the convoluted logic of the slave system, she could not inherit herself.

36. The people enslaved by the Tracys say comparatively little in the novel, but we learn that they "regarded her wonderingly, and talked mysteriously of somebody and something Claire knew not what"—a suggestion that these people know some of the secrets Juno knows (15). Nonetheless, it seems to me that Jim's amazing interaction with young Nellie marks both a key gesture in the novel toward African Americans in the South and a starting point for talking about how the newly freed people who accessed the novel might have read it.

37. It also might be better to call Juno and Martin's farm "rural" rather than "isolated," and there is no suggestion in the text that they do not interact with a broader community. A hint of that possible circle of interaction is seen when a "nice looking colored man" named Thomas, directs Richard to Miss Ellwood and knows Juno's name even though he claims to "not know much about her myself" (98).

38. His 1885 *Treatise on Domestic Education* was even more specific, claiming that "two young women who were spoiled by their parents, yet in their teens, [were] sent to Wilberforce to be subdued and rendered good" and "were, for repeated acts of insubordination, punished by the lady principal and matron with solitary confinement for two or three days. This kind of discipline was revenged by them in setting the central building on fire, involving us in the loss of the entire edifice, and compelling us to erect another at the cost of about $40,000" (101).

{WORKS CITED}

Nineteenth-Century Periodicals

African Methodist Episcopal Church Magazine, Brooklyn.
Le Bijou, Cincinnati.
Christian Recorder, Pittsburgh and Philadelphia.
Colored Citizen, Cincinnati.
Courier, Syracuse.
Daily Pantagraph, Bloomington, IL.
Empire, Sydney, Australia.
Evening Telegraph, Philadelphia.
Frederick Douglass's Paper, Rochester.
Freedom's Journal, New York City.
The Liberator, Boston.
Lutheran and Missionary, Philadelphia.
Maitland Mercury and Hunter River General Advertiser, Maitland, Australia.
Morning Herald, Sydney, Australia.
The Mystery, Pittsburgh.
Newark Evening Courier, Newark, NJ.
New York Herald, New York City.
New York Times, New York City.
New York Tribune, New York City.
The North Star, Rochester.
Pacific Appeal, San Francisco.
The Palladium of Liberty, Columbus, OH.
Provincial Freeman, Toronto.
Repository of Religion and Literature, and of Science and Art, Indianapolis, Philadelphia, and Baltimore.
True Royalist and Weekly Intelligencer, Windsor, Ontario.
Weekly Anglo-African, New York City.

Manuscript Sources and Government Records

American Missionary Association Archives, Amistad Research Center.
Bloomington, Illinois Court Records and Marriage Records.
Censuses of Canada for 1861 and 1871.
Essex County, New Jersey Wills.
Illinois State Censuses for 1855, 1865, 1875.
Plymouth Congregational Church Records, Syracuse University Library.
US Federal Censuses for 1840, 1850, 1860, 1870, 1880, 1890, 1900, 1910, 1920, 1930.
US Military Service and Pension Records for the Civil War.

Books and Articles

African Methodist Episcopal Church. *The Doctrines and Discipline of the African Methodist Episcopal Church*. Philadelphia: Richard Allen and Jacob Tapisco, 1817.

Allen, Richard, and Absalom Jones. *A Narrative of the Proceedings of the Black People during the Late Awful Calamity in Philadelphia*. Philadelphia: William W. Woodward for the Authors, 1794.

Anbinder, Tyler. "James W. Barker." *American National Biography*. Ed. John A. Garraty and Mark C. Carnes. New York: Oxford University Press, 1999. 21: 573–574.

Anderson, Benedict. *Imagined Communities: Reflections on the Origin and Spread of Nationalism*. New York: Verso, 1983.

Angell, Stephen. *Bishop Henry McNeal Turner and African American Religion in the South*. Knoxville: University of Tennessee Press, 1992.

Angell, Stephen, and Anthony Pinn, eds. *Social Protest Thought in the African Methodist Episcopal Church, 1862–1939*. Knoxville: University of Tennessee Press, 2000.

Apap, Chris. "'Let No Man of Us Budge One Step': David Walker and the Rhetoric of African American Emplacement." *Early American Literature* 46.2 (2011): 319–350.

Bacon, Jacqueline. *Freedom's Journal: The First African American Newspaper*. Lanham, MD: Lexington Books, 2007.

Bailey, Julius. *Around the Family Altar: Domesticity in the African Methodist Episcopal Church, 1865–1900*. Gainesville: University Press of Florida, 2005.

———. *Race Patriotism: Protest and Print Culture in the AME Church*. Knoxville: University of Tennessee Press, 2012.

Baker, Nicholson. *Double Fold: Libraries and the Assault on Paper*. New York: Random House, 2001.

Ball, Wendy, and Tony Martin. *Rare Afro-Americana: A Reconstruction of the Adger Library*. Boston: G.K. Hall, 1981.

Barrett, Faith. *To Fight Aloud Is Very Brave: American Poetry and the Civil War*. Amherst: University of Massachusetts Press, 2012.

Barrett, Faith, and Christianne Miller, eds. *"Words for the Hour": A New Anthology of Civil War Poetry*. Amherst: University of Massachusetts Press, 2005.

Bassard, Katherine Clay. *Spiritual Interrogations: Culture, Gender, and Community in Early African American Women's Writing*. Princeton: Princeton University Press, 1999.

———. *Transforming Scriptures: African American Women Writers and the Bible*. Athens: University of Georgia Press, 2010.

Bennett, Paula Bernat. *Poets in the Public Sphere: The Emancipatory Project of American Women's Poetry, 1800–1900*. Princeton: Princeton University Press, 2003.

Bentley, Nancy. "Introduction, In the Spirit of the Thing: Critique as Enchantment." *J19: The Journal of Nineteenth-Century Americanists* 1.1 (Spring 2013): 147–153.

Bernstein, Robin. *Racial Innocence: Performing American Childhood from Slavery to Civil Rights*. New York: New York University Press, 2011.

Biddle, Daniel R., and Murray Dubin. *Tasting Freedom: Octavius Catto and the Battle for Equality in Civil War America*. Philadelphia: Temple University Press, 2010.

Blight, David. *Race and Reunion: The Civil War in American Memory*. Cambridge: Harvard University Press, 2001.

Blum, Hester. *The View from the Masthead: Maritime Imagination and Antebellum American Sea Narratives*. Chapel Hill: University of North Carolina Press, 2008.

Brasher, Glenn David. *The Peninsula Campaign and the Necessity of Emancipation: African Americans and the Fight for Freedom*. Chapel Hill: University of North Carolina Press, 2012.

Bray, Robert. *Reading with Lincoln*. Carbondale: Southern Illinois University Press, 2010.

Bristol, Douglas W. Jr. *Knights of the Razor: Black Barbers in Slavery and Freedom*. Baltimore: Johns Hopkins University Press, 2009.

Bromley, George W., and Walter S. Bromley. *Atlas of the City of Philadelphia, 1885*. Philadelphia: G. W. Bromley, 1885. Available via the Greater Philadelphia GeoHistory Network at http://www.philageohistory.org/geohistory/.

Brown, Candy Gunther. *The Word in the World: Evangelical Writing, Publishing, and Reading in America, 1789–1880*. Chapel Hill: University of North Carolina Press, 2004.

Brown, Canter Jr. *Florida's Black Public Officials, 1867–1924*. Tuscaloosa, AL: University of Alabama Press, 1998.

———. "'Where Are Now the Hopes I Cherished?': The Life and Times of Robert Meacham." *Florida Historical Quarterly* 69 (July 1990): 1–36.

Brown, Matthew. "The Tiger's Leap and the Dog's Paw: Method, Matter, and Meaning in the History of the Book." *Early American Literature* 44.3 (2009): 657–675.

Bullock, Penelope. *The Afro-American Periodical Press, 1838–1909*. Baton Rouge: Louisiana State University Press, 1981.

Burlingame, Michael. *Abraham Lincoln: A Life*. Baltimore: Johns Hopkins University Press, 2008.

Cabak, Melanie A., Mark D. Groover, and Scott J. Wagers. "Health Care and the Wayman A.M.E. Church." *Historical Archaeology* 29.2 (1990): 55–76.

Callahan, Allen Dwight. *The Talking Book: African Americans and the Bible*. New Haven: Yale University Press, 2006.

Campbell, James T. *Songs of Zion: The African Methodist Episcopal Church in the United States and South Africa*. New York: Oxford University Press, 1995.

Carter, Tomeiko Ashford. "The Sentiment of the Christian Serial Novel: *The Curse of Caste; or The Slave Bride* and the AME *Christian Recorder*." *African American Review* 40.4 (Winter 2006): 717–730.

Case, Jay Riley. *An Unpredictable Gospel: American Evangelicals and World Christianity, 1812–1920*. New York: Oxford University Press, 2012.

Cavitch, Max. *American Elegy: The Poetry of Mourning from the Puritans to Walt Whitman*. Minneapolis: University of Minnesota Press, 2007.

Chatterjee, Partha. *The Nation and Its Fragments: Colonial and Postcolonial Histories*. Princeton, NJ: Princeton University Press, 1993.

Clark-Lewis, Elizabeth. *First Freed: Washington, D.C. in the Emancipation Era*. Washington, DC: Howard University Press, 2002.

Clinton, Catherine. *Mrs. Lincoln: A Life*. New York: Harper Collins, 2009.

Cohen, Lara Langer. "'The Emancipation of Boyhood': Postbellum Teenage Subculture and the Amateur Press." *Common-place* 14.1 (Fall 2013). www.common-place.org/vol-14/no-01/cohen/.

Cohen, Lara Langer, and Jordan Stein, eds. *Early African American Print Culture*. Philadelphia: University of Pennsylvania Press, 2012.

Cohen, Michael. "Contraband Singing: Poems and Songs in Circulation during the Civil War." *American Literature* 82.2 (2010): 271–304.

Coker, Daniel. *A Dialogue between a Virginian and an African Minister*. Baltimore: Benjamin Edes, 1810.

Cole, Jean Lee. "Information Wanted: *The Curse of Caste, Minnie's Sacrifice,* and the *Christian Recorder*." *African American Review* 40.4 (Winter 2006): 731–742.

Collins, Julia C. *The Curse of Caste*. Eds. William L. Andrews and Mitch Kachun. New York: Oxford University Press, 2006.

Danky, James P., ed. *African American Newspapers and Periodicals: A National Bibliography*. Cambridge: Harvard University Press, 1998.

Dann, Martin E., ed. *The Black Press, 1827–1890: The Quest for National Identity*. New York: G. P. Putnam, 1971.

Davidson, Cathy. *Revolution and the Word: The Rise of the Novel in America*. New York: Oxford University Press, 1986.

DeLombard, Jeannine Marie. "African American Cultures of Print." *A History of the Book in America: Volume 3, The Industrial Book, 1840–1880*. Eds. Scott E. Casper, Jeffrey D. Groves, Steven W. Nissenbaum, and Michael Winship. Chapel Hill: University of North Carolina Press, 2007. 360–373.

Dodson, Jualynne E. *Engendering Church: Women, Power, and the AME Church*. Lanham, MD: Rowman and Littlefield, 2002.

Doesticks, Philander [Mortimer Thomson]. *The Witches of New York*. Philadelphia: T. B. Peterson, 1858.

Douglass, Frederick. *Autobiographies*. Ed. Henry Louis Gates Jr. New York: Library of America, 1994.

Eastman, Carolyn. *A Nation of Speechifiers: Making an American Public after the Revolution*. Chicago: University of Chicago Press, 2009.

Emancipation in the District of Columbia: Letter from the Secretary of the Treasury. [Washington] 1864.

Ernest, John. "Artless Stories, Simple Facts." Paper given at the Conference on Editorial Problems, University of Toronto, 2012 ("Editing Early African American Literature").

———. "Canals and Rivers." *African American Review* 44.4 (Winter 2011): 573–575.

———. *Liberation Historiography: African American Writers and the Challenge of History, 1794–1861*. Chapel Hill: University of North Carolina Press, 2004.

———. *A Nation within a Nation: Organizing African American Communities before the Civil War*. Lanham, MD: Ivan R. Dee, 2011.

Faust, Drew Gilpin. *This Republic of Suffering: Death and the American Civil War*. New York: Knopf, 2008.

Fishel, Leslie H. "Benjamin Lynch." *African American National Biography*. Eds. Henry Louis Gates Jr. and Evelyn Brooks Higginbotham. New York: Oxford University Press, 2008. 5: 336–338.

———. "George Thomas Downing." *African American National Biography*. Eds. Henry Louis Gates Jr. and Evelyn Brooks Higginbotham. New York: Oxford University Press, 2008. 3: 55–56.

Fleishner, Jennifer. *Mrs. Lincoln and Mrs. Keckly: The Remarkable Story of the Friendship between a First Lady and a Former Slave*. New York: Broadway Books, 2003.

Foreman, P. Gabrielle. "The *Christian Recorder*, Broken Families, and Educated Nations in Julia C. Collins's Civil War Novel *The Curse of Caste*." *African American Review* 40.4 (Winter 2006): 705–716.

———. "A Riff, A Call, and A Response: Reframing the Problem That Led to Us Being Tokens in Ethnic and Gender Studies; or Where Are We Going Anyway and with Whom Will We Travel?" *Legacy* 30.2 (2013): 306–322.

Foster, Frances Smith. "A Narrative of the Interesting Origins and (Somewhat) Surprising Developments of African American Print Culture." *American Literary History* 17.4 (Winter 2005): 714–740.

———. *'Til Death or Distance Do Us Part: Love and Marriage in Early African America*. New York: Oxford University Press, 2010.

———. *Written by Herself: Literary Production by African American Women, 1746–1892*. Bloomington: Indiana University Press, 1993.

Foster, Frances Smith, ed. *Love and Marriage in Early African America*. Lebanon, NH: Northeastern University Press, 2008.

Foster, Frances Smith, and Chanta Haywood. "Christian Recordings: Afro-Protestantism, Its Press, and the Production of African American Literature." *Religion and Literature* 27.1 (Spring 1995): 15–33.

Fraser, Rod. *The Champion of the Seas*. Glen Waverly, Victoria, Australia: Pilgrim Printing, 1999.

Gardner, Eric. "African American Women's Poetry in the *Christian Recorder*, 1855–1865: A Bio-Bibliography with Sample Poems." *African American Review* 40.4 (Winter 2006): 813–831.

———. "*The Complete Fortune Teller and Dream Book*: An Antebellum Text 'By Chloe Russel, A Woman of Colour.'" *New England Quarterly* 78.2 (June 2005): 259–288.

———. "'Each Atomic Part': Edmonia Goodelle Highgate's African American Transcendentalism." *Toward A Female Genealogy of Transcendentalism*. Eds. Jana Argersinger and Phyllis Cole. Athens: University of Georgia Press, 2014. 277–299.

———. "A 'New' Chapter from Frances Ellen Watkins Harper's *Sowing and Reaping*." *Common-place* 13.1 (October 2012). http://www.common-place.org/vol-13/no-01/gardner/.

———. "Remembered (Black) Readers: Subscribers to the *Christian Recorder*, 1864–1865." *American Literary History* 23.2 (Summer 2011): 229–259.

———. "Susan Paul Smith Vashon." *African American National Biography*. Eds. Henry Louis Gates Jr. and Evelyn Brooks Higginbotham. New York: Oxford University Press, 2008.

———. "Two Texts on Children and Christian Education by Maria W. Stewart." *PMLA* 123.1 (January 2008): 156–165.

———. *Unexpected Places: Relocating Nineteenth-Century African American Literature*. Jackson: University Press of Mississippi, 2009.

———. "'Yours for the Cause': The *Christian Recorder* Writings of Lizzie Hart." *Legacy, A Journal of American Women Writers* 27.2 (2010): 367–391.

Garvey, Ellen Gruber. *Writing with Scissors: American Scrapbooks from the Civil War to the Harlem Renaissance*. New York: Oxford University Press, 2012.

Gates, Henry Louis Jr., and R. J. Ellis. "Introduction" to Harriet Wilson's *Our Nig*. New York: Vintage, 2011. xiii–lxviii.

Gellner, Ernest. *Nations and Nationalism*. Ithaca, NY: Cornell University Press, 1983.

Gerber, David A. "Peter Humphries Clark." *African American National Biography*. Eds. Henry Louis Gates Jr. and Evelyn Brooks Higginbotham. New York: Oxford University Press, 2008. 2: 299–300.

Glaude, Eddie. *Exodus! Religion, Race, and Nation in Early 19th Century Black America*. Chicago: University of Chicago Press, 2000.

Gooding, James Henry. *On the Altar of Freedom: A Black Soldier's Civil War Letters from the Front*. Amherst: University of Massachusetts Press, 1991.

Green, Augustus. *A Brief Account of the Re-Organization of the BME Church*. Detroit: O.S. Gulley, 1872.

———. *A Discourse for the Times, on Our Condition as It Is and Might Be*. Philadelphia: Hughes and Company, 1853.

———. *The Life of the Rev. Dandridge F. Davis of the African M. E. Church*. Pittsburgh: B. F. Peterson, 1850.

———. *A Treatise on the Episcopacy of the African M. E. Church*. Pittsburgh: N. M. Poindexter, 1845.

Greeson, Jennifer. "'Ruse It Well': Reading, Power, and the Seduction Plot in *The Curse of Caste*." *African American Review* 40.4 (Winter 2006): 769–778.

Gutjahr, Paul. *An American Bible: A History of the Good Book in the United States, 1777–1880*. Stanford, CA: Stanford University Press, 1999.

Hack, Daniel. "Close Reading at a Distance: The African Americanization of *Bleak House*." *Critical Inquiry* 34.4 (Summer 2008): 729–753.

Hall, Stephen G. *A Faithful Account of the Race: African American Historical Writing in Nineteenth-Century America*. Chapel Hill: University of North Carolina Press, 2009.

Handy, James A. *Scraps of African Methodist Episcopal History*. Philadelphia: AME Book Concern, 1902.

Hanses, Mathias. "Wiley Lane." *African American National Biography*. Eds. Henry Louis Gates Jr. and Evelyn Brooks Higginbotham. New York: Oxford University Press, 2008. Online supplement accessed through http://o-www.oxfordaasc.com.library.svsu.edu/article/opr/t0001/e4683.

Harper, Frances Ellen Watkins. *A Brighter Coming Day: A Frances Ellen Watkins Harper Reader*. Ed. Frances Smith Foster. New York: Feminist Press of CUNY, 1990.

Harrison, Thomas G. *The Career and Reminiscences of an Amateur Journalist and a History of Amateur Journalism*. Indianapolis: Thomas G. Harrison, 1883.

Haywood, Chanta. "Constructing Childhood: The *Christian Recorder* and Literature for Black Children, 1854–1865." *African American Review* 36.3 (Autumn 2002): 417–428.

———. *Prophesying Daughters: Black Women Preachers and the Word, 1823–1913*. Columbia: University of Missouri Press, 2003.

Herz, Walter. "Peter H. Clark." *Dictionary of Unitarian and Universalist Biography*. Eds. Barry Andrews et. al. Scituate, MA: Unitarian Universalist History and Heritage Society, 2006. http://uudb.org/articles/peterclark.html.

Hewitt, Elizabeth. *Correspondence and American Literature, 1770–1865*. Cambridge: Cambridge University Press, 2005.

Hobson, Christopher Z. *The Mount of Vision: African American Prophetic Tradition, 1800–1950*. New York: Oxford University Press, 2012.

Hollandsworth, James G. Jr. *An Absolute Massacre: The New Orleans Race Riot of July 30, 1866*. Baton Rouge: Louisiana State University, 2001.

Hoover, Ethel D. "Retail Prices after 1850." *Trends in the American Economy in the Nineteenth Century*. Ed. William N. Parker. Washington, DC: National Bureau of Economic Research, 1960. 141–190.

Hovde, David M. "The Library Is a Valuable Hygienic Appliance." *Reading for Moral Progress, University of Illinois Occasional Papers* 207 (1997): 19–42.

——— "The U.S. Christian Commission's Library and Literacy Programs for the Union Military Forces in the Civil War." *Libraries & Culture* 24.3 (Summer 1989): 295–316.

Hutton, Frankie. *The Early Black Press in America, 1827–1860*. Westport, CT: Greenwood Press, 1993.

Irvine, Russell W. "Martin H. Freeman of Rutland: America's First Black College Professor and Pioneering Black Social Activist." *Rutland Historical Society Quarterly* 26.3 (1996): 71–99.

Ito, Akiyo. "Olaudah Equiano and the New York Artisans: The First American Edition of *The Interesting Narrative of the Life of Olaudah Equiano, or Gustavus Vassa, the African*." *Early American Literature* 32.1 (1997): 82–101.

Jackson, Cassandra. "Frances Ellen Watkins Harper." *African American National Biography*. Eds. Henry Louis Gates Jr. and Evelyn Brooks Higginbotham. New York: Oxford University Press, 2008. 4: 69–70.

Jackson, Leon. *The Business of Letters: Authorial Economies in Antebellum America*. Stanford, CA: Stanford University Press, 2008.

———. "The Talking Book and the Talking Book Historian: African American Cultures of Print—The State of the Discipline." *Book History* 13 (2010): 251–308.

James, Jennifer. *A Freedom Bought with Blood: African American War Literature from the Civil War to World War II*. Chapel Hill: University of North Carolina Press, 2007.

Jeffrey, Julie Roy. *Abolitionists Remember: Antislavery Autobiographers and the Unfinished Work of Emancipation*. Chapel Hill: University of North Carolina Press, 2008.

Johnson, Abby Arthur, and Ronald Maberry Johnson. *Propaganda and Aesthetics: The Literary Politics of Afro-American Magazines in the Twentieth Century*. Amherst: University of Massachusetts Press, 1979.

Johnson, Robert, and Alan Roberts, "Young, John (1827–1907)." *Australian Dictionary of Biography*, National Centre of Biography, Australian National University, http://adb.anu.edu.au/biography/young-john-4904/text8211.

Jun, Helen. "Black Orientalism: Nineteenth Century Narratives of Race and US Citizenship." *American Quarterly* 58.4 (December 2006): 1047–1066.

Kachun, Mitch. "Interrogating the Silences: Julia C. Collins, 19th-Century Black Readers and Writers, and the *Christian Recorder*." *African American Review* 40.4 (Winter 2006): 649–659.

Kaser, David. *Books and Libraries in Camp and Battle: The Civil War Experience*. Westport, CT: Greenwood Press, 1984.

Lee, Mary E. Ashe. "Afmerica." *Nineteenth-Century American Women Poets: An Anthology*. Ed. Paula Bernat Bennett. Malden, MA: Blackwell, 1998. 466–471.

Leonard, Keith. *Fettered Genius: The African American Bardic Poet from Slavery to Civil Rights*. Charlottesville: University of Virginia Press, 2006.

Levander, Carolyn. "Sutton Griggs and the Borderlands of Empire." *American Literary History* 22.1 (Spring 2010): 57–84.

Levine, Robert. "The Early African American Novel." *The Cambridge History of the American Novel*. Eds. Leonard Cassuto, Claire Virginia Eby, and Benjamin Reiss. Cambridge: Cambridge University Press, 2011. 267–282.

——. *Martin R. Delany: A Documentary Reader*. Chapel Hill: University of North Carolina Press, 2003.

Levstik, Frank. "George Boyer Vashon." *African American National Biography*. Eds. Henry Louis Gates Jr. and Evelyn Brooks Higginbotham. New York: Oxford University Press, 2008. 8: 23–24.

Lincoln, C. Eric, and Lawrence H. Mamiya. *The Black Church in the African American Experience*. Durham, NC: Duke University Press, 1990.

Little, Lawrence S. *Disciples of Liberty: The African Methodist Episcopal Church in the Age of Imperialism, 1884–1916*. Knoxville: University of Tennessee Press, 2000.

Loghran, Trish. *The Republic in Print: Print Culture in the Age of U. S. Nation Building, 1770–1870*. New York: Columbia University Press, 2007.

Looby, Christopher. *Voicing America: Language, Literary Form, and the Origins of the United States*. Chicago: University of Chicago Press, 1996.

Lorang, Elizabeth, and R. J. Weir. "'Will Not These Days Be by Thy Poets Sun': Poems of the *Anglo-African* and *National Anti-Slavery Standard*, 1863–1864." *Scholarly Editing* 34 (2013). http://www.scholarlyediting.org/2013/editions/intro.cwnewspaperpoetry.html.

Lutes, Jean Marie. "Beyond the Bounds of the Book: Periodical Studies and Women Writers of the Late Nineteenth and Early Twentieth Centuries." *Legacy* 27.2 (2010): 336–356.

Maffly-Kipp, Laura. *Setting Down the Sacred Past: African American Race Histories*. Cambridge: Harvard University Press, 2010.

Masur, Kate. *An Example for All the Land: Emancipation and the Struggle over Equality in Washington, D.C.* Chapel Hill: University of North Carolina Press, 2010.

——. "A Filmmaker's Imagination, and a Historian's." *Chronicle of Higher Education* November 30, 2012.

——. "In Spielberg's *Lincoln*, Passive Black Characters." *New York Times* November 12, 2012.

May, Cedric. *Evangelism and the Black Atlantic, 1760–1835*. Athens: University of Georgia Press, 2008.

McElroy, A. *McElroy's Philadelphia City Directory*. Philadelphia: A. McElroy, 1842–1877.

McGill, Meredith. *American Literature and the Culture of Reprinting, 1834–1853*. Philadelphia: University of Pennsylvania Press, 2003.

McHenry, Elizabeth. *Forgotten Readers: Recovering the Lost History of African American Literary Societies*. Durham, NC: Duke University Press, 2002.

McPherson, James M. *The Negro's Civil War: How American Negroes Felt and Acted during the War for Union*. New York: Pantheon, 1965.

Menard, J. Willis. *Lays from Summer Lands*. Eds. Larry Eugene Rivers, Richard Matthews, and Canter Brown Jr. Tampa: University of Tampa Press, 2002.

Meyer, Lars. "Safeguarding Collections at the Dawn of the 21st Century: Describing Roles & Measuring Contemporary Preservation Activities in ARL Libraries." Washington,

DC: Association of Research Libraries, 2009. http://www.libqual.org/documents/admin/safeguarding-collections.pdf.

Miall, David S. "Empirical Approaches to Studying Literary Readers." *Book History* 9 (2006): 291–311.

Middleton, Stephen. *The Black Laws in the Old Northwest: A Documentary History.* Westport, CT: Greenwood Press, 1993.

Miller, Monica. *Slaves to Fashion: Black Dandyism and the Styling of Black Diasporic Identity.* Durham, NC: Duke University Press, 2009.

Mitchell, Koritha. *Living with Lynching: African American Lynching Plays, Performance, and Citizenship, 1890–1930.* Urbana: University of Illinois Press, 2011.

Montague, W. L. *Biographical Record of the Alumni of Amherst College during the First Half Century, 1821-1871.* Amherst: np, 1883.

Moody, Joycelyn. *Sentimental Confessions: Spiritual Narratives of Nineteenth-Century African American Women.* Athens: University of Georgia Press, 2003.

Mossell, Gertrude. *The Work of Afro-American Women.* New York: Oxford University Press, 1988.

Mulvey, Christopher. "Liberating an African American Text: Editing *Clotel* for an Electronic Century." *Critical Voicings of Black Liberation: Resistance and Representations in the Americas.* Eds. Kimberly L. Phillips et. al. Munster, Germany: LIT Verlag, 2003. 163–175.

Nerone, John. "Newspapers and the Public Sphere." *A History of the Book in America: Volume 3, The Industrial Book, 1840–1880.* Eds. Scott E. Casper, Jeffrey D. Groves, Steven W. Nissenbaum, and Michael Winship. Chapel Hill: University of North Carolina Press, 2007. 230–248.

Newman, Richard. *Freedom's Prophet: Bishop Richard Allen, the AME Church, and the Founding Fathers.* New York: New York University Press, 2009.

Newman, Richard, Patrick Rael, and Phillip Lapsansky, eds. *Pamphlets of Protest: An Anthology of Early African American Protest Literature, 1790–1860.* New York: Routledge, 2001.

Nord, David Paul. *Communities of Journalism: A History of American Newspapers and Their Readers.* Urbana: University of Illinois Press, 2001.

———. *Faith in Reading: Religious Publishing and the Birth of Mass Media in America, 1790–1860.* New York: Oxford University Press, 2004.

———. "A Republican Literature: A Study of Magazine Reading and Readers in Late Eighteenth-Century New York." *American Quarterly* 40.1 (1988): 42–64.

Nwankwo, Ifeoma. *Black Cosmopolitanism: Racial Consciousness and Transnational Identity in the Nineteenth Century Americas.* Philadelphia: University of Pennsylvania Press, 2005.

O'Brien, Colleen. "What the Dickens?: Representations of Slavery and Intertextual Influence in Julia Collins's *The Curse of Caste; or, The Slave Bride*." *African American Review* 40.4 (Winter 2006): 661–685.

Owens, A. Nevell. *Formation of the African Methodist Episcopal Church in the Nineteenth Century: Rhetoric of Identification.* New York: Palgrave Macmillan, 2014.

Pawley, Christine. "Beyond Market Models and Resistance: Organizations as a Middle Layer in the History of Reading." *Library Quarterly* 79.1 (January 2009): 73–93.

Payne, Daniel. *Biography of Rev. David Smith of the AME Church*. Xenia, OH: Xenia Gazette Office, 1881.

———. *History of the African Methodist Episcopal Church*. Nashville: AME Sunday School Union, 1891.

———. *Recollections of Seventy Years*. Nashville: AME Sunday School Union, 1888.

———. *Semi-Centenary and Retrospection of the African Methodist Episcopal Church*. Baltimore: Sherwood and Company, 1866.

———. *A Treatise on Domestic Education*. Cincinnati: Cranston and Stowe for the Author, 1885.

Pearce, Larry Wesley. "Enoch K. Miller and the Freedmen's Bureau." *Arkansas Historical Quarterly* 31 (Winter 1972): 305–327.

Penn, I. Garland. *The Afro-American Press and Its Editors*. Springfield, MA: Wiley and Company, 1891.

Peterson, Carla. *"Doers of the Word": African American Women Speakers and Writers in the North (1830–1880)*. New York: Oxford University Press, 1995.

Pierce, Yolanda. *"Hell without Fires": Slavery, Christianity, and the Antebellum Spiritual Narrative*. Gainesville: University Press of Florida, 2005.

Pratt, Lloyd. "Stranger History." *J19: The Journal of Nineteenth-Century Americanists* 1.1 (Spring 2013): 154–160.

Price, Leah. "Reading: The State of the Discipline." *Book History* 7 (2004): 303–320.

Pride, Armistead S., and Clint C. Wilson II. *A History of the Black Press*. Washington, DC: Howard University Press, 1997.

Quarles, Benjamin. *Lincoln and the Negro*. New York: Oxford University Press, 1962.

Raboteau, Albert. *Slave Religion: The "Invisible Institution" in the Antebellum South*. New York: Oxford University Press, 1979.

Redkey, Edwin, ed. *A Grand Army of Black Men: Letters from African American Soldiers in the Union Army, 1861–1865*. Cambridge: Cambridge University Press, 1992.

Reno, Lydia M. *Early Buds*. Boston: James Monroe and Co., 1853.

Richards, Eliza. "Correspondent Lines: Poetry, Journalism, and the US Civil War." *ESQ* 54 (2008): 145–170.

Rivers, Larry, and Canter Brown Jr. *Laborers in the Vineyard of the Lord: The Beginnings of the AME Church in Florida, 1865–1895*. Gainesville: University Press of Florida, 2001.

Rooks, Noliwe. *Ladies' Pages: African American Women's Magazines and the Culture That Made Them*. New Brunswick, NJ: Rutgers University Press, 2004.

Rowell, George P. *American Newspaper Directory*. New York: George P. Rowell and Company, 1869–1887. Available online at http://www.loc.gov/rr/news/news_research_tools/ayersdirectory.html.

Rusert, Britt. "Types of Mankind: Visualizing Kinship in Afro-Native America." *Common-place* 13.1 (October 2012). http://www.common-place.org/vol-13/no-01/tales/.

Sandweiss, Martha. *Passing Strange: A Tale of Gilded Age Love and Deception across the Color Line*. New York: Penguin, 2009.

Savage, Kirk. *Standing Soldiers, Kneeling Slaves: Race, War, and Monument in Nineteenth Century America*. Princeton, NJ: Princeton University Press, 1997.

Schuetze, Sarah. "Ill Fated: The Disease of Racism in Julia Collins's *The Curse of Caste*." *Legacy* 30.1 (2013): 82–100.

Scruggs, Lawson A. *Women of Distinction, Remarkable in Works and Invincible in Character.* Raleigh, NC: L.A. Scruggs, 1893.
Seraile, William. *Fire in His Heart: Benjamin Tucker Tanner and the AME Church.* Knoxville: University of Tennessee Press, 1998.
———. *Voice of Dissent: Theophilus Gould Steward (1843–1924) and Black America.* Brooklyn: Carlson Publishing, 1991.
Sherman, Joan. *African American Poetry of the Nineteenth-Century.* Urbana: University of Illinois Press, 1992.
———. *Invisible Poets: Afro-Americans of the Nineteenth Century.* Second Ed. Urbana: University of Illinois Press, 1989.
Sicherman, Barbara. "Ideologies and Practices of Reading." *A History of the Book in America: Volume 3, The Industrial Book, 1840–1880.* Eds. Scott E. Casper, Jeffrey D. Groves, Steven W. Nissenbaum, and Michael Winship. Chapel Hill: University of North Carolina Press, 2007. 279–302.
Sinha, Manisha. "Allies for Emancipation?: Lincoln and Black Abolitionists." *Our Lincoln: New Perspectives on Lincoln and His World.* Ed. Eric Foner. New York: W.W. Norton, 2008. 167–196.
———. "Lincoln Again." *History Workshop Online* February 24, 2013. Online at http://www.historyworkshop.org.uk/lincoln-again/.
Smith, C. S. *A History of the African Methodist Episcopal Church.* Philadelphia: Book Concern of the AME Church, 1922.
Smith, Dinitia. "A Slave Story is Rediscovered." *New York Times* October 28, 2006.
Smith, Theophus. *Conjuring Culture: Biblical Formations of Black America.* New York: Oxford University Press, 1994.
Spady, James. "Robert Mara Adger." *Africana: The Encyclopedia of the African and African American Experience.* Eds. Kwame Anthony Appiah and Henry Louis Gates Jr. New York: Oxford University Press, 2005. 34–35.
Steele, Jeffrey. "The Gender and Racial Politics of Mourning." *An Emotional History of America.* Eds. Peter N. Stearns and Jan Lewis. New York: New York University Press, 1998. 91–106.
Steinroetter, Vanessa. "'Reading the List': Casualty Lists and Civil War Poetry." *ESQ* 59.1 (Spring 2013): 48–78.
Sterling, Dorothy. *We Are Your Sisters: Black Women in the Nineteenth Century.* New York: W. W. Norton, 1984.
Stoddard, Richard Henry. *Abraham Lincoln: An Horatian Ode.* New York: Bunce and Huntington, 1865.
Swift, David. *Black Prophets of Justice: Activist Clergy before the Civil War.* Baton Rouge: Louisiana State University Press, 1989.
Tanner, Benjamin Tucker. *Apology for African Methodism.* Baltimore: np, 1867.
———. *Outline of Our History and Government.* Philadelphia: Grant, Faires, and Rodgers, 1884.
Thorpe, Sheldon B. *The History of the 15th Connecticut Volunteers in the War for the Defense of the Union, 1861–1865.* New Haven, CT: Price, Lee, and Adkins, 1893.
Tilmon, Levin. *A Brief Miscellaneous Narrative of the More Early Part of the Life of L. Tilmon.* Jersey City, NJ: W.W. and L.A. Pratt, 1853.

Townsend, Craig D. *Faith in Their Own Color: Black Episcopalians in Antebellum New York City*. New York: Columbia University Press, 2005.

Tripp, Bernell. *Origins of the Black Press, New York, 1827–1847*. Northport, AL: Vision, 1992.

Turner, Henry McNeal. *Freedom's Witness: The Civil War Correspondence of Henry McNeal Turner*. Ed. Jean Lee Cole. Morgantown: West Virginia University Press, 2013.

———. *The Genius and Theory of Methodist Polity*. Philadelphia: Publication Department, AME Church, 1885.

Turner, Justin G., and Linda Levitt Turner. *Mary Todd Lincoln: Her Life and Letters*. New York: Alfred A. Knopf, 1972.

U[nited]. S[tates]. C[hristian]. C[omission]. *Facts, Principles, and Progress*. Philadelphia: C. Sherman and Son, 1863.

Vashon, George Boyer. "Vincent Ogé" in *Autographs for Freedom*. Ed. Julia Griffiths. Auburn, NY: Alden, Beardsley, and Co., 1854. 44–60.

Vogel, Todd, ed. *The Black Press: New Literary and Historical Essays*. New Brunswick, NJ: Rutgers University Press, 2001.

Walker, Clarence E. *A Rock in a Weary Land: The African Methodist Episcopal Church during the Civil War and Reconstruction*. Baton Rouge: Louisiana State University Press, 1982.

Warner, Michael. *Letters of the Republic: Publication and the Public Sphere in Eighteenth-Century America*. Cambridge: Harvard University Press, 1990.

Warren, Joyce. *Fanny Fern: An Independent Woman*. New Brunswick, NJ: Rutgers University Press, 1992.

Warren, Kenneth. *What Was African American Literature?* Cambridge: Harvard University Press, 2011.

Washington, John E. *They Knew Lincoln*. New York: E. P. Dutton, 1942.

Wayman, Alexander. *Cyclopedia of African Methodism*. Baltimore: Methodist Episcopal Book Depository, 1882.

———. *My Recollections of African M. E. Ministers*. Philadelphia: AME Book Rooms, 1881.

White, Charles Frederick. *Who's Who in Philadelphia: A Collection of Thirty Biographical Sketches of Philadelphia Colored People*. Philadelphia: AME Book Concern, 1912.

Williams, Gilbert Anthony. The Christian Recorder, *Newspaper of the African Methodist Episcopal Church: History of a Forum for Ideas, 1854–1902*. Jefferson, NC: McFarland, 1996.

Williams, Heather Andrea. *Help Me to Find My People: The African American Search for Family Lost in Slavery*. Chapel Hill: University of North Carolina Press, 2012.

[Willson, Joseph.] *Sketches of the Higher Classes of Colored Society in Philadelphia*. Philadelphia: Merrihew and Thompson, 1841.

Wilson, Keith P. *Campfires of Freedom: The Camp Life of Black Soldiers During the Civil War*. Kent, OH: Kent State University Press, 2002.

Winch, Julie. *The Elite of Our People: Joseph Willson's Sketches of Black Upper-Class Life in Antebellum Philadelphia*. University Park, PA: Pennsylvania State University Press, 2000.

Wittenborg, Karin. "A Librarian Looks at Preservation." Paper presented at "Do We Want to Keep our Newspapers?" Conference, University of London, March 2001. http://www.arl.org/preserv/presresources/wittenborg.shtml.

Wong, Edlie. "'Neither is Memory Always Thus Avenging': Longing for Kinship in Julia C. Collins's *Curse of Caste* and the *Christian Recorder*." *African American Review* 40.4 (Winter 2006): 687–704.

Wood, Joseph R. *The Moral of Molliston Madison Clark*. Lewiston, NY: E. Mellen, 1990.

Wood, Marcus. *The Horrible Gift of Freedom: Atlantic Slavery and the Representation of Emancipation*. Athens: University of Georgia Press, 2010.

Woseley, Roland E. *The Black Press USA*. Ames: Iowa State University Press, 1971.

Wright, Richard R. *Centennial Encyclopedia of the African Methodist Episcopal Church*. Philadelphia: [AME Book Concern], 1916.

Yacovone, Donald. "Lewis Henry Douglass." *African American National Biography*. Eds. Henry Louis Gates Jr. and Evelyn Brooks Higginbotham. New York: Oxford University Press, 2008. Online supplement accessed through http://0-www.oxfordaasc.com.library.svsu.edu/article/opr/t0001/e4717.

———. "Mark Réné De Mortie and Louisa De Mortie." *African American National Biography*. Eds. Henry Louis Gates Jr. and Evelyn Brooks Higginbotham. New York: Oxford University Press, 2008. Online supplement accessed through http://0-www.oxfordaasc.com.library.svsu.edu/article/opr/t0001/e4715.

Yellin, Jean Fagan. *The Pen Is Ours: A Listing of Works by and about African American Women before 1910*. New York: Oxford University Press, 1991.

Zboray, Ronald J., and Mary Saracino Zboray. *Literary Dollars and Social Sense: A People's History of the Mass Market Book*. New York: Routledge, 2005.

{ INDEX }

Note: Locators followed by the letter 'n' refer to notes.

"A. B.," 135–136
"A. C. W.," 213–215
Accessible Archives, 28, 257n15, 263n11, 265n15, 278n13
Adger, Daniel
   Recorder letters of, 19, 168, 179–187, 189–192, 292n17, 292n19–20, 293n25, 293n27–33, 294n34
   life and circle of, 179–187, 292n21, 293n27–28
Adger, Elizabeth, 179, 292n18
Adger, James, 181, 292n21–26, 294n34
Adger, John George, 292n21
Adger, Joseph, 292n21
Adger, Mary Ann Morong, 179, 182
Adger, Robert, 64, 179–180, 182, 292n19–21
Adger, Robert Mara, 179, 292n18
Adger, William, 179
"Afamerica," 211, 297n22
African American Newspapers and Periodicals, 29, 38, 259n21
African American soldiers,
   in the 4th USCI (also 4th National Guard and 4th Corps de Afrique), *127*, 128
   in the 6th USCI, 115
   in the 14th USCI, 136
   in the 22nd USCI, 152
   in the 25th USCI, 112, 128–129, 205, 296n6
   in the 26th USCI, 136, 224, 285n2
   in the 27th USCI, 90, 144
   in the 28th USCI, 129–130
   in the 29th USCI, 144
   in the 32nd USCI, 297n19
   in the 35th USCI, 297n19
   in the 43rd USCI, 224
   in the 76th USCI, 128, 276n68
   in the 102nd USCI, 297n19
   in the Massachusetts 54th, 154, 162, 297n19, 296n6
   in the Massachusetts 55th, 297n19
   in the New York 185th, 191
   campaigns to send the *Recorder* to, 54, 76, 88–91, 274n48
   reading and writing of, 11, 19, 28, 72, 77, 127–131, 135–137, 151–158, *154*, 164, 178, 223, 227–228, 234–235, 251, 254, 274n46, 276n68, 288n26, 288n28, 289n30
   See also specific soldiers listed by name.
African Civilization Society, 284n66
African Methodist Episcopal Church
   Bishops of, 3, 15–16, 24, 26–27, 31–32, 41, 44–45, 49, 52–54, 56–57, *58*, 59, 132, 140, 142, 177, 262n3, 266n19
   Book Concern of, 26–27, 31, 34–41, 45–68, 63, 71–80, 84, 87, 92–93, 98, 100, 105, 107, 131, 142, 144, 146, 213, 266n19, 267n28, 269n46, 269n50, 269n52, 271n13, 271n18, 272n26, 273n36, 274n38, 275n51, 278n11, 286n8, 292n20
   Discipline of, 14–15, 26–27, 33–34, 37, 41, 49–50, 54, 59, 65, 68, 78, 94, 140–142, 176, 265n17, 266n20, 267n37, 272n20, 272n26, 286n9
   structure of, 14–16, 26–27, 30–34
   See also individual figures, entities, and events listed by name.
African Methodist Episcopal Church General Conference
   of 1844, 75, 140–141, 266n19
   of 1852, 27, 31, 36
   of 1856, 37, 39, 51
   of 1860, 40–41
   of 1864, 31, 49–52, 68, 72, 269n48–50
   of 1868, 41, 56–59, 213
   of 1872, 44
African Methodist Episcopal Church Magazine, 24, 34, 262n4, 266n22
Allabach, Peter H., 233
Allegheny Institute, 113
Allen, Richard, 26–27, 30, *58*, 144, 149, 256n9, 279n17
"Aleph," 148, 288n22
Alexander, James M., 123
"Alexandrina Lucilla Morimer" *see* Harriet Reynolds Krauth
Alternative medicine, 80–82, 242, 275n56
American Missionary Association (AMA), 187, 194, 276n72, 285n72
Amherst College, 23, 128

Anderson, Benedict, 14, 34, 260n25
Anderson, Mary J. C., 277n73
Andrews, William L., 10–11, 227, 230–235, 248, 259n20, 299n4, 300n8, 300n11, 301n18
Angell, Steven, 26–27, 256n9
Anglo-African Magazine, 227
Appomattox, 191, 253
Arnett, Benjamin W., 3
Ashe, Adelia, 297n22
Ashe, Mary E., 165, 211–212, 297n22, 298n23
Ashe, Simon, 297n22
Ashmun Institute, 287n18
Australia, 168, 179–186, 192, 292n17, 292n21–294n34
Avery College, 79

Bacon, Jacqueline, 10
Bailey, Julius, 24, 26, 113, 165, 256n9
Baker, Nicholson, 265n16
Ball and Thomas, 126
Ballard, John, 270n6
Banneker Institute, 69, 180
Banton, William C., 273n36
Barker, J. W., 115, 282n42
Barrett, Edward, 191
Bassard, Katherine Clay, 11
Beard, John W., 115–116, 282n43
Beecher, Lyman, 131
Bell, James Madison, 131
Bell, Philip, 91, 188, 290n5
Beman, Amos, 37
Bennett, Mrs. M., 80
Bennett, Paula Bernat, 197, 211
Bentley, Nancy, 17
Bernstein, Robin, 128, 285n70
Berry, George, 116
Bethel AME Church (Baltimore), 15
Bethel AME Church (Philadelphia; "Mother Bethel"), 28–29, 33, 51, 55, 62, 75, 266n23, 276n63, 279n17
Bethel Sabbath School (Hamilton, OH), 156
Bible, 27, 65, 78, 140–142, 151, 155–156, 162, 230, 286n7, 288n28
Biddle, Daniel R., 180–181
Billings, John D., 152
Bird School (Philadelphia), 180
Black Abolitionist Papers, 10, 28, 259n20, 263n11
Black Periodical Literature Project, 10, 28, 259n20
Blake, 227, 299n3
Bland, Julie, 283n52
Blassingame, John, 12
Bleak House, 226, 299n2
Bloomington, IL, 96–102, 132, 142, 277n1–278n11, 280n18, 281n28, 286n13

Blue, Belle *see* Belle Blue Claxton
Blue, Richard, 102, 278n9
Boling, Thomas H., 273n36
Bondwoman's Narrative, 227, 299n5, 302n33
Booth, Edwin, 274n47
Booth, John Wilkes, 251, 253, 274n47
Bowers, Thomas J., 80
Brayman, Mason, 114, 123, 284n61, 284n63
Breckinridge, R. J., 15
Bristol, Charles, 113
Bristol, Douglas, 124, 283n50
British Methodist Episcopal (BME) Church, 31, 49, 84, 107, 121, 144–145, 266n21, 267n37
Brock, John, 224
Brodie, G. W., 284n67
Brown, Candy Gunther, 73, 94, 276n71, 291n11
Brown, Canter Jr., 145, 286n4
Brown, Hallie Quinn, 297n22
Brown, Henry "Box," 282n42
Brown, James W., 80
Brown, John, 275n51
Brown, John Mifflin
    life and circle of, 3, 47, 50, 57–58, 142–145, 267n28
    work with the *Repository of Religion*, 47–48, 50, 178, 291n15
Brown, Lois, 11, 260n24
Brown, Mary Louisa, 47
Brown, Morris, 58, 141
Brown, Oliver Phelps, 81, 275n55
Brown, Solomon G., 295n6
Brown, William Wells, 131, 187, 227, 271n14, 275n51
Browning, Elizabeth Barrett, 191, 294n45
Browning, Orville Hickman, 2
Bruce, Blanche K., 116
Bruce, Dickson D., 11
Buchanan, Lewis, 129, 285n71
Buell, Kilbourne Ambrose, 282n40
Bullock, Penelope, 262n4, 267n35–36
Burch, Charles, 44–45
Burlingame, Michael, 2, 255n2, 255n6, 256n8
Burris, Andrew, 91
Burton, John, 136
Bustill, Joseph, 80–81, 238, 275n53
Bustill, Sarah, 80–81, 238, 275n53
Buttles, A. B., 104
Byron, Lord, 230

Cain, Richard, 93, 123, 298n22
Camp William Penn, 115
Campbell, J. G., 104
Campbell, Jabez Pitt
    at 1856 AME General Conference, 38–39
    at 1860 AME General Conference, 41, 46

Index

at 1864 AME General Conference, 50
collection of *Recorder* issues, 24, 28–30, 263n13–265n15, 267n31, 278n13, 298n25
educational efforts and writing of, 37, 142–144, 177–178, 286n11, 291n15
life and circle of, *38*, *58*, 188, 214, 278n14
as *Recorder* editor, 38–39, 45, 62, 65, 70, 267n31–33, 271n18, 273n33
Campbell, Mary A., *38*
Campbell, Robert, 66–67, 293n30
Carter, Alice, 113
Carter, James E., 211
Carter, Tomeiko, 237
Case, Jay, 144, 261n26, 302n26
Catto, Octavius, 180
Catto, William T., 36–37
Cavitch, Max, 197–198, 206, 214, 216–220, 223, 296n15–297n18, 298n30, 298n33
"Cerberus," 290n6
Champion of the Seas, 182–185
Charnock, Thomas, 80
Chesnutt, Charles, 13
Christian, Barbara, 11
Christian Herald, The, 24, 34–36, 267n27–28
Christian Recorder, The
advertisements in, 66, 71–72, 77–82, 100, 238, 242, 272n21, 275n51–56, 286n12
agents of, 5–6, 11, 36, 39, 43, 64, 77, 85–94, 100, 103, 123, 132, 144, 176, 232, 257n10, 269n52, 275n60, 276n66, 276n69, 276n73, 282n39
Campbell run of, 24, 28, 30, 263n13, 264n14, 265n15, 267n31, 278n13, 298n25
carriers of, 66, 86, 89, 275n62, 276n63
cataloging of, 29–30, 263n12–265n16, 273n33
distribution of, 89–132, 275n59, 275n61–285n77
early (pre-1860) history of, 24, 26–28, 31, 33–40, 262n4, 266n19–267n33
extant presences of, 28–30, 263n7–265n16
"Information Wanted" notices in, 11, 65, 82–83, 130, 136, 185, 247, 259n22 275n58, 298n30, 300n10
look and feel of, 70–72, 78, 273n33–35
notices (including marriage notices and obituaries) in, 11, 72, 82–83, 140, 170–171, 198, 275n57–59
offices of, 61–67, *63*, 270n1–11, 271n13, 271n19, 272n21–22
and periodical exchange, 83–84, 275n60
"Philadelphia Resolution," 44–45
printing of, 35–36, 39, 66–72, 269n45, 271n13, 271n16, 271n19–20
reprinting in, 70, 72, 77, 84–85, 174, 199, 219, 223–227, 287n16, 294n43, 295n3, 296n6

subscribers to, 8, 18–19, 45, 48, 51, 54, 59, 64, 66, 70, 73–80, 84–133, 138–139, 154–155, 160, 164, 168–170, 176, 180, 196, 205, 211, 220, 275n56, 276n73–285n77
by age, 115–116, 118–120, 282n43–45, 287n47–48
by gender, 111–112, 118–120, 281n32–33
by household configuration, 117–120, 147, 283n47–49
institutional, 131–132, 284n74–77
literacy of, 138–139
by location, 64, 86, 105–111, 281n27–31, 292n19
by marital status, 116–120, 282n45–283n49
via military groups, 127–131, 284n68–285n73
by occupation, 120–124, 283n50–58
by property reported, 124–126, 283n59–284n64
by race, 112–115, 281n34–282n42
See also individuals, texts, and entities listed by name.
Chronicling America, 29
Claflin, William, 114–115, 284n61, 284n63
Clark, Herbert, 271n17
Clark, James C., 80
Clark, Madison Molliston
life and circle of, 39, 50–51, 267n28, 267n30, 267n34
as *Recorder* editor, 36–39, 65, 67, 70, 74, 267n29, 267n31
Clark, Peter Humphries, 67, 271n15, 271n17
Claxton, Belle Blue, 102, 280n20
Claxton, James, 102
Clinton, Catherine, 8
Clotel, 131, 227, 299n3
Cohen, Lara Langer, 261n29, 271n17
Coker, Daniel, 26
Colder, Georgianna, 200, 203
Cole, Jean Lee, 236, 250, 256n9, 257n15, 260n24, 300n10
Collins, Annie, 301n17
Collins, Julia, 147, 158, 226–236, 248–251, 277n73, 300n14–301n17
See also Curse of Caste
Collins, Sarah C. ("Sadie"), 301n17
Collins, Simon C. *see* Stephen C. Collins
Collins, Stephen C., 232–235, 300n16, 301n17
Colored American, 66, 290n5
Colored Citizen (Cincinnati), 156, 163–164
Cook, George F., 123
Cook, Henry, 149
Cooper, Emily, 97, 102
Cooper, Daniel, 206
Cooper, Frisby J., 149, 288n20–21

Cooper, Nancy, 97–99, 101–102, 113, 120–122, 132, 278n9, 278n11, 281n28
Coppin, Fannie Jackson, 132
Cornell, John, 118, 283n47
Cornell, Mary, 118, 283n47
Crafts, Hannah, 227, 302n33
Craighead, James Geddes, 23
Curse of Caste, 11, 14, 20, 77, 80, 153, 158, 199, 294n43
   and education, 227, 230–231, 235–236, 247–251, 300n10, 300n13, 302n26
   and fortune telling, 236–245, 301n23, 302n32
   publication circumstances of, 226–228, 230–231, 234, 237, 240–242, 299n3–5, 302n34
   See also Curse of Caste, characters in
Curse of Caste, characters in
   Ellwood, Miss, 243–250, 302n31, 303n37
   Hays, Alfred, 229, 238, 301n21
   Hays, Juno 20, 228–230, 236–254, 300n10, 300n21, 302n27, 302n29–n32, 303n36–37
   Hays, Laura Tracy, 229, 238, 250, 301n21
   Jim, 248, 303n36
   Manville, 229, 238–239, 243, 247, 250, 302n35
   Neville, Claire, 20, 80, 228–230, 236–240, 242–251, 296n9, 300n7, 302n27, 302n31–32, 302n35, 303n36
   Ray, Martin, 243–245, 250, 302n29, 303n37
   Sayvord, Count, 229, 249
   Tracy, Colonel, 229, 238, 243, 246, 248, 301n21, 302n27, 302n35
   Tracy, Isabelle, 248
   Tracy, Lina, 228–229, 237–239, 242–244, 246–247, 249–251, 296n9, 302n35
   Tracy, Nellie Thornton, 248, 301n21–302n32
   Tracy, Nellie, 248
   Tracy, Richard, 229, 237–239, 242–250, 301n21, 302n35, 303n37

D'Aubigne, Jean Henri Merle, 141, 286n12
Daffin, Sarah ("Sallie"), 187–188, 213, 215–216, 236, 249, 294n38, 298n28, 300n13
Daniel A. Payne Literary Society, 148–149
Davis, Henderson, 205, 207
Davis, Henry, 107
Davis, James W., 205, 207
Davis, William J., 96–98, 101–102, 278n8
Dawson, James A., 288n28
Dawson, John, 152–153
"De Profundis," 191, 294n45
Decordover's Periodical Depot, 79, 86, 87
Deeper, E., 292n23
Delany, Martin, 11, 35–36, 66, 227, 253, 266n25–266n26, 281n36, 297n22
Demby, Angeline R., 219–222, 299n35

DeMortie, Lousia, 188, 283n56, 294n35
DeMortie, Mark Rene, 283n56
Devine, Jesse W., 111
Dickens, Charles. 226, 299n2
Dickinson, Andrew, 271n14
Divination, *see* fortune telling
Documenting the American South, 259n20, 266n21
Dodson, Jualynne, 165, 265n17, 300n12
Doolittle, John Birge, 282n41
Douglass, Frederick
   journalism of, 35, 66–67, 226, 266n26, 271n15, 273n33, 290n5, 299n2
   life and circle of, 23, 56, 77, 81, 128, 144, 180, 187–188, 198, 201, 218, 262n29, 287n13, 294n37, 294n40, 297n17, 298n33
   Narrative, 12–13, 16, 259n23
Douglass, Frederick Jr., 123
Douglass, Lewis, 67, 271n17
Douglass, Sarah M., 37, 39
Douglass Literary Society, 288n22
Dove, William A., 58, 93
Dowden, Mary, 65
Downing, Cordelia, 283n56
Downing, George, 283n56
Downing, Peter, 125, 283n59
Downing, Thomas, 104, 125, 283n59
Dowman, Mary M., 149
Drake, Joseph Rodman, 162
Draper, Daniel, 176
Drew University, 29, 263n12
Duerte, Mrs. H. S., 80
Duval, George, 224

Elegies, 19, 135, 191, 196–225
Elevator, 91
Ellis, Elsie, 296n6
Emancipation in DC, 2, 256n4
Emancipation Proclamation, 2, 173, 193, 233–234
Embry, J. C., 266n23
Emerson, Ralph Waldo, 12, 192
Equiano, Olaudah, 13, 279n17
Ernest, John, 12, 260n24, 262n29
Evans, Edward, 149

Fairweather, George, 276n66
Farrah, Bernard, 114, 284n61
Faust, Drew Gilpin, 204–207
Female Publication Society, 75
Fern, Fanny, 188, 294n42
Ferris, Stephen J., 216
Field, Abraham, 276n63
Fishel, Leslie, 55
Fisk University, 263n12
Fitzhugh, Nelson, 114, 276n66, 282n40, 284n64

Fletcher, Ryland, 114, 284n61
Flipper, Henry Ossian, 290n39
Foreman, Gabrielle, 12, 248, 261n29, 300n10
Fort Barrancas, 128
Fort Duane, 137, 285n2
Fort Morgan, 136
Fort Pickens, 129, 205
Fort Pillow, 136, 155, 158, 222
Fortunetelling, 236–245, 301n23, 302n32
Foster, Frances Smith, 10–12, 26–27, 140, 201, 258n19, 263n12, 265n15
Franklin, John Hope, 12
Frederick Douglass's Paper, 271n15, 273n33
Frederick Douglass School, 166
Freed people in the post-war South, 3, 52, 55, 90, 255n4, 269n53, 282n41, 285n72, 296n6
  and "contraband" relief efforts, 6–8, 214, 242
  and *Curse of Caste*, 234, 240, 242, 248–249, 303n36
  Recorder advice to, 145–146, 149, 151, 287n14
  teaching of, 160, 162, 164, 166–167, 186–188, 194
  See also individuals listed by name.
Freedmen's Aid Society (Xenia, OH), 160
Freedom's Journal, 10, 26
Freeman, Joseph, 149
Freeman, Martin H., 112, 123, 281n36
Frisby, Samuel C., 207

Gaddis, Maxwell, 78
Gaines, Wesley J., 3, 302n26
Gaiter, John, 124
Gaiter, Susan, 124
Gardiner, Peter, 72, 273n37
Garey, E. E., 34
Garnet Equal Rights League, 148
Garnet, Henry Highland, 186, 201, 287n18
Garrison, William Lloyd, 66, 180, 275n51
Gates, Henry Louis Jr., 12, 227,
George, George Freudberg, 219
Gettysburg, 128
Gibbs, Mary Eliza, 270n6
Gibbs, Peter, 123
Giddings, Joshua, 78
Gilchrist, Enoch, 231–232, 234, 250, 300n15, 301n18
Gleaves, Georgina, 80
Gooding, James Henry, 154
Goodrich, Charles Augustus, 141, 143
Gossin, Andrew J., 295n1
Gould, Theodore, 36, 64, 93, 269n52
Graham, Grafton H., 45
Grant, Abraham, 3
Grant, Nelson T., 125
Green, Augustus R., 24, 34–37, 40–41, 66, 84, 266n21–22, 267n27–29

Green, Julia, 232, 300n15
Greenwood, Mary E., 149
Greeson, Jennifer, 236, 245, 300n10
Grimes, Leonard, 257n15
Grimes, William W., 51
Gross, Ann E., 282n43

Habersham, Maria Ann, 284n65
Hall, Abraham Thompson, 96–98, 142, 147, 269n56, 277n1
Hamilton, Gail, 188, 294n42
Hamilton, Robert, 66, 91, 227, 299n3
Hamilton, Thomas, 66, 91, 227, 299n3
Hammon, Jupiter, 259n24
Hammond, Savage L., 39, 47, 126, 142, 284n64
Handy, James A., 3, 5, 257n11
"Hannibal," 269n54
Harding, Mrs. C. E., 80
Harding, Charlotte, 270n3
Harper, Frances Ellen Watkins
  life and circle of, 13, 66, 81, 104, 139, 142, 150–151, 187, 201, 275n52, 295n4, 298n26
  Recorder writings of, 37, 39, 150–151, 165, 196–197, 226, 228, 249, 259n24, 263n12, 265n15
Harper's New Monthly Magazine, 276n64
Harper's Weekly, 79
Hart, Julia, 135–136, 203, 208
Hart, Lizzie
  life and circle of, 76, 111, 135–137, 203, 207–210, 274n47, 285n1, 290n38
  Recorder writings of, 135–137, 156, 158–161, 194, 207–210, 214, 216, 218–220, 222, 231, 235, 285n2, 289n35, 298n34
Hartman, Saidiya, 12
Hawkins, S. Shorter, 80
Hawthorne, Nathaniel, 219
Hay, John, 256n8
Haywood, Chanta, 10, 26–27, 256n9, 258n19, 266n24, 267n32, 287n16
Hedden, Francis, 43–44, 268n42
Hedden, Sarah, 43, 268n42
Henry, John F., 97
Henson, Ann Eliza, 136
Henson, Oliver C., 122
Herley, John L., 206–207
Herman, Henry S., 289n34
Hewlett, Aaron Molineaux, 123, 283n57
Hidden Hand, The, 301n24
Highgate, Caroline, 187
Highgate, Charles (father of Edmonia G. Highgate), 186–187, 294n36–37
Highgate, Charles (brother of Edmonia G. Highgate, "Charlie"), 190–192

Highgate, Edmonia Goodelle
  life and circle of, 186–187, 190–195, 201, 249,
    294n36–37, 294n39–40, 296n13
  Recorder writing of, 19, 160, 166–168, 179,
    186–194, 203, 231, 235–236, 241, 244,
    290n1–4, 294n35, 294n43–46, 300n13
  and Transcendentalism, 13, 166–167, 192–193
Highgate, Hannah Francis, 186–187, 294n36
Hill, I. J., 144
Hobbs, Barnabas Coffin, 42
Hogarth, George, 34, 39, 266n22
Hogue, W. Lawrence, 12
Holcomb, Shepherd, 65
Holmes, John and Company, 81
Homeopathy, *see* alternative medicine
Hopkins, William H., 187
Horne, Thomas Hartwell, 141, 143
Houston, C. J., 273n36
Hovde, David, 152–153, 276n67
Howard, Oliver O., 114
Howard, Shadrach, 301n25
Howard University, 23, 29
Howe, Julia Ward, 222
Hughes, William, 132
Hunter, William, 64, 131, 135, 137, 271n18

"In the Cars," 196–204, 215, 225, 296n15
Incidents in the Life of a Slave Girl, 13
Indiana AME Literary Society, 267n34
Institute for Colored Youth, 66, 180, 237,
  269n45, 273n36, 287n17
Israel Church Reading Room (DC), 131–132, 135
Ito, Akiyo, 279n17

Jackson, Andrew, 4
Jackson, Mrs. E. A., 267n28
Jackson, Leon, 17, 84, 91, 261n29, 276n64, 276n71
Jackson, Thomas H., 161, 211
Jacobs, Harriet, 13, 16, 241, 262n29
Jeffrey, Julie Roy, 164, 251
Jenifer, John T., 211
Johnson, Andrew, 8, 56
Johnson, Ezra Rust, 123, 284n64
Johnson, J. H., 210–211
Johnson, J. R., 296n6
Johnson, J. W., 138
Johnson, Jacob S., 129
Johnson, James H. A., 263n9
Johnson, Jane, 80
Johnson, Joseph R., 299n2
Jones, Absalom, 26
Jones, Alfred, 124
Jones, Catherine, 136
Jones, Delilah, 124
Jones, William H., 36, 38–39

Jones, William T., 276n63
Jordan, Johnny, 136
Jun, Helen, 293n33

Kachun, Mitch, 10, 27, 227, 230–235, 248, 256n9,
  300n8, 300n11, 301n18
Kean, Charles, 182, 184, 293n32
Kean, Mrs. Charles (Ellen Tree), 184, 293n32
Keckley, Elizabeth, 6–9, 7, 132, 251, 254,
  257n13–15
Keene, Laura, 288n28
Ketchum, Alexander, 114
"Knitting the Socks," 289n35
Knox, Thomas E., 126
Krauth, Charles Porterfield, 172, 291n9–10
Krauth, Harriet Reynolds, 70, 164, 172–174, 176,
  178, 188, 291n10, 291n12–14

L'Ouverture Literary Assembly, 213
L'Ouverture, Toussaint, 275n51, 277n73, 293n30
Ladies Union Association, 81
Lane Seminary, 131, 285n76
Lane, Wiley, 23–24, 26, 36, 262n1, 262n3
Langston, John Mercer, 162, 187, 201
Lankford, W. S., 277n4–5, 286n13
Lapsansky, Phillip, 262n30
Lawrence, Thomas, 266n23
Lee, Benjamin F., 3, 211
Lee, Jarena, 158
Lee, Mary E. Ashe *see* Mary E. Ashe
Lee, Robert E., 252
Leekin, John, 150
Leonard, Keith, 197
"Letters from Olympus," 70, 164, 172–174, 176,
  178, 188, 291n10, 291n12–14
Levine, Robert, 35, 266n25, 299n5
Lewis, Abram D., 141
"A Life Day," 296n10
Lincoln, Abraham
  elegies to, 19, 190, 196–198, 210, 213, 217–225
  life and circle of, 6–8, 132, 251–253, 255n6,
    256n8, 258n16
  and Daniel Payne, 1–2, 4–9, 20, 255n1–2,
    255n7
  representations of, 4, 9, 56, 72, 160, 216, 254,
    256n7, 258n17, 288n23, 289n37, 298n32–34
Lincoln, Mary Todd, 6, 257n13
Lincoln, Willie, 1, 6
Lincoln University, 143–144
Literary Society of Wilmington (DE) AME
  Church, 149
Little Wesley AME Church (Philadelphia), 45,
  149
Little Wesley AME Church Literary Society,
  149

Index

Loguen, Jermain, 186–187
Longfellow, Henry Wadsworth, 230
Longfellow, William A., 80, 275n53
Lorang, Elizabeth, 296n7, 299n3
Lorde, Audre, 296n12
Loughran, Trish, 14, 260n25
Lovejoy, Elijah, 271n14
Loyal Georgian, 84
Lutheran and Missionary, 70, 164, 172–173, 291n10
Lynch, James
  as *Recorder* editor, 52–56, 61–62, 69–70, 72, 76, 82, 84–86, 88, 93–95, 99–100, 115, 131, 145–146, 170, 175–176, 257n12, 271n18, 274n38–39, 275n57, 275n60, 279n15
  life and circle of, 5, 52–54, 53, 64, 67, 88, 93, 142, 257n10, 269n52–53, 270n11, 285n75, 297n19

Mabines, William, 113
"Madam Julian," 242
Magarge, Charles, 80
Magee, John, 104
Malone, J. W., 98
Martin, J. Sella, 126
Massachusetts Anti-Slavery Society, 4
Massachusetts Female Anti-Slavery Society, 194
Masur, Kate, 9–10, 17
May, Cedric, 259n24
May, Frederick W. G., 114, 126, 284n61, 284n63
May, Samuel Joseph, 186–187
Mayhew, Isaiah, 273n36
McCaskill, Barbara, 12
McClellan, George B., 1
McCormick Theological Seminary, 285n76
McCown, Julie, 259n24
McDonald, William, 115, 282n41
McGill, Meredith, 84
McHenry, Elizabeth, 105, 131, 138, 148, 262n30, 286n3
McIntosh, Aeneas, 51
McKay, Nellie, 12
Meacham, Robert, 138–140, 144–146, 150–151
Melville, Herman, 13
Menard, John Willis, 69, 196, 295n4
Mercantile Library (Philadelphia), 285n76
Middlebury College, 113
Miller, Edward, 283n47
Miller, Enoch K., 112, 128–130, 285n72
Miller, Leah, 283n47
Miller, Louisa, 42, 213, 268n38
Miller, Mary *see* Mary Weaver
Miller, Monica, 120
Miranda see Clotel.
Mitchell, Koritha, 261n25

Mitchell, Samuel Augustus, 141
Mitchem, Johnston, 113, 142, 277n5
Moody, Joycelyn, 12
Moore, Charles O., 5, 257n11
Moore, Daniel W., 5, 131, 142, 257n10–11
Moral and Mental Improvement Association (Baltimore), 131
Morel, Junius C., 113, 123
Morgan, Albert T., 194, 295n47
Morgan, Caroline Highgate *see* Caroline Highgate
Morris, Mrs. E., 205, 296n6
Morris, Jared, 116
Morrison, Toni, 296n12
Mother Bethel AME Church (Philadelphia) *see* Bethel AME Church (Philadelphia)
Muirhead, Jack, 277n2
Myers, Frederick, 97, 142
Mystery, The, 11, 34–35, 66–67, 266n23, 266n25

National Convention of Colored Men of 1864, 187, 201–202
National Lincoln Monument Association, 224
Nazrey, Willis
  and the BME Church (Canada), 31, 40–42, 49–51, 144, 176–178, 267n37, 291n15
  life and circle of, 36–38, 45–46, 49–51, 58
Neale, John Mason, 77, 172
New York Ledger, 79, 301n24
New York Observer, 288n28
Newark AME Church, 43
Newman, Richard, 30, 262n30, 263n5, 279n17
Nichols, William, 122, 283n54
Nielsen, Aldon, 197
Norfolk, VA, 136, 187, 213, 215
North Star, The, 35, 115, 266n26, 282n42
Northup, Solomon, 79

Oberlin College, 42, 131, 187, 210, 212, 285n74
Obi, 241, 244
Olive Branch Boarding House, 80
Oswego (NY) Gentlemen and Ladies' Literary and Lyceum Association, 149
Otter, Samuel, 19
Our Nig, 227
Outridge, James Manly, 182–184

Pacific Appeal, 84, 91, 219, 223, 301n25
Paley, William, 141
Pardoe, Julia, 277n73
Parham, William, 123
Parker, Byrd, 266n23
Parker, Theodore, 114
Patent medicine, *see* alternative medicine
Patterson, Leonard, 51

Pawley, Christine, 18, 262n30
Payne, Daniel
  at 1844 AME General Conference, 140–141
  at 1860 AME General Conference, 41, 45
  at 1864 AME General Conference, 49–51
  and education, 27, 140–141, 151, 286n6
  life and circle of, 3, 15, 27, 36, 41–42, 49, 52, 58, 96, 141–142, 144–145, 148–149, 177, 252, 267n34, 268n37, 269n47, 291n15, 302n26
  and Abraham Lincoln, 1–2, 4–9, 20, 256n1–2, 256n7
  and Wilberforce, 252–253
  writing and editing of, 24, 34, 36–37, 39–40, 140–141, 176–177, 262n3, 263n10, 267n29, 267n33, 296n10
  See also Daniel A. Payne Literary Society
Payne, Eliza Jane, 252
Payne, James H., 90, 155–157, 289n31–n33
Pearce, Charles H., 145
Peck, Francis J., 148–149
Penn, I. Garland, 259n21
Pennington, James W. C., 37
Pennsylvania, University of, 179
Pennsylvania State Equal Rights League, 81
"Peregrinator," 219, 223, 299n37
"Periwinkle," 173
Peter, 206, 296n14
Peters, Charles, 115–116
Peterson, Carla, 12, 258n19
Philadelphia, 26, 36, 38–41, 49, 77–82, 128, 143, 148, 172, 179–182, 193, 214–215, 219, 242, 268n43, 271n29, 273n36, 274n41, 274n47, 276n72, 282n39, 289n35, 301n24
  Recorder subscribers in, 66, 84, 86–87, 91–92, 281n27, 292n19
  See also individuals and locations listed by name.
Philadelphia Conference (AME), 31, 37–45, 51–55, 59, 72–73, 76–77, 147, 269n50, 270n7, 286n11
Philadelphia Evening Telegraph, 85
Philadelphia Tribune, 84
"Philander Doesticks" *see* Mortimer Thompson
Philips, Mary J., 211
Phillips, H. S., 242
Phillips, Wendell, 275n51, 277n73
Pilkington, Mark, 115
Pinn, Anthony, 26–27, 256n9
Pitts, Reginald, 232–233, 300n15–301n17
Plymouth Congregational Church, 186–187
Port Hudson, 128
Porter, James, 123
Porter, Ebenezer, 141
Pratt, Lloyd, 17, 261n27–28
Presbyterian Herald, 228

Price, Henry, 207
Price, Mary, 207
Price, Rachel, 207
Princeton Journal, 147
Provincial Freeman, 42, 115, 282n42

Quarles, Benjamin, 1, 12, 255n1
Quinn Chapel (Chicago), 96
Quinn, William Paul, 34, 41–42, 51, 58, 90, 125, 266n23

Rachel, 209–210
Rael, Patrick, 262n30
Ralley, Anne, 115
Ranciere, Jacques, 17, 261n27
Randolph, Paschal Beverly, 188
Ray, Charles, 243
"Raymond" *see* Jacob A. Raymond.
Raymond, Jacob A., 136, 296n6
Read, Philander, 127–128, 276n68, 284n68
"Rector," 56
"Rectus," 56, 57
Redkey, Edwin, 130, 154
Redpath, James, 131, 227
Reno, Lydia M., 295n3
Repository of Religion and Literature
  in competition with the *Recorder*, 47–50
  history and content of, 1, 39–42, 178, 214, 226, 231, 256n7, 262n4, 267n36, 268n45, 291n15, 299n1
Revels, Hiram, 39, 123
Revels, Willis, 39–40, 50, 56, 142
Rhodes, Henry J., 5, 257n11
Riley, Girard, 114
Roberson, Richard, 202, 272n23
Roberts, Benjamin F., 66, 271n17
Rock, John S., 4, 123, 217
Rodgers, Anna, 272n26
Rodgers, James B., 68, 271n13, 272n24, 272n26
Ro(d)gers, Theodore, 136–137, 156, 285n2
Rooks, Noliwe, 263n12
Rose Cottage, 229, 243, 250
Ross, Liberty, 45
Rowell's *Newspaper Directory*, 85, 273n33
Rue, George, 93
Russel, Chloe, 241
Rutledge, William J., 280n18

Salter, Moses B., 3
Sampson, B. K., 163–164
Saxon, Armstead, 276n66
Saxton, Rufus, 114
Savage, Kirk, 251
Schieffelin, Samuel, 272n26
Schmucker, Samuel Simon, 141

Schuetze, Sarah, 300n10, 302n30
Scott, Dred, 104, 180, 303n35
Shakespeare, William, 148, 230, 288n28
"Shalom," 213
Shelley, Percy Bysshe, 174
Sherman, Joan, 12, 295n5, 296n10
Shorter, James, 57–58
Shurz, Carl, 255n7
Sickles, Martha D., 138, 145
Simms, Laura, 6, 257n11, 276n66
Simpson, Joshua McCarter, 123
Simpson, Sarah T., 255n4
Singleton, Grayson, 135–136
Singleton, Primos, 283n51
Singleton, Tamar, 283n51
Sinha, Manisha, 255n1
Slade, William, 6, 8–9, 132, 251, 254, 258n16
Slave narratives, 12–13, 16, 83, 259n20
Smalls, Robert, 123
Smith, Mrs. A. M., 120, 283n49
Smith, Anna Eliza, 207
Smith, Annie M.
    and other *Recorder* writers, 172, 178, 186, 199, 228, 235, 290n38
    Recorder subscriptions of, 120, 283n49
    Recorder writings of, 159–165, 289n36–37
Smith, Charles S., 49–50, 267n33 269n56, 278n11
Smith, Daniel, 253
Smith, David S., 5, 257n10–11
Smith, Edward, 207
Smith, Gerrit, 194
Smith, Harriet, 207
Smith, James McCune, 188, 260n24, 290n5, 294n41
Smith, Rachel A., 267n28
Smith, Roswell Chamberlain, 141
Social, Civil and Statistical Association of the Colored People of Pennsylvania, 81
Southworth, E. D. E. N., 301n24
Spaeth, Adolph, 291n10
Spaeth, Harriet Reynolds Krauth *see* Harriet Reynolds Krauth
Spellman, James J., 80, 275n53
Spencer, Ann, 124
Spencer, James, 124
Spielberg, Steven, 9
Spriggs, John, 232, 301n17
Spiritualism, 81–82, 193, 240–242, 301n25, 302n32
Stanford, Anthony
    life and circle of, 46, 51, 268n43
    as *Recorder* editor, 45–49, 54, 68, 76, 95, 142, 214, 268n43, 268n45, 269n46, 271n18, 272n30
Statia, Isaac, 42

Statia, Martha (mother of Martha Statia Weaver), 42, 44, 268n40–41, 277n73
Steele, Jeffrey, 204, 297n17
Stein, Jordan, 261n29
Sterling, Dorothy, 12, 295n47
Stevenson, John W., 104, 139–141, 143–144, 146, 150
Stewart, Maria, 39, 226, 299n1
Stiles, William, 271n13
Still, Mary, 75, 78, 91–92, 123
Still, Peter, 180
Still, William, 75, 91, 275n52
Stoddard, Richard H., 219, 224–225, 298n34
Stokes, Darius, 15
Streiby, Michael, 187
Strother, Thomas, 144, 177–178, 290n6, 291n16
Stowe, Harriet Beecher, 201, 295n3
Stuart, George H., 87–88
Syracuse, NY, 186–187, 191, 194, 199, 201–202, 294n36, 299n2
Syracuse High School, 186

Tanner, Benjamin ("Benny"), 208–210, 216–217
Tanner, Benjamin Tucker
    elegy to Benjamin "Benny" Tanner ("Benny's Gone"), 208–210, 216–217
    elegy to Mary Weaver, 213–215, 298n25
    life and circle of, 3, 25, 28, 44, 104, 142, 262n3, 298n22
    as *Recorder* editor, 23–26, 28, 36, 43, 50–51, 59, 66–68, 71, 73, 85, 95, 165, 169, 256n9, 262n4, 263n9, 264n14, 270n11, 271n13, 271n18, 272n26, 273n33, 273n36, 286n12
    writings of, 34, 39, 42, 49, 55, 64, 76, 96, 144, 263n5, 277n73
Tanner, Henry Ossawa, 67, 104
Tanner, Sarah Elizabeth Miller
    and "Benny's Gone," 208–210, 216
    life and circle of, 104, 209
Tates, Emma A., 206
Taylor, Eliza J., 277n73
Telly, Madison, 122
Thernstrom, Stephan, 124
Thomas, Alexander, 126
Thompson, Jane E., 213, 216–217
Thompson, Mortimer, 241, 301n24
Thoreau, Henry David, 13, 167, 189, 193
Thorpe, Sheldon, 282n41
Three-Fingered Jack, 241
Tibbs, John, 93
Tillman, James, 147
Tilmon, Levin, 36, 266n27
Toombs, Robert, 130
Tougaloo College, 194
True Royalist, 84, 266n21

Tucker, Richard, 123
Turner, Henry McNeal
    life and circle of, 3, 44, 122–123, 144, 228, 283n54, 286n9, 298n22, 302n26
    Recorder letters of, 8, 72, 77, 154–155, 157, 169, 174, 188, 208–209, 213–214, 256n9, 257n15, 260n24, 273n35, 274n40, 276n66, 289n29
Turner, John, 188
Turner, Nat, 180
Turpin, Amanda, 232–236, 250, 300n14
Turpin, James H., 213
Turpin, Nelson, 147, 232–235, 301n18
"Two-Cent Money," 75, 93, 176, 266n19
Tyler, Page, 93

Uncle Tom's Cabin, 180, 238
"Uncle William's Pulpit," 299n2
Underground Railroad, 91, 223, 232, 285n71
Underwood, J. P., 94
Union Bethel AME Church (DC), 6
United States Christian Commission (USCC), 87–89, *88*, 129–130, 137, 152–153, 191, 245, 272n24, 276n67–68, 284n66, 288n25

Van Hauser, Robert, 139
Vashon, Anne Paul, 19, 196–204, 254, 295n1, 296n9, 297n15
Vashon, Emma, 295n1
Vashon, Emma Prestina Story, 295n1
Vashon, Fannie Brooks, 295n1
Vashon, Frank, 295n1
Vashon, George (son of George Boyer Vashon), 295n1
Vashon, George Boyer
    "In the Cars," 196–210, 214–216, 225, 254, 296n15, 297n16
    life and circle of, 14, 79, 187, 196–204, 295n1, 296n8, 296n10, 296n13
Vashon, John Boyer, 295n1
Vashon, Susan Paul
    elegy to Mary Weaver, 213, 215, 217–218, 221–222, 298n31, 299n38
    life and circle, 196, *200*, 215, 295n1, 298n29
Vesey, Denmark, 180
Vicksburg Campaign, 114
"Vincent Ogé," 199, 296n11
Virgil, 160, 237, 302n28
Vosburg, John Henry, 194

Washburne, Elihu, 255n7
Walden Pond, 167, 193
Walker, William S., 276n66
Waller, Albert, 278n8
Ward, P. H., 96
Ward, Samuel Ringgold., 186
Ward, Thomas M. D., 3, 37, 51, *58*, 267n29, 268n43
Warren, John A., 50
Warren, Kenneth, 260n24
"Washington and Lincoln (Apotheosis)," 216
Washington, John E., 9, 258n16
Waters, Edward, *58*
Waters, James C., 144
Watkins, Frances Ellen *see* Frances Ellen Watkins Harper.
Watkins, George T., 142
Watson, Richard, 141, 286n8
Watts, Samuel, 51
Waugh, Frederick
    elegies to, 20, 197–198, 210–215, 218, 220–223
    life and circle of, 210–211, 252–254, 295n6, 297n21
Waugh, John T., 211, 213
Wayman, Alexander
    at 1864 AME General Conference, 50
    life and circle of, 3, 39, 42, 45, 51, *58*, 102, 142–143, 145, 269n52
    writings of, 24, 52, 141, 262n3, 263n10
Wayman AME Church (Bloomington, IL), 96–97, *98*, 101, 132, 142, 277n2–5, 278n6, 278n8, 278n11, 286n13
Wear, Ann, 80
Weaver, David, 41
Weaver, Elisha, 4, 5, 8–11, 18, 25, 187, 211, 214, 256n9, 263n10, 269n54, 271n18, 272n23, 285n2, 298n25, 299n37
    at AME General Conference of 1860, 40–41
    at AME General Conference of 1864, 49–52
    at AME General Conference of 1868, 56–59, 269n56
    at AME General Conference of 1872, 44
    business practices of, 61–68, 73–95, 99–100, 107, 127–132, 169, 180–181, 270n4, 270n6, 270n9, 272n20, 273n36, 274n41–44, 274n48, 274n49, 275n52, 275n55, 275n62, 276n65–66, 279n15, 281n39, 283n49, 285n76, 287n14, 293n30
    early life of, 41–42
    editorial appointments outside of General Conferences, 44–49, 52–56
    editorial practices of, 69–73, 84, 90–92, 99, 137, 142, 145–147, 158–159, 163–164, 169–178, 196, 199, 218–224, 227–228, 230–231, 264n14, 269n45, 269n47, 272n28, 273n33, 271n16, 274n37, 288n23, 290n6, 291n8–9, 291n16, 292n20
    family of, *see individuals listed by name*
    later life of, 42–44, 268n40–42
    and the *Repository of Religion*, 39–40, 267n34–36
    and the USCC, 87–89

Weaver, Elisha (son of Elisha and Mary Weaver), 42
Weaver, Joseph G., 42
Weaver, Martha (daughter of Martha Statia and Elisha Weaver), 42, 268n41
Weaver, Martha Statia, 42, 268n40–41
Weaver, Mary
  elegies to 20, 197–198, 210, 213–218, 220–223, 234, 298n25–27, 298n31
  life and family of 42, 61, 65–66, 72, 120, 268n38–39, 268n45, 270n1
Weaver, Nellie, 42
Webb, Elijah, 297n21
Weekly Anglo-African, 85, 227
Weir, George, 93
Weir, R. J., 296n7, 299n3
Weld, Theodore, 180
Wells, Charlotte, 278n8
Wells, Frances, 101
Wells, Martha Ann, 97–99, 101, 103, 110–111, 113, 117, 132, 278n7–8, 278n11, 281n28
Wells, William, 97, 101, 113, 117, 278n7–8, 278n11, 280n18
Wesley, Charles, 295n2
Wesley, Dorothy Porter, 12
Wesley, John, 141
Wheatley, Phillis, 13
Whipper, William, 125
White, Garland H., 129–130, 285n73
White House, 1–4, 6, 8–9, 11, 132, 217, 251–254, 256n7
Whitman, Walt, 194, 220–221
Whittier, John Greenleaf, 188, 295n3
Wiggins, James, 276n63
Wilberforce College, 108, 111, 161, 164–165, 210–212, 257n15, 285n74, 297n22
Wilberforce College fire, 28, 211, 252–253, 303n38
Wilberforce Missionary Association, 161
Wilkinson, J. F., 132
Williams, Anna Louisa, 115, 282n43
Williams, Ebenezer T., 45
Williams, Gilbert Anthony, 256n9
Williams, Heather Andrea, 259n22, 275n58
Williams, James M., 45
Williams, Samuel B., 219–223, 299n36, 299n38
Williamsport, PA, 147, 226, 228, 231–235, 300n14–16, 301n18
Willson, Joseph, 116, 120, 123, 260n24, 282n44
Willson, Josephine, 116
Wil[l]son, Emily., 116, 282n44
Wilson, Frank T., 233
Wilson, Harriet, 227, 241
Wilson, Ivy, 198, 260n24
Wilson, Keith P., 154, 289n30
Wilson, William J., 39, 188, 290n5
Winch, Julie, 260n24, 282n44
Winston and Thomas, 79, 81
Wise, Daniel, 78
Witches of New York, 241, 244, 301n24
Wittenborg, Karin, 265n16
Wombaugh, Charles H., 233
Wood, Marcus, 2, 17, 256n5
Woodfork, Austin, 96
Woodlin, Joshua, 37, 59, 271n18
Wordsworth, William, 173
Worthy, Ellen, 255n4
Wright, Richard, 70, 85, 269n55, 271n18, 273n33, 277n1, 286n9

Xenia, OH, 108, 120, 159–164
Xenia (Ohio) Female Benevolent Society, 163

Yancy, Helen, 96–99, 101–102, 111, 113, 122, 123, 132, 277n1, 277n3, 278n11, 281n28
Yancy, Lewis, 96–97, 101–102, 122, 277n1, 277n3, 278n11, 280n19
Yancy, Mary Jane, 102, 117
Yellin, Jean Fagan, 12–13, 298n22
Young, George Washington, 255n4
Young, Henry J., 131
Young, John, 293n26
Young, William S., 67–68, 271n20

Zafar, Rafia, 12
Zuille, John J., 66